5th Workshop on Argument Mining 2018

Brussels, Belgium
1 November 2018

ISBN: 978-1-5108-7424-4

EMNLP 2018

**Proceedings of the
5th Workshop on Argument Mining**

November 1, 2018
Brussels, Belgium

Order copies of this and other ACL proceedings from:

Association for Computational Linguistics (ACL)
209 N. Eighth Street
Stroudsburg, PA 18360
USA
Tel: +1-570-476-8006
Fax: +1-570-476-0860
acl@aclweb.org

Introduction

Argument mining (also, "argumentation mining") is a relatively new research field within the rapidly evolving area of Computational Argumentation. The tasks pursued within this field are highly challenging with many important practical applications. These include automatically identifying argumentative structures within discourse, e.g., premises, conclusion, and argumentation scheme of each argument, as well as relationships between pairs of arguments and their components. To date, researchers have investigated a plethora of methods to address these tasks in various areas, including legal documents, user generated Web discourse, on-line debates, product reviews, academic literature, newspaper articles, dialogical domains, and Wikipedia articles. Relevant manually annotated corpora are released at an increasing pace, further enhancing the research in the field. In addition, argument mining is inherently tied to sentiment analysis, since an argument frequently carries a clear sentiment towards its topic. Correspondingly, this year's workshop will be coordinated with the corresponding WASSA workshop, aiming to have a joint poster session.

Argument mining can give rise to various applications of great practical importance. For instance, by developing methods that can extract and visualize the main pro and con arguments raised in a collection of documents towards a query of interest, one can enhance data-driven decision making. In instructional contexts, argumentation is a pedagogically important tool for conveying and assessing the students' command of course material, as well as for advancing critical thinking. Written and diagrammed arguments by students represent educational data that can be mined for purposes of assessment and instruction. This is especially important given the wide-spread adoption of computer-supported peer review, computerized essay grading, and large-scale online courses and MOOCs. Additionally, mining pros and cons may be useful in multiple business applications, for instance, for researching a company or considering the potential of a possible investment.

Success in argument mining requires interdisciplinary approaches informed by natural language processing technology, artificial intelligence approaches, theories of semantics, pragmatics and discourse, knowledge of discourse of domains such as law and science, argumentation theory, computational models of argumentation, and cognitive psychology. The goal of this workshop is to provide a follow-on forum to the last four years' Argument Mining workshops at ACL and EMNLP, the major research forum devoted to argument mining in all domains of discourse.

Organizers:

Noam Slonim, IBM Research AI (chair)
Ranit Aharonov, IBM Research AI (chair)
Kevin Ashley, University of Pittsburgh
Claire Cardie, Cornell University
Nancy Green, University of North Carolina Greensboro
Iryna Gurevych, Technische Universität Darmstadt
Ivan Habernal, Technische Universität Darmstadt
Diane Litman, University of Pittsburgh
Georgios Petasis, National Center for Scientific Research (NCSR) "Demokritos"
Chris Reed, University of Dundee
Vern R. Walker, Maurice A. Deane School of Law at Hofstra University, New York

Program Committee:

Ahmet Aker, University of Duisburg-Essen
Carlos Alzate, IBM Research AI
Roy Bar-Haim, IBM Research AI
Yonatan Bilu, IBM Research AI
Katarzyna Budzynska, Polish Academy of Sciences (Poland) & University of Dundee (UK)
Elena Cabrio, Université Côte d'Azur, Inria, CNRS, I3S, France
Leshem Choshen, IBM Research AI
Johannes Daxenberger, Technische Universität Darmstadt
Liat Ein Dor, IBM Research AI
Matthais Grabmair, Carnegie Mellon University
Graeme Hirst, University of Toronto
Vangelis Karkaletsis, National Center for Scientific Research (NCSR) "Demokritos"
John Lawrence, Centre for Argument Technology - University of Dundee
Ran Levy, IBM Research AI
Beishui Liao, Zhejiang University
Robert Mercer, The University of Western Ontario
Marie-Francine Moens, The Katholieke Universiteit Leuven
Smaranda Muresan, Columbia University
Elena Musi, Columbia University
Matan Orbach, IBM Research AI
Joonsuk Park, Williams College
Simon Parsons, King's College London
Ariel Rosenfeld, Weizmann Institute of Science
Patrick Saint-Dizier, Centre National de la Recherche Scientifique (CNRS)
Jodi Schneider, University of Illinois at Urbana-Champaign
Eyal Shnarch, IBM Research AI
Christian Stab, Technische Universität Darmstadt
Benno Stein, Bauhaus-Universität Weimar
Serena Villata, Centre National de la Recherche Scientifique (CNRS)
Henning Wachsmuth, Bauhaus-Universität Weimar
Zhongyu Wei, Fudan University

Invited Speaker:

Hugo Mercier, Institut Jean Nicod, CNRS

Table of Contents

Conference Program

Thursday, November 1, 2018

09:00–09:10   **Openings**

Session 1

09:10–10:10   *Keynote Talk: Argumentation and Human Reason*
Hugo Mercier

10:10–10:30   *Argumentative Link Prediction using Residual Networks and Multi-Objective Learning*
Andrea Galassi, Marco Lippi and Paolo Torroni

10:30–11:00   *Coffee Break*

Session 2

11:00–11:20   *End-to-End Argument Mining for Discussion Threads Based on Parallel Constrained Pointer Architecture*
Gaku Morio and Katsuhide Fujita

11:20–11:40   *ArguminSci: A Tool for Analyzing Argumentation and Rhetorical Aspects in Scientific Writing*
Anne Lauscher, Goran Glavaš and Kai Eckert

11:40–12:00   *Evidence Type Classification in Randomized Controlled Trials*
Tobias Mayer, Elena Cabrio and Serena Villata

12:00–12:20   *Predicting the Usefulness of Amazon Reviews Using Off-The-Shelf Argumentation Mining*
Marco Passon, Marco Lippi, Giuseppe Serra and Carlo Tasso

12:20–14:30   ***Lunch and Poster Presentations***

An Argument-Annotated Corpus of Scientific Publications
Anne Lauscher, Goran Glavaš and Simone Paolo Ponzetto

Argumentative Link Prediction using Residual Networks and Multi-Objective Learning

Andrea Galassi[1], Marco Lippi[2], and Paolo Torroni[1]

[1]Department of Computer Science and Engineering DISI
University of Bologna
{a.galassi, paolo.torroni}@unibo.it
[2]Department of Sciences and Methods for Engineering
University of Modena and Reggio Emilia
marco.lippi@unimore.it

Abstract

We explore the use of residual networks for argumentation mining, with an emphasis on link prediction. The method we propose makes no assumptions on document or argument structure. We evaluate it on a challenging dataset consisting of user-generated comments collected from an online platform. Results show that our model outperforms an equivalent deep network and offers results comparable with state-of-the-art methods that rely on domain knowledge.

1 Introduction

Argumentation mining is a growing sub-area of artificial intelligence and computational linguistics whose aim is to automatically extract arguments from generic textual corpora (Lippi and Torroni, 2016a). The problem is typically broken down into focused sub-problems such as the identification of sentences containing argument components like claims and premises, of the boundaries of argument components within such sentences, and the prediction of the argumentative structure of the document at hand.

In spite of significant results achieved in component identification tasks, such as claim/evidence detection (Rinott et al., 2015; Lippi and Torroni, 2015; Park and Cardie, 2014; Park et al., 2015b; Stab and Gurevych, 2014), classification (Eckle-Kohler et al., 2015; Niculae et al., 2017) and boundary detection (Sardianos et al., 2015; Levy et al., 2014; Lippi and Torroni, 2016b; Habernal and Gurevych, 2017), comparatively less progress has been made in the arguably more challenging argument structure prediction task (Cabrio and Villata, 2012; Stab and Gurevych, 2014).

Again due to the challenging nature of the general argumentation mining problem, solutions have typically addressed a specific genre or application domain, such as legal texts (Mochales Palau and Moens, 2011), persuasive essays (Stab and Gurevych, 2017), or Wikipedia articles (Levy et al., 2014; Rinott et al., 2015) and have heavily relied on domain knowledge. One particular aspect of the domain is the argument model. While argumentation as a discipline has developed rather sophisticated argument models, such as Toulmin's (1958), the majority of the available argumentation mining data sets refer to ad-hoc, usually simpler argument models, often in an effort to obtain a reasonable inter-annotator agreement. Another crucial aspect is the document structure. For instance, in some domains, certain argument components occupy a specific position in the document.

Moreover, until recently, approaches have mostly used traditional methods such as support vector machines, logistic regression and naive Bayes classifiers. Only in the last couple of years the field has started to look more systematically into neural network-based architectures, such as long short-memory networks and convolutional neural networks, and structured output classifiers.

The aim of this study is to investigate the application of residual networks–a deep neural network architecture not previously applied to this domain–to a challenging structure prediction task, namely link prediction. Our ambition is to define a model that does not exploit domain-specific, highly engineered features, or information on the underlying argument model, and could thus be, at least in principle, of general applicability. Our results match those of state-of-the-art methods that rely on domain knowledge, but use much less a-priori information.

The next section reviews recent applications of neural networks to argumentation mining. Section 3 presents our model, Section 4 the benchmark, and Section 5 discusses results. Section 6 concludes.

Proceedings of the 5th Workshop on Argument Mining, pages 1–10
Brussels, Belgium, November 1, 2018. ©2018 Association for Computational Linguistics

2 Related work

The application of neural network architectures in argumentation mining is relatively recent. A study most closely related to ours was presented by Niculae et al. (2017) and will be described in greater detail in Section 4. The authors propose a structured learning framework based on factor graphs. Their approach imposes constraints to the graph according to the underlying argument model, and it includes a joint optimization method based on the AD3 algorithm (Martins et al., 2015), structured Support Vector Machines (Tsochantaridis et al., 2005) and Recurrent Neural Networks (Rumelhart et al., 1986). Link prediction and argument component classification are performed jointly, reaching state-of-the-art results on two distinct corpora. In contrast to our method, Niculae et al.'s heavily relies on a-priori knowledge.

In the domain of persuasive essays, Eger et al. (2017) consider several sub-tasks of argumentation mining, making use of various neural architectures. These include neural parsers (Dyer et al., 2015; Kiperwasser and Goldberg, 2016), LSTMs for joint entity and relation extraction (LSTM-ER) (Miwa and Bansal, 2016), and Bidirectional LSTM coupled with Conditional Random Fields and Convolutional Neural Networks (BLCC) (Ma and Hovy, 2016) in a multi-task learning framework (Søgaard and Goldberg, 2016). Eger et al. conclude that neural networks can outperform feature-based techniques in argumentation mining tasks.

Convolutional Neural Networks and LSTMs have been used by Guggilla et al. (2016) to perform claim classification, whereas bidirectional LSTMs have been exploited by Habernal and Gurevych (2016) to assess the persuasiveness of arguments. More recently, neural networks have been applied to the task of topic-dependent evidence detection (Shnarch et al., 2018), improving the performance on a manually labelled corpus through the use of unsupervised data. Potash et al. (2017) have applied Pointer Networks (Vinyals et al., 2015) to argumentation mining.

Looking beyond argumentation mining, Lei et al. (2018) reviews the application of several deep learning techniques for sentiment analysis, while Conneau et al. (2017) for the first time applies very deep residual networks to NLP-related task and successfully performs text classification at the character level. Small residual convolutional networks have been successfully applied by Zhang et al. (2018) to multi-label classification on medical notes and by Huang and Wang (2017) to distantly-supervised relation extraction, where a knowledge base is used to generate a noisy set of positive relations among unlabeled data.

3 Residual networks for argument mining

Residual networks (He et al., 2016a,b) are a recent family of deep neural networks that achieved outstanding results in many machine learning tasks, in particular in computer vision applications such as medical imaging (Yu et al., 2017), computational linguistics (Bjerva et al., 2016), crowd flow prediction (Zhang et al., 2017), and game playing (Cazenave, 2018; Chesani et al., 2018).

The core idea behind residual networks, illustrated by Figure 1, is to create shortcuts that link neurons belonging to distant layers, whereas standard feed-forward networks typically link neurons belonging to subsequent layers only. This kind of architecture usually results in a speedier training phase, and it usually allows to train networks with a very large number of layers. The original architecture exploits convolutional layers, but it can be generalized to dense (fully-connected) layers. The motivation behind residual networks is that if multiple non-linear layers can asymptotically approximate a complex function $H(x)$, they can also asymptotically approximate its residual function $F(x) = H(x) - x$. The original function is therefore obtained by simply adding back the residual value: $H(x) = F(x) + x$.

The architecture we propose in this paper makes use of the dense residual network model, along with an LSTM (Hochreiter and Schmidhuber, 1997), to jointly perform link prediction and argument component classification. More specifically, our approach works at a local level on pairs of sentences, without any document-level global optimization, and without imposing model constraints induced, e.g., by domain-specific or genre-specific hypotheses. For that reason, it lends itself to integration with more complex systems.

3.1 Model description

One of our aims is to propose a method that abstracts away from a specific argument model. We thus reason in terms of abstract entities, such as

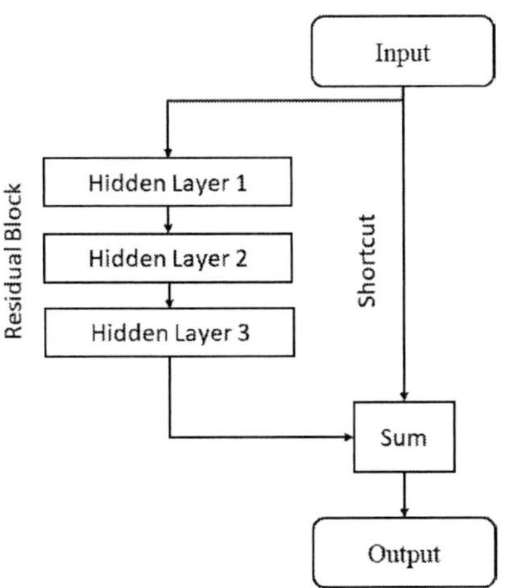

Figure 1: General schema of a residual network with a single residual block with three hidden layers.

argumentative propositions and the links among them. Such abstract entities are instantiated into concrete categories, such as claims and premises, supports or attacks, as soon as we apply the method to a domain described by a specific dataset whose annotations follow a concrete argument model. In particular, in this work we instantiate our model with the categories proposed by Niculae et al. (2017) for the annotation of the CDCP corpus.

In general, a document D is a sequence of *tokens*, i.e., words and punctuation marks. An argumentative proposition a is a sequence of contiguous tokens within D, which represents an argument, or part thereof. A labeling of propositions is induced by the chosen argument model. Such a labeling associates each proposition with the corresponding category of the argument component it contains.

Given two propositions a and b belonging to the same document, a directed relation from the former (*source*) to the latter (*target*) is represented as $a \rightarrow b$. Reflexive relations ($a \rightarrow a$) are not allowed.

Each relation $a \rightarrow b$ is characterized by two labels: a (Boolean) *link label*, $L_{a \rightarrow b}$, and a *relation label*, $R_{a \rightarrow b}$. The link label indicates the presence of a link, and is therefore *true* if there exists a directed link from a to b, and *false* otherwise. The relation label instead contains information on the nature of the link connecting a and b. In particular, it represents the direct or inverse relation between the two propositions, according to the links

that connect a to b or b to a. In other words, its domain is composed, according to the underlying argument model, not only by all the possible link types (e.g., *attack* and *support*), but also by their opposite types (e.g., *attackedBy* and *supportedBy*) as well as by a category, *none*, meaning absence of link in either direction.[1]

One objective is to establish the value of the link label $L_{a \rightarrow b}$ for each possible input pair of propositions (a, b) belonging to the same document D. Such a *link prediction* task can be considered as a sub-task of argument structure prediction. Another objective is the *classification* of propositions and relations, i.e., the prediction of labels P_a, P_b, $R_{a \rightarrow b}$. That is also jointly performed, as in (Niculae et al., 2017). Notice, however, that Niculae et al. do not predict $R_{a \rightarrow b}$ relations, but only link and proposition labels.

3.2 Embeddings and features

Since the purpose of this work is to evaluate deep residual networks as an instrument for argumentation mining, without resorting to domain- or genre-specific information, the system relies on a minimal set of features that do not require elaborate processing.

Any input token is transformed into a 300-dimensional embedding by exploiting the GloVe pre-trained vocabulary (Pennington et al., 2014). Input sequences are zero-padded to the length of the longest sequence (153 tokens). The distance between two propositions could also be relevant to establishing whether two components are linked. We thus employed the number of propositions that separate two given propositions as an additional feature. Following previous works in the game domain, where scalar values have been encoded in binary form (Silver et al., 2016; Cazenave, 2018; Chesani et al., 2018), we represented distance using as a 10-bit array, where the first 5 bits are used in case that the source precedes the target, and the last 5 bits are used in the opposite case. In both cases, the number of consecutive "1" values encodes the value of the distance (distances are capped by 5). For example, if the target precedes the source by two sentences, the distance is -2, which produces encoding 0001100000; if the source precedes the target by three sentences, the distance is 3, with encoding 0000011100. In this

---

[1]Given the *none* category, label $L_{a \rightarrow b}$ could, in principle, be induced by label $R_{a \rightarrow b}$, but it is still convenient to keep both during the optimization process.

way, the Hamming distance between two distance value encodings is equal to the difference between the two distance values.

3.3 Residual Network Architecture

The network architecture is illustrated in Figure 2. It is composed by the following macro blocks:

- two deep embedders, one for sources and one for targets, that manipulate token embeddings;

- a dense encoding layer for feature dimensionality reduction;

- an LSTM to process the input sequences;

- a residual network;

- the final-stage classifiers.

Source and target propositions are encoded separately by the first three blocks, then they are concatenated together, along with the distance, and given as input to the residual network.

The deep embedders refine the token embeddings, thus creating new, more data-specific embeddings. Relying on deep embedders instead of on pre-trained autoencoders, aims to achieve a better generality, at least in principle, and avoid excessive specialization, thus limiting overfitting. The dimensionality reduction operated by the dense encoding layer allows to use an LSTM with fewer parameters, which has two positive effects: it reduces the time needed for training, and again it limits overfitting.

The deep embedders are residual networks composed by a single residual block, composed by 4 pre-activated time-distributed dense layers. Accordingly, each layer applies the same transformation to each embedding, regardless of their position inside the sentence. All the layers have 50 neurons, except the last one, which has 300 neurons.

The dense encoding layer reduces the size of the embedding sequences by applying a time-distributed dense layer, which reduces the embedding size to 50, and a time average-pooling layer (Collobert et al., 2011), which reduces the sequence size to $1/10$ of the original. The resulting sequences are then given as input to a single bidirectional LSTM, producing a representation of the proposition of size 50. Thus, for each proposition, 153 embeddings of size 300 are transformed first into 153 embeddings of size 50, then into 15 embeddings of size 50, and finally in a single feature of size 50.

Source and target features, computed this way, alongside with the distance encoding, are then concatenated together and given as input to the residual network. The first level of the network is a dense encoding layer with 20 neurons, while the residual block is composed by a layer with 5 neurons and one with 20 neurons. The sums of the results of the first and the last layers of the residual networks are provided as input to the classifiers.

The final layers of the system are three independent softmax classifiers used to predict the source, the target, and the relation labels. The output of each classifier is a probability distribution along all the possible classes of that label. The predicted class is the one with the highest score. All these three classifiers, which predict labels for two different tasks, contribute simultaneously to our learning model. The link classifier is obtained by summing the relevant scores produced by the relation classifier.[2]

All the dense layers use the rectifier activation function (Glorot et al., 2011), and they randomly initialize weights with He initialization (He et al., 2015). The application of all non-linearity functions is preceded by batch-normalization layers (Ioffe and Szegedy, 2015) and by dropout layers (Srivastava et al., 2014), with probability $p = 0.1$.

4 Benchmark

4.1 Dataset

We evaluated our model against the Cornell eRule-making Corpus (CDCP) (Niculae et al., 2017). This consists of 731 user comments from a eRule-making website, for a total of about 4,700 propositions, all considered to be argumentative.[3] The argument model adopted is the one proposed by Park et al. (2015a), where links are constrained to form directed graphs. Propositions are divided into 5 classes: POLICY (17%), VALUE (45%), FACT

---

[2]For instance, if our model considers *attack* and *support* relations as the only possible links, and the relation classifier scores are *attack* = 0.15, *support* = 0.2, *attackedBy* = 0.1, *supportedBy* = 0.05, *none* = 0.5, then the link classifier scores are: *true* = 0.35, *false* = 0.65.

[3]In an effort to obtain comparable results, we applied same preprocessing steps described in (Niculae et al., 2017), enforcing transitive closure and removing nested proposition, even though our approach does not take into account the argumentation model, nor its properties.

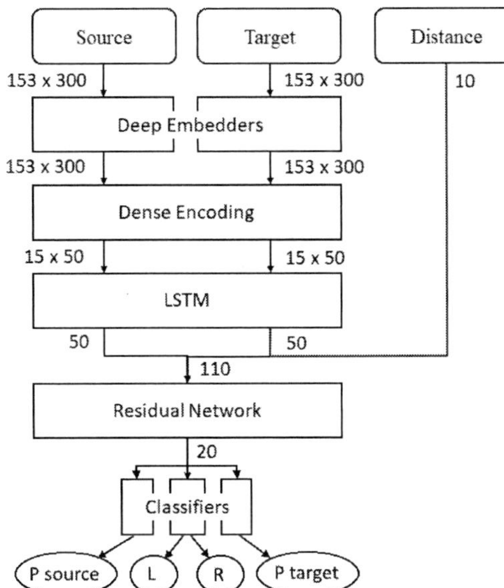

Figure 2: A block diagram of the proposed architecture. The figure shows, next to each arrow, the dimensionality of the data involved, so as to clarify the size of the inputs and the outputs of each block.

(16%), TESTIMONY (21%) and REFERENCE (1%). Links are divided between REASON (97%) and EVIDENCE (3%). Figure 3 shows an annotated document from the CDCP corpus.

Link prediction is a particularly difficult task in the CDCP dataset, where only 3% of all the possible proposition pairs (more than 43,000) are linked. A preliminary analysis of the data suggests that the number of propositions separating source and target (*distance*) could be a relevant feature, since most linked propositions are not far from each other. Indeed, as Figure 4 shows, around 70% of links are between adjacent propositions.

We tokenized documents using a hand-crafted parser based on the progressive splitting of the tokens and search within the GloVe vocabulary. We preferred not to use existing tools because of the nature of the data, since the CDCP documents often do not follow proper writing conventions (such as the blank space after the period mark), leading in some cases to a wrong tokenization. As a result, the number of tokens not contained in the GloVe dictionary dramatically reduced from 384, originally obtained with the software provided by Niculae et al. (2017), to 84. Each of these tokens was mapped into a randomly-generated embedding.

Table 1: Experimental dataset composition.

Split	Train	Valid.	Test	Total
Documents	513	68	150	731
Propositions	3,338	468	973	4,779
Values	1438	231	491	2160
Policies	585	77	153	815
Testimonies	738	84	204	1026
Facts	549	73	124	746
References	28	3	1	32
Couples	30,056	3,844	9,484	43,384
Links	923	143	272	1,338
Reasons	888	139	265	1292
Evidences	35	4	7	46

4.2 Structured Learning

The state of the art for the CDCP corpus is the work described by the corpus authors themselves (Niculae et al., 2017). They use a structured learning framework to jointly classify all the propositions in a document and determine which ones are linked together. To perform the classification, the models can rely on many factors and constraints. The unary factors represent the model's belief in each possible class for each proposition or link, without considering any other proposition or link. For each link between two propositions, the compatibility factors influence link classification according to the proposition classes, taking into account adjacency between propositions and precedence between source and target. The second-order factors influence the classification of pairs of links that share a common proposition, by modeling three local argumentation graph structures: grandparent, sibling and co-parent. Furthermore, constraints are introduced to enforce adherence to the desired argumentation structure, according to the argument model and domain characteristics.

The authors discuss experiments with 6 different models, which differ by complexity (the type of factors and constraints involved) and by how they model the factors (SVMs and RNNs). The RNN models compute sentence embeddings, by exploiting initialization with GloVe word vectors, while the SVMs models rely on many specific features. The first-order factors rely on the same features used by Stab and Gurevych (2017), both for the propositions and the links. These are, among the others, unigrams, dependency tuples, token statistics, proposition statistics, propo-

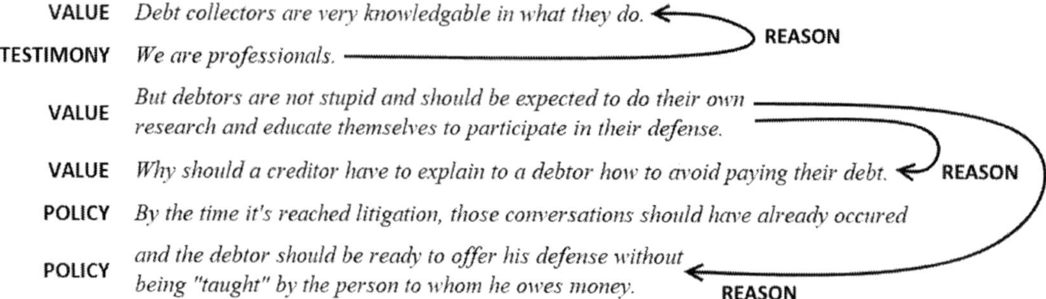

Figure 3: Argumentation structure in one of the documents of the CDCP corpus.

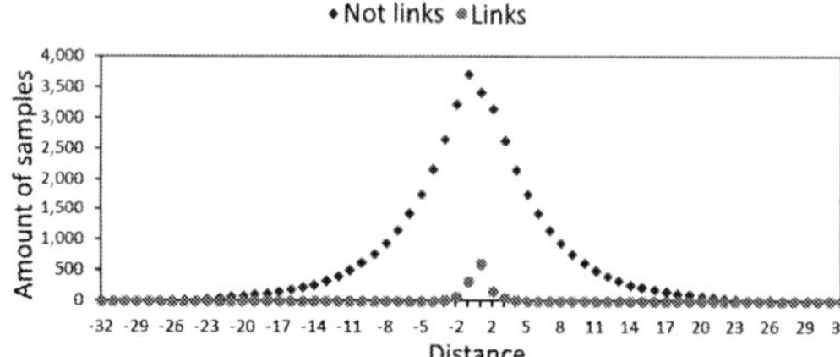

Figure 4: Link distribution in the CDCP dataset with respect to distance. The distance is considered positive when the source precedes the target, negative otherwise.

sition location, indicators from hand-crafted lexicons and handcrafted ones, shared phrases, subclauses, depth of the parse tree, tense of the main verb, modal verbs, POS, production rules, type probability, discourse triplets (Lin et al., 2014), and average GloVe embeddings. The higher-order factors exploit the following features between all three propositions and between each pair: same sentence indicators, proposition order, Jaccard similarity, presence of any shared nouns, and shared noun ratios. The overall feature dimensionality is reportedly 7000 for propositions and 2100 for links, not counting 35 second-order features.

5 Results

5.1 Experimental setting

We created a validation set by randomly selecting documents from the original training split with 10% probability. We used the remaining documents as training data and the original test split as is. Table 1 reports the statistics related to the three splits.

We defined the learning problem as a multi-objective optimization problem, whose loss function is given by the weighted sum of four different components: the categorical cross-entropy on three labels (source and target categories, link relation category) and an L_2 regularization on the network parameters. The weights of these components were, respectively, 1, 1, 10, 10^{-4}.

We performed mini-batch optimization using Adam (Kingma and Ba, 2014) with parameters $b_1 = 0.9$ and $b_2 = 0.9999$, and by applying proportional decay of the initial learning rate $\alpha_0 = 5 \times 10^{-3}$. Training was early-stopped after 200 epochs with no improvements on the validation data. We chose the numerous hyper-parameters of the architecture and of the learning model after an initial experimental setup phase, based on the performance on the validation set for the link prediction task. Results obtained in this phase confirmed that the presence of the deep embedder block and of the distance feature lead to better results.

We compared the results of the residual network model against an equivalent deep network with the same number of layers and the same hyper-parameters, but without the shortcut that characterize the residual network block. We applied two different training procedures for both this deep network baseline and the residual network. In particular, as the criterion for early stopping we used once the error on link prediction and once the error on proposition classification. In the presentation of our results we will refer to these two models as link-guided (LG) and proposition-guided (PG).

Following (Niculae et al., 2017), we measured the performance of the models by computing the F_1 score for links, propositions, and the average between the two, in order to provide a summary evaluation. More specifically, for the links we measured the F_1 of the positive classes (as the harmonic mean between precision and recall), whereas for the propositions we used the score of each class and then we computed the macro-average. We also reported the F_1 score for each direct relation class, alongside with their macro-average.

Since each proposition is involved in many pairs, both as a source and as a target, its classification is performed multiple times. To classify it uniquely, we considered the average probability score assigned to each class and we have assigned the most probable class. That is of course not the only option. Another possibility could be to assign the class that results to be the most probable in most of the cases, thus relying on a majority vote. A further option could be to simply consider the label with highest confidence. However, this procedure might be more sensitive to outliers, because the misclassification of a sentence in just one pair would lead to the misclassification of the sentence, regardless of all the other pairs. A deeper analysis of different techniques to address this issues is left to future research.

5.2 Discussion and analysis

Table 2 summarizes the evaluation of baselines and residual networks,[4] also showing the best scores obtained by the structured learning configurations presented in (Niculae et al., 2017).

Results highlight how the proposed approach based on residual networks outperforms the state of the art for what concerns link prediction. In addition, residual link-guided network training consistently performs better than both deep networks baselines in all the three tasks.

As for proposition label prediction, the results obtained through structured approaches still maintain a slight advantage over residual networks. This could be partially explained by the fact that hyper-parameter tuning was done with the aim to select the best model for link prediction. It should also be considered that we perform proposition classification relying on the merging of labels obtained through local optimization, while the structured learning approach exploits a global optimization. Nonetheless, the average score of residual networks is better than that of structured

---

[4]We report the results obtained on just one trained model. As explained in (Reimers and Gurevych, 2017), due to the non-deterministic behavior of the neural networks, this scores are influenced by the random seed of the training. Evaluating the same model trained many times with different seeds, and reporting the average scores would clearly yield a more robust evaluation.

Baseline LG	Predicted				
True	P	F	T	V	R
P	0.78	0.00	0.01	0.21	0.00
F	0.08	0.00	0.04	0.88	0.00
T	0.00	0.00	0.70	0.30	0.00
V	0.08	0.00	0.09	0.82	0.00
R	0.00	0.00	1.00	0.00	0.00

Baseline PG	Predicted				
True	P	F	T	V	R
P	0.74	0.00	0.02	0.24	0.00
F	0.03	0.00	0.08	0.89	0.00
T	0.01	0.00	0.63	0.35	0.00
V	0.05	0.00	0.09	0.86	0.00
R	0.00	0.00	0.00	0.00	1.00

ResNet LG	Predicted				
True	P	F	T	V	R
P	0.76	0.06	0.01	0.17	0.00
F	0.06	0.42	0.08	0.44	0.00
T	0.00	0.06	0.75	0.18	0.00
V	0.07	0.12	0.10	0.70	0.00
R	0.00	0.00	0.00	0.00	1.00

ResNet PG	Predicted				
True	P	F	T	V	R
P	0.78	0.07	0.02	0.12	0.00
F	0.06	0.45	0.09	0.40	0.00
T	0.02	0.08	0.69	0.22	0.00
V	0.08	0.16	0.13	0.64	0.00
R	0.00	0.00	0.00	0.00	1.00

Structured SVM full	Predicted				
True	P	F	T	V	R
P	0.76	0.05	0.04	0.16	0.00
F	0.04	0.44	0.10	0.42	0.00
T	0.01	0.06	0.72	0.21	0.00
V	0.05	0.11	0.08	0.76	0.00
R	0.00	0.00	0.00	0.00	1.00

Structured RNN basic	Predicted				
True	P	F	T	V	R
P	0.73	0.10	0.00	0.17	0.00
F	0.07	0.48	0.06	0.38	0.00
T	0.01	0.08	0.73	0.19	0.00
V	0.05	0.15	0.08	0.71	0.00
R	0.00	0.00	0.00	0.00	1.00

Figure 5: Confusion matrix for proposition prediction. Top: baseline networks; middle: residual networks; bottom: structured prediction by (Niculae et al., 2017).

RNNs, thus proving the generality of the approach.

We shall also remark that our approach can achieve such results without exploiting any specific hypothesis or a-priori knowledge of the genre or domain. This could be an added value in contexts where arguments may be laid out freely, without following a pre-determined argument model, yet it would be interesting to uncover the underlying argumentation's structure.

Results also indicate that the most common mistake regards the prediction of facts as values (see Figure 5). That should come as no surprise, since VALUE is by far the largest class in the corpus, and it is therefore also affected by many false positives. Interestingly, baselines completely avoid to classify any proposition as a FACT.

As far as relation label prediction is concerned, this model apparently fails to predict the EVIDENCE relation. That negative result was also to be expected, since such a class is scarcely present in the whole dataset (less than 1%).

6 Conclusion and future work

We presented the first application of residual networks in the argumentation mining domain. We proposed a model that outperforms an equivalent deep network and competes with state-of-the-art techniques in a challenging dataset.

Considering that the model makes use of only one simple feature – the argumentative distance between two proposition – a natural extension of

Table 2: F_1 scores computed on the test set. For each class, the number of instances is reported in parenthesis. For the comparison with structured learning, the best scores obtained by any of the structured configurations are reported.

Metric	Deep Baseline		Deep Residual		Structured	
	LG	PG	LG	PG	SVM	RNN
Average (Link and Proposition)	33.18	42.88	47.28	46.37	**50.0**	43.5
Link (272)	22.56	22.45	**29.29**	20.76	26.7	14.6
Proposition (973)	43.79	63.31	65.28	71.99	**73.5**	72.7
VALUE (491)	73.77	74.45	72.19	73.24	76.4	73.7
POLICY (153)	73.85	76.09	74.36	76.43	77.3	76.8
TESTIMONY (204)	71.36	65.98	72.86	68.63	71.7	75.8
FACT (124)	0	0	40.31	41.64	42.5	42.2
REFERENCE (1)	0	100	66.67	100	100	100
Relation (272)	11.68	11.52	**15.01**	10.31		
REASON (265)	23.35	23.04	30.02	20.62		
EVIDENCE (7)	0	0	0	0		

this study would be its integration in a more structured and constrained argumentation framework.

Since in argumentation it is often the case that single propositions cannot contain all the relevant information to predict argument components and relations, it could be useful to provide also the context of argumentation as an input. Hence, another interesting direction of investigation could be the integration of the whole document text in the model.

References

Johannes Bjerva, Barbara Plank, and Johan Bos. 2016. Semantic tagging with deep residual networks. In *Proceedings of COLING 2016, the 26th International Conference on Computational Linguistics: Technical Papers*, pages 3531–3541.

Elena Cabrio and Serena Villata. 2012. Combining textual entailment and argumentation theory for supporting online debates interactions. In *Proceedings of the 50th annual meeting of the Association for Computational Linguistics (ACL 2012)*, pages 208–212, Jeju, Korea. Association for Computational Linguistics.

T. Cazenave. 2018. Residual networks for computer go. *IEEE Transactions on Games*, 10(1):107–110.

F. Chesani, A. Galassi, M. Lippi, and P. Mello. 2018. Can deep networks learn to play by the rules? a case study on nine men's morris. *IEEE Transactions on Games*, pages 1–1.

Ronan Collobert, Jason Weston, Léon Bottou, Michael Karlen, Koray Kavukcuoglu, and Pavel Kuksa. 2011. Natural language processing (almost) from scratch. *Journal of Machine Learning Research*, 12(Aug):2493–2537.

Alexis Conneau, Holger Schwenk, Loïc Barrault, and Yann Lecun. 2017. Very deep convolutional networks for text classification. In *Proceedings of the 15th Conference of the European Chapter of the Association for Computational Linguistics: Volume 1, Long Papers*, volume 1, pages 1107–1116.

Chris Dyer, Miguel Ballesteros, Wang Ling, Austin Matthews, and Noah A Smith. 2015. Transition-based dependency parsing with stack long short-term memory. In *Proceedings of the 53rd Annual Meeting of the Association for Computational Linguistics and the 7th International Joint Conference on Natural Language Processing (Volume 1: Long Papers)*, volume 1, pages 334–343.

Judith Eckle-Kohler, Roland Kluge, and Iryna Gurevych. 2015. On the role of discourse markers for discriminating claims and premises in argumentative discourse. In *Proceedings of the 2015 Conference on Empirical Methods in Natural Language Processing (EMNLP)*, page to appear, Lisbon, Portugal. Association for Computational Linguistics.

Steffen Eger, Johannes Daxenberger, and Iryna Gurevych. 2017. Neural end-to-end learning for computational argumentation mining. In *Proceedings of the 55th Annual Meeting of the Association for Computational Linguistics (Volume 1: Long Papers)*, volume 1, pages 11–22.

Xavier Glorot, Antoine Bordes, and Yoshua Bengio. 2011. Deep sparse rectifier neural networks. In *Proceedings of the Fourteenth International Conference on Artificial Intelligence and Statistics*, volume 15 of *Proceedings of Machine Learning Research*, pages 315–323, Fort Lauderdale, FL, USA. PMLR.

Chinnappa Guggilla, Tristan Miller, and Iryna Gurevych. 2016. CNN-and LSTM-based claim classification in online user comments. In *Proceedings of COLING 2016, the 26th International Conference on Computational Linguistics: Technical Papers*, pages 2740–2751.

Ivan Habernal and Iryna Gurevych. 2016. Which argument is more convincing? analyzing and predicting convincingness of web arguments using bidirectional lstm. In *Proceedings of the 54th Annual Meeting of the Association for Computational Linguistics (Volume 1: Long Papers)*, volume 1, pages 1589–1599.

Ivan Habernal and Iryna Gurevych. 2017. Argumentation mining in user-generated web discourse. *Computational Linguistics*, 43(1):125–179.

Kaiming He, Xiangyu Zhang, Shaoqing Ren, and Jian Sun. 2015. Delving deep into rectifiers: Surpassing human-level performance on imagenet classification. In *Proceedings of the IEEE international conference on computer vision*, pages 1026–1034.

Kaiming He, Xiangyu Zhang, Shaoqing Ren, and Jian Sun. 2016a. Deep residual learning for image recognition. In *Proceedings of the IEEE Conference on Computer Vision and Pattern Recognition*, pages 770–778.

Kaiming He, Xiangyu Zhang, Shaoqing Ren, and Jian Sun. 2016b. Identity mappings in deep residual networks. In *European Conference on Computer Vision*, pages 630–645. Springer.

Sepp Hochreiter and Jürgen Schmidhuber. 1997. Long short-term memory. *Neural computation*, 9(8):1735–1780.

YiYao Huang and William Yang Wang. 2017. Deep residual learning for weakly-supervised relation extraction. In *Proceedings of the 2017 Conference on Empirical Methods in Natural Language Processing*, pages 1803–1807.

Sergey Ioffe and Christian Szegedy. 2015. Batch normalization: Accelerating deep network training by reducing internal covariate shift. In *Proceedings of the 32nd International Conference on Machine Learning*, volume 37 of *Proceedings of Machine Learning Research*, pages 448–456, Lille, France. PMLR.

Diederik Kingma and Jimmy Ba. 2014. Adam: A method for stochastic optimization. *arXiv preprint arXiv:1412.6980*.

Eliyahu Kiperwasser and Yoav Goldberg. 2016. Simple and accurate dependency parsing using bidirectional LSTM feature representations. *Transactions of the Association for Computational Linguistics*, 4:313–327.

Zhang Lei, Wang Shuai, and Liu Bing. 2018. Deep learning for sentiment analysis: A survey. *Wiley Interdisciplinary Reviews: Data Mining and Knowledge Discovery*, 0(0):e1253.

Ran Levy, Yonatan Bilu, Daniel Hershcovich, Ehud Aharoni, and Noam Slonim. 2014. Context dependent claim detection. In *COLING 2014, Dublin, Ireland*, pages 1489–1500. ACL.

Ziheng Lin, Hwee Tou Ng, and Min-Yen Kan. 2014. A pdtb-styled end-to-end discourse parser. *Natural Language Engineering*, 20(2):151–184.

Marco Lippi and Paolo Torroni. 2015. Context-independent claim detection for argument mining. In *Proceedings of the Twenty-Fourth International Joint Conference on Artificial Intelligence, IJCAI 2015, Buenos Aires, Argentina, July 25-31, 2015*, pages 185–191. AAAI Press.

Marco Lippi and Paolo Torroni. 2016a. Argumentation mining: State of the art and emerging trends. *ACM Trans. Internet Technol.*, 16(2):10:1–10:25.

Marco Lippi and Paolo Torroni. 2016b. Margot. *Expert Syst. Appl.*, 65(C):292–303.

Xuezhe Ma and Eduard Hovy. 2016. End-to-end sequence labeling via bi-directional LSTM-CNNs-CRF. In *Proceedings of the 54th Annual Meeting of the Association for Computational Linguistics (Volume 1: Long Papers)*, volume 1, pages 1064–1074.

André FT Martins, Mário AT Figueiredo, Pedro MQ Aguiar, Noah A Smith, and Eric P Xing. 2015. Ad 3: Alternating directions dual decomposition for map inference in graphical models. *The Journal of Machine Learning Research*, 16(1):495–545.

Makoto Miwa and Mohit Bansal. 2016. End-to-end relation extraction using LSTMs on sequences and tree structures. In *Proceedings of the 54th Annual Meeting of the Association for Computational Linguistics, ACL 2016, August 7-12, 2016, Berlin, Germany, Volume 1: Long Papers*.

Raquel Mochales Palau and Marie-Francine Moens. 2011. Argumentation mining. *Artificial Intelligence and Law*, 19(1):1–22.

Vlad Niculae, Joonsuk Park, and Claire Cardie. 2017. Argument mining with structured SVMs and RNNs. In *Proceedings of the 55th Annual Meeting of the Association for Computational Linguistics, ACL 2017, Vancouver, Canada, July 30 - August 4, Volume 1: Long Papers*, pages 985–995. Association for Computational Linguistics.

Joonsuk Park, Cheryl Blake, and Claire Cardie. 2015a. Toward machine-assisted participation in eRulemaking: An argumentation model of evaluability. In *Proceedings of the 15th International Conference on Artificial Intelligence and Law*, pages 206–210. ACM.

Joonsuk Park and Claire Cardie. 2014. Identifying appropriate support for propositions in online user comments. In *Proceedings of the First Workshop on Argumentation Mining*, pages 29–38, Baltimore, Maryland. Association for Computational Linguistics.

Joonsuk Park, Arzoo Katiyar, and Bishan Yang. 2015b. Conditional random fields for identifying appropriate types of support for propositions in online user comments. In *Proceedings of the Second Workshop on Argumentation Mining*. Association for Computational Linguistics.

Jeffrey Pennington, Richard Socher, and Christopher Manning. 2014. GloVe: Global Vectors for word representation. In *Proceedings of the 2014 conference on empirical methods in natural language processing (EMNLP)*, pages 1532–1543.

Peter Potash, Alexey Romanov, and Anna Rumshisky. 2017. Here's my point: Joint pointer architecture for argument mining. In *Proceedings of the 2017 Conference on Empirical Methods in Natural Language Processing*, pages 1364–1373.

Nils Reimers and Iryna Gurevych. 2017. Reporting score distributions makes a difference: Performance study of lstm-networks for sequence tagging. In *Proceedings of the 2017 Conference on Empirical Methods in Natural Language Processing*, pages 338–348.

Ruty Rinott, Lena Dankin, Carlos Alzate Perez, Mitesh M. Khapra, Ehud Aharoni, and Noam Slonim. 2015. Show me your evidence - an automatic method for context dependent evidence detection. In *Proceedings of the 2015 Conference on Empirical Methods in Natural Language Processing, EMNLP 2015, Lisbon, Portugal, September 17-21, 2015*, pages 440–450. The Association for Computational Linguistics.

David E Rumelhart, Geoffrey E Hinton, and Ronald J Williams. 1986. Learning representations by back-propagating errors. *Nature*, 323(6088):533.

Christos Sardianos, Ioannis Manousos Katakis, Georgios Petasis, and Vangelis Karkaletsis. 2015. Argument extraction from news. pages 56–66.

Eyal Shnarch, Carlos Alzate, Lena Dankin, Martin Gleize, Yufang Hou, Leshem Choshen, Ranit Aharonov, and Noam Slonim. 2018. Will it blend? blending weak and strong labeled data in a neural network for argumentation mining. In *Proceedings of the 56th Annual Meeting of the Association for Computational Linguistics (Volume 2: Short Papers)*, volume 2, pages 599–605.

David Silver, Aja Huang, Chris J Maddison, Arthur Guez, Laurent Sifre, George Van Den Driessche, Julian Schrittwieser, Ioannis Antonoglou, Veda Panneershelvam, Marc Lanctot, et al. 2016. Mastering the game of go with deep neural networks and tree search. *nature*, 529(7587):484.

Anders Søgaard and Yoav Goldberg. 2016. Deep multi-task learning with low level tasks supervised at lower layers. In *Proceedings of the 54th Annual Meeting of the Association for Computational Linguistics (Volume 2: Short Papers)*, volume 2, pages 231–235.

Nitish Srivastava, Geoffrey E Hinton, Alex Krizhevsky, Ilya Sutskever, and Ruslan Salakhutdinov. 2014. Dropout: a simple way to prevent neural networks from overfitting. *Journal of Machine Learning Research*, 15(1):1929–1958.

Christian Stab and Iryna Gurevych. 2014. Identifying argumentative discourse structures in persuasive essays. In *EMNLP 2014, Doha, Qatar*, pages 46–56. ACL.

Christian Stab and Iryna Gurevych. 2017. Parsing argumentation structures in persuasive essays. *Computational Linguistics*, 43(3):619–659.

Stephen Edelston Toulmin. 1958. *The Uses of Argument*. Cambridge University Press.

Ioannis Tsochantaridis, Thorsten Joachims, Thomas Hofmann, and Yasemin Altun. 2005. Large margin methods for structured and interdependent output variables. *Journal of machine learning research*, 6(Sep):1453–1484.

Oriol Vinyals, Meire Fortunato, and Navdeep Jaitly. 2015. Pointer networks. In *Advances in Neural Information Processing Systems*, pages 2692–2700.

L. Yu, H. Chen, Q. Dou, J. Qin, and P. A. Heng. 2017. Automated melanoma recognition in dermoscopy images via very deep residual networks. *IEEE Transactions on Medical Imaging*, 36(4):994–1004.

Junbo Zhang, Yu Zheng, and Dekang Qi. 2017. Deep spatio-temporal residual networks for citywide crowd flows prediction. In *AAAI*, pages 1655–1661.

Xinyuan Zhang, Ricardo Henao, Zhe Gan, Yitong Li, and Lawrence Carin. 2018. Multi-label learning from medical plain text with convolutional residual models. *arXiv preprint arXiv:1801.05062*.

End-to-End Argument Mining for Discussion Threads
Based on Parallel Constrained Pointer Architecture

Gaku Morio and **Katsuhide Fujita**

Tokyo University of Agriculture and Technology

2-24-16, Koganei, Tokyo, Japan

morio@katfuji.lab.tuat.ac.jp, katfuji@cc.tuat.ac.jp

Abstract

Argument Mining (AM) is a relatively recent discipline, which concentrates on extracting claims or premises from discourses, and inferring their structures. However, many existing works do not consider micro-level AM studies on discussion threads sufficiently. In this paper, we tackle AM for discussion threads. Our main contributions are follows: (1) A novel combination scheme focusing on micro-level inner- and inter- post schemes for a discussion thread. (2) Annotation of large-scale civic discussion threads with the scheme. (3) *Parallel constrained pointer architecture* (PCPA), a novel end-to-end technique to discriminate sentence types, inner-post relations, and inter-post interactions simultaneously.[1] The experimental results demonstrate that our proposed model shows better accuracy in terms of relations extraction, in comparison to existing state-of-the-art models.

1 Introduction

Argument Mining (AM) is a discipline which concentrates on extracting claims or premises, and inferring their structures from a discourse. In (Palau and Moens, 2009; Stab and Gurevych, 2014; Peldszus and Stede, 2013), they construed an argument as the pairing of a single claim and a (possibly empty) set of premises, which justifies the claim.

Generally, identifying structures for argument components (i.e., premises and claims) is categorized as a micro-level approach, and among complete arguments as a macro-level approach. There are some micro-level approaches (Palau and Moens, 2009; Stab and Gurevych, 2014, 2017), however, few AM studies aggressively consider a scheme of micro-level reply-to

interactions in a thread. Though Hidey et al. (2017) provided a micro-level thread structured dataset, they considered an entire thread as a discourse. Thus, they allowed a premise that links to a claim in another post, while a post should be considered as a stand-alone discourse because a writer for each post is different. Also, we need to consider post-to-post interactions with the stand-alone assumption as a backdrop. Moreover, the dataset of (Hidey et al., 2017) with only 78 threads is too small to apply state-of-the-art neural discrimination models.

In addition to the shortage of micro-level anotations for discussion threads, no empirical study on end-to-end discrimination models which tackle discussion threads exist, to the best of our knowledge.

Motivated by the weaknesses above, this paper commits to the empirical study for discussion threads. Our main three contributions are as follows: (1) A novel combination scheme to apply AM to discussion threads. We introduce *inner-post* and *inter-post* schemes in combination. This combination enables us to discriminate arguments per post, rather than per thread as in (Hidey et al., 2017). In the former scheme, a post is assumed as a stand-alone discourse and a micro-level annotation is provided. In the second scheme, we introduce inter-post micro-level interactions. The introduction of the interactions allows us to capture informative argumentative relations between posts. (2) Large-scale online civic discussions are annotated by the proposed scheme. Specifically, we provide two phase annotation, and evaluate inter-annotator agreements. (3) A **parallel constrained pointer architecture** (PCPA) is proposed, which is a novel end-to-end neural model. The model can discriminate types of sentences (e.g., claim or premise), inner-post relations and inter-post interactions, simultaneously. In particu-

---

[1] Available at:
https://github.com/EdoFrank/EMNLP2018-ArgMining-Morio
including source codes.

Proceedings of the 5th Workshop on Argument Mining, pages 11–21

Brussels, Belgium, November 1, 2018. ©2018 Association for Computational Linguistics

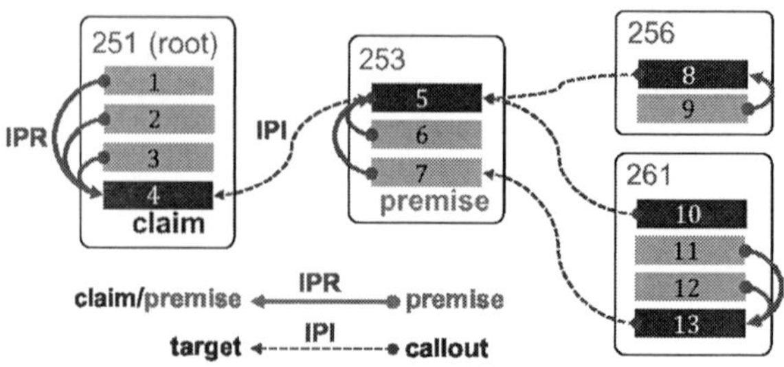

Figure 1: Example of our scheme for a thread.

lar, our PCPA achieved a significant improvement on challenging relation extractions in comparison to the existing state-of-the-art models (Eger et al., 2017; Potash et al., 2017). An advantage of our model is that the constraints of a thread structure are considered. The constraints make our architectures effective at learning and inferring, unlike existing pointer models.

While our dataset of discussion threads will make further advances in AM, the proposed PCPA will make end-to-end AM studies going forward.

2   Related Works

Stab and Gurevych (2017) argue that the task of AM is divided into the following three subtasks:

- **Component identification** focuses on separation of argumentative and non-argumentative text units and identification of argument component boundaries.
- **Component classification** addresses the function of argument components. It aims at classifying argument components into different types, such as claims and premises.
- **Structure identification** focuses on linking arguments or argument components. Its objective is to recognize different types of argumentative relations, such as support or attack relations.

The structure identification can also be divided to macro- and micro-level approaches. The macro-level approach as in (Boltužić and Šnajder, 2014; Ghosh et al., 2014; Murakami and Raymond, 2010) addresses relations between complete arguments and ignores the micro-structure of arguments (Stab and Gurevych, 2017). In (Ghosh et al., 2014), the authors introduced a scheme to represent relations between two posts by *target* and *callout*; however, their study discards micro-level structures in arguments because of their macro-level annotation. The micro-level approach as in (Palau and Moens, 2009; Stab and Gurevych, 2014, 2017) focuses on the relations between argument components.

In (Palau and Moens, 2009), arguments are considered as trees. In (Stab and Gurevych, 2017), the authors also represented relations of argument components in essays as tree structures. However, they addressed discourses of a single writer (i.e., an essay writer) rather than multiple authors in a discussion thread. Therefore, we can't simply apply their scheme to our study.

Recently, the advances of automatic detection of argument structures have been seen in the discipline of AM. Some recent papers (Lippi and Torroni, 2015; Eckle-Kohler et al., 2015) propose argument component identification to extract argumentative components in the entire discourse. These works (Persing and Ng, 2016; Eger et al., 2017; Potash et al., 2017) showed link extraction task to find argumentative relations between argument components.

End-to-end discrimination models are also highlighted in AM. The reason is low error propagation compared with the other ends (pipeline). The pipeline models have to discriminate argument component identification and link extraction subtasks independently, and thus cause the error propagation (Eger et al., 2017). The authors propose manners to apply multi-task learning (Søgaard and Goldberg, 2016; Martínez Alonso and Plank, 2017) and LSTM-ER (Miwa and Bansal, 2016) to the end-to-end AM. Another end-to-end work for AM, Potash et al. (2017) argues that Pointer Networks (Vinyals et al., 2015; Katiyar and Cardie, 2017) which incorporate a sequence-to-sequence model in their classifier is a state-of-the-art model for argument component type prediction and link extraction tasks.

3 Argument Mining for Discussion Thread

3.1 Scheme

In this work, we present a novel scheme combining *inner-post* scheme of a stand-alone post with *inter-post* scheme that considers a reply-to argumentative relation. In the inner-post scheme (e.g., claim/premise types and inner-post relations), "one-claim" approach from (Stab and Gurevych, 2017) is adopted. In the inter-post scheme, the micro-level interaction in the spirit of (Ghosh et al., 2014) is employed. The definitions of inner-post relation and inter-post interaction are follows:

- **Inner-post relation (IPR)** is a directed argumentative relation in a post. Each IPR:$(target \leftarrow source)$ indicates that the *source* component is either a justification for or a refutation of the *target* component. Thus, a *source* should be a premise, and each premise has a single outgoing link to another premise or claim (Eger et al., 2017).
- **Target** is a head of IPI that has been called out by a subsequent claim in another post that replies to the post of the target.
- **Callout** is a tail of IPI that refers back to a prior target. In addition to referring back to the target, a callout must be a claim.[2]
- **Inter-post interaction (IPI)** is the micro-level relationship of two posts: parent post and child post that replies to the parent post. A relation $(parent \leftarrow child)$ represents the *child* is a **callout** and *parent* is a **target**.

Figure 1 shows our combination scheme for a discussion thread.

3.2 Dataset

To develop a sufficient AM corpus for discussion threads, we have annotated an original large-scale online civic discussion (Morio and Fujita, 2018a). The civic discussion data is obtained by an online civic engagement on the *COLLAGREE* (Ito et al., 2014; Morio and Fujita, 2018b) including a thread structure. The discussion was held from the end of 2016 to the beginning of 2017, and co-hosted by the government of Nagoya City, Japan. The accumulated data includes 204 citizens, 399 threads, 1327 posts, 5559 sentences and 120241 tokens spelled in Japanese.[3] To the best of our knowl-

edge, this work is the first approach which annotates large-scale civic discussions for AM.[4]

3.3 Annotation Design

In (Peldszus and Stede, 2013), the authors argue that the annotation task for AM contains the following three subtasks: (1) segmentation, (2) segment classification and (3) relationship identification. The segmentation requires extensive human resources, time, and cost. Therefore, we apply a rule-based technique for the segmentation. Then, we consider each sentence as an argument component candidate (ACC). For classifying the argument component, the ACC types (claim, premise or non-argumentative (NonArg)) for each ACC are annotated. Finally, the relationship identification needs to annotate IPRs and IPIs.

Using multiple processes for multiple annotation subtasks is common (Meyers and Brashers, 2010; Stab and Gurevych, 2014, 2017). To annotate our data, we provide two phases. In the first phase, we concentrate on annotating ACC type and IPR, and create a temporal gold standard. In the second phase, IPI is annotated using the temporal gold standard.

We employed a majority vote to create the gold standard. All three annotators independently annotated in this work. The procedure of the first phase for compiling the temporal gold standard is as follows.

A1: Each ACC type is decided on a majority vote. When the ACC type of the sentence cannot be decided by majority vote, NonArg is assigned to them.
A2: Each IPR (link existence) is decided on a majority vote.
A3: Merging the results from A1 and A2, and obtaining trees where root is a claim. Thus, we have trees to the number of claims in a post.
A4: Eliminating premise tags that do not belong to any trees, assigning them to NonArg, and eliminating their IPR.

3.4 Annotation Result

Inter-annotator agreement for ACC type, IPR and IPI annotations are calculated using Fleiss's κ (Fleiss, 1971). First, we attempt to evaluate the agreement of the first phase annotations, however, the κ of IPR is relatively low: 0.420. The annotators are less likely to agree on serial arguments (Stab and Gurevych, 2017) like $(premise \leftarrow premise)$ relations.[5]

---

[2]To restrict a callout to a claim makes our problem more simple because the number of outgoing links from a claim becomes one at a maximum. Thus, we introduced the restriction.

[3]The average of the number of posts per thread is 3.33 (standard deviation is 3.29), the depth of threads is 1.09 (standard deviation is 1.19), the number of sentences per post is 4.19 (standard deviation is 3.33) and the number of words per sentence is 21.63 (standard deviation is 19.92).

[4]Recently, Park and Cardie (2018) provide a similar dataset of civic engagement, while their dataset doesn't consider post-to-post relations sufficiently.

[5]Unlike with Persuasive Essays (Stab and Gurevych, 2017), citizen's documents for civic discussions are seldom

Corpus	Type	Size	κ
COLLAGREE	Claim	1449	.531
	Premise	2762	.554
	NonArg	1348	.529
	IPR w/ A0	2762	.466
	IPI	745	.430
Persuasive Essays	Claim	1506	.635
	Premise	3832	.833
	Inner-essay rel	3832	.708-.737

Table 1: Inter-annotator agreement scores for the two corpora.

Therefore, we introduce an initial process A0, transforming $(premise1 \leftarrow premise2)$ into $(root\ claim\ of\ premise2 \leftarrow premise2)$, before A1.[6]

Table 1 summarizes the number of each type of relation and inter-annotator agreement.[7] For comparison, we also mention the annotation results of Persuasive Essays (Stab and Gurevych, 2017). Unlike the essay dataset, our datasets contain badly-structured writings, resulting in low agreement. However, classification tasks can be applied as (Landis and Koch, 1977) refers to the κ value from 0.41 to 0.61 as "moderate agreement". Moreover, the agreement of IPR is improved by providing the process A0.

4 Discriminating ACC Type, Inner-Post Relation and Inter-Post Interaction

This section describes the study on our end-to-end discrimination model, which identifies ACC type, IPR and IPI for our annotated dataset.

4.1 Thread Representation as a Sequence

If the thread itself contains flow of its argument, only the thread itself is considered as the desirable input for a discrimination model. Thus, we describe a way of representing a thread with an input sequence.

In this work, we extend the sequence representation of (Eger et al., 2017; Potash et al., 2017).

---

well-structured. Thus, we don't see the point in providing a more complex scheme (i.e., allowing $(premise \leftarrow premise)$ relations).

[6]For example, two IPRs $\{(claim1 \leftarrow premise1), (premise1 \leftarrow premise2)\}$ are transformed to $\{(claim1 \leftarrow premise1), (claim1 \leftarrow premise2)\}$.

[7]Outgoing IPI links are composed of 574 claims, 109 premises, and 62 NonArgs. Considering that a callout should be a claim, the $(claim \leftarrow claim)$ interaction accounts for 77% of the total. The results indicate that IPIs are pretty argumentative. In addition, we annotated support/attack relations (Cocarascu and Toni, 2017). The results show support accounts for 86% and attacks for 7% of the total IPIs.

The creation of thread representation as an input sequence consists of the following two steps. First, we assume each element of the input sequence for recurrent neural network is a sentence representation, rather than a word representation. Second, we sort the sentence representations by the thread depth order. In addition, for each thread depth, we in turn order them according to the timestamp of their post, and insert separator representations. The first one makes it possible to input a short sequence to LSTM units (Hochreiter and Schmidhuber, 1997). The second makes a classifier easy to discriminate considering the hierarchy of a thread and reply relations. Figure 2 shows an example of a thread representation as sequence.

4.2 Parallel Constrained Pointer Architecture

One of the main technical contributions of our approach is to provide a discrimination model that classifies ACC type, IPR and IPI simultaneously via end-to-end learning. A Pointer Network (PN) for end-to-end AM achieves state-of-the-art results (Potash et al., 2017), which leads to applying a PN based technique to our scheme. Unfortunately, the naive PN did not achieve the result expected (the quantitative results are shown in Section 5), because the simple PN is unable to constrain its search space for thread structures. For instance, an inner-post relation classifier could discriminate with no need to search out of its post, or an inter-post interaction classifier could classify with no need to search out of the parent post and child post. Therefore, we propose a novel neural model named *parallel constrained pointer architecture* (PCPA). PCPA provides two parallel pointer architectures: IPR and IPI discrimination architectures that adopt the apparent constrains of threads.

Sentence Representation as Input

First, we introduce the input representation. Given N threads $(T_1, \ldots, T_N)$, we denote T_i's posts which are sorted in thread depth order, and then timestamp order as described in Section 4.1 as $(P_1^{(i)}, \ldots, P_{N_i}^{(i)})$, where N_i represents the number of posts in T_i. In addition to the thread and post representations, write $(S_1^{(i,j)}, \ldots, S_{N_{i,j}}^{(i,j)})$ for sentences in post $P_j^{(i)}$, where $N_{i,j}$ represents the number of sentences in $P_j^{(i)}$. Note that separator rep-

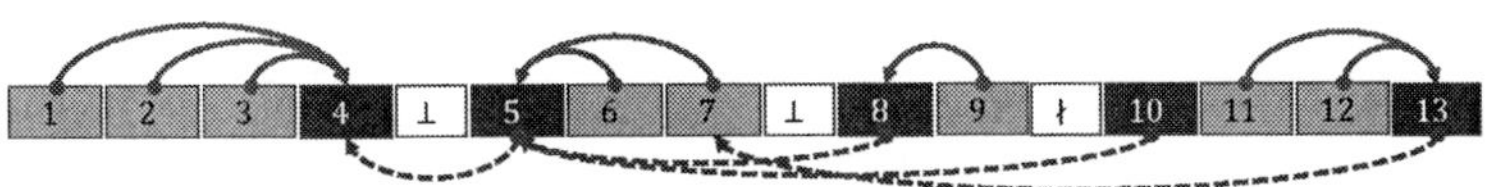

Figure 2: Sequence representation from Figure 1. $\perp$ and $\not{/}$ denotes a separator representation of thread depth and posts.

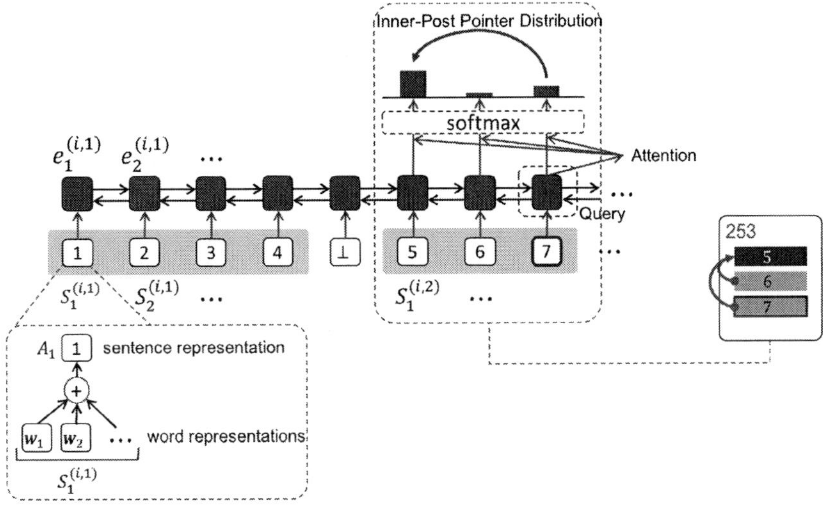

Figure 3: Example of the constrained pointer architecture of inner-post relation (IPR) identification, discriminating the IPR target from the ACC "7".

resentations are not considered in the notation.

Then, w_n is given initially, an embedding vector of nth word in a sentence $S_k^{(i,j)}$, a sentence representation for an input of LSTM is represented as: $A_k = \sum_n w_n$, where w_n is gained from bag-of-words (BoW) or word embeddings (Mikolov et al., 2013; Pennington et al., 2014; Stab and Gurevych, 2017). In our study, we employed BoW and a fully connected layer with a trainable parameter to learn word embeddings. Subsequently, we provide Bidirectional LSTM (BiLSTM) (Graves and Schmidhuber, 2005) because PN requires encoding steps. At each time step of the encoder BiLSTM, PCPA considers a representation of an ACC. Thus, the hidden representation e_i of BiLSTM becomes the concatenation of forward and backward hidden representations. To simplify the explanation, we denote the hidden representations of $(S_1^{(i,j)}, \ldots, S_{N_{i,j}}^{(i,j)})$ as $(e_1^{(i,j)}, \ldots, e_{N_{i,j}}^{(i,j)})$. For better understanding, we show notations in Figure 3.

Discriminating Inner-Post Relation

The general PN of (Potash et al., 2017) uses all hidden states e_i. Alternately, PCPA can limit the states to improve the accuracies, since each premise has a single outgoing link to another sentence in its post. Hence, we provide an approach to discriminate IPR using only inner-post hidden states of the BiLSTM.

Figure 3 shows the example IPR discrimination in thread T_i; for example, we assume that the inner-post relation of the sentence written as "7" in the 3rd ACC of post $P_2^{(i)}$ is classified. The general PN needs to consider all e_i, therefore, the search space is large. On the other hands, our proposed PCPA can consider $(e_1^{(i,2)}, e_2^{(i,2)}, e_3^{(i,2)})$, which needs to use the hidden states of its post only. Therefore, our constrained architecture can reduce the search space significantly.

In general, given W_1, W_2, and v_1, parameters of attention model (Luong et al., 2015) for PN,

$$u_l^{(i,j,k)} = v_1^\top \tanh \left(W_1 e_l^{(i,j)} + W_2 e_k^{(i,j)} \right) \quad (1)$$

represents a degree that kth ACC in post $P_j^{(i)}$ has an outgoing link to lth ACC. Moreover, we can assume $e_k^{(i,j)}$ as a query vector. Supposing the ACC has no outgoing link, we can consider the ACC learned to point to itself. Although equation (1) is real-value, a distribution over the IPR input is

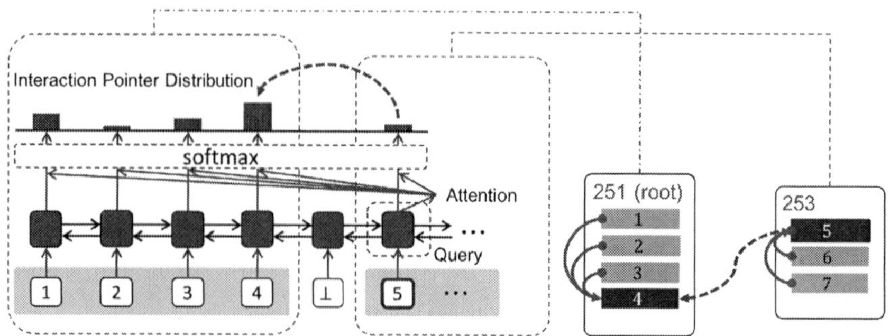

Figure 4: Example of the constrained pointer architecture of inter-post interaction (IPI) identification, discriminating the IPI target that is called out from the ACC "5".

considered by taking softmax function, i.e.,

$$p(y_k^{ipr} \mid P_j^{(i)}) = \mathrm{softmax}(u^{(i,j,k)}) \quad (2)$$

representing the probability that kth ACC in post $P_j^{(i)}$ has an outgoing link to lth ACC in $P_j^{(i)}$. Therefore, the objective for IPR in thread T_i is calculated by taking the sum of log-likelihoods for all posts:

$$L_i^{ipr} = \sum_{j=1}^{N_i} \sum_{k=1}^{N_{i,j}} \log p(y_k^{ipr} \mid P_j^{(i)}) \quad (3)$$

Discriminating Inter-Post Interaction

As the definition of target and callout in our scheme, IPI exists between a parent post and child post that replies to the parent. Thus, PCPA can discriminate IPI with no need to use all of the hidden representations of the LSTM. In other words, it can discriminate IPI without searching outside of the two posts.

Hence, we design an output layer that requires only a set of reply pairs in thread T_i. Specifically, we assume that $R^{(i)} = \{(j_1, j_2), \cdots \}$ where $j_1 \neq j_2 \wedge j_1 < j_2$ for a set of parent-child pairs in thread T_i. Supposing j_1 is the index of a parent post and j_2 represents the index of the child post that replies to the j_1. Note that when thread T_i does not have any reply pairs, $R^{(i)} = \varnothing$. Considering the above, a technique that is similar to the IPR's technique is introduced.

Figure 4 shows the example IPI discrimination in thread T_i; supposing that we are going to discriminate a target that is called out from ACC "5" in the figure. In this case, the search space is limited by the parent post $(e_1^{(i,1)}, \ldots, e_4^{(i,1)})$. Moreover, we add an element $e_1^{(i,2)}$ so that a callout can point itself if there's no target in its parent post. The left four outputs in the "Interaction Pointer Distribution" indicate a discrete probabilistic distribution that the callout ACC "5" links to target sentences in its parent post, and an output on the far right represents a probability that the callout links to itself.

The equation (1) uses a query in the PN, so we in turn concentrate on using a query vector for the callout in IPI. Herein, we introduce an additional PN for IPI using new attention parameters, W_3, W_4 and v_2, as:

$$q_l^{(i,j,k)} = v_2^\top \tanh\left(W_3 e_l^{(i,j)} + W_4 e_k^{(i,j)}\right) \quad (4)$$

where $e_k^{(i,j)}$ is the query from the callout. Supposing that the reply pair is (j_1, j_2), a target of kth ACC of the child post $P_{j_2}^{(i)}$ is searched. The expanded vector $\left[q^{(i,j_1,k)}; q_k^{(i,j_2,k)}\right]$ is obtained by concatenating the attention vectors $q^{(i,j_1,k)}$ from the parent post and a vector $q_k^{(i,j_2,k)}$ from the callout. This expansion process is the same as the process of (Merity et al., 2016). Finally, given all reply pairs of thread T_i, the log-likelihood is calculated as follows:

$$p(y_k^{ipi} \mid P_{j_1}^{(i)}, P_{j_2}^{(i)}) = \mathrm{softmax}([q^{(i,j_1,k)}; q_k^{(i,j_2,k)}])$$

$$L_i^{ipi} = \sum_{(j_1,j_2)\in R^{(i)}} \sum_{k=1}^{N_{i,j_2}} \log p(y_k^{ipi} \mid P_{j_1}^{(i)}, P_{j_2}^{(i)})$$

$$(5)$$

Discriminating ACC Type

At each time step of the BiLSTM, the type classification task predicts whether it is claim, premise, or NonArg. The ACC type of sentence $S_k^{(i,j)}$ can be classified by taking softmax of $z_k^{(i,j)} = W_{type} e_k^{(i,j)} + b_{type}$, where W_{type} and b_{type} are parameters. An objective for the type classifier

16

can also be described by taking the sum of log-likelihoods for all posts as:

$$p(y_k^{type} \mid P_j^{(i)}) = \mathrm{softmax}(z_k^{(i,j)})$$

$$L_i^{type} = \sum_{j=1}^{N_i} \sum_{k=1}^{N_{i,j}} \log p(y_k^{type} \mid P_j^{(i)}) \qquad (6)$$

Joint Learning

Combining objectives of IPR (equation (3)), IPI (equation (5)) and the ACC type (equation (6)), the training objective of PCPA is shown as follows:

$$Loss = \frac{1}{N} \sum_i (-\alpha L_i^{ipr} - \beta L_i^{ipi}$$

$$- (1 - \alpha - \beta) L_i^{type}) \qquad (7)$$

where α and β are hyperparameters which adjust the weight of tasks in our cost function. Note that $\alpha, \beta \in [0, 1] \wedge \alpha + \beta < 1$.

5 Experiments

5.1 Experimental Settings

Evaluation Metric

For the evaluation of ACC types, IPR and IPI discrimination, we adopt precision, recall and F1 scores. To obtain the precision and recall, we introduce a way to compute positive and negative cases by creating relations (Stab and Gurevych, 2017), excluding self-pointers. [8] [9]

Baselines

First, we employ state-of-the-art PN techniques from (Potash et al., 2017) as baselines. The use of these baselines was decided because our model PCPA (**Our Model**) employs pointer architectures. As the authors proposed two techniques, sequence-to-sequence model (**PN with Seq2Seq**) and w/o sequence-to-sequence model (**PN without Seq2Seq**), we have the two models for comparison.

To analyze how a *non* PN model works, multi-task learning is employed to the baseline (Søgaard and Goldberg, 2016) (**STagBLSTM**) by (Eger et al., 2017). STagBLSTM is composed of shared BiLSTM layers for subtasks, and output layers for each subtask. In (Eger et al., 2017), the authors provided a BIO tagging task, however, the task is not required in our work because BiLSTM handles an input as sentence representation rather than as word representation. In this paper, we use one BiLSTM.[10]

To show end-to-end learning models are effective for AM on thread structures, we provide the following three task specific baselines. First, feature-based SVM (Stab and Gurevych, 2017) (**SVM - T**) is introduced. T indicates each subtask of the claim classifier, premise classifier, IPR classifier, and IPI classifier. In addition, random forest (**RF - T**) and the logistic regression technique (Peldszus and Stede, 2015) (**Simple - T**) are also introduced. For each task specific model, BoW features the top 500 most frequent words [11].

We assume that each output of PN with Seq2Seq, PN without Seq2Seq or STagBLSTM does not satisfy the constraints as a self-pointer. This is because inappropriate outputs with constraint violations of IPR and IPI by these approaches will happen, i.e., they can predict IPI out of parent and child posts. The assumption maintains the false positive (FP) of baselines, since a self-pointer which results from a chance is not counted as FP. This condition gives the baselines the advantage of precision over our models. Therefore, this assumption is convincing.

The following describes our implementation details. The implementation of neural models are by Chainer (Tokui et al., 2015). The hyperparameters are the same as (Potash et al., 2017) for the PN baselines and our models[12]. In the interest of time,

---

[8]For example, supposing there is a post which contains three sentences, (S_1, S_2, S_3), and two gold standard IPRs, $(S_1 \leftarrow S_2)$ and $(S_1 \leftarrow S_3)$. This is exactly the case that positive cases of IPR are $\{(S_1 \leftarrow S_2), (S_1 \leftarrow S_3)\}$, and negative cases are all sentence pairs excluding self-pointers. That is, negatives are $\{(S_2 \leftarrow S_1), (S_2 \leftarrow S_3), (S_3 \leftarrow S_1), (S_3 \leftarrow S_2)\}$. In this case, self-pointer cases are $\{(S_1 \leftarrow S_1), (S_2 \leftarrow S_2), (S_3 \leftarrow S_3)\}$.

[9]For IPI, we are also able to create sentence pairs. For instance, suppose there is a parent post which contains three sentences (S_1, S_2, S_3), a child post that contains two sentences (S_4, S_5), and a gold standard IPI, $(S_2 \leftarrow S_5)$. The positive case of IPI is exactly $\{(S_2 \leftarrow S_5)\}$, and negative cases are all sentence pairs excluding self-pointers, that is, $\{(S_1 \leftarrow S_4), (S_1 \leftarrow S_5), (S_2 \leftarrow S_4), (S_3 \leftarrow S_4), (S_3 \leftarrow S_5)\}$.

[10]Though there are some variation models other than the single BiLSTM model, our preliminary experiments show a non-significant improvement.

[11]In fact (Stab and Gurevych, 2017) and employs rich features such as structural features. We only use BoW for comparison because the properties of COLLAGREE corpus substantially differ from their corpus.

[12]Hidden input dimension size 512, hidden layer size 256 for the BiLSTMs, hidden layer size 512 for the LSTM decoder of PN without Seq2Seq, and high dropout rate of 0.9 (Srivastava et al., 2014; Zarrella and Marsh, 2016). All models are trained with the Adam optimizer (Kingma and Ba,

Model type	Model name	Type classification			Link extraction			
		Claim F1	Premise F1	NonArg F1	IPR Precision	IPR F1	IPI Precision	IPI F1
Joint learning	Our Model	58.5	68.7	36.0	33.8	***40.8**	19.6	***24.8**
	Our Model - Hyp	58.1	**71.5**	**58.8**	***45.8**	***44.3**	***30.4**	***26.9**
	STagBLSTM	54.2	65.6	56.9	14.3	14.9	21.0	12.6
	PN with Seq2Seq	58.3	70.8	48.6	35.7	27.2	13.0	19.4
	PN without Seq2Seq	**60.1**	71.3	53.1	36.6	35.0	26.5	20.8
Task specific	SVM - T	53.3	64.4	52.3	13.8	22.4	6.4	11.5
	RF - T	41.0	66.8	38.3	0	0	100	1.4
	Simple - T	41.1	66.1	38.3	0	0	0	0
Joint learning w/o separator	Our Model w/o separator	43.1	66.3	29.6	30.0	36.1	9.9	13.7
	STagBLSTM w/o separator	51.8	66.1	55.2	13.9	14.5	16.1	10.8
	PN with Seq2Seq w/o separator	40.7	67.8	52.7	30.4	23.2	10.8	14.6
	PN without Seq2Seq w/o separator	43.4	67.6	53.7	29.5	21.1	19.0	6.0

Table 2: **Top**: Our models vs. joint baselines (%). * indicates significant. at $p < 0.01$, two-sided Wilcoxon signed rank test (Derryberry et al., 2010), compared with each baseline. **Middle**: Performances of task specific baselines. **Bottom**: Performances of joint models w/o separator representations.

we ran 50 epochs, and used the trained model for testing. The COLLAGREE dataset is divided into training threads and testing threads at $8 : 2$. In addition, we use the following hyperparameters in equation (7): $\alpha = \beta = 1/3$. However, total loss of L^{ipr} and L^{ipi} tends to enlarge since they have to calculate a sum of the sentence pairs. Hence, we provide a model with tuned hyperparameters $\alpha = \beta = 0.15$ (**Our Model - Hyp**) for comparison.

5.2 Experimental Results

Table 2 summarizes the results of our models and baselines. For each model, we showed the best F1 score in the table. Due to limitations of space, we omitted recalls and some precisions. Surprisingly, all models performed as well as we expected in our dataset, in spite of low agreements (see Table 1). Although the basis of the ACC type classifier of PCPA is the same as the PN model, our model with tuned hyperparameters is better at NonArg identification than the baseline PN models.

Both of our models significantly outperform all baselines for the IPR and IPI discrimination tasks. "Our Model - Hyp" achieves F1 $+9.3\%$ in IPR identification in comparison with the best baseline PN without Seq2Seq. This is the most important result because it indicates that incorporating constrains of thread structures with the PNs makes relation classifiers easy to learn and discriminate.

STagBLSTM shows lower scores in terms of both IPR and IPI identification, implying the difficulty of the use of the multi-task learning of BiL-

2014) with a mini batch size of 16.

Model	IPR - F1	IPI - F1
Our Model	±0.7	±1.8
PN with Seq2Seq	±2.3	±1.2
PN without Seq2Seq	±2.7	±3.9

Table 3: Standard deviations of F1 scores (%)

STM. In addition, Table 2 (Middle) also illustrates that most neural models yield better F1 scores in comparison with the task specific models. In addition, the logistic regression and RF are overfitted, despite that cross validations are employed. Thus, end-to-end learning assumes an important role for AM, even in thread structures.

Effectiveness of Separator Representation

To demonstrate the effectiveness of the separator representations, we conducted an experiment. In Table 2 (Bottom), the models without the separator input representations are indicated as "w/o separator". It shows that separator representations dramatically improve scores of PN based models. This remarkable result is from the ability to learn the structural information of a thread by encoding separators in the BiLSTM.

Stability

To analyze the stability of our models, we compare standard deviations among three selected models. Table 3 shows standard deviations for the three models. These results indicate that our model has lower standard deviations for IPR than baseline PN models. The reason for this is the size of search space: our models can effectively limit the search space based on thread structures.

Model	IPR - F1	IPI - F1
Our Model	*39.6	*22.6
Our Model with Param Share	36.7	11.9

Table 4: The effect of parameter sharing of the two pointer architectures.

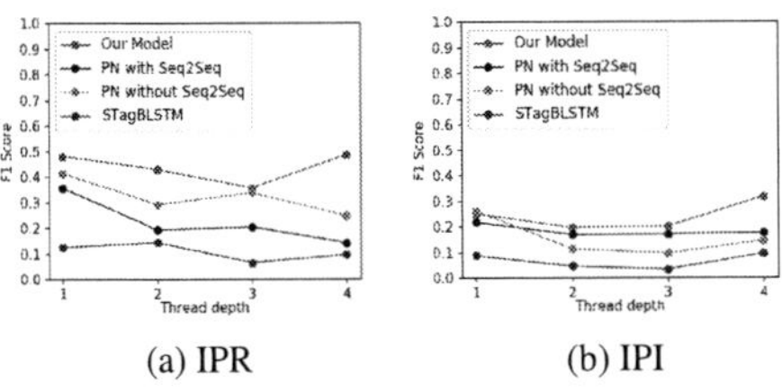

(a) IPR   (b) IPI

Figure 5: Performances on different thread depths.

Analysis for Parallel Design

Next, we show how our models improve their performance by employing our parallel pointer architecture. Herein, we provide a new model of PCPA with a single PN (**Our Model with Param Share**), which shares v_1, W_1 and W_2 in equation (1) and v_2, W_3 and W_4 in equation (4), respectively. Table 4 demonstrates the mean of F1 scores for our model and Our Model with Param Share. Note that the average performances are lower than the best performances in Table 2. The scores indicate that sharing the two pointer architecture parameters is not effective in our proposed model. We estimate this is because poor association (Caruana, 1997) between the IPR and IPI identification tasks exists. Therefore, our approach of using two parallel pointer architectures is effective.

Performance Specialized in Threads

We examine how our models are specialized in thread structures. Specifically, we limit the threads in test datasets by specific thresholds, and then analyze performance transitions. We conduct two experiments as the thread depth is limited (Figure 5a and 5b). While the baselines performances decrease as the thread depth increases, our model keeps its F1 score because of the separators and the search space. The separator representations for an input increase according to the thread depth, and the baseline PN models need to use wider range of hidden states in comparison with the PCPA model. In other words, our models are extremely effective, even for deeper threads.

We also limit the threads that we can use in test data by the number of posts (Figure 6a, and

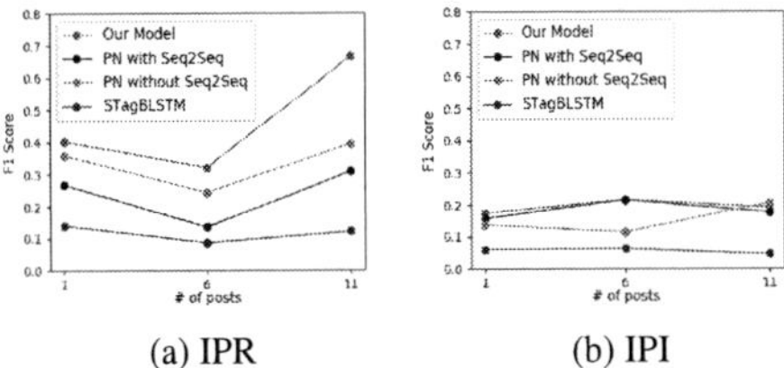

(a) IPR   (b) IPI

Figure 6: Performances on different number of posts. When the horizontal value is 1, we test using threads which contains [1-5] posts.

6b). For discriminating IPR, our model increasingly outperforms others in accordance with the number of posts. Figure 6b indicates that the difference between our model and baselines is minimal. This is because the number of posts does not affect the thread depth, necessarily. Most of *COLLAGREE*'s threads have a depth of at most 2. In other words, Figure 6b also implies the depth of threads affects the improvement of IPI identifications.

6 Conclusion

This paper presented an end-to-end study on discussion threads for argument mining (AM). We proposed an AM scheme that is composed of micro-level inner- and inter- post scheme for a discussion thread. The annotation result shows we acquire the valid and pretty argumentative corpus. To structuralize the discourses of threads automatically, we propose a neural end-to-end AM technique. Specifically, we presented a novel technique to utilize constraints of the thread structure for pointer networks. The experimental results demonstrated that our proposed model outperformed state-of-the-art baselines in terms of relation identifications.

Possible future work includes enhancing our scheme for less restricted conditions, i.e., multiple targets from one callout.

Acknowledgments

This work was supported by CREST, JST (JP-MJCR15E1), Japan and JST AIP-PRISM Grant Number JPMJCR18ZL, Japan. We thank Takayuki Ito, Eizo Hideshima, Takanori Ito and Shun Shiramatsu for providing us with the COLLAGREE data.

References

Filip Boltužić and Jan Šnajder. 2014. Back up your stance: Recognizing arguments in online discussions. In *Proceedings of the First Workshop on Argumentation Mining*, pages 49–58, Baltimore, Maryland. Association for Computational Linguistics.

Rich Caruana. 1997. Multitask learning. *Mach. Learn.*, 28(1):41–75.

Oana Cocarascu and Francesca Toni. 2017. Identifying attack and support argumentative relations using deep learning. In *Proceedings of the 2017 Conference on Empirical Methods in Natural Language Processing*, pages 1374–1379. Association for Computational Linguistics.

DeWayne R. Derryberry, Sue B. Schou, and W. J. Conover. 2010. Teaching rank-based tests by emphasizing structural similarities to corresponding parametric tests. *Journal of Statistics Education*, 18(1).

Judith Eckle-Kohler, Roland Kluge, and Iryna Gurevych. 2015. On the role of discourse markers for discriminating claims and premises in argumentative discourse. In *Proceedings of the 2015 Conference on Empirical Methods in Natural Language Processing*, pages 2236–2242, Lisbon, Portugal. Association for Computational Linguistics.

Steffen Eger, Johannes Daxenberger, and Iryna Gurevych. 2017. Neural end-to-end learning for computational argumentation mining. In *Proceedings of the 55th Annual Meeting of the Association for Computational Linguistics (Volume 1: Long Papers)*, pages 11–22, Vancouver, Canada. Association for Computational Linguistics.

Joseph L Fleiss. 1971. Measuring nominal scale agreement among many raters. *Psychological Bulletin*, 76(5):378–382.

Debanjan Ghosh, Smaranda Muresan, Nina Wacholder, Mark Aakhus, and Matthew Mitsui. 2014. Analyzing argumentative discourse units in online interactions. In *Proceedings of the First Workshop on Argument Mining, hosted by the 52nd Annual Meeting of the Association for Computational Linguistics, ArgMining@ACL 2014, June 26, 2014, Baltimore, Maryland, USA*, pages 39–48.

Alex Graves and Jürgen Schmidhuber. 2005. Framewise phoneme classification with bidirectional lstm and other neural network architectures. *NEURAL NETWORKS*, pages 5–6.

Christopher Hidey, Elena Musi, Alyssa Hwang, Smaranda Muresan, and Kathy McKeown. 2017. Analyzing the semantic types of claims and premises in an online persuasive forum. In *Proceedings of the 4th Workshop on Argument Mining*, pages 11–21, Copenhagen, Denmark. Association for Computational Linguistics.

Sepp Hochreiter and Jürgen Schmidhuber. 1997. Long short-term memory. *Neural Comput.*, 9(8):1735–1780.

Takayuki Ito, Yuma Imi, Takanori Ito, and Eizo Hideshima. 2014. Collagree: A faciliator-mediated large-scale consensus support system. In *Proceedings of the 2nd International Conference of Collective Intelligence*.

Arzoo Katiyar and Claire Cardie. 2017. Going out on a limb: Joint extraction of entity mentions and relations without dependency trees. In *Proceedings of the 55th Annual Meeting of the Association for Computational Linguistics (Volume 1: Long Papers)*, pages 917–928. Association for Computational Linguistics.

Diederik P. Kingma and Jimmy Ba. 2014. Adam: A method for stochastic optimization. *CoRR*, abs/1412.6980.

J. Richard Landis and Gary G. Koch. 1977. The measurement of observer agreement for categorical data. *Biometrics*, 33(1).

Marco Lippi and Paolo Torroni. 2015. Context-independent claim detection for argument mining. In *Proceedings of the 24th International Conference on Artificial Intelligence*, IJCAI'15, pages 185–191. AAAI Press.

Thang Luong, Hieu Pham, and Christopher D. Manning. 2015. Effective approaches to attention-based neural machine translation. In *EMNLP*, pages 1412–1421. The Association for Computational Linguistics.

Héctor Martínez Alonso and Barbara Plank. 2017. When is multitask learning effective? semantic sequence prediction under varying data conditions. In *Proceedings of the 15th Conference of the European Chapter of the Association for Computational Linguistics: Volume 1, Long Papers*, pages 44–53, Valencia, Spain. Association for Computational Linguistics.

Stephen Merity, Caiming Xiong, James Bradbury, and Richard Socher. 2016. Pointer sentinel mixture models. *CoRR*, abs/1609.07843.

Renee A. Meyers and Dale Brashers. 2010. Extending the conversational argument coding scheme: Argument categories, units, and coding procedures. *Communication Methods and Measures*, 4(1-2):27–45.

Tomas Mikolov, Ilya Sutskever, Kai Chen, Greg S Corrado, and Jeff Dean. 2013. Distributed representations of words and phrases and their compositionality. In C. J. C. Burges, L. Bottou, M. Welling, Z. Ghahramani, and K. Q. Weinberger, editors, *Advances in Neural Information Processing Systems 26*, pages 3111–3119. Curran Associates, Inc.

Makoto Miwa and Mohit Bansal. 2016. End-to-end relation extraction using lstms on sequences and tree structures. In *Proceedings of the 54th Annual Meeting of the Association for Computational Linguistics (Volume 1: Long Papers)*, pages 1105–1116. Association for Computational Linguistics.

Gaku Morio and Katsuhide Fujita. 2018a. Annotating online civic discussion threads for argument mining. In *2018 IEEE/WIC/ACM International Conference on Web Intelligence (WI)*, page (to appear).

Gaku Morio and Katsuhide Fujita. 2018b. Predicting argumentative influence probabilities in large-scale online civic engagement. In *Companion Proceedings of the The Web Conference 2018*, WWW '18, pages 1427–1434, Republic and Canton of Geneva, Switzerland. International World Wide Web Conferences Steering Committee.

Akiko Murakami and Rudy Raymond. 2010. Support or oppose?: Classifying positions in online debates from reply activities and opinion expressions. In *Proceedings of the 23rd International Conference on Computational Linguistics: Posters*, COLING '10, pages 869–875, Stroudsburg, PA, USA. Association for Computational Linguistics.

Raquel Mochales Palau and Marie-Francine Moens. 2009. Argumentation mining: The detection, classification and structure of arguments in text. In *Proceedings of the 12th International Conference on Artificial Intelligence and Law*, ICAIL '09, pages 98–107, New York, NY, USA. ACM.

Joonsuk Park and Claire Cardie. 2018. A corpus of erulemaking user comments for measuring evaluability of arguments. In *Proceedings of the Eleventh International Conference on Language Resources and Evaluation, LREC 2018, Miyazaki, Japan, May 7-12, 2018*.

Andreas Peldszus and Manfred Stede. 2013. From argument diagrams to argumentation mining in texts: A survey. *Int. J. Cogn. Inform. Nat. Intell.*, 7(1):1–31.

Andreas Peldszus and Manfred Stede. 2015. Joint prediction in mst-style discourse parsing for argumentation mining. In *Proceedings of the 2015 Conference on Empirical Methods in Natural Language Processing*, pages 938–948, Lisbon, Portugal. Association for Computational Linguistics.

Jeffrey Pennington, Richard Socher, and Christopher Manning. 2014. Glove: Global vectors for word representation. In *Proceedings of the 2014 Conference on Empirical Methods in Natural Language Processing (EMNLP)*, pages 1532–1543. Association for Computational Linguistics.

Isaac Persing and Vincent Ng. 2016. End-to-end argumentation mining in student essays. In *Proceedings of Human Language Technologies: The 2016 Annual Conference of the North American Chapter of the Association for Computational Linguistics*, pages 1384–1394.

Peter Potash, Alexey Romanov, and Anna Rumshisky. 2017. Here's my point: Joint pointer architecture for argument mining. In *Proceedings of the 2017 Conference on Empirical Methods in Natural Language Processing*, pages 1375–1384. Association for Computational Linguistics.

Anders Søgaard and Yoav Goldberg. 2016. Deep multi-task learning with low level tasks supervised at lower layers. In *Proceedings of the 54th Annual Meeting of the Association for Computational Linguistics*, volume 2, pages 231–235. Association for Computational Linguistics.

Nitish Srivastava, Geoffrey Hinton, Alex Krizhevsky, Ilya Sutskever, and Ruslan Salakhutdinov. 2014. Dropout: A simple way to prevent neural networks from overfitting. *Journal of Machine Learning Research*, 15:1929–1958.

Christian Stab and Iryna Gurevych. 2014. Annotating argument components and relations in persuasive essays. In *COLING 2014, 25th International Conference on Computational Linguistics, Proceedings of the Conference: Technical Papers, August 23-29, 2014, Dublin, Ireland*, pages 1501–1510.

Christian Stab and Iryna Gurevych. 2017. Parsing argumentation structures in persuasive essays. *Computational Linguistics*, 43(3):619–659.

Seiya Tokui, Kenta Oono, Shohei Hido, and Justin Clayton. 2015. Chainer: a next-generation open source framework for deep learning. In *Proceedings of Workshop on Machine Learning Systems (LearningSys) in The Twenty-ninth Annual Conference on Neural Information Processing Systems (NIPS)*.

Oriol Vinyals, Meire Fortunato, and Navdeep Jaitly. 2015. Pointer networks. In C. Cortes, N. D. Lawrence, D. D. Lee, M. Sugiyama, and R. Garnett, editors, *Advances in Neural Information Processing Systems 28*, pages 2692–2700. Curran Associates, Inc.

Guido Zarrella and Amy Marsh. 2016. Mitre at semeval-2016 task 6: Transfer learning for stance detection. In *Proceedings of the 10th International Workshop on Semantic Evaluation (SemEval-2016)*, pages 458–463, San Diego, California. Association for Computational Linguistics.

ArguminSci: A Tool for Analyzing Argumentation and Rhetorical Aspects in Scientific Writing

Anne Lauscher,[1,2] Goran Glavaš,[1] and Kai Eckert[2]

[1]Data and Web Science Research Group
University of Mannheim, Germany
[2]Web-based Information Systems and Services
Stuttgart Media University, Germany

```
{anne, goran, simone}@informatik.uni-mannheim.de
{lauscher, eckert}@hdm-stuttgart.de
```


Abstract

Argumentation is arguably one of the central features of scientific language. We present *ArguminSci*, an easy-to-use tool that analyzes argumentation and other rhetorical aspects of scientific writing, which we collectively dub *scitorics*. The main aspect we focus on is the fine-grained argumentative analysis of scientific text through identification of argument components. The functionality of *ArguminSci* is accessible via three interfaces: as a command line tool, via a RESTful application programming interface, and as a web application.

1 Introduction

Scientific publications are primary means for convincing scientific communities of the merit of one's scientific work and importance of research findings (Gilbert, 1976). To this end, authors typically present their work by embracing and exploiting established practices and specific tools related to the scientific discourse, such as citations (Gilbert, 1977), that facilitate building persuading argumentation lines. Consequently, scientific texts are abundant with different interrelated rhetorical and argumentative layers. In this work, we refer to this set of mutually-related rhetorical aspects of scientific writing as *scitorics*.

Numerous research groups have already proposed computational models for analyzing scientific language with respect to one or multiple of these aspects. For example, Teufel and Moens (1999) presented experiments on the automatic assignment of *argumentative zones*, i.e., sentential discourse roles, to sentences in scientific articles. Similarly, there has been work on automatic classification of citations with respect to their polarity and purpose (Jha et al., 2017; Lauscher et al., 2017b). It has also been shown that through analyses of *scitorics* higher-level computational tasks

can be supported, such as the attribution of scientific statements to authors (Teufel and Moens, 2000), identification of research trends (McKeown et al., 2016), or automatic summarization of scientific articles (Abu-Jbara and Radev, 2011; Lauscher et al., 2017a).

In this work, we present *ArguminSci*[1] a tool that aims to support the holistic analyses of scientific publications in terms of *scitorics*, including the identification of argumentative components. We make *ArguminSci* publicly available for download.[2] In its core, it relies on separate neural models based on recurrent neural networks with the long short-term memory cells (LSTM) (Hochreiter and Schmidhuber, 1997) pre-trained for each of the five tasks in the area of scientific publication mining that *ArguminSci* adresses, namely (1) argumentative component identification, (2) discourse role classification, (3) subjective aspect classification, (4) summary relevance classification, and (5) citation context identification. *ArguminSci* is available as a command line tool, through a RESTful HTTP-based application programming interface, and as a web-based graphical user interface (i.e., as a web application).

2 Related Work

We divide the overview of related tools and systems into two categories: (1) systems targeting the analysis of scitorics and (2) tools for argument mining (in other domains).

Tools for the Analysis of Scitorics. Ronzano and Saggion (2015) presented the *Dr. Inventor Framework*, which provides end-to-end analysis of scientific text starting with the extraction of text

---

[1]Pronounced like a Polish name and dedicated to Marvin Minsky (`https://de.wikipedia.org/wiki/Marvin_Minsky`): [aɹgjumˈɪnski].

[2]`https://github.com/anlausch/ArguminSci`

Proceedings of the 5th Workshop on Argument Mining, pages 22–28
Brussels, Belgium, November 1, 2018. ©2018 Association for Computational Linguistics

from PDF documents. The system embeds several modules for mining scientific text, e.g., for the discourse role characterization of sentences. Saggion et al. (2017) presented *MultiScien*, a tool that analyzes scientific text collections in English and Spanish and offers a visualization of discourse categories and summaries. Also, several systems analyzing *argumentative zones* (Teufel et al., 1999) have been made publicly available (e.g., Guo et al., 2012; Simsek et al., 2013). However, to the best of our knowledge, *ArguminSci* is the first publicly available system that provides fine-grained argumentative analysis of scientific publications, and allows for a joint analysis of *scitorics* – argumentation and several other rhetorical aspects of scientific language.

Argument Mining Tools. Apart from new research models and approaches, several systems and software tools have been proposed for argument mining in other domains, mainly using machine-learning models at their core. Wachsmuth et al. (2017) developed *args.me*, an argument search engine that aims to support users in finding arguments and forming opinions on controversial topics.[3] Another similar system is *ArgumenText* (Stab et al., 2018). In contrast to *args.me*, the search engine of *ArgumenText* provides access to sentential arguments extracted from large amounts of arbitrary text. The system most similar to *ArguminSci* is *MARGOT* (Lippi and Torroni, 2016),[4] which extracts argumentative components from arbitrary text provided by the user. However, *MARGOT* is not tuned for a particular domain and does not perform well on scientific text (i.e., it cannot account for peculiarities of argumentative and rhetorical structures of scientific text). While *MARGOT* focuses only on argumentative components, *ArguminSci* allows for parallel analysis of four other rhetorical aspects of scientific writing.

3 System Overview

We first describe the five annotation tasks that *ArguminSci* covers and the models we train for addressing these tasks. Next, we provide a technical overview of the system capabilities and interfaces through which it is possible to access *ArguminSci*.

<hr>

[3]http://www.argumentsearch.com/
[4]http://margot.disi.unibo.it

3.1 Annotation Tasks and Dataset

Annotation Tasks. Our system supports the following aspects of rhetorical analysis (i.e., automatic annotation) of scientific writing: (1) argument component identification, (2) discourse role classification, (3) subjective aspect classification, (4) citation context identification, and (5) summary relevance classification. Out of these tasks – in accordance with the structure of the annotations in our training corpus – argument component identification and citation context identification are token-level sequence labeling tasks, whereas the remaining three tasks are cast as sentence-level classification tasks.

- *Argument Component Identification (ACI):* The task is to identify argumentative components in a sentence. That is, given a sentence $\mathbf{x} = (x_1, \ldots, x_n)$ with individual words x_i assign a sequence of labels $\mathbf{y_{aci}} = (\mathbf{y_1}, \ldots, \mathbf{y_n})$ out of the set of token tags Y_{aci}. The label set is a combination of the standard B-I-O tagging scheme and three types of argumentative components, namely *background claim*, *own claim*, and *data*.

- *Discourse Role Classification (DRC):* Given a sentence $\mathbf{x}$ the task is to classify the role of the sentence in terms of the discourse structure of the publication. The classes are given by the set $Y_{drc} = \{Background, Unspecified, Challenge, FutureWork, Approach, Outcome\}$.

- *Subjective Aspect Classification (SAC):* Given a sentence $\mathbf{x}$ the task is to assign a single class out of eight possible categories in $Y_{sac} = \{None, Limitation, Advantage, Disadvantage-Advantage, Disadvantage, Common Practice, Novelty, Advantage-Disadvantage\}$.

- *Summary Relevance Classification (SRC):* Out of the set of possible relevance classes Y_{src}, choose one given a sentence $\mathbf{x}$, with $Y_{src} = \{Very relevant, Relevant, May appear, Should not appear, Totally irrelevant\}$.

- *Citation Context Identification (CCI):* The task is to identify textual spans corresponding to citation contexts. More specifically, given a sentence $\mathbf{x} = (x_1, \ldots, x_n)$ the task is to decide on a label for each of the tokens x_i. The possible labels are *Begin_Citation_Context*, *Inside_Citation_Context*, and *Outside*.

23

Annotation Layer	Labels
Argument Component	*Background claim, Own claim, Data* (coupled with B-I-O scheme)
Discourse Role	*Background, Challenge, Approach, Outcome, Future work*
Citation Context	*Begin citation context, Inside citation context, Outside*
Subjective Aspect	*Advantage, Disadvantage, Adv.-disadv., Disadv.-adv., Novelty, Common practice, Limitation*
Summarization Relevance	*Totally irrelevant, Should not appear, May appear, Relevant, Very relevant*

Table 1: Labels of *ArguminSci*'s annotation layers.

Dataset. For training our models, we used an extension of the Dr. Inventor Corpus (Fisas et al., 2015, 2016), which we annotated with fine-grained argumentation structures (Lauscher et al., 2018). The corpus consists of 40 scientific publications in the field of computer graphics and, besides our annotations of argumentative components, offers four layers of annotation, three of which are on the sentence level (DRC, SAC, SRC). Our argument annotation scheme includes three types of argumentative components:

- *Background claim*: A statement of argumentative nature, which is about or closely related to the work of others or common practices in a research field or about background facts related to the topic of the publication.

- *Own claim*: A statement of argumentative nature, which related to the authors own work and contribution.

- *Data*: A fact that serves as evidence pro or against a claim.

More details on the argument-extended corpus we use to train our models can be found in the accompanying resource paper (Lauscher et al., 2018). For more details on the original annotation layers of the Dr. Inventor Corpus, we refer the reader to (Fisas et al., 2015, 2016). In Table 1, we provide the overview of all labels for all five *scitorics* tasks that *ArguminSci* is capable of recognizing.

3.2 Annotation Models.

At the core of *ArguminSci* is a collection of bidirectional recurrent networks with long short-term memory cells (Bi-LSTMs) (Hochreiter and Schmidhuber, 1997), one pre-trained for each of the five annotation tasks on our argumentatively extended Dr. Inventor corpus (Fisas et al., 2015, 2016; Lauscher et al., 2018).

Model Descriptions. As *ArguminSci* addresses (1) two token-level sequence tagging tasks and (2) three sentence-level classification tasks, the system implements two types of models:

- *Token-level Sequence Labeling*: Given a sentence $\mathbf{x} = (x_1, \ldots, x_n)$ with words x_i, we first lookup the vector representations e_i (i.e., pre-trained word embeddings) of the words x_i. Next, we run a Bi-LSTM and obtain the sentence-contextualized representation h_i for each token:

$$h_i = [\overrightarrow{LSTM}(e_1, \ldots, e_i); \overleftarrow{LSTM}(e_n, \ldots, e_i)].$$

Finally, we feed the vector h_i into a single-layer feed-forward network and apply a softmax function on its output to predict the label probability distribution for each token:

$$y_i = \mathrm{softmax}(W h_i + b),$$

with $W \in \mathbb{R}^{2K \times |Y|}$ being the weight matrix, $b \in \mathbb{R}^{|Y|}$ the bias vector, and K being the state size of the LSTMs.

- *Sentence-level Classification*: The sentence-level classification builds upon the output of the Bi-LSTM described above: Following Yang et al. (2016), we first obtain a sentence representation by aggregating the individual hidden representations of the words h_i using an intra-sentence attention mechanism defined as

$$s_i = \sum_j \alpha_i h_i.$$

The individual weights α_i are computed as follows:

$$\alpha_i = \mathrm{softmax}(U \, u_{att}),$$

with u_{att} as the trainable attention head vector and the matrix U containing the Bi-LSTM-contextualized token representations, transformed through a single-layer feed-forward network with non-linear activation (i.e., we first non-linearly transform vectors h_i and stack the transformations to form the matrix U):

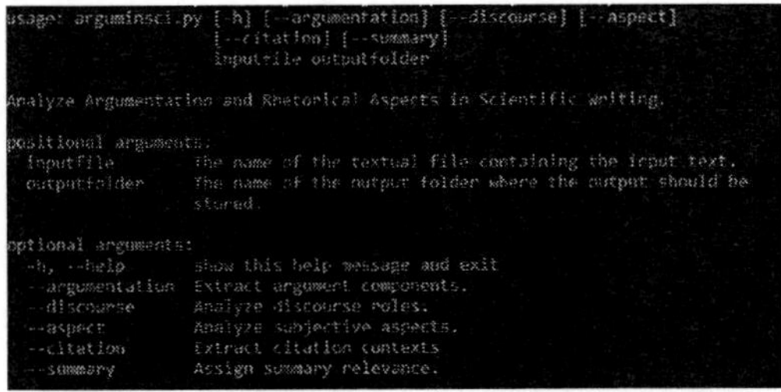

Figure 1: Help text of *ArguminSci*'s command line interface.

Figure 2: The *ArguminSci* web application offers a simple interfaces for easy analysis of *scitorics*.

$$U_i = \tanh(W_{att}h_i + b_{att}) .$$

Analogous to the above-mentioned token-level sequence tagging model, in the last step we apply a feed-forward net with a softmax layer to get the class predictions from the obtained attention-based sentence representation s_i.

We implemented all models in Python, using the Tensorflow framework.[5]

Model Performance. We evaluated the performance of our models on a held-out test set, which comprises 12 randomly selected publications in our corpus (roughly 30% of the corpus, totaling in 2874 sentences). In Table 2 we report the results in terms of F_1 score, macro-averaged over the task labels.

3.3 Interfaces

We offer three different modes of access to *ArguminSci*: (1) using a command line tool, (2) via an RESTful application programming interface, and (3) using a web application.

---

[5]https://www.tensorflow.org/

Task	F1 (%)
Token-level	
Argument Component Identification	43.8
Citation Context Identification	47.0
Sentence-level	
Discourse Role Classification	42.7
Subjective Aspect Classification	18.8
Summary Relevance Classification	33.5

Table 2: Tagging and classification performances.

Command Line Tool. The first interface *ArguminSci* offers is a command line tool, invokable with Python. The script should be provided with two mandatory arguments defining the path to the input file containing the text to be annotated and the path to the output folder where the processing results (i.e., annotated text) will be stored. Furthermore, there are five optional flags which define the type of analysis to perform, each corresponding to one of the *scitorics* tasks. For example, if the user wants to run ACI and DRC on the input text, she should set the flags `--argumentation` and `--discourse`, respectively. Figure 1 shows the help content for the command line tool.

RESTful Application Programming Interface. The application programming interface (API) provides one main HTTP POST end point, which expects a string parameter `text` to be submitted. A second parameter `api_mode` acts as a flag for setting the output format of the predictions (i.e., annotated text) to JSON. A `cURL` request to our RESTful interface has the following format:

```
curl  --request POST
--url http://<host>/predict
--data 'text=<text>&api_mode=True'
```

For example, given the text *"Our model performs best."*, the API will return a JSON object with the following nested structure:

```
{
  "argumentation":
  [
    [
      [
        "our",
        "BEGIN_OWN_CLAIM"
      ],
      [
        "model",
        "INSIDE_OWN_CLAIM"
```

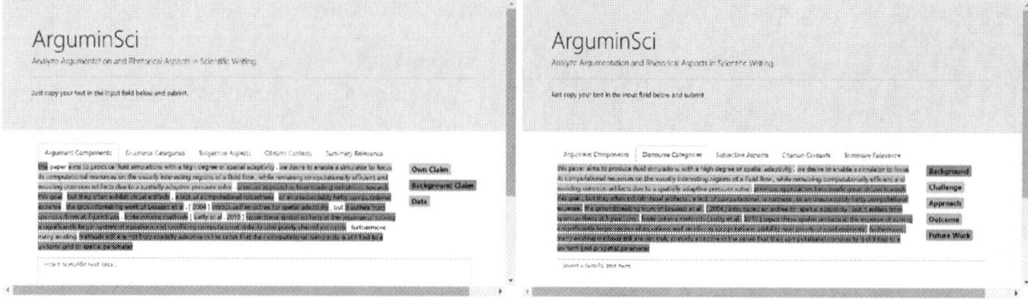

(a) Result of the argument component identification.
(b) Result of the discourse role classification.

Figure 3: The *ArguminSci* web application visualizes the result of the analysis by highlighting the text in different colors. The user can navigate among the different *scitorics* by using the tab control.

```
    ],
    [
        "performs",
        "BEGIN_OWN_CLAIM"
    ],
    [
        "best",
        "INSIDE_OWN_CLAIM"
    ],
    [
        ".",
        "OUTSIDE"
    ]
   ], ...
 ],
 "citation": [...],
 "discourse": [...],
 "aspect": [...],
 "summary": [...]
}
```

In order to enable developers and researchers to use *ArguminSci* as an HTTP service, we make the RESTful API publicly accessible[6]. For the implementation of the API we used the Flask framework in Python.[7]

Web application. Finally, the third option for accessing *ArguminSci* is the web application, based on the template rendering engine Jinja2[8] and the front-end library Bootstrap.[9] We adopt a lean and simple design with a a single interaction screen. Here, the user can enter the text she desires to annotate with *ArguminSci*'s scitorics annotation models (see Figure 2). Figures 3a and 3b depict the results of the processing. The result is displayed in a tab control in the middle of the screen – different annotation layers can be accessed via the tab navigation. The spans of the input text are highlighted with colors indicating different labels, as predicted by the *ArguminSci*'s neural models.

4 Conclusion

Scientific publications, as tools of persuasion (Gilbert, 1977), are highly argumentative and carefully composed texts in which explicit arguments are intertwined with other rhetorical aspects of scientific writing. In this paper, we presented *ArguminSci*, a tool that offers a holistic analysis of scientific publications through a set of rhetorical and argumentative aspects of scientific writing we collectively dub *scitorics*. The *ArguminSci* tool encompasses pre-trained recurrent neural models for two different token-level sequence tagging (identification of argumentative components and citation contexts) and three sentence classification tasks (discourse roles, subjective aspect, and summary relevance).

ArguminSci's functionality can be accessed in three different ways: as a command line tool, via a RESTful application programming interface, and as a web application. In future work, we intend to expose the training phase for the models as well. We also plan to allow for different annotation schemes and to extend the tool with models for other *scitorics* tasks, such as citation purpose and citation polarity classification.

Acknowledgments

This research was partly funded by the German Research Foundation (DFG) with the grant number EC 477/5-1 (LOC-DB). We thank the anonymous reviewers for their constructive and insightful comments.

---

[6]We keep the service endpoint address updated at https://github.com/anlausch/ArguminSci

[7]http://flask.pocoo.org/

[8]http://jinja.pocoo.org/docs/2.10/

[9]https://getbootstrap.com/

References

Amjad Abu-Jbara and Dragomir Radev. 2011. Coherent citation-based summarization of scientific papers. In *Proceedings of the 49th Annual Meeting of the Association for Computational Linguistics: Human Language Technologies: Volume 1*, pages 500–509, Portland, OR, USA. Association for Computational Linguistics.

Beatriz Fisas, Francesco Ronzano, and Horacio Saggion. 2016. A multi-layered annotated corpus of scientific papers. In *Proceedings of the International Conference on Language Resources and Evaluation*, pages 3081–3088, Portorož, Slovenia. European Language Resources Association.

Beatriz Fisas, Horacio Saggion, and Francesco Ronzano. 2015. On the discoursive structure of computer graphics research papers. In *Proceedings of The 9th Linguistic Annotation Workshop*, pages 42–51, Denver, CO, USA. Association for Computational Linguistics.

G Nigel Gilbert. 1976. The transformation of research findings into scientific knowledge. *Social Studies of Science*, 6(3-4):281–306.

G Nigel Gilbert. 1977. Referencing as persuasion. *Social Studies of Science*, 7(1):113–122.

Yufan Guo, Ilona Silins, Roi Reichart, and Anna Korhonen. 2012. Crab reader: A tool for analysis and visualization of argumentative zones in scientific literature. In *Proceedings of the 24th International Conference on Computational Linguistics: Demonstration Papers*, pages 183–190, Mumbai, India. The COLING 2012 Organizing Committee.

Sepp Hochreiter and Jürgen Schmidhuber. 1997. Long Short-Term Memory. *Neural Computation*, 9(8):1735–1780.

Rahul Jha, Amjad-Abu Jbara, Vahed Qazvinian, and Dragomir R. Radev. 2017. NLP-driven citation analysis for scientometrics. *Natural Language Engineering*, 23(1):93–130.

Anne Lauscher, Goran Glavaš, and Kai Eckert. 2017a. University of mannheim@ clscisumm-17: Citation-based summarization of scientific articles using semantic textual similarity. In *CEUR workshop proceedings*, volume 2002, pages 33–42. RWTH.

Anne Lauscher, Goran Glavaš, and Simone Paolo Ponzetto. 2018. An argument-annotated corpus of scientific publications. In *Proceedings of the 5th Workshop on Mining Argumentation*, Brussels, Belgium. Association for Computational Linguistics. To appear.

Anne Lauscher, Goran Glavaš, Simone Paolo Ponzetto, and Kai Eckert. 2017b. Investigating convolutional networks and domain-specific embeddings for semantic classification of citations. In *Proceedings of the 6th International Workshop on Mining Scientific Publications*, pages 24–28, Toronto, ON, Canada. Association for Computing Machinery.

Marco Lippi and Paolo Torroni. 2016. MARGOT: A web server for argumentation mining. *Expert Systems with Applications*, 65:292–303.

Kathy McKeown, Hal Daume, Snigdha Chaturvedi, John Paparrizos, Kapil Thadani, Pablo Barrio, Or Biran, Suvarna Bothe, Michael Collins, Kenneth R. Fleischmann, Luis Gravano, Rahul Jha, Ben King, Kevin McInerney, Taesun Moon, Arvind Neelakantan, Diarmuid O'Seaghdha, Dragomir Radev, Clay Templeton, and Simone Teufel. 2016. Predicting the impact of scientific concepts using full-text features. *Journal of the Association for Information Science and Technology*, 67(11):2684–2696.

Francesco Ronzano and Horacio Saggion. 2015. Dr. inventor framework: Extracting structured information from scientific publications. In *Discovery Science*, pages 209–220, Cham. Springer International Publishing.

Horacio Saggion, Francesco Ronzano, Pablo Accuosto, and Daniel Ferrés. 2017. Multiscien: a bi-lingual natural language processing system for mining and enrichment of scientific collections. In *Proceedings of the 2nd Joint Workshop on Bibliometric-enhanced Information Retrieval and Natural Language Processing for Digital Libraries*, volume 1888, pages 26–40, Tokyo, Japan. CEUR-WS.

Duygu Simsek, Simon Buckingham Shum, Agnes Sandor, Anna De Liddo, and Rebecca Ferguson. 2013. Xip dashboard: visual analytics from automated rhetorical parsing of scientific metadiscourse. In *Proceedings of the 1st International Workshop on Discourse-Centric Learning Analytics*, Leuven, Belgium. Association for Computing Machinery.

Christian Stab, Johannes Daxenberger, Chris Stahlhut, Tristan Miller, Benjamin Schiller, Christopher Tauchmann, Steffen Eger, and Iryna Gurevych. 2018. ArgumenText: Searching for arguments in heterogeneous sources. In *Proceedings of the 2018 Conference of the North American Chapter of the Association for Computational Linguistics: Demonstrations*, pages 21–25. Association for Computational Linguistics.

Simone Teufel, Jean Carletta, and Marc Moens. 1999. An annotation scheme for discourse-level argumentation in research articles. In *Proceedings of the 9th Conference on European Chapter of the Association for Computational Linguistics*, pages 110–117, Bergen, Norway. Association for Computational Linguistics.

Simone Teufel and Marc Moens. 1999. Discourse-level argumentation in scientific articles: Human and automatic annotation. In *Towards Standards and Tools for Discourse Tagging, Workshop*, Maryland, MA, USA. Association for Computational Linguistics.

Simone Teufel and Marc Moens. 2000. What's yours and what's mine: Determining intellectual attribution in scientific text. In *Proceedings of the 2000 Joint SIGDAT Conference on Empirical Methods in Natural Language Processing and Very Large Corpora: Held in Conjunction with the 38th Annual Meeting of the Association for Computational Linguistics-Volume 13*, pages 9–17, Hong Kong. Association for Computational Linguistics.

Henning Wachsmuth, Martin Potthast, Khalid Al Khatib, Yamen Ajjour, Jana Puschmann, Jiani Qu, Jonas Dorsch, Viorel Morari, Janek Bevendorff, and Benno Stein. 2017. Building an argument search engine for the web. In *Proceedings of the 4th Workshop on Argument Mining*, pages 49–59, Copenhagen, Denmark. Association for Computational Linguistics.

Zichao Yang, Diyi Yang, Chris Dyer, Xiaodong He, Alex Smola, and Eduard Hovy. 2016. Hierarchical attention networks for document classification. In *Proceedings of the 2016 Conference of the North American Chapter of the Association for Computational Linguistics: Human Language Technologies*, pages 1480–1489, San Diego, CA, USA. Association for Computational Linguistics.

Evidence Type Classification in Randomized Controlled Trials

Tobias Mayer and **Elena Cabrio** and **Serena Villata**
Université Côte d'Azur, CNRS, I3S, Inria, France
{tmayer,cabrio,villata}@i3s.unice.fr

Abstract

Randomized Controlled Trials (RCT) are a common type of experimental studies in the medical domain for evidence-based decision making. The ability to automatically extract the *arguments* proposed therein can be of valuable support for clinicians and practitioners in their daily evidence-based decision making activities. Given the peculiarity of the medical domain and the required level of detail, standard approaches to argument component detection in *argument(ation) mining* are not fine-grained enough to support such activities. In this paper, we introduce a new sub-task of the argument component identification task: *evidence type classification*. To address it, we propose a supervised approach and we test it on a set of RCT abstracts on different medical topics.

1 Introduction

Evidence-based decision making in medicine has the aim to support clinicians and practitioners to reason upon the arguments in support or against a certain treatment, its effects, and the comparison with other related treatments for the same disease. These approaches (e.g., (Hunter and Williams, 2012; Craven et al., 2012; Longo and Hederman, 2013; Qassas et al., 2015)) consider different kinds of data, e.g., Randomized Controlled Trials or other observational studies, and they usually require transforming the unstructured textual information into structured information as input of the reasoning framework. This paper proposes a preliminary step towards the issue of providing this transformation, starting from RCT, i.e., documents reporting experimental studies in the medical domain. More precisely, the research question we answer in this paper is: *how to distinguish different kinds of evidence in RCT, so that fine-grained evidence-based decision making activities are supported?*

To answer this question, we propose to resort on *Argument Mining* (AM) (Peldszus and Stede, 2013; Lippi and Torroni, 2016a), defined as "the general task of analyzing discourse on the pragmatics level and applying a certain argumentation theory to model and automatically analyze the data at hand" (Habernal and Gurevych, 2017). Two stages are crucial: *(1)* the detection of argument components (e.g., claim, premises) and the identification of their textual boundaries, and *(2)* the prediction of the relations holding between the arguments. In the AM framework, we propose a new task called *evidence type classification*, as a sub-task of the argument component identification task. The distinction among different kinds of evidence is crucial in evidence-based decision making as different kinds of evidence are associated to different weights in the reasoning process. Such information need to be extracted from raw text.

To the best of our knowledge, this is the first approach in AM targeting evidence type classification in the medical domain. The main contributions of this paper are: (i) we propose four classes of evidence for RCT (i.e., *comparative, significance, side-effect,* and *other*), and we annotate a new dataset of 169 RCT abstracts with such labels, and (ii) we experiment with supervised classifiers over such dataset obtaining satisfactory results.

2 Evidence type classification

In (Mayer et al., 2018), as a first step towards the extraction of argumentative information from clinical data, we extended an existing corpus (Trenta et al., 2015) on RCT abstracts, with the annotations of the different argument components (evidence, claim, major claim). The structure of RCTs should follow the CONSORT policies to ensure a minimum consensus, which makes the studies

Proceedings of the 5th Workshop on Argument Mining, pages 29–34
Brussels, Belgium, November 1, 2018. ©2018 Association for Computational Linguistics

comparable and ideal for building a corpus[1]. RCT abstracts were retrieved directly from PubMed[2] by searching for the disease name and specifying that it has to be a RCT. This version of the corpus with coarse labels contains 927 argument components (679 evidence and 248 claims) from 159 abstracts comprising 4 different diseases (glaucoma, hypertension, hepatitis b, diabetes).

In particular, an *evidence* in a RCT is an observation or measurement in the study (ground truth), which supports or attacks another argument component, usually a *claim*. Those observations comprise side effects and the measured outcome of the intervention and control arm. They are observed facts, and therefore credible without further justifications, since this is the ground truth the argumentation is based on. In Example 1, *evidence* are in italic, underlined and surrounded by square brackets with subscripts, while claims are in bold.

Example 1: To compare the intraocular pressure-lowering effect of latanoprost with that of dorzolamide when added to timolol. [...] [*The diurnal intraocular pressure reduction was significant in both groups $(P < 0.001)$*]$_1$. [*The mean intraocular pressure reduction from baseline was 32% for the latanoprost plus timolol group and 20% for the dorzolamide plus timolol group*]$_2$. [*The least square estimate of the mean diurnal intraocular pressure reduction after 3 months was -7.06 mm Hg in the latanoprost plus timolol group and -4.44 mm Hg in the dorzolamide plus timolol group $(P < 0.001)$*]$_3$. Drugs administered in both treatment groups were well tolerated. This study clearly showed that **[the additive diurnal intraocular pressure-lowering effect of latanoprost is superior to that of dorzolamide in patients treated with timolol]**$_1$.

Example 1 shows different reports of the experimental outcomes as evidence. Those can be results without concrete measurement values (see evidence 1), or exact measured values (see evidence 2 and 3). Different measures are annotated as multiple evidence. The reporting of side effects and negative observations are also considered as evidence. Traditionally evidence-based medicine (EBM) focuses mainly on the study design and

risk of bias, when it comes to determining the quality of the evidence. As stated by (Bellomo and Bagshaw, 2006) there are also other aspects of the trial quality, which impinge upon the truthfulness of the findings. As a step forward, in this work we extend the corpus annotation, specifying four classes of *evidence*, which are most prominent in our data and assist in assessing these complex quality dimensions, like reproducibility, generalizability or the estimate of effect:

comparative: when there is some kind of comparison between the control and intervention arms (Table 1, example 2). Supporting the search for similarities in outcomes of different studies, which is an important measure for the reproducibility.

significance: for any sentence stating that the results are statistically significant (Table 1, example 3). Many comparative sentences also contain statistical information. However, this class can be seen more as a measure for the strength of beneficial or potentially harmful outcomes.

side-effect: captures all evidence reporting any side-effect or adverse drug effect to see if potential harms outweigh the benefits of an intervention (Table 1, example 4).

other: all the evidence that do not fall under the other categories, like non-comparative observations, risk factors or limitations of the study (too rare occurrences to form new classes). Especially the latter can be relevant for the generalizability of the outcome of a study (Table 1, example 5).

Table 2 shows the statistics of the obtained dataset. Three annotators have annotated the data after a training phase. Inter Annotator Agreement has been calculated on 10 abstracts comprising 47 evidence, resulting in a Fleiss' kappa of 0.88.

3 Proposed methods

In (Mayer et al., 2018), we addressed the argument component detection as a supervised text classification problem: given a collection of sentences, each labeled with the presence/absence of an argument component, the goal is to train a classifier to detect the argumentative sentences. We retrainedT an existing system, i.e. MARGOT (Lippi and Torroni, 2016b), to detect evidence and claims from clinical data. The methods we used are SubSet Tree Kernels (SSTK) (Collins and Duffy, 2002),

---

[1] http://www.consort-statement.org/
[2] https://www.ncbi.nlm.nih.gov/pubmed/

1.	Brimonidine provides a sustained long-term ocular hypotensive effect, is well tolerated, and has a low rate of allergic response.
2.	The overall success rates were 87% for the 350-mm2 group and 70% for the 500-mm2 group ($P = 0.05$).
3.	All regimens produced clinically relevant and statistically significant ($P < .05$) intraocular pressure reductions from baseline.
4.	Allergy was seen in 9 % of subjects treated with brimonidine.
5.	Risk of all three outcomes was higher for participants with chronic kidney disease or frailty.

Table 1: Sample of each class represented in the corpus (*claim, comparative, significance, side-effect, other*).

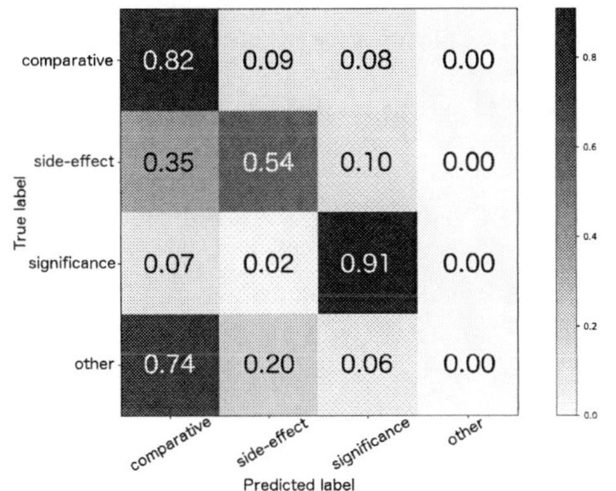

Figure 1: Normalized confusion matrix of the combined test set.

which offer a reasonable compromise between expressiveness and efficiency (Lippi and Torroni, 2016b). In SSTK, a fragment can be any subtree of the original tree, which terminates either at the level of pre-terminal symbols or at the leaves. Data was pre-processed (tokenisation and stemming), and the constituency parse tree for each sentence was computed. Furthermore, the Bag-of-Words (BoW) features with Term Frequency and Inverse Document Frequency (TF-IDF) values were also computed. All the pre-processing steps were performed with Stanford CoreNLP (version 3.5.0). We conducted experiments with different classifiers and feature combinations. Two datasets were prepared to train two binary classifiers for each approach: one for claim detection, and one for evidence detection. Both training sets only differ in the labels, which were assigned to each sentence. 5-fold cross validation was performed optimizing for the F_1-score. The model was evaluated on the test set in Table 2 obtaining 0.80 and 0.65 F_1-score for evidence and claim detection respectively.

As a step forward - after the distinction between argumentative (claims and evidence) and non-argumentative sentences - we address the task of distinguishing the different types of evidence (see Section 2). We cast it as a multi-class classification problem. For that we use Support Vector Machines (SVMs)[3] with a linear kernel and different strategies to transform the multi-class into a binary classification problem: *(i)* ONEVSREST, and *(ii)* ONEVSONE. The first strategy trains one classifier for each class, where the negative examples are all the other classes combined, outputting a confidence score later used for the final decision. The second one trains a classifier for each class pair and only uses the correspondent subset of the data for that. As features, we selected lexical ones, like TF-IDF values for BoW, n-grams and the MedDRA[4] dictionary for adverse drug effects. As for the argument component classification, the model was evaluated on different test sets with respect to the weighted average F_1-score for multi-class classification. The models were compared against a random baseline, based on the class distribution in the training set and a majority vote classifier, which always assigns the label of the class with the highest contingent in the training set. The first dataset consisting only of the glaucoma data, and the second one comprising all the other maladies as well (see Table 2).

4   Results and Discussion

We run two sets of experiments. In the first one, we test the evidence type classifier on the gold standard annotations of the evidence. In the second one, we test the whole pipeline: the evidence type classifier is run on the output of the argument component classifier described in the previous section. In both cases, the best feature combination was a mix of BoW and bi-grams. The dictionary of adverse drug effects did not increase the performance. Together with the fact that the data contains just a small group of reoccurring side-effects, this suggests that the expected discriminative information from the dictionary is captured within the uni- and bi-gram features. This might change for bigger datasets with a broader range of adverse effects. Results of the best feature combinations and the random baseline are reported in Table 3. For the evidence type classifier on gold stan-

---

[3]scikit-learn, version 0.19.1
[4]https://www.meddra.org/

Dataset	Topic	#abstract	#comp.	#sign.	#side-eff.	#other
Training set	glaucoma	79	151	83	65	10
Test set	glaucoma, diabetes, hepatitis, hypertension	90 (resp. 30, 20, 20, 20)	160	98	79	33

Table 2: Statistics on the dataset showing the class distributions.

Dataset	Method	glaucoma	combined.
Gold standard	RANDOM	0.33	0.32
	MAJORITY	0.27	0.26
	N-GRAMS	0.80	0.74
whole pipeline	RANDOM	0.38	0.38
	MAJORITY	0.38	0.39
	N-GRAMS	0.71	0.66

Table 3: Results (weighted average F_1-score).

dard annotations, the observed results regarding the different multi-class strategies did not differ significantly. A F_1-score of 0.80 and 0.74 respectively for the glaucoma and combined test set was achieved. Reviewing the best n-grams, they contain very specific medical terminology, explaining the performance difference between the two test sets. For the future, another pre-processing step with better abstraction capability, e.g., substituting concrete medical related terms with more general tags, could provide benefits for the trained model on the out-of-domain task. The F_1-score of the whole pipeline is 0.71 for the glaucoma and 0.66 for the combined test set. As expected, the errors of the argument component classifier have an impact on the performances of the second step, but that corresponds to a more realistic scenario.

Error analysis. As shown in Figure 1, *side-effect* were often misclassified as *comparative*. Certain types of *side-effect* comprise comparisons of side-effects between the two groups including statements of their non-existence. The structure and wording of those sentences are very similar to correct *comparative* examples and only differ in the comparison criteria (side-effect vs. other measurement), see Examples 2 and 3. Furthermore, *comparative* and *significance* labels were often confused. As explained above, comparisons can also state information about the statistical significance and could therefore belong to both classes, see Example 4. For future work, we plan to adopt a multi-label approach to overcome this problem.

Example 2: Headache, fatigue, and drowsiness were similar in the 2 groups.

Example 3: The number of adverse events did not differ between treatment groups, with a mean (SD) of 0.21 (0.65) for the standard group and 0.32 (0.75) for the intensive group (P=0.44).

Example 4: The clinical success rate was 86.2% in the brimonidine group and 81.8% in the timolol group, making no statistically significant difference between them (p=0.817).

5 Concluding remarks

We have presented a first step towards mining fine-grained evidence from RCTs, contributing in *i)* the definition of the AM sub-task of evidence type classification for medical data, *ii)* a new dataset of RCT annotated with claims and four kinds of evidence, and *iii)* a supervised classifier to address this task.

A similar task is comparative structure identification in clinical trials. It relies on under-specified syntactic analysis and domain knowledge (Fiszman et al., 2007). (Gupta et al., 2017) applied syntactic structure and dependency parsers to extract comparison structures from biomedical texts. (Trenta et al., 2015) built an information extraction system based on a maximum entropy classifier with basic linguistic features for the tasks of extracting the patient group, the intervention and control arm, and the outcome measure description. Differently from us, they extract information to fill in evidence tables, ignoring the linguistic phrases to reconstruct the whole argumentation. (Dernoncourt et al., 2017) developed a neural network with word embeddings to assign PubMed RCT abstract labels to sentences showing that considering sequential information to jointly predict sentence labels improves the results. However, their task differs from ours as they predict the abstracts structure, which depends on contextual information. Concerning the evidence classification, (Rinott et al., 2015) tackled this problem on Wikipedia based data, dividing the evidence into *study, anecdotal and expert* evidence. This taxonomy is not applicable for the here presented type of data. Beside the extraction of evidence, another relevant task is their qualitative evaluation. The traditional quality-based hierarchy for medical evidence grades them based on the employed research method, e.g., the applied statistical principles (Schünemann et al., 2008). Top ranked methods comprise systematic reviews and meta-analyses of RCTs (Manchikanti et al., 2009). While they focus on collecting and using metadata from the studies to draw general conclusions to define, e.g., recommendation guidelines, they do not consider 'why' an author came to certain conclusion. This issue is tackled in our paper.

For future work, we plan to weight the argument strength based on the different evidence types (similar to the categories proposed in (Wachsmuth et al., 2017) and (Gurevych and Stab, 2017)). A scale for side-effects could be based on a weighted taxonomy of adverse drug effects. Furthermore, we plan to mine the full RCT reports, to get relevant information on the limitations of the study and risk factors, currently annotated with the *other* label since they rarely appear in the abstracts.

References

Rinaldo Bellomo and Sean M. Bagshaw. 2006. Evidence-based medicine: Classifying the evidence from clinical trials – the need to consider other dimensions. *Critical Care*, 10(5):232.

Michael Collins and Nigel Duffy. 2002. New ranking algorithms for parsing and tagging: Kernels over discrete structures, and the voted perceptron. In *ACL*, pages 263–270. ACL.

Robert Craven, Francesca Toni, Cristian Cadar, Adrian Hadad, and Matthew Williams. 2012. Efficient argumentation for medical decision-making. In *KR*. AAAI Press.

Franck Dernoncourt, Ji Young Lee, and Peter Szolovits. 2017. Neural networks for joint sentence classification in medical paper abstracts. In *EACL*, pages 694–700.

Marcelo Fiszman, Dina Demner-Fushman, François-Michel Lang, Philip Goetz, and Thomas C. Rindflesch. 2007. Interpreting comparative constructions in biomedical text. In *BioNLP@ACL*, pages 137–144.

Samir Gupta, A. S. M. Ashique Mahmood, Karen Ross, Cathy H. Wu, and K. Vijay-Shanker. 2017. Identifying comparative structures in biomedical text. In *BioNLP 2*, pages 206–215.

Iryna Gurevych and Christian Stab. 2017. Recognizing insufficiently supported arguments in argumentative essays. In (Lapata et al., 2017), pages 980–990.

Ivan Habernal and Iryna Gurevych. 2017. Argumentation mining in user-generated web discourse. *Comput. Linguist.*, 43(1):125–179.

Anthony Hunter and Matthew Williams. 2012. Aggregating evidence about the positive and negative effects of treatments. *Artificial Intelligence in Medicine*, 56(3):173–190.

Mirella Lapata, Phil Blunsom, and Alexander Koller, editors. 2017. *Proceedings of the 15th Conference of the European Chapter of the Association for Computational Linguistics, EACL 2017, Valencia, Spain, April 3-7, 2017, Volume 1: Long Papers*. Association for Computational Linguistics.

Marco Lippi and Paolo Torroni. 2016a. Argumentation mining: State of the art and emerging trends. *ACM Trans. Internet Techn.*, 16(2):10.

Marco Lippi and Paolo Torroni. 2016b. MARGOT: A web server for argumentation mining. *Expert Systems with Applications*, 65:292–303.

Luca Longo and Lucy Hederman. 2013. Argumentation theory for decision support in health-care: A comparison with machine learning. In *BHI*, pages 168–180.

Laxmaiah Manchikanti, Sukdeb Datta, Howard Smith, and Joshua A Hirsch. 2009. Evidence-based medicine, systematic reviews, and guidelines in interventional pain management: part 6. systematic reviews and meta-analyses of observational studies. *Pain physician*, 12 5:819–50.

Tobias Mayer, Elena Cabrio, Marco Lippi, Paolo Torroni, and Serena Villata. 2018. Argument mining on clinical trials. In *Proceedings of COMMA'18*.

Andreas Peldszus and Manfred Stede. 2013. From argument diagrams to argumentation mining in texts: A survey. *Int. J. Cogn. Inform. Nat. Intell.*, 7(1):1–31.

Malik Al Qassas, Daniela Fogli, Massimiliano Giacomin, and Giovanni Guida. 2015. Analysis of clinical discussions based on argumentation schemes. *Procedia Computer Science*, 64:282–289.

R. Rinott, L. Dankin, C. Alzate Perez, M. M. Khapra, E. Aharoni, and N. Slonim. 2015. Show me your evidence - an automatic method for context dependent evidence detection. In *EMNLP*.

Holger Schünemann, Andrew D Oxman, Jan Brozek, Paul Glasziou, Roman Jaeschke, Gunn Vist, John Williams, Regina Kunz, Jonathan Craig, Victor M Montori, Patrick Bossuyt, and Gordon Guyatt. 2008. Grading quality of evidence and strength of recommendations for diagnostic tests and strategies. *BMJ (Clinical research ed.)*, 336:1106–10.

Antonio Trenta, Anthony Hunter, and Sebastian Riedel. 2015. Extraction of evidence tables from abstracts of randomized clinical trials using a maximum entropy classifier and global constraints. *CoRR*, abs/1509.05209.

Henning Wachsmuth, Benno Stein, Graeme Hirst, Vinodkumar Prabhakaran, Yonatan Bilu, Yufang Hou, Nona Naderi, and Tim Alberdingk Thijm. 2017. Computational argumentation quality assessment in natural language. In (Lapata et al., 2017), pages 176–187.

Predicting the Usefulness of Amazon Reviews
Using Off-The-Shelf Argumentation Mining

Marco Passon[†], Marco Lippi[‡], Giuseppe Serra[†], Carlo Tasso[†]

[†]Università degli Studi di Udine
[‡]Università degli Studi di Modena e Reggio Emilia
`marco.passon@spes.uniud.it`
`marco.lippi@unimore.it`
`{giuseppe.serra, carlo.tasso}@uniud.it`

Abstract

Internet users generate content at unprecedented rates. Building intelligent systems capable of discriminating useful content within this ocean of information is thus becoming a urgent need. In this paper, we aim to predict the usefulness of Amazon reviews, and to do this we exploit features coming from an off-the-shelf argumentation mining system. We argue that the usefulness of a review, in fact, is strictly related to its argumentative content, whereas the use of an already trained system avoids the costly need of relabeling a novel dataset. Results obtained on a large publicly available corpus support this hypothesis.

1 Introduction

In our digital era, reviews affect our everyday decisions. More and more people resort to digital reviews before buying a good or deciding where to eat or stay. In fact, helpful reviews allow users to grasp more clearly the features of a product they are about to buy, and thus to understand whether it fits their needs. The same can be said for users who want to book hotels or restaurants.

Companies have started to exploit the importance of reviews. For example, when browsing for a specific product, we are usually presented reviews that have been judged helpful by other users. Moreover, we are often given the possibility to sort reviews according to the number of people who judged them as helpful. That said, a review can also be helpful for companies who want to monitor what people think about their brand. Being able to identify helpful reviews has thus many important applications, both for users and for companies, and in multiple domains.

The automatic identification of helpful reviews is not as easy as it may seem, because the review content has to be semantically analyzed. There-fore, this process is traditionally done by asking users for a judgment.

To overcome this issue, some approaches have been proposed. One of the earliest studies (Kim et al., 2006) aims to rank Amazon reviews by their usefulness by training a regressor with a combination of different features extracted from text and metadata of the reviews, as well as features of the product. Similar approaches employ different sets of features (Ngo-Ye and Sinha, 2012), for example including the reputation of reviewers too (Baek et al., 2012). Another significant work (Mudambi and Schuff, 2010) builds a customer model that describes which features of an Amazon review affect its perceived usefulness, and then it uses such features to build a regression model to predict the usefulness, expressed as the percentage of the number of people who judged a review to be useful. A hybrid regression model (Ngo-Ye and Sinha, 2014) combines text and additional features describing users (recency, frequency, monetary value) to predict the number of people who judged as useful reviews taken from Amazon and Yelp. A more complete work considers both regression and classification (Ghose and Ipeirotis, 2011). It proves different hypotheses, starting with expressing the usefulness of an Amazon review as a function of readability and subjectivity cues, and then converting the usefulness, expressed with a continuous value, into a binary usefulness, that is predicting if a review is useful or not useful.

Another recent work (Liu et al., 2017) presents an approach that explores an similar assumption to ours: helpful reviews are typically *argumentative*. In fact, what we hope to read in a review is something that goes beyond plain opinions or sentiment, being rather a collection of reasons and evidence that motivate and support the overall judgment of the product or service that is reviewed. These characteristics are usually cap-

35

Proceedings of the 5th Workshop on Argument Mining, pages 35–39
Brussels, Belgium, November 1, 2018. ©2018 Association for Computational Linguistics

tured by an argumentation analysis, and could be automatically detected by an argumentation mining system (Lippi and Torroni, 2016a). The work in (Liu et al., 2017) considers a set of 110 hotel reviews, it presents a complete and manual labeling of the arguments in such reviews, and it exploits such information as additional features for a machine learning classifier that predicts usefulness. In this paper, instead, we investigate the possibility to predict the usefulness of Amazon reviews by using features coming from an automatic *argumentation mining system*, thus not directly using human-annotated arguments. A preliminary experimental study conducted on a large publicly dataset (117,000 Amazon reviews) confirms that this could be really doable and a very fruitful research direction.

2 Background

Argumentation is the discipline that studies the way in which humans debate and articulate their opinions and beliefs (Walton, 2009). Argumentation mining (Lippi and Torroni, 2016a) is a rapidly expanding area, at the cross-road of many research fields, such as computational linguistics, machine learning, artificial intelligence. The main goal of argumentation mining is to automatically extract arguments and their relations from plain textual documents.

Among the many approaches developed in recent years for argumentation mining, based on advanced machine learning and natural language processing techniques, the vast majority is in fact genre-dependent, or domain-dependent, as they exploit information that is highly specific of the application scenario. Due to the complexity of these tasks, building general systems capable of processing unstructured documents of any genre, and of automatically reconstructing the relations between the arguments contained in them, still remains an open challenge.

In this work, we consider a simple definition of argument, inspired by the work by Douglas Walton (2009), that is the so-called claim/premise model. A *claim* can be defined as an assertion regarding a certain topic, and it is typically considered as the conclusion of an argument. A *premise* is a piece of evidence that supports the claim, by bringing a contribution in favor of the thesis that is contained within the claim itself.

3 Methodology

Our goal is to develop a machine learning system capable of predicting the usefulness of a review, by exploiting information related to its argumentative content. In particular, we consider to enrich the features of a standard text classification algorithm with features coming from an argumentation mining system. To this aim, we use MARGOT (Lippi and Torroni, 2016b), a publicly available argumentation mining system[1] that employs the claim/premise model (to our knowledge, there are no other off-the-shelf systems that perform argumentation mining). Two distinct classifiers, based on Tree Kernels (Moschitti, 2006) are trained to detect claims and premises (also called evidence), respectively. When processing a document, MARGOT returns two scores for each sentence, one computed by each kernel machine, that are used to predict the presence of a claim or a premise within that sentence (by default, MARGOT uses a decision threshold equal to zero).

Consider for example the following excerpt of a review, where the proposition in italics is identified by MARGOT as a claim:

> The only jam band I ever listen to now is Cream, simply because they were geniuses. They were geniuses because the spontaneity, melodicism, and *fearlessness in their improvisation has never been equaled in rock*, and rarely so in jazz.

Clearly, such a review is very informative, since it comments on very specific aspects of the product, bringing motivations that can greatly help users in taking their decisions. Similarly, the following excerpt of another review brings very convincing arguments in favor of an overall positive judgment of the product. In this case, both sentences are classified by MARGOT as argumentative.

> *The music indeed seems to transcend so many moods that most pianists have a very hard time balancing this act and there is an immense discography of these concertos of disjoint and loosely-knit performances. Pletnev pushes a straightforward bravura approach with lyrical interludes – and his performance pays off brilliantly.*

---

[1]`http://margot.disi.unibo.it`

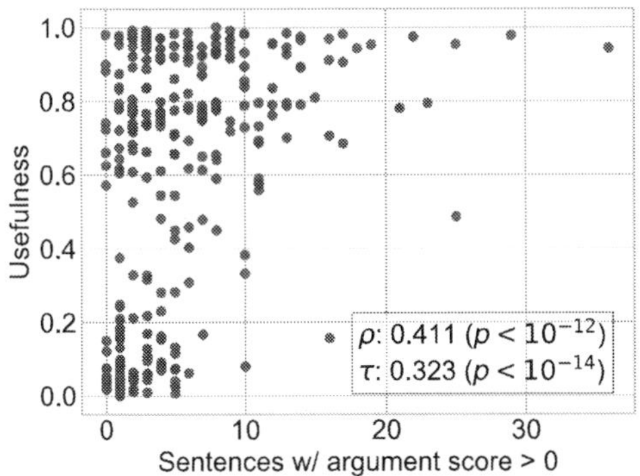

Figure 1: Relation between usefulness and number of sentences whose claim or evidence score is above zero for category "CDs and Vinyl".

Within this work, we compute simple statistics from the output of MARGOT: the average claim/evidence/argument score, the maximum claim/evidence/argument score, the number and the percentage of sentences whose claim/evidence/argument score is above 0 (that is, the number and the percentage of sentences that contain a claim, an evidence or simply one of those). From a preliminary analysis, in fact, we observed how the presence of arguments within a review is highly informative of its usefulness. Figure 1, for example, shows the correlation of the number of sentences whose claim or evidence score, according to MARGOT, is above 0, with the usefulness for a subset of 200 reviews in the Amazon category "CDs and Vinyl". While it is true that a low number of sentences that contain a claim or an evidence does not necessarily mean that the review is useless, yet the figure shows that a review with a high number of sentences containing a claim or an evidence is most likely a useful review, which confirms our intuition that useful reviews are in fact argumentative. We use these simple statistics as an additional set of features to be used within a standard text classification algorithm, in order to assess whether the presence of argumentative content can help in predicting how useful is a review.

We hereby remark that using MARGOT within this framework is not optimal, because MARGOT was trained on a completely different genre of documents, that is Wikipedia articles. Therefore, we are dealing with a *transfer learning* task, where the argumentation mining system is tested on a different domain with respect to the one it was originality trained on. Using such a classifier adds a challenge to our approach, but it has the advantage of not needing a labeled corpus of argumentative reviews to train a new argumentation mining system from scratch. Indeed, more sophisticated systems that take into account argumentation could be developed: here, we just want to exploit a straightforward combination of features in order to test our hypothesis.

4 Experimental Results

To evaluate the proposed approach we use the public Amazon Reviews dataset (McAuley and Leskovec, 2013), in particular, we worked with the so called "5-core" subset, that is, a subset of the data in which all users and items have at least five reviews. Each element of this dataset contains a product review and metadata related to it.

Since we aim to predict usefulness, for each review we compute the ratio between the number of people who voted and judged that review as useful, and the total number of people who expressed a judgment about that review. Then, we define useful reviews as the ones whose percentage of usefulness is equal or above 0.7 (that means that at least 70% of the people who judged a review, judged it as useful), while the remaining are considered not to be useful, and thus they represent our negative class.

The Amazon Review dataset is split into product categories. For our experiments we picked three of them, chosen among those with the highest number of reviews. Our choice has fallen upon the "CDs and Vinyl" "Electronics" and "Movies and TV" categories. We further selected only the reviews having at least 75 rates, in order to assess usefulness on a reasonably large set of samples. Finally, we randomly selected 39,000 reviews for each category, ending up with an almost balanced number of helpful and unhelpful reviews.

Our goal in executing the experiments is to predict whether a review is considered useful, by taking into account either its textual content only, or, additionally, also the argumentation mining data coming from MARGOT. In other words, we are working in a binary classification scenario.

In these experiments we use a stochastic gradient descent classifier[2] with a hinge loss, which is a classic solution in binary classification tasks. We

---

[2] We used `SGDClassifier` in *scikit-learn*.

Table 1: Performance on three Amazon categories using different sets of features: Margot features (M), Bag-of-Words (BoW), Bag-of-Words weighted by TF-IDF (TF-IDF), and combinations thereof.

Category	Data	A	P	R	F_1
CDs and Vinyl	M	.600	.544	.772	.638
	BoW	.756	.716	.769	.742
	BoW + M	.784	.744	**.799**	.771
	TF-IDF	.769	.736	.767	.752
	TF-IDF + M	**.787**	**.751**	.797	**.773**
Electronics	M	.583	.529	**.744**	.618
	BoW	.676	.639	.656	.648
	BoW + M	**.689**	.640	.714	**.675**
	TF-IDF	.672	**.651**	.612	.631
	TF-IDF + M	**.689**	.649	.684	.666
Movies and TV	M	.564	.517	.792	.625
	BoW	.745	.705	.748	.726
	BoW + M	.773	**.741**	.767	.754
	TF-IDF	.757	.719	.761	.740
	TF-IDF + M	**.777**	.739	**.784**	**.761**

performed the tuning of the α and ϵ parameters with a 5-fold cross validation over the training set, and we then used the best model to predict over the test set. From the original set of 39,000 reviews, 50% of them is used as training set, and the other half as the test set. Each category is treated singularly.

We run experiments both employing a plain Bag-of-Words model, and with TF-IDF features. Both preprocessing variants perform tokenization and stemming[3] and exclude stopwords and words that do not appear more than five times in the whole training set. To regularize the different magnitude of the features, both textual features and argumentation mining features are normalized using the L2 normalization in all our experiments. Textual and argumentative features are simply concatenated into a single vector. The performance is measured in terms of accuracy (A), precision (P), recall (R), and F_1, as in standard text classification applications.

Table 1 shows that, even using only the features obtained from MARGOT, thus completely ignoring the textual content of the review, the accuracy of the classifier is far above a random baseline. Moreover, results clearly highlights how the improvement obtained by using argumentative features is consistent across all product categories, both using plain BoW and TF-IDF weighting. For the "CDs and Vinyl"and "Electronics"categories

the difference between the classifier exploiting TF-IDF with MARGOT and the one using TF-IDF only is statistically significant according to a McNemar's test, with p-value < 0.01. The same holds for the BOW classifier, for the "Electronics"and "Movies and TV"categories.

It is interesting to notice that, while the "CDs and Vinyl" and the "Movies and TV" categories have similar performance, even when using textual data only, the category "Electronics" results to be the most difficult to predict. One plausible explanation for this is the heterogeneity of such category, that includes many different types of electronic devices. The other two categories, instead, include more homogeneous products. It would be very interesting to further investigate whether certain product categories result to be more suitable for argumentation studies.

5 Conclusions

When reading online reviews of products, restaurants, and hotels, we typically appreciate those that bring motivations and reasons rather than plain opinions. In other words, we often look for *argumentative* reviews. In this paper, we proposed a first experimental study that aims to show how features coming from an off-the-shelf argumentation mining system can help in predicting whether a given review is useful.

We remark that this is just a preliminary study, which yet opens the doors to several research directions that we aim to investigate in future works. First, we certainly plan to use more advanced machine learning systems, such as deep learning architectures, that have achieved significant results in many applications related to natural language processing. In addition, we aim to address different learning problems, for example moving to multi-class classification, or directly to regression.

The combination of textual and argumentative features exploited in this work was effective in confirming our intuition, but it can certainly be improved. While building a dedicated argumentation mining system for product reviews could require an effort in terms of corpus annotation, we believe that transfer learning here could play a crucial role. Beyond using statistics obtained from the output of an argumentation mining system as an additional input for a second-stage classifier, a unified model combining the two steps could result to be a smart compromise for this kind of application.

---

[3]We used `Snowball` from python `nltk` library.

References

Hyunmi Baek, JoongHo Ahn, and Youngseok Choi. 2012. Helpfulness of online consumer reviews: Readers' objectives and review cues. *International Journal of Electronic Commerce*, 17(2):99–126.

A. Ghose and P. G. Ipeirotis. 2011. Estimating the helpfulness and economic impact of product reviews: Mining text and reviewer characteristics. *IEEE Transactions on Knowledge and Data Engineering*, 23(10):1498–1512.

Soo-Min Kim, Patrick Pantel, Tim Chklovski, and Marco Pennacchiotti. 2006. Automatically assessing review helpfulness. In *Proceedings of the 2006 Conference on empirical methods in natural language processing*, pages 423–430. Association for Computational Linguistics.

Marco Lippi and Paolo Torroni. 2016a. Argumentation mining: State of the art and emerging trends. *ACM Trans. Internet Technol.*, 16(2):10:1–10:25.

Marco Lippi and Paolo Torroni. 2016b. MARGOT: A web server for argumentation mining. *Expert Syst. Appl.*, 65:292–303.

Haijing Liu, Yang Gao, Pin Lv, Mengxue Li, Shiqiang Geng, Minglan Li, and Hao Wang. 2017. Using argument-based features to predict and analyse review helpfulness. In *Proceedings of the 2017 Conference on Empirical Methods in Natural Language Processing, EMNLP 2017, Copenhagen, Denmark, September 9-11, 2017*, pages 1358–1363. Association for Computational Linguistics.

Julian McAuley and Jure Leskovec. 2013. Hidden factors and hidden topics: understanding rating dimensions with review text. In *Proceedings of the 7th ACM conference on Recommender systems*, pages 165–172. ACM.

Alessandro Moschitti. 2006. Efficient convolution kernels for dependency and constituent syntactic trees. In Johannes Frnkranz, Tobias Scheffer, and Myra Spiliopoulou, editors, *Machine Learning: ECML 2006*, volume 4212 of *LNCS*, pages 318–329. Springer Berlin Heidelberg.

Susan M Mudambi and David Schuff. 2010. Research note: What makes a helpful online review? a study of customer reviews on amazon. com. *MIS quarterly*, pages 185–200.

Thomas L Ngo-Ye and Atish P Sinha. 2012. Analyzing online review helpfulness using a regressional relieff-enhanced text mining method. *ACM Transactions on Management Information Systems (TMIS)*, 3(2):10.

Thomas L Ngo-Ye and Atish P Sinha. 2014. The influence of reviewer engagement characteristics on online review helpfulness: A text regression model. *Decision Support Systems*, 61:47–58.

Douglas Walton. 2009. Argumentation theory: A very short introduction. In Guillermo Simari and Iyad Rahwan, editors, *Argumentation in Artificial Intelligence*, pages 1–22. Springer US.

An Argument-Annotated Corpus of Scientific Publications

Anne Lauscher,[1,2] Goran Glavaš,[1] and **Simone Paolo Ponzetto[1]**
[1]Data and Web Science Research Group
University of Mannheim, Germany
[2]Web-based Information Systems and Services
Stuttgart Media University, Germany
{anne, goran, simone}@informatik.uni-mannheim.de
lauscher@hdm-stuttgart.de

Abstract

Argumentation is an essential feature of scientific language. We present an annotation study resulting in a corpus of scientific publications annotated with argumentative components and relations. The argumentative annotations have been added to the existing Dr. Inventor Corpus, already annotated for four other rhetorical aspects. We analyze the annotated argumentative structures and investigate the relations between argumentation and other rhetorical aspects of scientific writing, such as discourse roles and citation contexts.

1 Introduction

With the rapidly growing amount of scientific literature (Bornmann and Mutz, 2015), computational methods for analyzing scientific writing are becoming paramount. To support learning-based models for automated analysis of scientific publications, potentially leading to better understanding of the different rhetorical aspects of scientific language (which we dub *scitorics*), researchers publish manually-annotated corpora. To date, existing manually-annotated scientific corpora already reflect several of these aspects, such as sentential discourse roles (Fisas et al., 2015), *argumentative zones* (Teufel et al., 1999, 2009; Liakata et al., 2010), subjective aspects (Fisas et al., 2016), and citation polarity and purpose (Jochim and Schütze, 2012; Jha et al., 2017; Fisas et al., 2016).

As tools of persuasion (Gilbert, 1976, 1977), scientific publications are abundant with argumentation. Yet, somewhat surprisingly, there is no publicly available corpus of scientific publications (in English), annotated with fine-grained argumentative structures. In order to support comprehensive analyses of rhetorics in scientific text (i.e., *scitorics*), argumentative structure of scientific publications should not be studied in isolation, but rather in relation to other rhetorical aspects, such as the discourse structure. This is why in this work we contribute a new argumentation annotation layer to an existing Dr. Inventor Corpus (Fisas et al., 2016), already annotated for several rhetorical aspects.

Contributions. We propose a general argument annotation scheme for scientific text that can cover various research domains. We next extend the Dr. Inventor corpus (Fisas et al., 2015, 2016) with an annotation layer containing fine-grained argumentative components and relations. Our efforts result in the first argument-annotated corpus of scientific publications (in English), which allows for joint analyses of argumentation and other rhetorical dimensions of scientific writing. We make the argument-annotated corpus publicly available.[1] Finally, we offer an extensive statistical and information-theoretic analysis of the corpus.

2 Related Work

Researchers have offered a plethora of argument annotation schemes and corpora for various domains, including Wikipedia discussions (Biran and Rambow, 2011), on-line debates (e.g., Abbott et al., 2016; Habernal and Gurevych, 2016), e-markets (e.g., Islam, 2007), persuasive essays (Stab and Gurevych, 2017), news editorials (Al Khatib et al., 2016), and law (Wyner et al., 2010). The corpus of Reed et al. (2008) covers multiple domains, including news and political debates.

The work on argumentative annotations in scientific writing is, however, much scarcer. Pioneering annotation efforts of Teufel and Moens (1999a,b); Teufel et al. (1999) focused on discourse-level argumentation (dubbed *argumentative zones*), denoting more the rhetorical structure of the publica-

---

[1]http://data.dws.informatik.
uni-mannheim.de/sci-arg/compiled_corpus.
zip

Proceedings of the 5th Workshop on Argument Mining, pages 40–46
Brussels, Belgium, November 1, 2018. ©2018 Association for Computational Linguistics

tions than fine-grained argumentation, i.e., there are no (1) fine-grained argumentative components (at sub-sentence level) and no (2) relations between components, giving rise to an argumentation graph. Blake (2010) distinguishes between explicit and implicit claims, correlations, comparisons, and observations in biomedical publications. In contrast, we are not interested in how the claim is made, but rather on what are the claims (and what is not a claim) and how they are mutually connected. Green et al. (2014); Green (2014, 2015, 2016) proposed methods for identifying and annotating argumentative structures in scientific publications, but released no publicly available annotated corpus. In the effort most similar to ours, Kirschner et al. (2015) annotated arguments in a corpus of educational research publications. Besides being quite small, this corpus is also written in German.

3   Annotation Scheme

A number of theoretical frameworks of argumentation have been proposed (Walton et al., 2008; Anscombre and Ducrot, 1983, *inter alia*).[2] Among the most widely used is the model of Toulmin (2003), from which we start in this work as well, because of its relative simplicity and adoption in artificial intelligence and argument mining (Bench-Capon, 1998; Verheij, 2005; Kirschner et al., 2015). The Toulmin model, originally developed for the legal domain, recognizes six types of argumentative components: *claim, data, warrant, backing, qualifier,* and *rebuttal*.

We conducted a preliminary annotation study using the Toulmin model with two expert annotators on a small corpus subset. Annotators did not identify any *warrant, backing, qualifier,* nor *rebuttal* components. The annotators also pointed to the interlinked argumentative structure of publications in which *claim* were often used as ground for (supporting or conflicting) another claim. Not foreseen by the Toulmin model, we realized that the relations between argumentative components can be of different nature. Finally, the annotators recognized two distinct claim types: those presented as common knowledge (or state of the art) in the research area and those relating to authors' own research.

Following the above observations from the preliminary annotation, we simplify the annotation scheme by removing the non-observed component

---

[2]For an extensive overview, we refer the reader to (Bentahar et al., 2010)

types. Our final annotation scheme has the following types of argumentative component:

(1) *Own Claim* is an argumentative statement that closely relates to the authors' own work, e.g.:

> *"Furthermore, we show that <u>by simply changing the initialization and target velocity, the same optimization procedure leads to running controllers.</u>"*

(2) *Background Claim* is an argumentative statement relating to the background of authors' work, e.g., about related work or common practices in the respective research field, e.g.:

> *"Despite the efforts, <u>accurate modeling of human motion remains a challenging tasks.</u>"*

(3) *Data* component represents a fact that serves as evidence for or against a claim. Note that references or (factual) examples can also serve as data, e.g.:

> *"[...], due to <u>memory and graphics hardware constraints</u> nearly all video game character animation is still done using traditional SSD."*

We follow Bench-Capon (1998) and allow for links between the arguments. We introduce three different relations types, similar to Dung (1995).

(1) A *Supports* relation holds between components a and b if the assumed veracity of b increases with the veracity of a;
(2) A *Contradicts* relation holds between components a and b if the assumed veracity of b decreases with the veracity of a;
(3) The *Semantically Same* relation is annotated between two mentions of effectively the same claim or data component. This relation can be seen as *argument coreference*, analogous to entity (Lee et al., 2011, 2017) and event coreference (Glavaš and Šnajder, 2013; Lu and Ng, 2018).

It is important to emphasize that we do not bind the spans of our argumentative components to sentence boundaries, but rather allow for argumentative components of arbitrary span lengths, ranging from a single token to multiple sentences.

4   Annotation study

Dataset. Believing that argumentation needs to be studied in combination with other rhetorical aspects of scientific writing, we enriched the existing Dr. Inventor corpus (Fisas et al., 2015, 2016), consisting of 40 publications from computer graphics, with argumentative information. The Dr. Inventor

Annotation Layer	Labels	%
Discourse Role	*Background*	20
	Challenge	5
	Approach	57
	Outcome	16
	Future Work	2
Citation Purpose	*Criticism*	23
	Comparison	9
	Use	11
	Substantiation	1
	Basis	5
	Neutral	53
Subjective Aspect	*Advantage*	33
	Disadvantage	16
	Adv.-Disadv.	3
	Disadv.-Adv.	1
	Novelty	13
	Common Practice	32
	Limitation	2
Summarization Relevance	*Totally irrelevant*	66
	Should not appear	6
	May appear	14
	Relevant	6
	Very relevant	8

Table 1: Annotation layers of the Dr. Inventor Corpus with label distributions.

corpus has four layers of rhetorical annotations: (1) discourse roles, (2) citation purposes with associated citation contexts, (3) judgments of subjective aspects, and (4) annotations of sentence relevance for a summary. Table 1 summarizes the different annotation layers and their label distributions.

Annotation Process. We hired one expert[3] and three non-expert annotators[4] for our annotation study. We trained the annotators in a calibration phase, consisting of five iterations, in each of which all annotators annotated one publication. After each iteration we computed the inter-annotator agreement (IAA), discussed the disagreements, and, if needed, adjourned the annotation guidelines.[5] We measured the IAA in terms of the F_1-measure because (1) it is easily interpretable and straight-forward to compute and (2) it can account for spans of varying length, allowing for computing relaxed agreements in terms of partial overlaps.[6] The evolution of IAA over the five calibration it-

---

[3]A researcher in computational linguistics, not in computer graphics.

[4]Humanities and social sciences scholars.

[5]http://data.dws.informatik.
uni-mannheim.de/sci-arg/annotation_
guidelines.pdf

[6]Note that the chance-corrected measures, e.g., Cohen's Kappa, approach F_1-measure when the number of negative instances grows (Hripcsak and Rothschild, 2005).

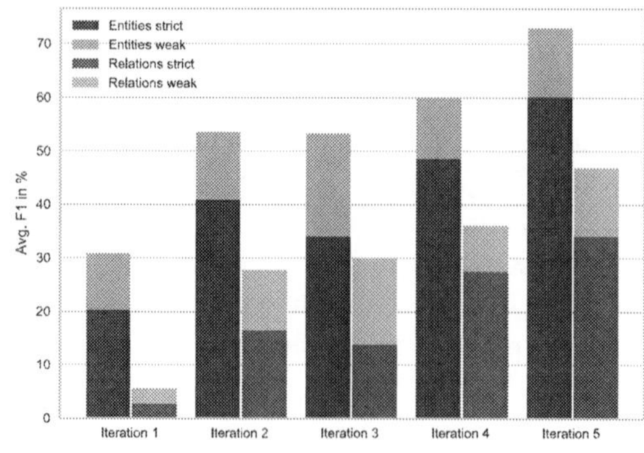

Figure 1: IAA evolution over the five calibration phases (*purple* for argumentative components; *blue* for relations; *dark* for the *strict* agreements; *light* for the *relaxed* agreements).

erations is depicted in Figure 1, in two variants: (1) A *strict* version in which components have to match exactly in span and type and relations have to match exactly in both components, direction and type of the link and (2) a *relaxed* version in which components only have to match in type and overlap in span (by at least half of the length of the shorter of them). Expectedly, we observe higher agreements with more calibration. The agreement on argumentative relations is 23% lower than on the components, which we think is due to the high ambiguity of argumentation structures, as previously noted by Stab et al. (2014). That is, given an argumentative text with pre-identified argumentative components, there are often multiple valid interpretations of an argumentative relation between them, i.e., it is "[...] hard or even impossible to identify one correct interpretation" (Stab et al., 2014). Additionally, disagreements in component identification are propagated to relations as well, since the agreement on a relation implies the agreement on annotated components at both ends of the relation.

5 Corpus Analysis

We first study the argumentation layer we annotated in isolation. Afterwards, we focus on the interrelations with other rhetorical annotation layers.

Analysis of Argumentation Annotations. Table 2 lists the number of components and relations in total and on average per publication. The number of *own claims* roughly doubles the amount of *background claims*, as the corpus consists only of original research papers, in which the authors mainly emphasize their own contributions. Interest-

Category	Label	Total	Per Publication
Component	*Background claim*	2,751	68.8 ± 25.2
	Own claim	5,445	136.1 ± 46.0
	Data	4,093	102.3 ± 32.1
Relation	*Supports*	5,790	144.8 ± 43.1
	Contradicts	696	17.4 ± 9.1
	Semantically same	44	1.1 ± 1.81

Table 2: Total and per-publication distributions of labels of argumentative components and relations in the extended Dr. Inventor Corpus.

Label	Min	Max	Avg (μ)	Std (σ)
Background claim	5	340	87.46	43.74
Own claim	3	500	85.70	44.03
Data	1	244	25.80	27.59

Table 3: Statistics on length of argumentative components (in number of characters) in the extended Dr. Inventor Corpus.

ingly, there are only half as many *data* components as claims. We can see two reasons for this – first, not all claims are supported and secondly, claims can be supported by other claims. There are many more *supports* than *contradicts* relations. This is intuitive, as authors mainly argue by providing *supporting* evidence for their own claims.

Table 3 shows the statistics on length of argumentative components. While the *background claims* and *own claims* are on average of similar length (85 and 87 characters, respectively), they are much longer than *data* components (average of 25 characters). This is intuitive given the domain of the corpus, as facts in computer science often require less explanation than claims. For example, we noticed that authors often refer to tables and figures as evidence for their claims. Similarly, when claiming weaknesses or strengths of related work, authors commonly provide references as evidence.

The argumentative structure of an individual publication corresponds to a forest of directed acyclic graphs (DAG) with annotated argumentative components as nodes and argumentative relations as edges. Thus, to obtain further insight into structural properties of argumentation in scientific publications, in Table 4 we provide graph-based measures like the number of connected components (i.e., subgraphs), the diameter, and the number of standalone claims (i.e., nodes without incoming or outgoing edges) and unsupported claims (i.e., nodes with no incoming *supports* edges). Our

Criterion	Min	Max	Avg (μ)	Std (σ)
Diameter	2	5	3.05	0.71
Max In-Degree	3	11	6.33	1.97
# standalone claims	27	127	63.00	21.40
# unsupp. claims	39	180	94.38	29.14
# unconn. subgraphs	78	231	147.23	35.78
# comp. per subgraph	1	17	2.09	1.5

Table 4: Graph-based analysis of the argumentative structures identified in the extended Dr. Inventor Corpus (per publication).

annotators identified an average of 141 connected component per publication, with an average diameter of 3. This indicates that either authors write very short argumentative chains or that our annotators had difficulties noticing long-range argumentative dependencies.

On the one hand, there are at least 27 standalone claims in each publication, that is claims, that are not connected with any other components. On the other hand, the maximum in-degree of a claim in a publication, on average, is 6, indicating that there are claims for which a lot of evidence is given. Intuitively, the claims for which more evidence is given should be more prominent. We next run PageRank (Page et al., 1999) on argumentation graphs of individual publications to identify most prominent claims. We list a couple of examples of claims with highest PageRank scores in Table 5. Somewhat unexpectedly, in 30 out of 40 publications in the dataset the highest ranked claim was a *background claim*. This suggests that in computer graphics authors emphasize more research gaps and motivation for their work than they justify its impact (for which empirical results often suffice).

Links to Other Rhetorical Aspects. We next investigate the interdependencies between the newly added argumentative annotations and the existing rhetorical annotations of the *Dr. Inventor Corpus*. An inspection of dependencies between different annotation layers in the corpus may indicate the usefulness of computational approaches that aim to exploit such interrelations. E.g., Bjerva (2017) recently showed that the measure of mutual information strongly correlates with performance gains obtained by multi-task learning models.

In this work, we employ the measure of normalized mutual information (NMI) (Strehl and Ghosh, 2003) to assess the amount of information shared between the five annotation layers. NMI is a variant of mutual information scaled to the interval $[0, 1]$

Type	Pub.	Claim with maximal PageRank score
background claim	A13 A21	'physical validity is often sacrificed for performance' 'a tremendous variety of materials exhibit this type of behavior'
own claim	A39	'the solution to the problem of asymmetry is to modify the CG method so that it can operate on equation (15), while procedurally applying the constraints inherent in the matrix W at each iteration'

Table 5: Claims with maximum PageRank score in a publication.

	AC	DR	SA	SR
AC	–	–	–	–
DR	**0.22**	–	–	–
SA	0.08	0.11	–	–
SR	0.04	0.10	0.13	–
CC	**0.18**	0.10	0.04	0.01

Table 6: Normalized mutual information between different annotation layers.

through normalization with the entropy of each of the two label sets. In Table 6 we show the NMI scores for all pairs of annotations layers: argument components (AC), discourse roles (DR), citation contexts (CC), subjective aspects (SA), and summary relevances (SR). The strongest association is found between argumentative components (AC) and discourse roles (DR). Looking at the labels of these two annotation layers, this seems plausible – *background claim* (AC) is likely to appear in a sentence of discourse role *background* (DR). Similarly, *own claims* more frequently appear in sections describing the *outcomes* of the work. To confirm this intuition, we computed co-occurrence matrices for pairs of label sets – indeed, the AC label *own claim* most frequently appears together with the discourse role *approach* and *outcome*, and the *background claim* with discourse roles *background* and *challenge*. Consider the following sentence:

> *"With the help of modeling tools or capture devices, complicated 3D character models are widely used in the fields of entertainment, virtual reality, medicine, etc."*

It contains a general claim about the research area (i.e., it is a *background claim*) and it also offers *background* information in terms of the discourse role. A similar set of intuitive label alignments justifies the higher NMI score between argumentative components (AC) and citation contexts (CC): *citation contexts* often appear in sentences with a *background claim*. Again, this is not surprising, as authors typically reference other publications and

in order to motivate their work:

> *"An improvement based on addition of auxiliary joints has been also proposed in [Weber 2000]. Although this reduces the artifacts, the skin to joints relationship must be re-designed after joint addition."*

In the above example, the wave-underlined text, i.e. the citation, serves as the *data* for the underlined text which is the *background claim* stating a research gap in the referenced work. At the same time, the underlined text can be seen as the *citation context* with the reference as target.

6 Conclusion

We presented an annotation scheme for argumentation analysis in scientific publications. We annotated the *Dr. Inventor Corpus* (Fisas et al., 2015, 2016) with an argumentation layer. The resulting corpus, which is, to the best of our knowledge, the first argument-annotated corpus of scientific publications in English, enables (1) computational analysis of argumentation in scientific writing and (2) integrated analysis of argumentation and other rhetorical aspects of scientific text. We further provided corpus statistics and graph-based analysis of the argumentative structure of the annotated publications. Finally, we analyzed the dependencies between different rhetorical aspects, which can inform computational models aiming to jointly address multiple aspects of scientific discourse. In the future, we plan to extend the corpus with publications from other domains and develop computational models for the integrated analysis of scientific writing.

Acknowledgments

This research was partly funded by the German Research Foundation (DFG), grant number EC 477/5-1 (LOC-DB). We thank our annotators for their very dedicated annotation effort.

References

Rob Abbott, Brian Ecker, Pranav Anand, and Marilyn A Walker. 2016. Internet argument corpus 2.0: An sql schema for dialogic social media and the corpora to go with it. In *Proceedings of the Tenth International Conference on Language Resources and Evaluation*, pages 4445–4452, Portorož, Slowenia. European Language Resources Association.

Khalid Al Khatib, Henning Wachsmuth, Johannes Kiesel, Matthias Hagen, and Benno Stein. 2016. A news editorial corpus for mining argumentation strategies. In *Proceedings of COLING 2016, the 26th International Conference on Computational Linguistics: Technical Papers*, pages 3433–3443, Osaka, Japan. The COLING 2016 Organizing Committee.

Jean-Claude Anscombre and Oswald Ducrot. 1983. *L'argumentation dans la langue*. Editions Mardaga.

Trevor JM Bench-Capon. 1998. Specification and implementation of toulmin dialogue game. In *Proceedings of the 11th Conference on Legal Knowledge Based Systems*, pages 5–20, Groningen, Netherlands. Foundation for Legal Knowledge Based Systems.

Jamal Bentahar, Bernard Moulin, and Micheline Blanger. 2010. A taxonomy of argumentation models used for knowledge representation. *Artificial Intelligence Review*, 33(3):211–259.

Or Biran and Owen Rambow. 2011. Identifying justifications in written dialogs. In *Fifth IEEE International Conference on Semantic Computing*, pages 162–168, Palo Alto, CA, USA. IEEE.

Johannes Bjerva. 2017. Will my auxiliary tagging task help? estimating auxiliary tasks effectivity in multi-task learning. In *Proceedings of the 21st Nordic Conference on Computational Linguistics*, pages 216–220, Gothenburg, Sweden. Association for Computational Linguistics.

Catherine Blake. 2010. Beyond genes, proteins, and abstracts: Identifying scientific claims from full-text biomedical articles. *Journal of Biomedical Informatics*, 43(2):173–189.

Lutz Bornmann and Rüdiger Mutz. 2015. Growth rates of modern science: A bibliometric analysis based on the number of publications and cited references. *Journal of the Association for Information Science and Technology*, 66(11):2215–2222.

Phan Minh Dung. 1995. On the acceptability of arguments and its fundamental role in nonmonotonic reasoning, logic programming and n-person games. *Artificial Intelligence*, 77(2):321–357.

Beatriz Fisas, Francesco Ronzano, and Horacio Saggion. 2016. A multi-layered annotated corpus of scientific papers. In *Proceedings of the International Conference on Language Resources and Evaluation*, pages 3081–3088, Portorož, Slovenia. European Language Resources Association.

Beatriz Fisas, Horacio Saggion, and Francesco Ronzano. 2015. On the discoursive structure of computer graphics research papers. In *Proceedings of The 9th Linguistic Annotation Workshop*, pages 42–51, Denver, CO, USA. Association for Computational Linguistics.

G Nigel Gilbert. 1976. The transformation of research findings into scientific knowledge. *Social Studies of Science*, 6(3-4):281–306.

G Nigel Gilbert. 1977. Referencing as persuasion. *Social Studies of Science*, 7(1):113–122.

Goran Glavaš and Jan Šnajder. 2013. Exploring coreference uncertainty of generically extracted event mentions. In *International Conference on Intelligent Text Processing and Computational Linguistics*, pages 408–422. Springer.

Nancy Green. 2014. Towards creation of a corpus for argumentation mining the biomedical genetics research literature. In *Proceedings of the First Workshop on Argumentation Mining*, pages 11–18, Baltimore, Maryland. Association for Computational Linguistics.

Nancy Green. 2015. Annotating evidence-based argumentation in biomedical text. In *2015 IEEE International Conference on Bioinformatics and Biomedicine*, pages 922–929, Washington, D.C., USA. IEEE.

Nancy Green. 2016. Implementing argumentation schemes as logic programs. In *The 16th Workshop on Computational Models of Natural Argument*, volume 30, New York, USA. CEUR-WS.

Nancy Green, E Cabrio, S Villata, and A Wyner. 2014. Argumentation for scientific claims in a biomedical research article. In *Proceedings of the Workshop on Frontiers and Connections between Argumentation Theory and Natural Language Processing*, pages 21–25, Forl-Cesena, Italy. CEUR-WS.

Ivan Habernal and Iryna Gurevych. 2016. Which argument is more convincing? Analyzing and predicting convincingness of web arguments using bidirectional LSTM. In *Proceedings of the 54th Annual Meeting of the Association for Computational Linguistics (Volume 1: Long Papers)*, page 1122, Berlin, Germany. Association for Computational Linguistics.

George Hripcsak and Adam S. Rothschild. 2005. Agreement, the F-measure, and reliability in information retrieval. *Journal of the American Medical Informatics Association*, 12(3):296–298.

Khandaker Shahidul Islam. 2007. An Approach to Argumentation Context Mining from Dialogue History in an e-Market Scenario. In *Proceedings of the 2Nd International Workshop on Integrating Artificial Intelligence and Data Mining - Volume 84*, AIDM '07, pages 73–81, Darlinghurst, Australia, Australia. Australian Computer Society, Inc.

Rahul Jha, Amjad-Abu Jbara, Vahed Qazvinian, and Dragomir R. Radev. 2017. NLP-driven citation analysis for scientometrics. *Natural Language Engineering*, 23(1):93–130.

Charles Jochim and Hinrich Schütze. 2012. Towards a generic and flexible citation classifier based on a faceted classification scheme. In *Proceedings of the 24th International Conference on Computational Linguistics*, pages 1343–1358, Mumbai, India. The COLING 2012 Organizing Committee.

Christian Kirschner, Judith Eckle-Kohler, and Iryna Gurevych. 2015. Linking the thoughts: Analysis of argumentation structures in scientific publications. In *Proceedings of the 2nd Workshop on Argumentation Mining*, pages 1–11, Denver, CO, USA. Association for Computational Linguistics.

Heeyoung Lee, Yves Peirsman, Angel Chang, Nathanael Chambers, Mihai Surdeanu, and Dan Jurafsky. 2011. Stanford's multi-pass sieve coreference resolution system at the conll-2011 shared task. In *Proceedings of the fifteenth conference on computational natural language learning: Shared task*, pages 28–34. Association for Computational Linguistics.

Kenton Lee, Luheng He, Mike Lewis, and Luke Zettlemoyer. 2017. End-to-end neural coreference resolution. In *Proceedings of the 2017 Conference on Empirical Methods in Natural Language Processing*, pages 188–197.

Maria Liakata, Simone Teufel, Advaith Siddharthan, and Colin R Batchelor. 2010. Corpora for the Conceptualisation and Zoning of Scientific Papers. In *Proceedings of the International Conference on Language Resources and Evaluation*.

Jing Lu and Vincent Ng. 2018. Event coreference resolution: A survey of two decades of research. In *IJCAI*, pages 5479–5486.

Lawrence Page, Sergey Brin, Rajeev Motwani, and Terry Winograd. 1999. The pagerank citation ranking: Bringing order to the web. Technical report, Stanford InfoLab.

Chris Reed, Raquel Mochales Palau, Glenn Rowe, and Marie-Francine Moens. 2008. Language resources for studying argument. In *Proceedings of the Sixth International Conference on Language Resources and Evaluation*, pages 2613–2618, Marrakesh, Marocco. European Language Resources Association.

Christian Stab and Iryna Gurevych. 2017. Parsing argumentation structures in persuasive essays. *Computational Linguistics*, 43(3):619–659.

Christian Stab, Christian Kirschner, Judith Eckle-Kohler, and Iryna Gurevych. 2014. Argumentation Mining in Persuasive Essays and Scientific Articles from the Discourse Structure Perspective. In *Proceedings of the Workshop on Frontiers and Connections between Argumentation Theory and Natural Language Processing*, pages 21–25.

Alexander Strehl and Joydeep Ghosh. 2003. Cluster ensembles – a knowledge reuse framework for combining multiple partitions. *Journal of Machine Learning Research*, 3:583–617.

Simone Teufel, Jean Carletta, and Marc Moens. 1999. An annotation scheme for discourse-level argumentation in research articles. In *Proceedings of the Ninth Conference on European Chapter of the Association for Computational Linguistics*, pages 110–117, Bergen, Norway. Association for Computational Linguistics.

Simone Teufel and Marc Moens. 1999a. Argumentative classification of extracted sentences as a first step towards flexible abstracting. In *Advances in automatic Text Summarization*, pages 155–171, Cambridge, MA, USA. MIT Press.

Simone Teufel and Marc Moens. 1999b. Discourse-level argumentation in scientific articles: Human and automatic annotation. In *Towards Standards and Tools for Discourse Tagging, Workshop*, Maryland, MA, USA. Association for Computational Linguistics.

Simone Teufel, Advaith Siddharthan, and Colin Batchelor. 2009. Towards discipline-independent argumentative zoning: Evidence from chemistry and computational linguistics. In *Proceedings of the 2009 Conference on Empirical Methods in Natural Language Processing: Volume 3*, pages 1493–1502, Edinburgh, Scotland. Association for Computational Linguistics.

Stephen E. Toulmin. 2003. *The Uses of Argument*, updated edition. Cambridge University Press.

Bart Verheij. 2005. Evaluating Arguments Based on Toulmins Scheme. *Argumentation*, 19(3):347–371.

Douglas Walton, Chris Reed, and Fabrizio Macagno. 2008. *Argumentation Schemes*. Cambridge University Press.

Adam Wyner, Raquel Mochales-Palau, Marie-Francine Moens, and David Milward. 2010. Approaches to Text Mining Arguments from Legal Cases. In *Semantic Processing of Legal Texts*, pages 60–79. Springer Berlin Heidelberg.

Annotating Claims in the Vaccination Debate

Benedetta Torsi, Roser Morante
Vrije Universiteit Amsterdam
De Boelelaan 1105, 1081 HV Amsterdam
The Netherlands
`b.torsi@student.vu.nl,r.morantevallejo@vu.nl`

Abstract

In this paper we present annotation experiments with three different annotation schemes for the identification of argument components in texts related to the vaccination debate. Identifying claims about vaccinations made by participants in the debate is of great societal interest, as the decision to vaccinate or not has impact in public health and safety. Since most corpora that have been annotated with argumentation information contain texts that belong to a specific genre and have a well defined argumentation structure, we needed to adjust the annotation schemes to our corpus, which contains heterogeneous texts from the Web. We started with a complex annotation scheme that had to be simplified due to low IAA. In our final experiment, which focused on annotating claims, annotators reached 57.3% IAA.

1 Introduction

Argumentation is an important aspect of human communication. The study of argumentation is an interdisciplinary research field that has been gaining momentum because of its relevance in cognitive sciences and its application in artificial intelligence. Because of the richness of information that it offers, data from the Web such as social media, on-line newspapers, forums, or blogs is often the subject of exploration (Lippi and Torroni, 2016). The availability of such data and the advancements in computational linguistics fostered the rise of a new research field called argumentation mining (AM) (Peldszus and Stede, 2013a), whose goal is to automatically extract argument components from text, generating structured data for computational models of argument.

Thus far, most corpora annotated with argumentation information are composed by a certain type of texts, such as argumentative essays (Stab and Gurevych, 2017) and news editorials (Al Khatib

et al., 2016), which usually have a specific structure. However, in order to understand public opinions, it is necessary to process textual data from the Web, which is generated by a diversity of users who do not follow a predefined template, resulting in texts of miscellaneous genres and registers.

Our research focuses on annotating argumentation components in a corpus of texts crawled from the Web. We chose this type of texts because they contain precious information about people's opinions and because existing argumentation schemes[1] are not directly applicable to Web data. Thus, one of our aims was to evaluate whether existing argumentation schemes can be applied to this data. Additionally, we focused on texts about the vaccination debate because of the importance of the topic from a societal and health perspective. A longer term goal of our work is to find out and analyze the claims that people make when they engage in the debate. Potential applications of both the analysis and the annotated data would be, for example, detecting misinformation about vaccinations to populate ontologies (Amith and Tao, 2018) or training agents (Rosenfeld and Kraus, 2016) to persuade hesitant users to vaccinate.

The vaccination debate is an exemplary case for the study of on-line debates and opinion forming processes. In 1998, a scientific paper was published by Andrew Wakefield, who argued that there was a link between the Measles Mumps and Rubella (MMR) vaccine and autism in children. The paper incited skepticism in the public about the safety and the effectiveness of vaccines, to such extent that more an more parents are deciding not to vaccinate their children, causing illnesses such as measles to spread and leading to a measles outbreak in the EU in 2017. Nowadays,

---

[1]By "argumentation schemes" we mean annotation schemes that have been used to annotate argumentation components.

Proceedings of the 5th Workshop on Argument Mining, pages 47–56
Brussels, Belgium, November 1, 2018. ©2018 Association for Computational Linguistics

with collaborative media, anyone can join in a discussion and share information and opinions. This makes it difficult to attest the reliability of on-line content (Zummo, 2017). Reports show that statistically significant positive correlations exist between monthly Measles cases and Google queries in most EU28 countries from January 2011 to August 2017 (Mavragani and Ochoa, 2018). Since the debate on immunization directly affects public health and safety, analyzing the way people engage in this discussion is of particular interest.

In this paper we present three annotation experiments with different annotation schemes. Our annotation studies were all performed on a corpus of texts related to the vaccination debate (Vax Corpus), which is composed of 294 documents automatically downloaded from the Internet adding up to 445,574 words. The documents that compose the corpus are heterogeneous in length, genre, and style: blog posts, editorials, news articles, and science articles. Below are some examples of statements found in the corpus:

1. These are child who can't be vaccinated. Children who have cancer. Children who are immunocompromised. Children who are truly allergic to a vaccine orpart of a vaccine (i.e anaphylaxis to egg). These children remain at risk. They cannot be protected ... except by vaccinating people around them.
2. Better believe if I ever have kids I won't be vaccinating.
3. Of course we were already blaming anti-vaxxers for bringing back measles and spreading them around Disneyland, but a fresh new study confirms that yup, is it definitely scientifically their fault, so let's blame them even harder now.
4. As we have already yelled, in all caps and with many exclamation points, JUST VACCINATE YOUR KIDS, DAMNIT!!!

After experimenting with several annotation schemes, we concluded that in order to model arguments in Web data, a simplified scheme is needed. We cannot rely on fine-grained models based on argumentation theory, as they are not directly applicable to heterogeneous texts. The simplified scheme was adopted for the annotation of our corpus, resulting in the annotated resource *VaxClaim Corpus*, which will be made publicly available. Since the simplified scheme does not contain domain-specific features, it should be applicable to other on-line debates. We will test this hypothesis in future work.

Section 2 presents related work. In Section 3 we introduce the pilot annotation studies and we discuss the results and main sources of disagreement. In Section 4 we describe the final annotation experiment, which focused on *claims*, and we also analyze the results and disagreements. Finally, in Section 5 we provide some conclusions.

2 Related Work

Numerous models have been developed to address and understand the internal (micro) structure of arguments (Lippi and Torroni, 2016). Walton adopted the notion of *argumentation scheme*, which allows to identify patterns in the arguments present in everyday discourse (Bentahar et al., 2010). Since then, several argumentation schemes have been put forward. For a general overview of argumentation schemes, refer to Lippi and Torroni (2016). Here we focus on the schemes used to annotate data for argumentation mining purposes.

Saint-Dizier followed a knowledge driven approach to tackle the task of mining arguments in Web data and concluded that it is possible to relate independent statements by means of lexical data, domain knowledge and reasoning schemes (Saint-Dizier, 2016).

Stab and Gurevych created a corpus of 402 argumentative essays selected from essayforum.com and annotated it with the following argument components: *major claims*, *claims*, and *premises* (Stab and Gurevych, 2017). They model the microstructure of arguments as a connected tree structure where the *major claim* is the root node which represents the author's standpoint. The *major claim* is expected to be contained either in the introduction or the conclusion of the essay. The rest of the essay contains *claims* (the cores of the arguments) and *premises*, which support the *claims*.

Al-Khatib et al. (2016) consider that in the editorial genre, the author generally does not only aim at persuading the audience, but she also wants to spread information about the topic. The author defends a thesis that conveys a stance on a controversial subject providing different kinds of evidence. They constructed a corpus by extracting 100 editorials from each of the following websites: aljazeera.com, foxnews.com and theguardian.com. They introduce an annotation task which consisted of dividing the corpus into segments. Then, each segment is assigned one of the following labels:

- *Common ground*: the segment contains a self-evident fact, it states common knowledge.

- *Assumption*: the segment contains a conclusion, an opinion or a judgment of the author.

- *Testimony*: the segment contains a statement made by some expert, witness or authority.

- *Statistics*: the segment contains the results of a quantitative study or data analyses.

- *Anecdote*: the segment expresses a personal experience, a specific instance, a concrete example.

- *Other*: the segment is not classifiable with any of the above classes.

These two argumentation schemes were adopted in the first pilot study presented in this work because the documents composing the Vax Corpus present characteristics of both argumentative essays and news editorials.

Habernal and Gurevych (2017) created a corpus of user-generated Web content collecting documents of different registers, such as articles, comments on articles, blog posts, forum posts, etc. Their scheme is based on the Toulmin model (Toulmin, 2003) and it is characterized by the following components argument components:

- *Claim*: the conclusion that the author is trying to establish.

- *Grounds*: the evidence and reasoning that constitute the foundation of the claim.

- *Backing*: the set of information that conveys the trustworthiness of the warrant.

- *Qualifiers*: they express the degree of cogency attached to the claim.

- *Rebuttal*: a statement expressing an instance in which the claim might be defeated.

- *Refutation*: a section of text that attacks the *Rebuttal*.

Their scheme was adopted for the second pilot study because it was designed to fit Web data. The belief was that the resulting annotation task would be feasible for the corpus at hand and that the scheme would allow for the identification of interesting argumentation patterns.

3 Annotating Argument Components: Pilot Studies

One of our research goals is to automatically extract claims related to the vaccination debate. In order to train a system, we first needed to annotate a corpus. We performed three annotation studies to test the feasibility of different annotation schemes. The first two studies served as pilots to discover strengths and weaknesses of previously proposed annotation schemes. For the two pilot studies, annotators were asked to annotate texts for 3 and 10 hours respectively. For the final annotation task, they were asked to annotate 100 randomly-selected documents from the Vax Corpus.

The annotation tasks were carried out by two annotators (A and B) with a background in Linguistics. Annotator A was more experienced with the topic of argumentation. Annotations were performed with the open source annotation tool eHOST, [2] which also provides options to calculate inter annotator agreement (IAA). IAA is calculated in eHOST by dividing the annotation matches by all annotations (matches + nonmatches). IAA was calculated with lenient matching in order not to penalize disagreements due to details such as punctuation.

3.1 First Pilot Study

We observed that some documents in the Vax Corpus present characteristics of argumentative essays. In particular, arguments are expressed in a hierarchical structure where there is a main claim, one or several sub-claims and premises providing backing for the claims. This is why for the first pilot study, we adopted the scheme put forward by Stab and Gurevych who found that, in argumentative essays, arguments are often characterized by a tree structure (Stab and Gurevych, 2017). Their markables were deemed appropriate and they were all adopted: *major claim*, *claim*, *premise*. Their approach had to be modified, however, to fit the

---

[2]http://blulab.chpc.utah.edu/content/ehost-extensible-human-oracle-suite-tools

characteristics of the Vax Corpus: more than one *claim* was allowed per paragraph. Furthermore, we allowed the *attack* relationship between *claim* and *major claim*. That means that the *major claim* does not have to be supported by all the *claims* present in the text and that some *claims* might play the role of *rebuttal*. The *rebuttal* presents opposing views to the author's *claim* and it is often presented with the intent of criticizing it, thus strengthening the claim (Habernal and Gurevych, 2017).

We also observed that the type of backing given by the authors in the Vax Corpus often fits with the descriptions of argument components proposed by Al-Khatib et al. (2016). We adopted their scheme with some modifications: (i) The definition of *assumption* seemed similar to the one of *claim*: they both constitute some sort of conclusion or judgment of the author. We left out this component, as it would overlap too much with the concept of *claim*. (ii) The definition of *common ground* seemed difficult to interpret and apply. It is unclear what should be considered common knowledge and what should not; consequently we left out this unit. (iii) The remaining units, *testimony*, *statistics*, *anecdote* and *other* correspond to the types of premise that were observed in the Vax Corpus. Furthermore, since according to the adopted definition of *claim*, the core statement of the argument can be attributed exclusively to the author of the text, the units *testimony* and *statistics* could only coincide with the *premise*. The *anecdote* corresponds to a recounting of a specific episode, thus it is uncommon that it fits the definition of *claim*. Considering all the factors mentioned above, we selected the four components *testimony*, *statistics*, *anecdote* and *other* as attributes for the component *premise*.

3.1.1 Results

The annotators were able to tackle one file per hour which resulted in 3 annotated documents. Table 1 presents the IAA scores. *Major claim* reached the highest agreement score (66.7%), but the annotators did not agree on the annotation of *premise* in any of the cases. Next we discuss cases of disagreement.

Major claims. An analysis of the disagreements revealed that it is difficult to establish which statement best summarizes the stance of the author, as exemplified by the example below, where each an-

Type	IAA	Matches	Non-matches
All	15.8%	6	77
Claim	6.9%	2	27
Premise	0.0%	0	48
MC	66.7%	4	2

Table 1: Two-way IAA Results (Pilot study 1). MC stands for "Major Claim".

notator marks a different *major claim* for the same text:

- **Annotator A**: If these diseases seem uncommon - or even unheard of - it's usually because these vaccines are doing their job.

- **Annotator B**: Childhood vaccines protect children from a variety of serious or potentially fatal diseases, including diphtheria, measles, polio and whooping cough (pertussis).

From Annotator A's perspective, the text conveys the effectiveness of vaccines in general. However, for Annotator B there is an emphasis on the importance of vaccinating children against the listed fatal diseases. Both interpretations are acceptable. The schema proposed is based on a hierarchy of claims, so when the ranking is not straightforward the annotation becomes prone to disagreement.

Claims. During a preliminary analysis of the corpus, it was noted that it is difficult to differentiate between *claims* and *premises*. *Claims* are controversial statements that express a certain stance or intention. Identifying controversy and intention in a statement is a process that can generate discrepancies in the annotations. Adopting the more restrictive definition of *claim* by Stab and Gurevych (2017), the goal was to limit the room for interpretation. The definition contains the requirements that the source of the *claim* should always be the author of the text and that *claims* should only be accepted if some backing is found in the text. Despite the restrictions and the example provided in the guidelines, the agreement was very low.

While the restriction about the source of the *claim* helped identifying the *claim*, there were no restrictions for the source of the *premise*: it could be attributable to the author or to another explicit source. Also, the granularity of annotation was approached differently in a few instances. Example 5 was marked as *claim* by Annotator A, while Annotator B marked it as *premise* considering that the source of "worry" is different from the author.

5. Some worry too about a preservative called thimerosal, which contained a very low concentration of a mercury compound.

Premise. The *premise* component achieved no matches. One reason is the difficulty of differentiating between *claims* and *premises*. Another plausible explanation is the fact that the merging of the two annotation guidelines concentrates in the *premise* component; the definition was drawn from Stab and Gurevych's work (2017) and the attributes where taken from Al-Khatib et al. (2016).

The high level of disagreement indicated that the guidelines did not describe and define properly the argument components. The definitions for *claim* and *premise* left too much room for interpretation.

3.2 Second Pilot Study

Habernal and Gurevych (2017)'s scheme was used in the second annotation study. The guidelines[3] had to be adapted because they require that annotators first conduct a round of annotations to identify all texts that are persuasive regarding the discussed topic. This step is not necessary because all texts in the Vax Corpus are about vaccinations and are considered on-topic. Furthermore, although the documents are not traditionally argumentative, it is possible to identify the intent to persuade in most of them. The second step required annotators to identify the following argument components: *claim, grounds, backing, rebuttal, refutation.*

This experiment was conducted to observe whether an argumentation scheme based on the Toulmin model and conceived as being applicable to Web data could indeed be applied to the Vax Corpus.

3.2.1 Results

The annotators were able to go through 37 documents in 10 hours. Table 2 presents the scores for IAA. The score for *refutation* was the lowest (10.0%), whereas the agreement for *backing* was the highest (25.8%). Considering the fact that the scheme was put forward to annotate Web data, the agreement reached is not satisfactory for any

---

[3]https://www.ukp.tu-darmstadt.de/data/argumentation-mining /argument-annotated-user-generated-web-discourse/

of the classes. Furthermore, the task was time-consuming.

Type	IAA	Matches	Non-matches
All classes	19.9%	210	843
Claim	19.7%	46	187
Backing	25.8%	92	264
Grounds	15.6%	56	303
Rebuttal	18.5%	12	53
Refutation	10.0%	4	36

Table 2: Two-way IAA Results (Pilot study 2).

Claims. Annotators were asked to annotate claims at sentence level, and only if there were other argument components in the sentence they should switch to the token level (Habernal and Gurevych, 2017). This indication caused several disagreements, as shown in the next example:

- **Annotator A**: [Some people have had concerns that ASD might be linked to the vaccines children receive but studies have shown that there is no link between receiving vaccines and developing ASD.]*Claim*

- **Annotator B**: [Some people have had concerns that ASD might be linked to the vaccines children receive]*Rebuttal* [but studies have shown that there is no link between receiving vaccines and developing ASD.]*Refutation*

Annotator A followed the suggestion to annotate at the sentence level and considered the whole section as a *claim* because she interpreted the first clause as a fact that the author needs to present in order to provide the context for his or her opinion on the matter. Annotator B followed the suggestion to switch to the token level in the presence of multiple components and identified two argument components within the sentence, *rebuttal* and *refutation*, which she related to the claim "There is no causal link between vaccination and autism." Both interpretations are acceptable, since it is difficult to determine which one is more appropriate on the basis of granularity criteria.

Claim and Grounds. The vagueness of the definitions and the nature of the texts caused annotators to assign different labels to the same fragments of text, suggesting that the task to differentiate between argument components in Web data is not an easy one. In particular, the distinction that annotators A and B struggled the most with is the one between *claim* and *grounds*. Even in the definition provided by Habernal and Gurevych (2017) the closeness of the two components is expressed: *"Grounds, can in fact, also be claims: subsidiary or secondary claims that are used to build up a larger argument. Grounds have to match your claims."*

Claim and Refutation The differentiation between *claim* and *refutation* caused disagreement as well. The guidelines define *refutation* as follows (Habernal and Gurevych, 2017): *"Rebuttal attacks the Claim by presenting opposing view (or contra-argument). Refutation attacks Rebuttal."* Consequently, the *refutation* and the *claim* convey similar ideas. The condition that allows for the identification of the *refutation* is the presence of the *rebuttal*. This means that if the annotators identify different argumentation structures in the text, one including a *rebuttal* and another excluding it, the first will very likely be annotated as *refutation* and the second will as *claim*.

Grounds and Backing The component *backing* reached the highest rate of agreement. This could be due to the fact that a large part of text could be identified as such. In fact, the guidelines simply state that *"Backing is additional evidence to support the argument."* (Habernal and Gurevych, 2017). Still, the differentiation between *backing* and *grounds* generated a lot of disagreement. Considering that they play a similar role in an argument, which is to support the *claim*, this was expectable. Reading the guidelines, one can understand that *grounds* is necessary evidence presented to provide good reasons for the *claim*, whereas *backing* is "additional", it does not seem to be necessary. In practice, this difference did not help the annotators, since it is difficult to determine what is necessary as support for an argument and what is futile.

From this second pilot study we learned that annotation schemes containing numerous components and guidelines that offer vague directives are not easily applicable to annotating argument components in heterogeneous texts where no clear patterns of argumentation structure are followed. The guidelines should contain precise directions, providing restrictions that can be used as reference in difficult cases like the ones presented above. As a result, we decided to simplify the annotation scheme in order to make the task feasible, given the type of texts that the Vax Corpus contains. The task would also become less time-consuming.

4 Annotating Claims

The third annotation task was simplified as much as possible. Since our final goal is to understand people's attitudes and gain insight in the process of opinion formation, we decided to focus on the core of the argument: the *claim*. This choice implicated that it was not possible to adhere to the traditional definition of argument. Conventionally, an argument is composed at least of two components: a *claim* and a *premise* (Palau and Moens, 2009; Peldszus and Stede, 2013b). Since premises are frequently claim-like statements and express the attitude of the source, they were not excluded from the annotation task and they were subsumed in the *claim* component. Therefore, the focus of this task was to identify all claim-like statements.

The definition of *claim* chosen was the following:

> *The claim is the central component of an argument. Claims are sections of text that express the stance of the author. Sometimes, claims are introduced by an explicit source in the text (different from the author). Since they are opinionated statements with respect to the topic, claims are often introduced by stance expressions, such as "In my opinion", "I think that".*

An important requirement is that the *claim* has to be a refutable statement. It follows that the following do not qualify as claims:

- **Rhetorical question**: "Wouldn't it be better to develop immunity naturally?"

- **Backing**: "I am a nurse."

- **Common ground**: "Measles can spread through airborne transmission."

- **Statistics**: "80% of vaccinated children experience serious side effects."

- **Anecdotes**: "I experienced hearing loss after being given the MMR vaccine."

- **Opinions**: "I am against vaccinations."

Additionally, when the person or entity to whom the *claim* could be attributed was an explicit source different from the author of the text, then annotators should also mark the *source* and the relation *Has_source* between *claim* and *source*.

The guidelines for the annotation task are provided as supplementary material.

4.1 Results

The annotators were able to annotate 100 files in 33.5 hours. Table 3 shows the IAA scores. Making a quantitative comparison with the IAA achieved by other related studies is not possible because they all use different evaluation measures. It is possible to compare the results of the main annotation study with the previous two that were carried out as part of this exploration.

Type	IAA	Matches	Non-matches
All	54.4%	2542	2130
Claim	57.3%	2224	1658
Source of Claim	40.3%	318	472

Table 3: Two-way IAA Results for the annotation of claims.

The *claim* component achieved 57.3% IAA, which is satisfactory as compared to the first (6.9%) and second experiments (19.7%). The higher IAA rate achieved in this experiment was predictable considering the fact that the annotation task was less restrictive. While in the second experiment *major claim* should be assigned to sections of text that fulfilled strict requirements, in the third experiment, the annotation of *claim* was not subject to such restrictions.

4.2 Error Analysis

Even if the IAA is acceptable for the task, the task remains difficult. In order to understand where its difficulty lies, we performed an error analysis focusing on the component *claim*. The main points of controversy noticed in the results are the following:

- *Debatability*, which refers to the degree of debatability that the *claim* needs to express in order to be considered as such.

- *Attributability and commitment*, which refer to the context the *claim* needs to be presented in, specifically looking at whether it can be attributed to a source and how strongly the source needs to commit to it.

- *Relatedness to topic*, which refers to deciding whether to annotate or not statements that fit the description of *claim*, but that do not have a direct relation to the topic of vaccination.

- *Granularity and sources*, which refer to different interpretations of the task of assigning sources to the *claim*, resulting in annotations with different degrees of granularity.

4.3 Debatability

The two annotators followed a different approach when annotating claim-like statements that could be accepted by both the anti-vaccination and the pro-vaccination audiences. These instances raised some questions about how open to discussion a statement should be in order to deserve the *claim* label. These sentences often contain modal verbs such as "may", "might" and "could". An example of this phenomenon can be observed in the following statements:

6. Vaccines, like any medicine, **can** have side effects.
7. The increased use of veterinary vaccines **may** be accompanied by an increase in human exposure to the vaccine strain, new methods of vaccine administration **may** result in an increased likelihood of inadvertent exposure, increased use of aerosol administration **may** result in greater human exposure to animal vaccines.

These examples deal with potentially negative situations that could take place as result of vaccine inoculation. At first glance, one might think that they reveal an anti-vaccination stance. However, they simply express the possibility that vaccines might have negative side effects, which is an idea that is welcomed by the pro-vaccination community as well. The statements express the capability of a certain occurrence to take place. This is difficult to debate, especially in the case of vaccinations. These examples are characterized by a high degree of acceptability and a low degree of debatability.

Annotator A had the tendency not to annotate such statements, while annotator B annotated them as *claims*. The approach of annotator A seemed to deem the debatability of *claim* very important because it directly results in the stance-expressiveness of the *claim*; if a statement could be accepted by both parties of the debate, it does not reveal the stance of the author. The proposed guidelines do not give information on how to approach these cases. Considering the fact that one of the goals of analyzing the vaccination debate is to identify the stance of the participating authors, future versions of the guidelines should suggest the identification of *claims* that are polarizing.

4.4 Attributability and Commitment

Annotators exhibited different behaviors in approaching instances where it was unclear to whom the claim-like statement could be attributed. Here are some examples:

8. If you run across someone claiming that **their religion is against vaccinations**, you can check here, although, admittedly, the article only covers mainstream religions
9. What if a parent makes a claim that they are Jewish, and one rabbi says that **vaccines are bad**?

Annotator B marked the tokens in bold as *claims*, whereas annotator A did not. The clauses in bold could, indeed, fit the definition of *claims*. Taking into consideration the context in which they are presented, it is difficult to attribute them to an explicit source or the author of the text. Their context expresses hypothetical situations where it could happen that someone makes those claims.

Other instances that raise similar questions are the following:

10. Some parents might worry that **the vaccine causes autism**.
11. Some people have had concerns that **ASD might be linked to the vaccines children receive**.

Annotator B marked the text in bold as *claim*, while annotator A did not. The statements also express hypothetical situations. Furthermore, they both deal with worries and concerns, which reveal a lower level of commitment to the claims in bold. The guidelines do not give directives on how to tackle the two groups of interesting cases. Although the examples contain clauses that fit the requirements of the class *claim*, it is not possible to attribute them to an author who is committed to them. One way to solve this issue would be to think about the end-goal of the project. If the goal is to capture the stances of the users who are participating in the vaccination debate by writing blog posts and comments, then the above-reported examples should be left unannotated. If the aim is to identify all the possible attitudes that people have regarding the debate, then it would make sense to mark those *claims*. Nonetheless, the examples express speculative claims. One could assume that those are real arguments that people brandish. Future versions of the guidelines will require annotators to mark as *claim* those statements that are attributable to a source and that reveal a high level of commitment.

4.5 Relatedness to the Topic

Annotators were asked to approach the texts focusing on finding all the statements that fit the description of *claim* without worrying about how related they were to the topic of vaccination. The choice was made because all documents in the Vax Corpus are considered on-topic. This directive was not always respected by both annotators leading to disagreement. Some examples are the following:

12. The gene is 'silent'.
13. God is going to save you.

These instances raised a critical objection. If one takes into account only the goal to capture the stance of the author, how useful is it to mark statements that are indirectly related to the topic of vaccination and that do not reveal information about the attitude of the source? The examples above do fit the description of *claim*. Since one of our goals is to gain insight in the process of opinion formation, these statements are helpful in forming a profile for the users, uncovering part of their background and some of their beliefs. Future versions of the guidelines will highlight more strongly the importance of such statements in order to avoid disagreement.

4.6 Granularity and Sources

The annotation of *sources* caused some disagreement, affecting the granularity of the *claim* annotations. Some examples exhibiting this kind of disagreement are the following:

14. **Annotator A**: [95% of Americans are brainwashed to believe they are doing this for us.]*claim*
    Annotator B: [95% of Americans]*source* are brainwashed to believe [they are doing this for us.]*claim*

15. **Annotator A**: [Government authorities also claim the sterilization chemical was an "accidental" contamination.]*claim*
Annotator B: [Government authorities]*source* also claim [the sterilization chemical was an "accidental" contamination.]*claim*

Because explicit sources are mentioned, one annotator decided to annotate *source* and *claim* whereas the other one annotated everything as *claim*. However, marking the explicit sources separately might exclude some information from the *claim*. In the case of Example 14, the author wants the audience to know that most Americans are brainwashed; identifying as the claim just the fragment "they are doing this for us" detracts details from the message that is being conveyed. In Example 15 Annotator B followed the same approach and annotated "Government authorities" as *source* and "the sterilization chemical was an "accidental" contamination" as *claim*. As a consequence the full *claim* made by the author of the text, which Annotator A annotated, is ignored. The reason why Annotator B exhibits this behavior is that she had been previously been trained to annotate attributions (Pareti, 2015) and sometimes she had the tendency to annotate attributions, which indicates that the guidelines should have been more explicit about how to deal with cases in which attributions are embedded in *claims*.

5 Conclusion

Our research goal was to test whether existing argumentation annotation schemes are applicable to heterogeneous texts from the Web in order to detect statements that are meaningful for the study of beliefs that motivate different stances towards a topic, in this case vaccinations.

Two pilot annotation studies were conducted with argumentation schemes used in previous annotation tasks (Stab and Gurevych, 2017; Habernal and Gurevych, 2017; Al Khatib et al., 2016). A quantitative and qualitative analysis of the results revealed that it was necessary to simplify the task because the annotation categories were not well defined and, consequently, the IAA was too low. This is why we decided to focus on annotating only *claims*. The new task was then tested by conducting a third annotation study, which resulted in 57.3% IAA.

The simplification of the annotation scheme made the annotation task more feasible and less time-consuming. Following the simplified scheme, annotators were better able to agree on fragments of text that are representative of the beliefs that people express when talking about vaccinations. Based on a qualitative error analysis we defined four sources of disagreement: debatability, attributability, relatedness to the topic and granularity of sources. Further research will evaluate how informative the fragments are for the analysis of the vaccination debate.

The simplified scheme had several weaknesses. The patterns of disagreement observed reveal the necessity to modify the guidelines for future experiments: (i) more annotated examples of difficult cases should be included; (ii) instructions should be provided on how to tackle instances where the granularity can be interpreted in different ways; (iii) it should also be stressed that claim-like statements that are not directly related to the topic need to be marked, as they are relevant; and (iv) the guidelines should be more restrictive. For example, the analysis of the errors related to *attributability* lead to the conclusion that *claims* should be attributable to a source and that the source should express a high level of commitment to the claim.

A general conclusion based on the quantitative results and the qualitative error analysis is that, even though the simplification of the scheme relieved some of the complexity of the task, agreeing on what a *claim* is still remains a difficult endeavor for human annotators. As future work we intend to propose a better definition of *claim*. Additionally, since the simplified scheme does not depend on domain dependent features, it should be applicable to any on-line debate. We plan to annotate similar corpora of other domains in order to test whether the same results can be obtained. Finally, we are currently developing a claim detection system as a means to measuring also the difficulty of performing this task automatically.

Acknowledgements

This research is supported by the Netherlands Organization for Scientific Research (NWO) via the Spinoza-prize awarded to Piek Vossen in the project "Understanding Language by Machines" (SPI 30-673, 2014-2019). We are also grateful to the anonymous reviewers for their valuable comments.

References

Khalid Al Khatib, Henning Wachsmuth, Johannes Kiesel, Matthias Hagen, and Benno Stein. 2016. A news editorial corpus for mining argumentation strategies. In *COLING*, pages 3433–3443.

Muhammad Amith and Cui Tao. 2018. Representing vaccine misinformation using ontologies. *Journal of Biomedical Semantics*, 9:22.

Jamal Bentahar, Bernard Moulin, and Micheline Bélanger. 2010. A taxonomy of argumentation models used for knowledge representation. *Artificial Intelligence Review*, 33(3):211–259.

Ivan Habernal and Iryna Gurevych. 2017. Argumentation mining in user-generated web discourse. *Computational Linguistics*, 43(1):125–179.

Marco Lippi and Paolo Torroni. 2016. Argumentation mining: State of the art and emerging trends. *ACM Transactions on Internet Technology (TOIT)*, 16(2):10.

Amaryllis Mavragani and Gabriela Ochoa. 2018. The internet and the anti-vaccine movement: Tracking the 2017 eu measles outbreak. *Big data and Cognitive Computing*, 2:2.

Raquel Mochales Palau and Marie-Francine Moens. 2009. Argumentation mining: the detection, classification and structure of arguments in text. In *Proceedings of the 12th international conference on artificial intelligence and law*, pages 98–107. ACM.

Silvia Pareti. 2015. *Attribution: A Computational Approach*. Ph.D. thesis, University of Edinburgh.

Andreas Peldszus and Manfred Stede. 2013a. From argument diagrams to argumentation mining in texts: A survey. *International Journal of Cognitive Informatics and Natural Intelligence (IJCINI)*, 7(1):1–31.

Andreas Peldszus and Manfred Stede. 2013b. From argument diagrams to argumentation mining in texts: A survey. *International Journal of Cognitive Informatics and Natural Intelligence (IJCINI)*, 7(1):1–31.

Ariel Rosenfeld and Sarit Kraus. 2016. Providing arguments in discussions on the basis of the prediction of human argumentative behavior. *ACM Transactions on Interactive Intelligent Systems (TiiS)*, 6(4):30.

Patrick Saint-Dizier. 2016. Argument mining: The bottleneck of knowledge and language resources. In *10th International Conference on Language Resources and Evaluation (LREC 2016)*, pages pp–983.

Christian Stab and Iryna Gurevych. 2017. Parsing argumentation structures in persuasive essays. *Computational Linguistics*, 43(3):619–659.

Stephen E Toulmin. 2003. *The uses of argument*. Cambridge university press.

Marianna Lya Zummo. 2017. A linguistic analysis of the online debate on vaccines and use of fora as information stations and confirmation niche. *International Journal of Society, Culture & Language*, 5(1):44.

Argument Component Classification for Classroom Discussions

Luca Lugini and **Diane Litman**
Computer Science Department & Learning Research and Development Center
University of Pittsburgh
Pittsburgh, PA 15260
{lul32,dlitman}@pitt.edu

Abstract

This paper focuses on argument component classification for transcribed spoken classroom discussions, with the goal of automatically classifying student utterances into claims, evidence, and warrants. We show that an existing method for argument component classification developed for another educationally-oriented domain performs poorly on our dataset. We then show that feature sets from prior work on argument mining for student essays and online dialogues can be used to improve performance considerably. We also provide a comparison between convolutional neural networks and recurrent neural networks when trained under different conditions to classify argument components in classroom discussions. While neural network models are not always able to outperform a logistic regression model, we were able to gain some useful insights: convolutional networks are more robust than recurrent networks both at the character and at the word level, and specificity information can help boost performance in multi-task training.

1 Introduction

Although there is no universally agreed upon definition, argument mining is an area of natural language processing which aims to extract structured knowledge from free-form unstructured language. In particular, argument mining systems are built with goals such as: detecting what parts of a text express an argument component, known as argument component identification; categorizing arguments into different component types (e.g. claim, evidence), known as argument component classification; understanding if/how different components are connected to form an argumentative structure (e.g. using evidence to support/attack a claim), known as argument relation identification. The development and release to the public of corpora and annotations in recent years have contributed to the increasing interest in the area.

One domain in which argument mining is rarely found in the literature is educational discussions. Classroom discussions are a part of students' daily life, and they are a common pedagogical approach for enhancing student skills. For example, student-centered classroom discussions are an important contributor to the development of students' reading, writing, and reasoning skills in the context of English Language Arts (ELA) classes (Applebee et al., 2003; Reznitskaya and Gregory, 2013). This impact is reflected in students' problem solving and disciplinary skills (Engle and Conant, 2002; Murphy et al., 2009; Elizabeth et al., 2012). With the increasing importance of argumentation in classrooms, especially in the context of student-centered discussions, automatically performing argument component classification is a first step for building tools aimed at helping teachers analyze and better understand student arguments, with the goal of improving students' learning outcomes.

Many current argument mining systems focus on analyzing argumentation in student essays (Stab and Gurevych, 2014, 2017; Nguyen and Litman, 2015, 2018), online dialogues (Swanson et al., 2015; McLaren et al., 2010; Ghosh et al., 2014; Lawrence and Reed, 2017), or in the legal domain (Ashley and Walker, 2013; Palau and Moens, 2009). A key difference between these studies and our work consists in the source of linguistic content: although we analyze written transcriptions of discussions, the original source for our corpora consists of spoken, multi-party, educational discussions, and the difference in cognitive skills and grammatical structure between written and spoken language (Biber, 1988; Chafe and Tannen, 1987) introduces additional complexity.

Our work and previous research studies on student essays share the trait of analyzing argumentation in an educational context. However, while

Proceedings of the 5th Workshop on Argument Mining, pages 57–67
Brussels, Belgium, November 1, 2018. ©2018 Association for Computational Linguistics

student essays are typically written by an individual student, in classroom discussions arguments are formed collaboratively between multiple parties (i.e. multiple students and possibly teachers). While our work shares the multi-party context in which arguments are made with research aimed at argument mining in online dialogues, prior online dialogue studies have not been contextualized in the educational domain.

Given these differences, we believe that argument mining models for student essays and online dialogues will perform poorly when directly applied to educational discussions. However, since similarities between the domains do exist, we expect that features exploited by such argument mining models can help us in classifying argument components in classroom discussions. Moreover, unlike the other two domains, we have access to labels belonging to a different (but related) class, specificity, which we can try to incorporate in argumentation models to boost performance.

Our contributions are as follows. We first experimentally evaluate the performance of an existing argument mining system developed for essay scoring (named wLDA) when applied off-the-shelf to predict argument component labels for transcribed classroom discussions. We then analyze the performance obtained when using the same features as wLDA to train a classifier specifically on our dataset. We combine the wLDA feature set with features used in argument mining in the context of online dialogues and show that they are able to capture some of the similarities between online dialogues and our domain, and considerably improve the model. We then evaluate two neural network models in several different scenarios pertaining to their input modality, the inclusion of handcrafted features, and the effect of multi-task learning when including specificity information.

2 Related Work

With respect to the educational domain, previous studies in argument mining were largely aimed at student essays. Persing and Ng (2015) studied argument strength with the ultimate goal of automated essay scoring. Stab and Gurevych (2014) performed argument mining on student essays by first jointly performing argument component identification and classification, then predicting argument component relations. Nguyen and Litman (2015) developed an argument mining system for analyzing student persuasive essays based on ar-

gument words and domain words. While domain words are used only in a specific topic, argument words are used across multiple topics and represent indicators of argumentative content. They later proposed an improved version of the system (2016), which we will refer to as wLDA, by exploiting features able to abstract over specific essay topics and improve cross-topic performance. While our current work is also aimed at developing argument mining systems in the educational context, we focus on educational discussion instead of student essays. Our work also differs in the argument component types used: we analyze claims, evidence, and warrants, while prior studies mostly focused on claims and premises. The inclusion of warrants is particularly important to explicitly understand how students use them to connect evidence to claims. As such, we do not expect prior models to work well on our corpus, although some of the features might still be useful. Also, while some of the previously proposed systems address multiple subproblems simultaneously, e.g. argument component identification and argument component classification, we only focus on argument component classification.

Swanson et al. (2015) developed a model for extracting argumentative portions of text from online dialogues, which were later used for summarizing the multiple argument facets. Misra et al. (2015) analyzed dyadic online forum discussions to detect central propositions and argument facets. Habernal and Gurevych (2017) analyzed user-generated web discourse data from several sources by performing micro-level argumentation mining. While these prior works analyze multi-party discussions, the discussions are neither originally spoken nor in an educational context.

Like other areas of natural language processing, argument mining is experiencing an increase in the development of neural network models. Niculae et al. (2017) used a factor graph model which was parametrized by a recurrent neural network. Daxenberger et al. (Daxenberger et al., 2017) investigated the different conceptualizations of claims in several domains by analyzing in-domain and cross-domain performance of recurrent neural networks and convolutional neural networks, in addition to other models. Schulz et al. (Schulz et al., 2018) analyzed the impact of using multitask learning when training on a limited amount of labeled data. In a similar way, we develop several convolutional neural network and recurrent neural network models, and also experiment with multi-task learning. More detailed comparisons will be given in Section 4.

3 Dataset

We collected 73 transcripts of text-based classroom discussions, i.e. discussions centered on a text or literature piece (e.g. play, speech, book), for ELA high school level classes. Some of the transcripts were gathered from published articles and dissertations, while the rest originated from videos which were transcribed by one of our annotators (see below). While detailed demographic information for students participating in each discussion was not available, our dataset consists of a mix of small group (16 out of 73) versus whole class (57/73) discussions, both teacher-mediated (64/73) versus student only (9/73). Additionally, the discussions originated in urban schools (28/73), suburban schools (42/73), and schools located in small towns (3/73).

The unit of analysis for our work is argument move, which consists of a segment of text containing an argumentative discourse unit (ADU) (Peldszus and Stede, 2013). Starting with transcripts broken down into turns at talk, an expert annotator segmented turns at talk into multiple argument moves when necessary: turns at talk containing multiple ADUs have been segmented into several argument moves, each consisting of a single ADU. Turn segmentation effectively corresponds to argument component identification, and it is carried out manually. We conducted a reliability study on turn segmentation with two annotators on a subset of the dataset consisting of 53 transcripts. The reliability analysis resulted in Krippendorff $\alpha_U = 0.952$ (Krippendorff, 2004), which shows that turns at talk can be reliably segmented.

After segmentation, the data was manually annotated to capture two aspects of classroom talk, argument component and specificity, using the ELA classroom-oriented annotation scheme developed by Lugini et al. (2018). The argument component types in this scheme, which is based on the Toulmin model (1958), are: (i) *Claim*: an arguable statement that presents a particular interpretation of a text or topic. (ii) *Evidence*[1]: facts, documentation, text reference, or testimony used to support or justify a claim. (iii) *Warrant*: rea-

sons explaining how a specific evidence instance supports a specific claim.

Chisholm and Godley (2011) observed how specificity has an impact on the quality of the discussion, while Swanson et al. (2015) noted that a relationship exists between specificity and the quality of arguments in online forum dialogues. For the purpose of investigating whether there exists a relationship between specificity and argument components, we additionally annotated data for specificity following the same coding scheme (Lugini et al., 2018). Specificity labels are directly related to four elements for an argument move: (1) it is specific to one (or a few) character or scene; (2) it makes significant qualifications or elaborations; (3) it uses content-specific vocabulary (e.g. quotes from the text); (4) it provides a chain of reasons. The specificity annotation scheme by Lugini et al. includes three labels along a linear scale: (i) *Low*: statement that does not contain any of these elements. (ii) *Medium*: statement that accomplishes one of these elements. (iii) *High*: statement that clearly accomplishes at least two specificity elements. Only student turns were considered for annotations; teacher turns at talk were filtered out and do not appear in the final dataset. Table 1 shows a coded excerpt of a transcript from a discussion about the movie *Princess Bride*.

The resulting dataset consists of 2047 argument moves from 73 discussions. As we can see from the label distribution shown in Table 2, students produced a high number of claims, while warrant is the minority class. We can also observe a class imbalance for specificity labels, though the ratio between majority and minority classes is lower than that for argument component labels.

We evaluated inter-rater reliability on a subset of our dataset composed of 1049 argument moves from 50 discussions double-coded by two annotators. Cohen's unweighted kappa for argument component labels was 0.629, while quadratic-weighted kappa for specificity labels (since they are ordered) was 0.641, which shows substantial agreement.

The average number of argument moves among the discussions is 27.3 while the standard deviation is 25.6, which shows a high variability in discussion length. The average number of words per argument move and standard deviation are 22.6 and 22.1, respectively, which also shows large variability in how much students speak.

---

[1]The "evidence" label is equivalent to "data" or "grounds" used in the original Toulmin model, though we use the label "evidence" to remain consistent with the annotation scheme.

Stu	Argument Move	Arg Comp	Spec
S1	Well Fezzik went back to how he was,	Claim	Low
S1	like how he gets lost. Then he goes like he needs to be around other people. And then finally when he does, he gets himself like relying on himself. But then right at the end, he doesnt know where hes at; he makes a wrong turn.	Evidence	Med
S1	cause he tried doing it by himself and he cant. So I think Fezzik went back to his normal ways, like after he changed.	Warrant	High

Table 1: Coded excerpt of a discussion of the movie *Princess Bride*. Student S1 first makes a claim about Fezzik's behavior, then provides evidence by listing a series of events, then connects such events to his claim using a warrant. As the argument progresses, the specificity level increases.

Argument Component		
Claim	Warrant	Evidence
1034	358	655

Specificity		
Low	Med	High
710	996	341

Table 2: Distribution of class labels for argument component type and specificity in our dataset.

4 Argument Component Classification

In this section we outline an existing argument component classification system that will serve as a baseline for our experiments, then propose several new models that use features extracted from neural networks and hand-crafted features, as well as models that use multi-task learning.

4.1 Existing Argument Mining System

The wLDA[2] system was developed for performing argument component identification, classification, and relation extraction from student essays. For the purpose of this study, we only consider the argument component classification subsystem. The model is based on a support vector machine classifier which exploits features able to improve cross-topic performance. The feature set consists of four main subsets: lexical features (argument words, verbs, adverbs, presence of modal verbs, discourse connectives, singular first person pronoun); parse features (argumentative subject-verb pairs, tense of the main verb, number of sub-clauses, depth of parse tree); structural features (number of tokens, token ratio, number of punctuation signs, sentence position, first/last paragraph, first/last sentence of paragraph); context features (number of tokens, number of punctuation signs, number of

sub-clauses, modal verb in preceding/following sentences) extracted from the sentences before and after the one considered; four additional features for abstracting over essay topics.

Since the model was trained on essays annotated for major claim, claim, and premise, but not on warrants, in our evaluation we did not take into account misclassification errors for argument moves in our dataset labeled as warrants. The pre-trained system performs argument component identification using a multiclass classification approach, such that each input will be classified as non argumentative, major claim, claim or premise. Since our goal is to evaluate performance related to the component classification problem, we ignored all the argument moves classified as non argumentative by wLDA. Considering the definitions of premise and evidence in the Toulmin model (1958), we made the assumption of the two labels being equivalent for this study, i.e. if the predicted class for an argument move is premise and its gold standard label in our dataset is evidence, we consider the prediction correct. In the same way we consider both claim and major claim labels as equivalent to claims in our dataset.

4.2 Neural Network Models

Since the pre-trained model did not work well on our dataset, and the features it is based on show a large gap in performance compared to the original work (see Section 5), we decided to use neural networks, and evaluate their ability to automatically extract meaningful features. The proposed models consist of variations of two basic neural network models, namely Convolutional Neural Network (CNN) and Recurrent Neural Network (RNN) models. All the choices regarding the models were made in order to keep complexity and the number of weights at a minimum, since neural net-

---

[2]The original name of wLDA+4 stands for "with LDA supported features and expanded with 4 features sets" compared to their previous system. We use wLDA for brevity.

work models require in general a large amount of training data, while we have a limited size dataset. The CNN model is based on a model proposed by Kim (2014) and already used for argument mining in the past (Daxenberger et al., 2017), with a difference in the number of convolutional/pooling layers. In particular, our model uses 3 convolutional/max pooling layers instead of 6, and only one fully connected layer after the convolutional ones, followed by a softmax layer used for classification. This choice resulted from observing significant overfitting when increasing the number of convolutional layers due to the increase in the number of model weights and the limited dataset size. Figure 1 shows diagrams for the different neural network setups used in our experiments.

The RNN model consists of a single Long-Short Term Memory (LSTM) network (Hochreiter and Schmidhuber, 1997). After propagating a complete argument move through the LSTM network, the resulting hidden state is the feature vector used as input to a softmax layer which outputs the predicted label. Recurrent neural networks have also been used in the context of argument mining (Daxenberger et al., 2017; Niculae et al., 2017). We set the size of the hidden state to 75 based on several factors. Following Bengio (Bengio, 2012), we decided to have an overcomplete network, i.e. one in which the size of the hidden state is bigger than the size of the input. Since the dimensionality of our character-based encoding is 37 and that for word-based embeddings is 50, we chose a hidden state with size greater than 50 (we use the same hidden state size for both models). Increasing the size introduced overfitting even quicker than the CNN model, given that the number of weights increases more quickly for our LSTM model.

When using text as input to a neural network, we can generally view an argument move as either a sequence of characters, or as a sequence of words. Unlike previous neural network-based argument mining models, each of our models was evaluated under both conditions: for character-based models we used a one-hot encoding (one-out of n) for each letter and number - special characters were filtered since they don't hold particular meaning in speech, and we cannot be sure of transcription conventions; for word-based models we used Global Vectors (GloVe) (Pennington et al., 2014) with dimensionality of 50. An important aspect to consider is that, while word-based models have some prior knowledge encoded in the word embeddings, character-based models do not.

Since neural network models usually require a large amount of training data to be effective, and we have relatively fewer number of argument moves compared to number of model weights, we also tested hybrid models in which a neural network output is combined with handcrafted features before the final softmax classification layer, as shown in Figure 1 (b) and Figure 1 (d). Both CNN and LSTM models used categorical cross-entropy as loss function, and the number of epochs was automatically selected at training time by monitoring performance on a validation set consisting of 10% of the training set for each fold.

4.3 Multi-task Learning

As we can see from Figure 2, the argument label distributions are different for the three specificity levels. This leads us to believe a relationship exists between the specificity and argumentation annotations, therefore we decided to see whether specificity labels can be used to improve the performance of our argument mining models.

Multi-task learning for neural network models has shown promising results in the machine learning field (Weston et al., 2012; Andrychowicz et al., 2016). It has recently been used in argument mining: Schulz et al. (2018) proposed a multi-task learning setup in which the primary task consists of jointly performing argument component identification and classification (framed as a sequence tagging problem), while the additional tasks consist of the same task applied to different datasets. They showed that the multi-task models achieved better performance than single-task learning especially when limited in-domain training data is available for the primary task.

Unlike (Schulz et al., 2018), we decided to implement as secondary task specificity prediction on the same data as the primary task. The underlying neural network setup was also different: while Schulz et al. used a bidirectional LSTM followed by a Conditional Random Field (CRF) classifier (Reimers and Gurevych, 2017), we were restricted to non-sequence classifiers. We implemented multi-task learning in one of the standard ways: the embeddings generated by the networks are completely shared for both tasks of predicting argumentation and specificity. For the CNN model, we added a second softmax layer for predicting specificity after the convolutional/pooling layers. Similarly, for the LSTM model we added

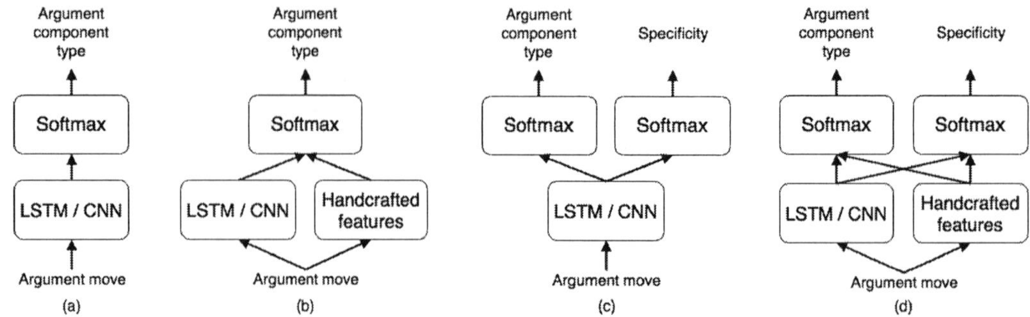

Figure 1: Neural network models used in this study: neural network only setup (a); model incorporating neural network and handcrafted features (wLDA and online dialogue sets) (b); multi-task setup for neural network only model (c); multi-task setup for model using neural network and handcrafted features (d).

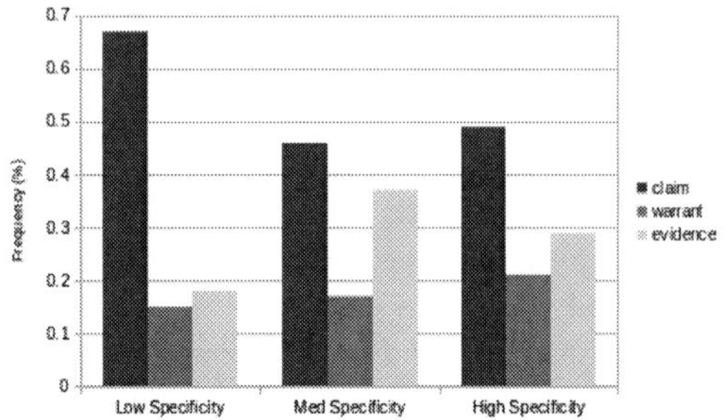

Figure 2: Argument labels by specificity levels.

a second softmax layer that operates on the final hidden state of the network to predict specificity. In both multi-task models specificity and argumentation are predicted at the same time, the loss function is computed as the sum of the individual loss functions for both tasks (the loss function for the specificity softmax layer is categorical cross-entropy as well), and gradient updates are backpropagated through the network. This process results in embeddings trained jointly for the two tasks, which can effectively capture information relevant to both specificity and argumentation.

4.4 Online Dialogue Features

Since our dataset is based on multi-party discussion, it shares similarities with prior argumentation work in multi-party online dialogues. Therefore we experiment with features from (Swanson et al., 2015), organized into three main subsets: semantic-density features (number of pronouns, descriptive word-level statistics, number of occurrences of words of different lengths), lexical features (tf-idf feature for each unigram and bigram, descriptive argument move-level statistics), and syntactic features (unigrams, bigrams and trigrams of part of speech tags). The only difference between the original features and the ones

we implemented consists in the use of Speciteller (Li and Nenkova, 2015). As observed by Lugini and Litman (Lugini and Litman, 2017), applying Speciteller as-is to domains other than news articles results in a considerable drop in performance. Therefore, instead of including the specificity score obtained by directly applying Specificity to an argument move, we decided to use Speciteller's features.

5 Experiments and Results

This section provides our experimental results. In Section 5.1 we will test our first hypothesis: using an argument mining system trained in a different domain will result in low performance, which can be improved by re-training on classroom discussions and by adding new features. Section 5.2 will be used to test our second hypothesis: neural network models can automatically extract important features for argument component classification. Our third hypothesis will be tested in Section 5.3: adding handcrafted features (i.e. online dialogue features, wLDA features) to the ones automatically extracted by neural networks will result in an increase of performance. Lastly, we will test our fourth hypothesis in Section 5.4: jointly learning to predict argument component type and specificity will result in more robust models and achieve a further performance improvement.

Our experiments evaluate every model using a leave-one-transcript-out cross validation: each fold contains one transcript as test set and the remaining 72 as training set. Cohen kappa, and unweighted precision, recall, and f-score were used as evaluation metrics.

The following python libraries were used for implementing and testing the different models: Scikit-learn (Pedregosa et al., 2011), Tensorflow

(Abadi et al., 2015), Keras (Chollet et al., 2015), NLTK (Bird et al., 2009).

Given that in our dataset warrants appear much less frequently than claims and evidence, data imbalance is a problem we need to address. If trained naively, the limited amount of training data and the unbalanced class distribution lead the neural network models to specialize towards claims and evidence, with much weaker performance on warrants. This is also the case for non neural network models, although the impact on performance is lower. To combat this phenomenon we decided to use oversampling (Buda et al., 2017) in order to create a balanced dataset, hoping to further reduce the performance gap between the different classes [3]. After computing the class frequency distribution on the training set, we randomly sampled moves from the two minority classes and added them to the current training set, repeating the process until the class distribution was completely balanced (i.e. until the number of argument moves for each class equals the number of moves in the majority class) [4], while the test set was unchanged.

Table 3 shows the results for all experiments. The statistical significance results in the table use the system in row 3 as the comparison baseline, as wLDA represents a system specifically designed for argument component classification (among other tasks). Additional statistical comparisons are provided in the text as well.

5.1 Using wLDA Off the Shelf

Since not all the argument moves were considered when computing results for the pre-trained out of the box wLDA model (see Section 4.1), the results in row 2 are not directly comparable to others. Nonetheless they show the upper bound in performance of the pre-trained model, and we can see that it is comparable to a majority baseline which always predicts the majority class in each fold. This result shows that claims and evidence expressed in written essays and classroom discussions have very little in common. This is clearer when we look at improvement obtained training a logistic regression model[5] using the same wLDA

features on our dataset (row 3), which outperforms the pre-trained wLDA in all metrics (row 2), and indicates that the wLDA features are still able to somewhat distinguish between claims and evidence while performing considerably worse on warrants. Additionally, if we add to this model the online dialogue feature set, the resulting model improves all results and obtains the best kappa overall (row 4). This confirms our hypothesis: given the similarity that exists between our domain and online dialogues, features developed for analyzing argumentation in online dialogues are also useful in classroom discussions.

5.2 Neural Network Models Alone

Our second hypothesis is validated by the results in Table 3 by comparing row 3 with rows 7, 11, 15, and 19, where we can see that the CNN models achieve performance comparable to a classifier trained on features specifically developed for argument component classification. This indicates that convolutional neural network models are able to extract useful features. Additionally, when comparing the best of these models (row 19, with respect to f-score) to the best performing model based only on handcrafted features (row 4), the difference in performance is not statistically significant for any of the metrics in Table 3.

Looking more closely at the results obtained using neural network models alone we can see two different trends. While LSTM models show performance comparable to random chance (e.g. row 5, with kappa close to zero and lower than the majority baseline), three of our four CNN models (rows 7, 15, 19) perform as well as or better than the wLDA based model (row 3) (except for precision in row 19 and F_e in row 7). Overall, under the same conditions CNN models almost always outperform LSTM models. One interesting difference between the two models is that the prior knowledge introduced by word embeddings in word-based models is essential for improving performance of LSTMs (e.g. row 5 vs row 9), while this is not the case for CNN models (e.g. row 7 vs row 11). The length of sequences (i.e. argument moves) for character-based models makes it extremely hard for LSTMs to capture long-term dependencies, especially with limited amount of training data. Convolutional models, on the other hand, learn kernels that effectively function as feature detectors and seem to be able to better distinguish important features, and do not always bene-

---

[3] We also tried setting class weights at training to influence the loss function, though it only improved results marginally.

[4] In the multi-task models oversampling was carried out only with respect to argument component labels since that is the primary task.

[5] We also experimented with random forest, naive Bayes and support vector machines, but they provided inferior results compared to logistic regression.

Row	Models / Features	Kappa	Precision	Recall	F-score	F_e	F_w	F_c
1	Majority baseline	0.068	0.265	0.406	0.314	0.109	0.004	0.532
2	Pre-trained wLDA	0.077	0.289	0.350	0.269	0.351	N/A	0.456
3	Logistic Regression (wLDA features)	0.142	0.412	0.394	0.379	0.390	0.211	0.540
4	Logistic Regression (wLDA features + online dialogue)	**0.283**	0.508	0.500	0.480	0.479	0.222	**0.693**
Character level NN models								
5	LSTM	-0.002	0.062	0.253	0.082	0.007	0.242	0.013
6	LSTM + wLDA + online dialogue	0.034	0.217	0.304	0.150	0.080	$0.272^{\ddagger}$	0.090
7	CNN	0.143	0.439	0.423	0.393	0.372	0.218	0.574
8	CNN + wLDA + online dialogue	$0.241^{\star}$	0.482	0.475	0.450	0.449	0.236	0.637
Word level NN models								
9	LSTM	0.069	0.408	0.399	0.218	0.161	0.198	0.295
10	LSTM + wLDA + online dialogue	0.181	0.462	0.447	0.391	0.362	$0.279^{\ddagger}$	0.522
11	CNN	0.125	0.410	0.404	0.378	0.370	0.231	0.526
12	CNN + wLDA + online dialogue	$0.241^{\star}$	$0.492^{\star}$	0.488	$0.455^{\dagger}$	0.468	$0.276^{\ddagger}$	0.622
Multi-task character level NN models								
13	LSTM	0.060	0.408	0.399	0.208	0.134	0.203	0.287
14	LSTM + wLDA + online dialogue	0.117	0.379	0.375	0.287	0.362	$0.279^{\ddagger}$	0.522
15	CNN	0.166	0.444	0.437	0.407	0.399	0.220	0.586
16	CNN + wLDA + online dialogue	$0.259^{\dagger}$	$0.506^{\dagger}$	0.488	$0.468^{\star}$	0.474	$0.262^{\dagger}$	0.640
Multi-task word level NN models								
17	LSTM	0.093	0.379	0.364	0.276	0.298	0.252	0.378
18	LSTM + wLDA + online dialogue	0.232	$0.497^{\dagger}$	0.482	0.440	0.419	$0.299^{\ddagger}$	0.583
19	CNN	0.164	0.351	0.443	0.441	0.476	0.249	0.598
20	CNN + wLDA + online dialogue	$0.276^{\ddagger}$	**$0.521^{\ddagger}$**	**$0.512^{\dagger}$**	**$0.485^{\dagger}$**	**0.484**	**$0.312^{\ddagger}$**	0.638

Table 3: Results obtained with the baseline model/features and the proposed neural network models using different feature sets. Each line represents the average of a transcript-wise cross validation. Best results are in bold. $\star$, $\dagger$, and $\ddagger$ indicate statistical significance at the 0.1, 0.05, and 0.01 levels respectively, compared to the model in row 3. The three right-most columns represent per-class F-score for evidence, warrants, and claims respectively.

fit from word level inputs.

5.3 Adding wLDA Features and Online Dialogue Features

It is clear from Table 3 that almost all neural network models benefit from additional handcrafted features (with the exception of precision and recall for rows 13 and 14). This is not surprising, given that neural networks require a large amount of data to be trained effectively, and although random oversampling helped, we still have a limited amount of training data. Even when including additional features the two architectures show slightly different trends: CNN usually outperform LSTM, however LSTM models benefit more from the additional features. This is at least in part due to LSTMs initially having lower performance without handcrafted features. We analyzed the importance of different subsets of the online dialogue features through a feature ablation study. For CNN models, removing any subset of features resulted in a decrease in performance, except for the *syntax* subset in the *character level CNN + wLDA + online dialogue* model in both single task and multi-task settings. For LSTM models, all feature subsets contributed to increasing performance in the multi-task settings, while that was not always true for the single task models.

5.4 Multi-task Learning

Finally, we analyze the impact of multi-task learning in argument component classification. Our findings are in line with the literature in other domains, with results showing that models trained on argumentation and specificity labels almost always outperform the ones trained only on argumentation. LSTMs benefit from the multi-task setup more than CNN models: among all combinations of LSTM models, the only one able to achieve kappa greater than 0.2 and f-score greater than 0.4 is a multi-task one. Additionally, the word-level CNN model using wLDA and online dialogue feature sets and trained using multi-task learning is the only model able to achieve f-score greater than 0.3 for warrants.

It should be noted that although the neural network based model at row 20 outperforms the logistic regression model at row 4 in terms of precision, recall, and F-score, the difference in performance is not statistically significant, and neither is the reduction in kappa and F_c.

6 Conclusions and Future Work

In this work we evaluated the performance of an existing argument mining system developed for a different educational application (i.e. student essays) on a corpus composed of spoken classroom discussions. Although the pre-trained system showed poor performance on our dataset, its features show promising results when used in a model specifically trained on classroom discussions. We extracted additional feature sets based on related work in the online dialogue domain, and showed that combining online dialogue and student essay features achieves the highest kappa on our dataset. We then developed additional models based on two types of neural networks, showing that performance can be further improved. We provided an experimental evaluation of the differences between convolutional networks and recurrent networks, and between character-based and word-based models. Lastly, we showed that argument component classification models can benefit from multi-task learning, when adding a secondary task consisting of predicting specificity.

Even though we were able to achieve better performance compared to a pre-trained system and a majority baseline, we are far from the performance of argument mining systems in other domains such as student essays or legal texts. Although the wLDA features extract information from previous argument moves, we plan to take advantage of the collaborative nature of our corpus by extending the feature sets in order to exploit contextual information and develop models that can explicitly take advantage of previous argument moves. Given the performance improvements obtained with multi-task models, we also plan to extend these models and include additional tasks at training time with the hope of further boosting performance. We also plan to add other types of cross validation, since leave-one-transcript-out introduces great variability in the composition of test sets, possibly attenuating the statistical significance for some results.

Acknowledgements

We want to thank Amanda Godley, Christopher Olshefski, Tazin Afrin, Huy Nguyen, and Annika Swallen for their contribution, and all the anonymous reviewers for their helpful feedback.

This work was supported by the Learning Research and Development Center.

References

Martín Abadi, Ashish Agarwal, Paul Barham, Eugene Brevdo, Zhifeng Chen, Craig Citro, Greg S. Corrado, Andy Davis, Jeffrey Dean, Matthieu Devin, Sanjay Ghemawat, Ian Goodfellow, Andrew Harp, Geoffrey Irving, Michael Isard, Yangqing Jia, Rafal Jozefowicz, Lukasz Kaiser, Manjunath Kudlur, Josh Levenberg, Dandelion Mané, Rajat Monga, Sherry Moore, Derek Murray, Chris Olah, Mike Schuster, Jonathon Shlens, Benoit Steiner, Ilya Sutskever, Kunal Talwar, Paul Tucker, Vincent Vanhoucke, Vijay Vasudevan, Fernanda Viégas, Oriol Vinyals, Pete Warden, Martin Wattenberg, Martin Wicke, Yuan Yu, and Xiaoqiang Zheng. 2015. TensorFlow: Large-scale machine learning on heterogeneous systems. Software available from tensorflow.org.

Marcin Andrychowicz, Misha Denil, Sergio Gomez, Matthew W Hoffman, David Pfau, Tom Schaul, Brendan Shillingford, and Nando De Freitas. 2016. Learning to learn by gradient descent by gradient descent. In *Advances in Neural Information Processing Systems*, pages 3981–3989.

Arthur N Applebee, Judith A Langer, Martin Nystrand, and Adam Gamoran. 2003. Discussion-based approaches to developing understanding: Classroom instruction and student performance in middle and high school english. *American Educational Research Journal*, 40(3):685–730.

Kevin D Ashley and Vern R Walker. 2013. Toward constructing evidence-based legal arguments using legal decision documents and machine learning. In *Proceedings of the Fourteenth International Conference on Artificial Intelligence and Law*, pages 176–180. ACM.

Yoshua Bengio. 2012. Practical recommendations for gradient-based training of deep architectures. In *Neural networks: Tricks of the trade*, pages 437–478. Springer.

Douglas Biber. 1988. *Variation across speech and writing*. Cambridge University Press.

Steven Bird, Ewan Klein, and Edward Loper. 2009. *Natural language processing with Python: analyzing text with the natural language toolkit.* "O'Reilly Media, Inc.".

Mateusz Buda, Atsuto Maki, and Maciej A Mazurowski. 2017. A systematic study of the class imbalance problem in convolutional neural networks. *arXiv preprint arXiv:1710.05381*.

W. Chafe and D. Tannen. 1987. The relation between written and spoken language. *Annual Review of Anthropology*, 16(1):383–407.

James S Chisholm and Amanda J Godley. 2011. Learning about language through inquiry-based discussion: Three bidialectal high school students talk about dialect variation, identity, and power. *Journal of Literacy Research*, 43(4):430–468.

François Chollet et al. 2015. Keras. `https://keras.io`.

Johannes Daxenberger, Steffen Eger, Ivan Habernal, Christian Stab, and Iryna Gurevych. 2017. What is the essence of a claim? cross-domain claim identification. In *Proceedings of the 2017 Conference on Empirical Methods in Natural Language Processing*, pages 2055–2066. Association for Computational Linguistics.

Tracy Elizabeth, Trisha L Ross Anderson, Elana H Snow, and Robert L Selman. 2012. Academic discussions: An analysis of instructional discourse and an argument for an integrative assessment framework. *American Educational Research Journal*, 49(6):1214–1250.

Randi A Engle and Faith R Conant. 2002. Guiding principles for fostering productive disciplinary engagement: Explaining an emergent argument in a community of learners classroom. *Cognition and Instruction*, 20(4):399–483.

Debanjan Ghosh, Smaranda Muresan, Nina Wacholder, Mark Aakhus, and Matthew Mitsui. 2014. Analyzing argumentative discourse units in online interactions. In *Proceedings of the First Workshop on Argumentation Mining*, pages 39–48.

Ivan Habernal and Iryna Gurevych. 2017. Argumentation mining in user-generated web discourse. *Computational Linguistics*, 43(1):125–179.

Sepp Hochreiter and Jürgen Schmidhuber. 1997. Long short-term memory. *Neural computation*, 9(8):1735–1780.

Yoon Kim. 2014. Convolutional neural networks for sentence classification. In *Proceedings of the 2014 Conference on Empirical Methods in Natural Language Processing (EMNLP)*, pages 1746–1751.

Klaus Krippendorff. 2004. Measuring the reliability of qualitative text analysis data. *Quality and Quantity*, 38:787–800.

John Lawrence and Chris Reed. 2017. Using complex argumentative interactions to reconstruct the argumentative structure of large-scale debates. In *Proceedings of the 4th Workshop on Argument Mining*, pages 108–117.

Junyi Jessy Li and Ani Nenkova. 2015. Fast and accurate prediction of sentence specificity. In *Proceedings of the Twenty-Ninth Conference on Artificial Intelligence (AAAI)*, pages 2281–2287.

Luca Lugini and Diane Litman. 2017. Predicting specificity in classroom discussion. In *Proceedings of the 12th Workshop on Innovative Use of NLP for Building Educational Applications*, pages 52–61.

Luca Lugini, Diane Litman, Godley Amanda, and Olshefski Christopher. 2018. Annotating stdent talk in text-based classroom discussions. In *Proceedings of the 13th Workshop on Innovative Use of NLP for Building Educational Applications*, pages 110–116.

Bruce M McLaren, Oliver Scheuer, and Jan Mikšátko. 2010. Supporting collaborative learning and e-discussions using artificial intelligence techniques. *International Journal of Artificial Intelligence in Education*, 20(1):1–46.

Amita Misra, Pranav Anand, Jean Fox Tree, and Marilyn Walker. 2015. Using summarization to discover argument facets in dialog. In *Proceedings of the 2015 Conference of the North American Chapter of the Association for Computational Linguistics: Human Language Technologies*.

P Karen Murphy, Ian AG Wilkinson, Anna O Soter, Maeghan N Hennessey, and John F Alexander. 2009. Examining the effects of classroom discussion on students comprehension of text: A meta-analysis. *Journal of Educational Psychology*, 101(3):740.

Huy Nguyen and Diane Litman. 2015. Extracting argument and domain words for identifying argument components in texts. In *Proceedings of the 2nd Workshop on Argumentation Mining*, pages 22–28.

Huy Nguyen and Diane J Litman. 2016. Improving argument mining in student essays by learning and exploiting argument indicators versus essay topics. In *FLAIRS Conference*, pages 485–490.

Huy V Nguyen and Diane J Litman. 2018. Argument mining for improving the automated scoring of persuasive essays. In *Proceedings of the Thirty-Second AAAI Conference on Artificial Intelligence*.

Vlad Niculae, Joonsuk Park, and Claire Cardie. 2017. Argument Mining with Structured SVMs and RNNs. In *Proceedings of ACL*.

Raquel Mochales Palau and Marie-Francine Moens. 2009. Argumentation mining: the detection, classification and structure of arguments in text. In *Proceedings of the 12th international conference on artificial intelligence and law*, pages 98–107. ACM.

F. Pedregosa, G. Varoquaux, A. Gramfort, V. Michel, B. Thirion, O. Grisel, M. Blondel, P. Prettenhofer, R. Weiss, V. Dubourg, J. Vanderplas, A. Passos, D. Cournapeau, M. Brucher, M. Perrot, and E. Duchesnay. 2011. Scikit-learn: Machine learning in Python. *Journal of Machine Learning Research*, 12:2825–2830.

Andreas Peldszus and Manfred Stede. 2013. From argument diagrams to argumentation mining in texts: A survey. *International Journal of Cognitive Informatics and Natural Intelligence (IJCINI)*, 7(1):1–31.

Jeffrey Pennington, Richard Socher, and Christopher Manning. 2014. Glove: Global vectors for word representation. In *Proceedings of the 2014 conference on empirical methods in natural language processing (EMNLP)*, pages 1532–1543.

Isaac Persing and Vincent Ng. 2015. Modeling argument strength in student essays. In *Proceedings of the 53rd Annual Meeting of the Association for Computational Linguistics and the 7th International Joint Conference on Natural Language Processing (Volume 1: Long Papers)*, volume 1, pages 543–552.

Nils Reimers and Iryna Gurevych. 2017. Argumentation mining in user-generated web discourse. In *Proceedings of the 2017 Conference on Empirical Methods in Natural Language Processing*, pages 338–348.

Alina Reznitskaya and Maughn Gregory. 2013. Student thought and classroom language: Examining the mechanisms of change in dialogic teaching. *Educational Psychologist*, 48(2):114–133.

Claudia Schulz, Steffen Eger, Johannes Daxenberger, Tobias Kahse, and Iryna Gurevych. 2018. Multi-task learning for argumentation mining in low-resource settings. In *Proceedings of the 2018 Conference of the North American Chapter of the Association for Computational Linguistics: Human Language Technologies, Volume 2 (Short Papers)*, pages 35–41. Association for Computational Linguistics.

Christian Stab and Iryna Gurevych. 2014. Annotating argument components and relations in persuasive essays. In *Proceedings of COLING 2014, the 25th International Conference on Computational Linguistics: Technical Papers*, pages 1501–1510.

Christian Stab and Iryna Gurevych. 2017. Parsing argumentation structures in persuasive essays. *Computational Linguistics*, 43(3):619–659.

Reid Swanson, Brian Ecker, and Marilyn Walker. 2015. Argument mining: Extracting arguments from online dialogue. In *Proceedings of the 16th Annual Meeting of the Special Interest Group on Discourse and Dialogue*, pages 217–226.

Stephen Toulmin. 1958. *The uses of argument*. Cambridge: Cambridge University Press.

Jason Weston, Frédéric Ratle, Hossein Mobahi, and Ronan Collobert. 2012. Deep learning via semi-supervised embedding. In *Neural Networks: Tricks of the Trade*, pages 639–655. Springer.

Evidence Types, Credibility Factors, and Patterns or Soft Rules for Weighing Conflicting Evidence: Argument Mining in the Context of Legal Rules Governing Evidence Assessment

Vern R. Walker, Dina Foerster, Julia Monica Ponce, Matthew Rosen
Research Laboratory for Law, Logic and Technology (LLT Lab)
Maurice A. Deane School of Law
Hofstra University; Hempstead, New York 11549, USA
Vern.R.Walker@Hofstra.edu

Abstract

This paper reports on the results of an empirical study of adjudicatory decisions about veterans' claims for disability benefits in the United States. It develops a typology of kinds of relevant evidence (argument premises) employed in cases, and it identifies factors that the tribunal considers when assessing the credibility or trustworthiness of individual items of evidence. It also reports on patterns or "soft rules" that the tribunal uses to comparatively weigh the probative value of conflicting evidence. These evidence types, credibility factors, and comparison patterns are developed to be inter-operable with legal rules governing the evidence assessment process in the U.S. This approach should be transferable to other legal and non-legal domains.

1 Introduction

Argument mining from the fact-finding portions of adjudicatory decisions in law presents several advantages. One advantage is analyzing careful reasoning by professional authors of unstructured natural language documents, which contain explanations of the reasoning of the decision maker from the evidence in the case to the factual conclusions. Another advantage is mining arguments and reasoning from documents that combine various types of evidence, such as lay testimony, expert opinions, medical records, and scientific publications. Yet another advantage is the societal importance of the subject matter, from disability claims to vaccine-injury compensation to medical malpractice.

If we can mine a large number of fact-specific cases for the arguments of the parties and the reasoning of the decision makers, then we could identify frequencies, trends, and success rates for different types of argument. We could also determine whether decision making among factually similar cases has been consistent. Native or web applications could use the data to recommend evidence and arguments to parties in new cases, and they could provide historically based support for legal decision makers.

But argument mining from adjudicatory decisions also faces significant challenges. Adjudicatory decisions occur within a complex legal process for resolving a dispute or deciding a case. In general, an adjudicatory process involves parties to the dispute, who raise issues to be decided, argue for or against specific outcomes on those issues, and often (especially in common law countries) produce the evidence on which the findings of fact are based. Another key participant in the adjudicatory process is the presiding official at the trial level (e.g., judge or administrative official), who presides over the creation of the official evidentiary record, decides which legal rules are applicable to the process, and decides how to enforce those legal rules. Another participant in the process is the fact-finder or trier of fact, who evaluates all the evidence produced, and officially declares the propositions that constitute the findings of fact for the proceeding. (Depending upon the tribunal and process, the same person may perform the roles of presiding official and of trier of fact.) In addition, there is almost always a reviewing authority (e.g., an appellate court), which oversees the decisions made at the trial level.

Such complexity of the adjudicatory process results in complex legal rules designed to govern the procedures. Substantive rules establish the issues to be decided, while process rules govern the procedures for deciding those issues (Walker, 2007). Some process rules govern various

Proceedings of the 5th Workshop on Argument Mining, pages 68–78
Brussels, Belgium, November 1, 2018. ©2018 Association for Computational Linguistics

participants and actions related to assessing the probative value of the evidence. For example, such rules may govern the admissibility of evidence into the evidentiary record, dictate the relevance or irrelevance of certain types of evidence for particular conclusions, establish what some evidence presumptively proves, or determine when a set of evidence is minimally sufficient to warrant a reasonable inference. If argument mining is performed for the purpose of recommending possible arguments in new legal cases, then we must ensure that those arguments are constructed within the constraints imposed by such legal rules.

Such process complexity also results in decision documents from fact-finding tribunals in which sentences have a range of rhetorical roles (Walker et al., 2017a). Some sentences report the procedural history of the case, while others state the legal rules that are applicable to the case, or they provide citations to legal authorities. Other sentences may state the rulings of law on motions made by the parties, or they may explain the bases for those rulings. In mining the fact-finding reasoning from the decision, it is necessary to identify and exclude most of these types of sentences from those that contain the fact-finding reasoning. The tribunal's assessment of the evidence is expressed in sentences that summarize the evidence presented, that state the arguments of the parties based on that evidence, that state the findings of fact, and that explain the tribunal's inferences from that evidence to those findings.

This paper reports on research to empirically derive a typology for arguments that is flexible enough to type most evidence assessment actually found in adjudicatory decisions, and transferable to many substantive areas of law. The typology should have a reasonable likelihood of automatic and accurate classification, so that software can identify trends and success rates with acceptably low error rates, and software can make recommendations about arguments in new cases. The argument types should also be inter-operable with the complex legal rules in the U.S. that constrain the evidence assessment process.

This paper reports on a typology based on adjudicatory decisions about veterans' claims for disability benefits in the United States. Section 2 summarizes prior work relevant to our research. Section 3 describes the dataset and our methodology. Section 4 reports the types of evidence that the tribunal considers relevant to the major issues litigated in these cases. Section 5 reports, for two primary types of evidence, the factors that triers of fact consider in assessing the credibility or trustworthiness of individual items of that type of evidence. Section 6 reports on patterns or "soft rules" that the tribunal uses to comparatively weigh the probative value of conflicting evidence. Section 7 discusses the usefulness of this approach and future work.

2   Prior Work

Prior work in argument mining directly related to our project is work aimed at classifying arguments into types, and especially by means of classifying the premises of the arguments into types. Researchers generally identify a unit of argument as containing a conclusion or claim, together with a set of one or more premises. (E.g., Palau and Moens, 2009; Walton, 2009; Stab and Gurevych, 2014; Lawrence and Reed, 2017; Wachsmuth et al., 2017.) One approach to classifying arguments is using the argumentative relation between premises and conclusion (e.g., support, opposition; pro, con; stance) (e.g. Lawrence and Reed, 2017; Wachsmuth et al., 2017). Another approach is to classify arguments by types of premises. Our work uses both approaches, but this paper reports only on the latter approach.

As we explain in Section 3, we distinguish two kinds of premise (or correspondingly, two types of sentence or clause): propositions stating the relevant evidence and propositions stating the reasoning from that evidence to the conclusion (the finding of fact). Stab and Gurevych (2014) classified clauses as major claim, claim, premise or non-argumentative, with directed argumentative relations possibly running from a premise to a major claim, a claim, or another premise. Liebeck et al. (2016) adapted this approach to mining suggestions or claims on options for actions or decisions.

Boltužic and Šnajder (2016) developed a typology for premises organized along three dimensions: premise type (fact, value, or policy), complexity (atomic, implication, or complex), and acceptance (universal or claim-specific). Hidey et al. (2017) classified premises as logos, pathos, or ethos. They defined an "ethos" premise as one that "appeals to the credibility established by personal experience/expertise." As we explain in Section 4, it is common in legal evidence assessment to evaluate the credibility or trustworthiness of sources of evidence. The adjudications in our dataset use a broad concept of credibility and a structured approach to determining credibility.

Some research directly related to our work is Rinott et al. (2015). They identified three different types of evidence: study results, expert testimony, and anecdotal descriptions. Also, Addawood and Bashir (2016) developed for Twitter data a typology of evidence having six types, including "expert opinion." We use somewhat related types, but we emphasize that our types are ones on which appellate courts have often predicated rules of law.

Finally, some research in argument mining has focused particularly on legal adjudicatory documents. Examples are U.S. court opinions (Jackson et al., 2003); judgments of the U.K. House of Lords (Hachey and Grover, 2006); U.S. trade secret cases (Ashley and Brüninghaus, 2009); extracts from legal texts of the European Court of Human Rights (Palau and Moens, 2009; Mochales and Moens, 2011); Indian court decisions (Saravanan and Ravindran, 2010); the process of argumentation from evidence to verdict in U.S. civil cases based on common law (Al-Abdulkarim et al., 2016); and judgment documents from Japanese civil trial courts (Yamada et al., 2017). However, to our knowledge, no research has developed a premise typology that is intended to be inter-operable with legal rules about evidence admissibility, irrelevance, minimal sufficiency, etc., particularly with such legal rules in the United States.

3 Dataset and Methodology

This section describes the sample of adjudicatory decisions we used in our study, as well as the methodology behind our results.

3.1 PTSD Dataset

We analyzed 30 fact-finding decisions issued by the U.S. Board of Veterans' Appeals ("BVA") from 2013 through 2016.[1] We arbitrarily selected those decisions from adjudicated disability claims by veterans for service-related post-traumatic stress disorder (PTSD). Individual claims for compensation for a disability usually originate at a Regional Office ("RO") of the U.S. Department of

Veterans Affairs ("VA"), or at another local office across the country (Allen, 2007; Moshiashwili, 2015). If the claimant is dissatisfied with the decision of the RO, she may file an appeal to the BVA. The BVA is an administrative appellate body that has the statutory authority to decide the facts of each case based on the evidence (Moshiashwili, 2015). The BVA must provide a written statement of the reasons or bases for its findings and conclusions, and that statement "must account for the evidence which [the BVA] finds to be persuasive or unpersuasive, analyze the credibility and probative value of all material evidence submitted by and on behalf of a claimant, and provide the reasons for its rejection of any such evidence." *Caluza v. Brown*, 7 Vet. App. 498, 506 (1995), *aff'd*, 78 F.3d 604 (Fed. Cir. 1996).[2]

3.2 Methodology

For purposes of mining different types of fact-finding arguments or reasoning from these decisions, we first developed annotation protocols for identifying those sentences that generally do not contribute critical information. Examples of such sentences are those that primarily state the procedural facts of the case, the applicable legal rules, any rulings as a matter of law, or rationales for such rulings. We focus primarily on sentences that play one of three reasoning roles in evidence assessment: the **conclusion** (a **finding of fact**), which states whether a propositional condition of a legal rule is determined to be true, false or undecided; the **foundations** for the reasoning (the **evidence** in the legal record, such as the testimony of a lay witness, the opinion of an expert witness, or exhibits such as a medical record, a photo, or a published scientific study); and the **reasoning** from the evidence to the findings of fact. We call these, respectively, **"finding sentences"**, **"evidence sentences"**, and **"reasoning sentences."** We developed detailed annotation protocols for these three sentence types.

Table 1 reports the frequencies of occurrence for these sentence types in the PTSD dataset. Many decisions involve claims for multiple disabilities, of which PTSD is one. Table 1 provides the total number of sentences for entire decisions in the dataset. For the PTSD portions of those decisions,

---

[2] We follow the U.S. legal convention of citing to statutes, regulations, decisions, or other legal documents within the text.

it reports the frequency of evidence sentences, reasoning sentences, and finding sentences.

Semantic Type	Frequency
Sentence	8,149
Evidence Sentence	1,412
Reasoning Sentence	442
Finding Sentence	310

Table 1: Frequency of Sentences in Dataset, and of Sentence Types in PTSD Portions of Decisions

Next, we identified which PTSD-related finding sentences were relevant to determining the three major substantive issues of fact to be decided in these cases. To obtain compensation for a present disability, the veteran must prove that she has a disability that is "service-connected" (Walker et al., 2017b). This requires proving three major issues of fact: (1) the veteran has a present disability; (2) while in active service, the veteran incurred an injury or disease, or the veteran suffered an aggravation of a pre-existing injury or disease, or there occurred an "in-service stressor" that is capable of causing PTSD; and (3) there is a causal relationship (or "nexus") between the present disability and the in-service incurrence, aggravation, or stressor. We then identified the evidence sentences relevant to each issue, and we catalogued the types of evidence the BVA considered relevant to each major issue. We report some of our results in Section 4, with examples.

For each type of evidence that we found, we then searched our decisions for sentences that describe how the BVA evaluated the credibility or trustworthiness of a single item of such evidence. Such sentences are reasoning sentences. We found that normally these decisions refer to a number of factors that tend to increase or decrease the credibility or trustworthiness of the particular evidence. We report some of our results on these factors in Section 5, with examples.

We then searched for reasoning sentences that weighed the comparative probative value of conflicting evidence relevant to the same issue of fact. In Section 6, we report a few of the patterns that we are finding, with examples.

Throughout these searches (for evidence types, credibility factors, and patterns for comparing probative value), we noted legal rules on evidence assessment that govern the argumentation. Legal rules have the logical form of conditions – "if p,

then q," where p states the condition of the rule and q its conclusion. We give examples of such rules in Sections 4, 5 and 6. We indicate in Section 7 how semantic typing of arguments should be inter-operable with governing legal rules.

4 Types of Evidence

We catalogued the types of evidence relied upon in the PTSD portions of the evidence assessment in the 30 BVA decisions. Table 2 lists the typology that we have developed. The Federal Rules of Evidence ("FRE") are typical of sets of rules adopted in U.S. jurisdictions to govern the admissibility of evidence in court. Broadly, evidence is admissible into the evidentiary record of a case, for consideration by the trier of fact, if it is "relevant," and not excluded by the U.S. Constitution, U.S. statutes, or rules of evidence. (Federal Rule of Evidence 402, 2017.) "Relevant evidence" is defined as evidence having "any tendency to make a fact [of consequence in determining the case] more or less probable than it would be without the evidence." (Federal Rule of Evidence 401, 2017.) In general, major categories of evidence are testimonial evidence (the testimony of a person), documentary evidence (evidence supplied by a writing or other document), and real evidence (physical evidence, such as clothing) (Black's Law Dictionary, 2014).

Evidence Type	Sub-Type
Lay Testimony	Veteran
	Veteran's spouse or partner
	Other veteran
	Other non-veteran
Medical Records	Pre-service
	In-service
	Post-service within the Veterans Administration
	Post-service not within Veterans Administration
Performance Evaluations	In-service
	Post-service
Other Service Records	
Other Expert Opinions	
Other Records	

Table 2: Types and Sub-Types of Evidence in the Sample of 30 BVA Decisions

Testimonial evidence in BVA cases includes lay testimony by the veteran filing the claim, a veteran's spouse or partner, another veteran, or other person. Such testimony often plays an important role in deciding the issues of fact. An example of an evidence sentence stating lay testimony is:

However, in written documents and in his Board hearing testimony, the Veteran contends that his acquired psychiatric disorder is the result of witnessing a shipmate fall overboard while stationed on the USS Constellation CVA 64 in approximately March 1975. [BVA 1554166]

Documentary evidence includes medical records, performance evaluations, and service or other records. Medical records, for example, can contain expert opinions, test results, or non-expert information. Examples of evidence sentences reporting the contents of medical records are:

With regard to positive evidence, in 2010 and 2011, a private psychologist, Dr. A.G., PhD., diagnosed the Veteran with PTSD due to his Vietnam experiences. [BVA 1400029]

The STRs [service treatment records] *showed no complaints, treatment, abnormalities or diagnosis for any psychiatric problems in service.* [BVA 1445540]

These examples of evidence sentences suggest the difficulty facing the BVA as trier of fact both in assessing the credibility of items of evidence taken individually (Section 5) and in resolving conflicts between items of evidence (Section 6).

5 Factors Affecting Credibility or Trustworthiness of Individual Items of Evidence

BVA decisions often take a factor-based approach to assessing the credibility of witness testimony or the trustworthiness of documentary evidence such as medical records. (For reasons we cannot discuss here, such factors are not identical to the issue-related "factors" common in the literature on case-based reasoning (e.g., Ashley and Brüninghaus, 2009; Al-Abdulkarim et al., 2016).) "Credibility" or "trustworthiness" denotes the quality of inspiring trust or belief. See, e.g., *Indiana Metal Products v. N.L.R.B.*, 442 F.2d 46, 51-52 (7th Cir. 1971). Appellate decisions often refer to "factors" as the characteristics of a witness that tend to make

her believable, or the characteristics of testimony or a document that tend to make it worthy of belief. See, e.g., *Southall-Norman v. McDonald*, 28 Vet. App. 346, 355 (Ct. App. Vet. Cl. 2016).

5.1 Lay Testimony

Table 3 lists some of the factors that can affect the credibility of lay testimony. There are legal rules governing the assessment of evidence using such factors. Some legal rules determine the relevance or irrelevance of such factors to proving particular issues of fact. For example, an appellate court has held that in assessing the credibility of oral testimony, a hearing officer may properly consider "the demeanor of the witness, the facial plausibility of the testimony, and the consistency of the witness' testimony with other testimony and affidavits." *Caluza v. Brown*, 7 Vet. App. 498 (1995), *aff'd*, 78 F.3d 604 (Fed. Cir. 1996). Such rules, however, tend to identify some but not all relevant factors.

Aspects of Lay Testimony	Factors Affecting Credibility
Source of Testimony (Witness)	Demeanor of witness while testifying
	Character of witness
	Consistency of witness
	Bias, personal interest
Basis of Testimony	Degree of personal knowledge
	Awareness of other evidence
	Competence relative to content
Content of Testimony	Facial plausibility
	Consistency with other evidence
	Corroboration from other evidence

Table 3: Factors Affecting Credibility of Lay Testimony

The **first set of factors** that we found in our sample of BVA decisions includes characteristics related to **the source** of the testimony – the witness herself. Such characteristics include: the demeanor of the witness while testifying at a hearing; some aspect of the witness's character (e.g., being considered a "malingerer" while on active duty); the consistency of the witness's own statements over time about the same events; or some bias of the witness, such as a personal interest in obtaining disability benefits at the time of the statement.

An example of a reasoning sentence that shows taking such factors into account is the following:

Additionally, the appellant has been extremely active in pursuing disability claims, including VA claims, EEOC claims, and workman's compensation claims. In the process of these claims, the appellant has provided testimony that is internally inconsistent and appears to frequently be shaped by the type of claim he is pursuing. [BVA 1413417]

The **second set of factors** concerns **the basis** for the testimony. These factors include: the degree of personal knowledge of the witness as the basis for the content of the testimony; the awareness by the witness of other evidence bearing on the testimony; and the competence of the witness to testify about the content. This last factor arises frequently in veterans' cases, as when the veteran seeks to testify about a psychological diagnosis but does not have the training to do so. An example is:

As a lay person, the Veteran is competent to report what comes to him through his senses, but he lacks the medical training and expertise to provide a complex medical opinion as to the etiology of an anxiety disorder. [BVA 1608262]

The **third set of factors** addresses **the content** of the testimony directly. Factors that affect credibility include: the plausibility (or implausibility) of the testimony on its face, such as internal inconsistencies; the extent of consistency or inconsistency with other evidence; and whether there is positive corroboration from other evidence. In addition to examples above, the following is an example of a reasoning sentence on corroboration:

Additionally, there are no medical records, police records, or changes in behavior that corroborate the Veteran's assertions. [BVA 1613894]

5.2 Medical Records

Table 4 lists some of the factors that affect the trustworthiness of information and expert opinions contained in medical records. There are legal rules governing evidence assessment, when it relies on such factors. For example, an appellate court has held that when assessing the probative value of documents for certain purposes, the BVA "may properly consider internal consistency, facial plausibility, and consistency with other evidence." *Caluza v. Brown*, 7 Vet. App. 498 (1995), *aff'd*, 78 F.3d 604 (Fed. Cir. 1996). However, such legal rules tend to state only some but not all relevant factors.

Aspects of Medical Records	Factors Affecting Trustworthiness
Source of Medical Record (author or source of content)	Relevant qualifications, expertise, etc.
	Bias, personal interest
Basis of Medical Record (e.g., physical examination, psychological evaluation)	Personal observation of patient
	Credibility or accuracy of other information relied upon
	Extent of patient's record taken into account
Content of Medical Record	Remarks that undermine conclusiveness
	Extent of detail
	Consistency with other evidence
	Corroboration from other evidence

Table 4: Factors Affecting Trustworthiness of Information within Medical Records

The **first set of factors** identified in our sample of BVA decisions includes characteristics related to **the author** of the medical record or **the source** of its content. Often, the author of the record is the same person who is asserting the proposition stated in the record. On occasion, however, the author states the assertion of some other person (e.g., of the veteran who recounts her medical history to a physician). Some factors are: the relevant qualifications, expertise, knowledge or skill of the medical or other expert to whom the content is attributed; or bias or personal interest of the expert. An example of a reasoning sentence is:

The Board finds that the clinician's opinion is competent because she is qualified through education, training, or experience to offer medical diagnoses, statements, or opinions. [BVA 1340434]

The **second set of factors** concerns **the basis** for the content of the medical record. Relevant factors for trustworthiness include: whether the content of the medical record is based on observations made personally by the source; the credibility or accuracy of other information that the expert relied upon (e.g., reports of personal history by the veteran); and the extent of the patient's record that the expert took into account in creating the content of the medical record. Some example reasoning sentences are:

This examiner's opinion was rendered following review of the claims file and interview of the Veteran. No deficiency is found in either respect. The Board notes that the Veteran's interview took a "great deal of time." That is shown by the examiner's use of that phrase and the fact that the summarization of the interview is around three pages in length. There is no indication of reliance on an inaccurate factual premise in formulating the opinion. A rationale for it was offered by the examiner. It further is sufficiently thorough and detailed. [BVA 1303141]

The above examples also illustrate some factors from the **third set of factors**, which address **the content** of the medical record. These factors include: remarks in the content that might serve to undermine the conclusiveness of the content (e.g., "possibly"); the extent of detail provided in the content; the degree of consistency or inconsistency with other evidence; and whether there is positive corroboration from other evidence, especially other medical evidence. Another example is:

The relevant evidence on this question includes a February 2007 VA examination report where the examiner opined that it was at least as likely as not that the Veteran suffered PTSD in her youth and that this was "possibly aggravated" by service. [BVA 1343153]

6 Patterns or Soft Rules for Comparing Conflicting Items of Evidence

Our study disclosed that the BVA has also developed recurring patterns of reasoning when comparing the probative value of conflicting evidence on the same issue of fact. In this section we provide examples of such patterns.

6.1 Comparing Evidence of Same Type

The lists of factors presented in Section 5 also supply an analytic approach to comparing conflicting evidence of the same type (e.g., conflicting medical records). In BVA 1400029, for example, on the issue of diagnosis of present PTSD, there was a conflict between VA treatment records (declining to diagnose PTSD) and a medical record by a private psychologist (diagnosing PTSD). After evaluating each of the available medical records on relevant factors, the Board reasoned:

Overall, the November 2010 and September 2011 VA psychological examinations in particular were thorough, supported by an explanation, and considered the Veteran's history and relevant longitudinal complaints. The VA opinions and treatment records outweigh the private treatment of record on the issue of whether the Veteran has a PTSD diagnosis in accordance with DSM-IV.

Because the same factors apply to each item of the same type of evidence, those factors provide an analytic framework for comparing conflicting items.

6.2 Comparing Evidence of Different Types

Several patterns or soft rules have developed for comparing credible evidence of different types. An assessment pattern can function as a "soft rule" if a reviewing court has explicitly stated that it is reasonable for the BVA to follow such a pattern in its decisions. (See Walker, 2007.) A legal rule stating that a pattern of assessment is reasonable is a permissive rule, stating in effect that the BVA may follow such a pattern without great risk of reversal by a higher court. But such a rule does not mandate following that pattern – it merely officially recognizes the pattern. At some later time, an appellate court might make using such a pattern mandatory (a normal legal rule), especially after the pattern becomes generally used. We mention and illustrate several of those patterns or soft rules.

Incompetent lay testimony vs. competent medical opinion. An important credibility factor for lay testimony is competence relative to the content. While a veteran is competent to testify concerning her own symptoms, the Board is skeptical concerning the veteran's competence to testify concerning diagnosis or etiology. The appellate courts have held that lay persons (non-experts) may be competent to testify about medical diagnoses under some conditions, e.g., *Davidson v. Shinseki*, 581 F.3d 1313, 1316 (Fed. Cir. 2009). However, the Board can consider a difference in competence between a lay witness and medical experts on an issue of diagnosis. In addition, the regulations on PTSD specifically require "medical evidence diagnosing the condition." Therefore, on the issue of diagnosis of present disability, we can find the Board deciding in accordance with the evidence in the medical records, despite testimony by the veteran to the contrary (e.g., BVA 1400029).

Lay testimony vs. contemporaneous documentary evidence. Given the possibility of bias or personal interest, together with the innate unreliability of human memory, the Board often favors contemporaneous documentary evidence over conflicting lay testimony made much later. While the appellate courts have held that the Board cannot automatically determine that competent lay testimony lacks credibility simply because it is uncorroborated by contemporaneous medical records, *Buchanan v. Nicholson*, 451 F.3d 1331, 1336 (Fed. Cir. 2006), the Board may weigh the absence of contemporaneous medical evidence against the lay testimony, *id.* at 1336-37. Thus, we find reasoning that states that contemporaneous documentary evidence outweighs later lay testimony, especially when the latter is discounted due to credibility factors. See, e.g., BVA 1340434.

The Benefit-of-the-Doubt Rule. Normally, the burden of proving the facts of a claim is on the party making the claim. When the probative value of supporting and opposing evidence is equally balanced, the party with the burden of proof must lose, as a matter of law. With veterans' claims, however, the statute places the burden of proof on the government, and it gives the benefit of the doubt to the veteran, 38 U.S.C.A. § 5107(b) (2018). Therefore, even when there is conflicting evidence of different types, if the Board considers the supporting and opposing evidence to be equally probative, then it must find the issue of fact for the veteran. E.g., BVA 1455333 (VA treatment records vs. VA examination record, on issue of present diagnosis of PTSD).

7 Discussion and Future Work

One important problem in argument mining is developing a useful typology for determining argument frequency, argument trends, or argument success rates. To predict argument outcomes in future cases, the argument typology should be based on the strength of the substantive evidence (the soundness of the argument), not merely on formal properties such as syllogistic form (the validity of the argument). In addition, a typology of arguments should be flexible enough to classify most evidence assessment actually found in adjudicatory decisions, and it should be transferable to many substantive areas of law. The typology should have a reasonable likelihood of automatic and accurate classification. Finally, for the use case of recommending arguments in actual cases, the arguments should comply with any applicable legal rules on evidence assessment.

Our future work includes developing such a typology for entire arguments, building upon the evidence types, credibility factors, and comparison patterns discussed in this paper. Evidence types provide a method not only for further classifying evidence sentences, but also for classifying arguments that rely in part on such evidence. Factors relevant to an evidence type provide independent variables for algorithms that predict the credibility or trustworthiness of a particular item of evidence. Patterns or soft rules for comparing different types of evidence provide methods for predicting the net probative value of a set of evidence that supports and opposes a conclusion on a particular substantive issue. Taken together, these layers of semantic classification provide a typology for arguments that identifies argument types in terms familiar to judges and lawyers, a methodology for predicting the strength of an argument, and a means of evaluating the status of an argument relative to any governing legal rules.

There are good reasons to think that our approach (evidence types, credibility factors, and comparison patterns) is sufficiently flexible, and transferable to areas of law outside veterans' claims. First, sets of rules such as the Federal Rules of Evidence govern (with some exceptions) many types of judicial cases, both criminal and civil (Federal Rule of Evidence 1101, 2017). Even where such rules of evidence admissibility do not govern (e.g., in many types of administrative adjudications), the basic conceptual categories from such rules are still employed. For example, distinguishing evidence into testimonial, documentary and real evidence is probably universal in the U.S., as well as classifying testimonial evidence into lay and expert. Moreover, even when the Federal Rules of Evidence do not apply, courts often consult them on questions that arise, such as what factors to consider in assessing the probative value of expert opinions (e.g., *Nieves-Rodriguez v. Peake*, 22 Vet.

App. 295 (2008)). Thus, our approach to classifying arguments by types of evidence should have broad applicability, even if a particular area of law tends to rely on different sub-types of evidence.

Second, appellate courts widely employ the concept of a "relevant factor" to establish rules governing the fact-finding process, in many different areas of law. (E.g., *Daubert v. Merrell Dow Pharmaceuticals, Inc.*, 509 U.S. 579 (1993).) Moreover, the factors relevant to evaluating the credibility of a witness's testimony are general in nature (see the examples in Section 5), and we expect them to be applicable across most substantive areas within law.

Finally, we have already found some patterns of comparing evidence types in areas of law outside veterans' claims. For example, the pattern of favoring contemporaneous documentary evidence over conflicting, later lay testimony is a recognized pattern in decisions about compensation for injuries allegedly caused by vaccinations. (E.g., *Walton v. Secretary of the Department of Health and Human Services*, No. 04-503V, 2007 WL 1467307 (2007).) In sum, there are good reasons to conclude that our approach will be widely useful across many areas of law.

In order to generate a sufficient amount of valid semantic data using our typology, we also develop annotation protocols (classification criteria and methods) to give precise meaning to the semantic type, to train new annotators, and to review the accuracy of human annotations. In our protocols, attribution verbs are strong discourse indicators for evidence and finding sentences (see Stab and Gurevych, 2014), especially when combined with signature grammatical subjects, such as "the Veteran" or "the Board" (see Walker et al., 2015). We also use such protocols to guide the development of rule-based software and linguistic features for automatically classifying legal texts (e.g., Savelka et al., 2017). Stab and Gurevych (2014) have classified such features into 5 groups. For example, the main verb of a finding sentence tends to be in present tense, while the main verbs of evidence sentences tend to be in past tense. Features derived from the protocols can drive the application of high-precision / low-recall techniques of the kind used successfully by Lawrence and Reed (2017). The system architecture described by Rinott et al. (2015) for ranking candidates for context-dependent evidence

might be promising in this regard. We will use the results of our present qualitative study as the framework for such future quantitative research.

The development of factors that increase or decrease either credibility or trustworthiness (Section 5) invites research into probabilistic models. Perhaps sufficient data could be obtained to develop models for predicting credibility and trustworthiness of evidence in new cases. If so, this approach would have applications beyond the legal domain.

Finally, we are developing techniques for achieving the inter-operability of the semantic types used for argument classification with the legal rules in the U.S. that constrain the evidence assessment process. We have provided examples of such legal rules throughout this paper, as well as elsewhere (Walker et al., 2017b). The semantic types used to classify arguments should include the concepts found in the conditions of such rules – e.g., rules governing "lay testimony," "expert opinion," or "medical record." Any analytic service that monitors or recommends arguments in legal cases would need to access and apply such legal rules.

The annotated dataset for this study will be publicly available on GitHub, at: https://github.com/LLTLab/VetClaims.

8 Conclusion

On the basis of an empirical study of veterans' disability claims in the United States, we are developing a typology for arguments. We think that our approach to evidence types, credibility factors, and patterns for comparing probative value will provide a useful typology for fact-finding arguments that is transferable to domains of law other than veterans' disability claims, and perhaps also to non-law domains.

Acknowledgements

We are grateful to the peer reviewers for this paper, whose comments led to significant improvements. This research was generously supported by the Maurice A. Deane School of Law at Hofstra University, New York, USA.

References

Aseel A. Addawood and Masooda N. Bashir. 2016. "What is Your Evidence?" A Study of Controversial Topics on Social Media. In

Proceedings of the 3rd Workshop on Argument Mining, pages 1-11. Berlin, Germany.

Latifa Al-Abdulkarim, Katie Atkinson, and Trevor Bench-Capon. 2016. Statement Types in Legal Argument. In Floris Bex and Serena Villata, editors, *Legal Knowledge and Information Systems (JURIX 2016)*, pages 3-12. IOS Press.

Michael P. Allen. 2007. Significant Developments in Veterans Law (2004-2006) and What They Reveal about the U.S. Court of Appeals for Veterans Claims and the U.S. Court of Appeals for the Federal Circuit. *University of Michigan Journal of Law Reform* 40: 483-568. University of Michigan.

Kevin D. Ashley and Stefanie Brüninghaus. 2009. Automatically classifying case texts and predicting outcomes. *Artificial Intelligence and Law* 17: 125-165.

Black's Law Dictionary. 2014. Bryan A. Garner, Editor in Chief. Thomson Reuters.

Filip Boltužic and Jan Šnajder. 2016. Fill the Gap! Analyzing Implicit Premises between Claims from Online Debates. In *Proceedings of the 3rd Workshop on Argument Mining*, pages 124-133. Berlin, Germany.

Federal Rules of Evidence. 2017. 28 United States Code Annotated.

Ben Hachey and Claire Grover. 2006. Extractive summarisation of legal texts. *Artificial Intelligence and Law*, 14: 305-345.

Christopher Hidey, Elena Musi, Alyssa Hwang, Smaranda Muresan and Kathleen McKeown. 2017. Analyzing the Semantic Types of Claims and Premises in an Online Persuasive Forum. In *Proceedings of the 4th Workshop on Argument Mining*, pages 11-21, Copenhagen, Denmark.

Peter Jackson, Khalid Al-Kofahi, Alex Tyrrell and Arun Vachher. 2003. Information extraction from case law and retrieval of prior cases. *Artificial Intelligence* 150: 239–290.

John Lawrence and Chris Reed. 2017. Mining Argumentative Structure from Natural Language Text Using Automatically Generated Premise-Conclusion Topic Models. In *Proceedings of the 4th Workshop on Argument Mining*, pages 39-48, Copenhagen, Denmark.

Matthias Liebeck, Katharina Esau and Stefan Conrad. 2016. What to Do with an Airport? Mining Arguments in the German Online Participation Project Tempelhofer Feld. In *Proceedings of the 3rd Workshop on Argument Mining*, pages 144-153. Berlin, Germany.

Raquel Mochales and Marie-Francine Moens. 2011. Argumentation mining. *Artificial Intelligence and Law*, 19(1):1–22. Springer.

Victoria Hadfield Moshiashwili. 2015. The Downfall of Auer Deference: Veterans Law at the Federal Circuit in 2014. *American University Law Review* 64: 1007-1087. American University.

Raquel Mochales Palau and Marie-Francine Moens. 2009. Argumentation mining: the detection, classification and structure of arguments in text. In *Proceedings of the 12th International Conference on Artificial Intelligence and Law (ICAIL 2009)*, pages 98–107, Barcelona, Spain.

Ruty Rinott, Lena Dankin, Carlos Alzate, Mitesh M. Khapra, Ehud Aharoni and Noam Slonim. 2015. Show Me Your Evidence – an Automatic Method for Context Dependent Evidence Detection. In *Proceedings of the 2015 Conference on Empirical Methods in Natural Language Processing*, pages 440-450, Lisbon, Portugal.

M. Saravanan and B. Ravindran. 2010. Identification of Rhetorical Roles for Segmentation and Summarization of a Legal Judgment. *Artificial Intelligence and Law*, 18(1):45–76.

Jaromir Savelka, Vern R. Walker, Matthias Grabmair and Kevin D. Ashley. 2017. Sentence Boundary Detection in Adjudicatory Decisions in the United States. *Revue TAL*, 58(2): 21-45.

Christian Stab and Iryna Gurevych. 2014. Identifying Argumentative Discourse Structures in Persuasive Essays. In *Proceedings of the 2014 Conference on Empirical Methods in Natural Language Processing (EMNLP)*, pages 46-56, Doha, Qatar.

Henning Wachsmuth, Martin Potthast, Khalid Al-Khatib, Yamen Ajjour, Jana Puschmann, Jiani Qu, Jonas Dorsch, Viorel Morari, Janek Bevendorff and Benno Stein. 2017. Building an Argument Search Engine for the Web. In *Proceedings of the 4th Workshop on Argument Mining*, pages 49-59, Copenhagen, Denmark.

Vern R. Walker. 2007. A Default-Logic Paradigm for Legal Fact-Finding. *Jurimetrics* 47: 193-243.

Vern R. Walker, Parisa Bagheri and Andrew J. Lauria. 2015. Argumentation Mining from Judicial Decisions: The Attribution Problem and the Need for Legal Discourse Models. Paper at the First Workshop on Automated Detection, Extraction and Analysis of Semantic Information in Legal Texts (ASAIL 2015), San Diego, California, USA. URL: https://people.hofstra.edu/vern_r_walker/WalkerEt Al-AttributionAndLegalDiscourseModels-ASAIL2015.pdf.

Vern R. Walker, Ji Hae Han, Xiang Ni and Kaneyasu Yoseda. 2017a. Semantic Types for Computational

Legal Reasoning: Propositional Connectives and Sentence Roles in the Veterans' Claims Dataset. In *Proceedings of the 16th International Conference on Artificial Intelligence and Law (ICAIL 2017)*, pages 217-26, London, UK.

Vern R. Walker, Ashtyn Hemendinger, Nneka Okpara and Tauseef Ahmed. 2017b. Semantic Types for Decomposing Evidence Assessment in Decisions on Veterans' Disability Claims for PTSD. In *Proceedings of the Second Workshop on Automatic Semantic Analysis of Semantic Information in Legal Text (ASAIL 2017)*, London, UK.

Douglas Walton. 2009. Argumentation theory: A very short introduction. In Guillermo Simari and Iyad Rahwan, editors, *Argumentation in Artificial Intelligence*, pages 1-22. Springer, US.

Hiroaki Yamada, Simone Teufel and Takenobu Tokunaga. 2017. Annotation of argument structure in Japanese legal documents. In *Proceedings of the 4th Workshop on Argument Mining*, pages 22-31, Copenhagen, Denmark.

Feasible Annotation Scheme for Capturing Policy Argument Reasoning using Argument Templates

Paul Reisert[†]   **Naoya Inoue**[†,‡]   **Tatsuki Kuribayashi**[‡]   **Kentaro Inui**[†,‡]

[†] RIKEN Center for Advanced Intelligence Project   [‡] Tohoku University
`paul.reisert@riken.jp`
`{naoya-i,kuribayashi,inui}@ecei.tohoku.ac.jp`

Abstract

Most of the existing works on argument mining cast the problem of argumentative structure identification as classification tasks (e.g. attack-support relations, stance, explicit premise/claim). This paper goes a step further by addressing the task of automatically identifying reasoning patterns of arguments using predefined templates, which is called *argument template (AT) instantiation*. The contributions of this work are three-fold. First, we develop a simple, yet expressive set of easily annotatable ATs that can represent a majority of writer's reasoning for texts with diverse policy topics while maintaining the computational feasibility of the task. Second, we create a small, but highly reliable annotated corpus of instantiated ATs on top of reliably annotated support and attack relations and conduct an annotation study. Third, we formulate the task of AT instantiation as structured prediction constrained by a feasible set of templates. Our evaluation demonstrates that we can annotate ATs with a reasonably high interannotator agreement, and the use of template-constrained inference is useful for instantiating ATs with only partial reasoning comprehension clues.

1   Introduction

Recognizing argumentative structures in unstructured texts is an important task for many natural language processing (NLP) applications. Argument mining is an emerging, leading field of argumentative structure identification in the NLP community. It involves a wide variety of subtasks for argumentative structure identification such as explicit premise and claim identification/classification (Reed et al., 2008; Rinott et al., 2015; Stab and Gurevych, 2014), stance classification (Hasan and Ng, 2014; Persing and Ng, 2016), and argumentative relation detection (Cocarascu

and Toni, 2017; Niculae et al., 2017; Peldszus and Stede, 2015b; Stab and Gurevych, 2017). These tasks have been useful for applications such as essay scoring, document summarization, etc. (Ghosh et al., 2016; Stab and Gurevych, 2017).

This paper addresses a feasible annotation scheme for the task of reasoning pattern identification in argumentative texts. Consider the following argument consisting of two argumentative segments S_1 and S_2 regarding the policy topic *Should Germany universities charge tuition fees?*:

(1) S_1: *German universities should not **charge tuition fees**.*
S_2: *Every German citizen has **a right to education**.*

In this work, we adopt Walton et al. (2008)'s argumentation schemes (ASs), one prominent theory used for identifying reasoning patterns in every day arguments. Using Walton et al. (2008)'s *Argument from Negative Consequences* scheme, the reasoning of Example 1 can be explained as follows:

- Premise : If action x is brought about, bad consequences y will occur.

- Conclusion: x should not be brought about.

where both x and y are slot-fillers and x="*charge tuition fees*" and y="*a right to education will be violated*". Each AS identifies a scheme (from 65 total schemes) and appropriate slot-fillers. Instantiations of such reasoning patterns for an argument have several advantages.

First, identifying such reasoning will be useful for a range of argumentation mining applications, such as aggregating multiple arguments for producing a logic-based abstractive summary. Second, we believe that it will contribute towards

79

Proceedings of the 5th Workshop on Argument Mining, pages 79–89
Brussels, Belgium, November 1, 2018. ©2018 Association for Computational Linguistics

automatically assessing the quality of the logical structure of a given argument, where identifying specific arguments can signify higher quality, especially for tasks such as essay scoring (Song et al., 2014; Wachsmuth et al., 2016). Third, it will be useful for generating support or attacks in application contexts where a human and machine are cooperatively engaged in a debate (for decision support or education). Furthermore, understanding the reasoning in an argumentative text can contribute towards determining implicit ARs not indicated with an explicit discourse marker.

Towards automatically identifying the underlying reasoning of argumentative texts, Reed (2006) created Araucaria, a corpus consisting of argumentative texts annotated with Walton et al. (2008)'s ASs. Feng and Hirst (2011) used Araucaria for creating a computational model for identifying the type of argumentation scheme.

Although Araucaria is a well-known corpus in the argumentation mining community, it suffers from complex annotation guidelines which makes the annotation task difficult.[1] A follow up study (Musi et al., 2016) reports that the inter-annotator agreement of annotating a simplified taxonomy of the *Argumentum Model of Topics* argumentation schemes (Rigotti, 2006; Palmieri, 2014) results in Fleiss' $\kappa = 0.31$ ("fair agreement") even if the annotators are trained and only a subset (8 types) of schemes are annotated. In this work, we assume the following: (i) annotating multiple types of ASs is difficult, and (ii) the reliability of annotating reasoning patterns for a single AS with implicit slot-fillers is low because when slot-fillers are not explicitly written in the original text, they must manually be generated by annotators using natural language sentences; this allows for a wide variety of possible, arbitrary candidates for each scheme (e.g. $y=$"a right to education is violated" in Example 1), making the annotation costly and difficult. Towards constructing a highly-reliable corpus for the task of automatic reasoning identification in argumentative texts, an annotation scheme that covers a wide-range of arguments as much as possible and simultaneously offers a simple way to specify implicit slot-fillers instead of manually creating natural language sentences is crucial.

This paper makes three important contributions towards automatically capturing a writer's reasoning in argumentative texts. First, we compose a simple, yet expressive set of easily annotatable templates (*argument templates* or *ATs*) that allow for writer's reasoning to be representable without the need for manual generation of natural language sentences when slot-fillers are implicit. Specifically, we propose a template/slot-filler based approach for instantiating reasoning patterns that capture the underlying reasoning between two argumentative segments in an argumentative relation (AR) using two types of causal labels (e.g. PROMOTE and SUPPRESS). Our annotation study demonstrates that we can annotate ATs with a reasonably high inter-annotator agreement (Cohen's κ=0.80) and ATs can represent a majority (74.6%) of writer's reasoning in a small essay corpus with multiple, diverse policy topics. Second, using ATs, we augment an existing, reliable corpus of argumentative texts (Peldszus and Stede, 2015a) with writer's reasoning and create a small, but useful corpus on top of pre-labeled argumentative relations. Third, towards creating a fully-automated argument template instantiation model, we create a preliminary computational model for instantiating ATs. We formulate the task of AT instantiation as structured prediction constrained by a feasible set of ATs. We hypothesize that the introduction of such constraints enables us to instantiate ATs with only partial reasoning comprehension clues. Our evaluation shows that template-constrained inference is indeed useful for instantiating ATs with only partial reasoning comprehension clues.

2 A Corpus of Instantiated Argument Templates

The key requirements for automatically capturing an argument's reasoning are four-fold: (i) capture a writer's implicit reasoning as much as possible, (ii) be machine-friendly, (iii) be useful for downstream applications, and (iv) keep human annotation simple. Towards this goal, as mentioned in Section 1, Reed (2006) created Araucaria, a corpus consisting of argumentative texts annotated with Walton et al. (2008)'s ASs. However, the annotation scheme requires annotators to manually generate natural language sentences for implicit slot-fillers (i.e. (ii) and (iv) are not considered).

To address this issue, we propose a method that allows annotators to avoid manual generation of natural language sentences when a slot-

---

[1] An inter-annotator agreement was not reported in Reed (2006).

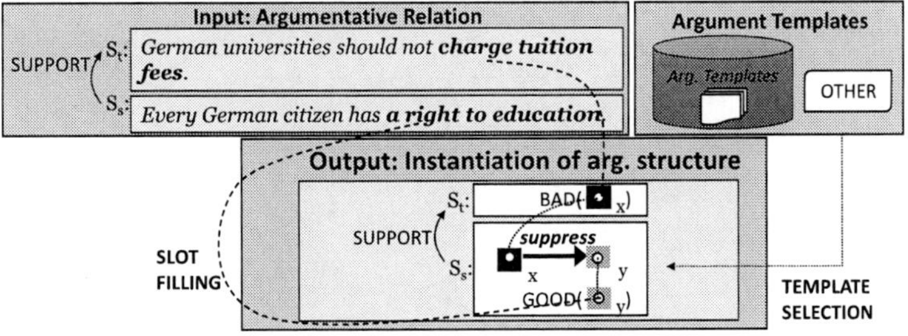

Figure 1: Overview of our argument template instantiation approach for capturing underlying reasoning.

filler is implicit. Given two argumentative statements with a known AR, our task is to identify the reasoning between them by (i) selecting a template from a predefined template set (*argument templates (ATs)*), where each template encodes a causal label, and (ii) instantiating the template via slot-filling, where the slot is linked with a relevant, arbitrary phrase in the input text. Figure 1 exemplifies our proposed approach, using the support relation from S_2 to S_1 in Example 1. The first step is to identify an AT: "S_1, *the target segment of the relation (i.e. S_t), states that x should not be brought about (i.e. bad)*[2] *, because S_2, the source segment of the relation (i.e. S_s), states that x is bad because when x happens, y, a good entity/event, will be suppressed.*". The second step is to instantiate the template by filling in the slots x, y with a phrase from the text: $x =$"*charge tuition fees*" and $y =$"*a right to education*". By encoding causal labels, annotators are no longer required to manually construct implicit slot-fillers (e.g. $y=$"a right to education will be violated" in Section 1).

The key insight about template design from previous work (Musi et al., 2016) is that if we annotate reasoning with coarse-grained reasoning types, the annotation becomes more difficult. In this work, we hypothesize that patterns for representing argumentation are not uniformly distributed but highly skewed, and create an inventory of major ATs, annotating only typical instances of reasoning with them. We label instances where a template cannot be instantiated as "OTHER". In fact, as we report in Section 2.3, the variety of reasoning underlying ARs in the corpus we use can be largely captured by only a small number of predefined templates. Although the ex-

pressibility of a slot-filler will be reduced by embedding causal labels into our templates, the feasibility of the computational task will be increased. In the future, we plan to capture the causal information lost by annotating other factors of the causality such as severity, truthfulness, likelihood, etc.

2.1 Dataset

We create our set of ATs using the arg-microtexts corpus[3] (Peldszus and Stede, 2015a), a corpus of manually composed arguments, due to its high reliability of annotated relations amongst 3 annotators (Fleiss $\kappa = 0.83$).[4] The corpus contains 112 argumentative texts, each consisting of roughly five segments composed of a policy topic question, a main claim, and several premises. Each argument in a text is comprised of a policy argument, where each topic supports that one should or should not do something. Additionally, each argumentative segment was annotated with its stance (i.e. *opponent* or *proponent*) towards the topic question. 357 ARs between segments have been manually annotated as either SUPPORT (i.e. a segment supports the acceptability of another argumentative segment), ATTACK (i.e. a segment attacks the acceptability of another argumentative segment), or UNDERCUT (i.e. a segment attacks another AR) relations, where each relation makes up 62.7% (224/357), 23.5% (84/357) and 13.8% (49/357), respectively.

In total, we used 89 texts[5], consisting of 23 diverse policy topics (e.g. *fines for dog dirt, waste separation*, etc.). We divided the corpus into two

---

[2] A target segment may either be a premise or conclusion in our dataset. Therefore, we consider the classification of x equivalent to its consequence (i.e. x=bad is equivalent to "x should not be brought about").

[3] https://github.com/peldszus/arg-microtexts

[4] Although the texts from the arg-microtexts corpus are controlled in a sense that they are not from "real" argumentative texts, we believe annotation on top of it is a good starting point due to its high reliability.

[5] The corpus has 112 texts, but we ignored 23 of the texts which did not include a topic question.

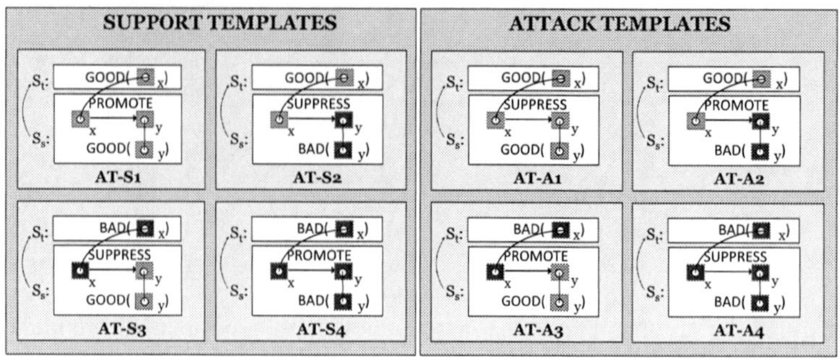

Figure 2: Some argument templates created and used in our corpus creation for SUPPORT and ATTACK relations, inspired by Walton et al. (2008)'s *Argument from Consequences* scheme.

disjoint sets: (i) a development set (20 texts, 87 relations) and (ii) test set (69 texts, 270 relations). We used the development set to induce the ATs described in Section 2.2 and conduct several trial annotations.

2.2 Argument Templates

We build our inventory of ATs based on Walton et al. (2008)'s argumentation schemes and analyze the development set for identifying the types of argumentation schemes. As the arg-microtexts corpus consists of policy arguments, we find that the most commonly used argumentation schemes from the corpus include the *Argument from Positive (Negative) Consequences* schemes, hereby referred to as the *Argument from Consequences* (AC) scheme. The scheme is as follows:

- Premise : If x is brought about, good (bad) consequences y will occur.

- Conclusion: x should (not) be brought about.

We create ATs for a SUPPORT relation by considering the relation between the premise and conclusion (e.g. S_s and S_t in Figure 1, respectively).

To represent ATTACK relations with argumentation schemes, we assume that a premise supports the opposite conclusion.

(2) S_t: *German universities should not **charge tuition fees.***
S_s: *However, tuition fees could promote **better education quality.***

For instance, in Example 2, an ATTACK relation exists from S_s to S_t. The premise, S_s, is in support

of the opposite conclusion (i.e. "German universities should charge tuition fees"). We represent this phenomena using the ATTACK templates shown in Figure 2.

AC-inspired templates As shown in Figure 2, we first create four ATs for a SUPPORT relation (AT-S1 to AT-S4). An example is as follows:

AT-S1: S_t, the target segment, implies/states that x, an entity/event, is GOOD and should be brought about. S_s, the source segment, implies/states that x is GOOD, because when x exists/happens (or existed/happened), y, a GOOD entity/event, will be (or was) PRO-MOTED (or NOT SUPPRESSED)[6]

In Example 1, the reasoning is instantiated by AT-S3, with x="*charge tuition fees*", a BAD thing, and y="*a right to education*", a GOOD thing.

The terms GOOD and BAD refer to the value judgment (VJ) a writer has towards a template slot. This differs from the original stance in the arg-microtexts corpus, which considers the stance of the whole argumentative segment towards the topic. PROMOTE and SUPPRESS refer to the causality between slot-fillers x and y, where PROMOTE refers to the activation of something (e.g. *smoking leads to cancer*) and SUPPRESS refers to the inactivation (e.g. *smoking destroys lives*) (Hashimoto et al., 2012). To reduce the complexity of the annotation study, we do not consider the modality of causality.

For an ATTACK relation, we create four ATs (AT-A1 to AT-A4), as illustrated in Figure 2.

---

[6]For our annotation, we consider both PROMOTED and NOT SUPPRESSED and both SUPPRESSED and NOT PRO-MOTED as equivalent in order to control the complexity of the task.

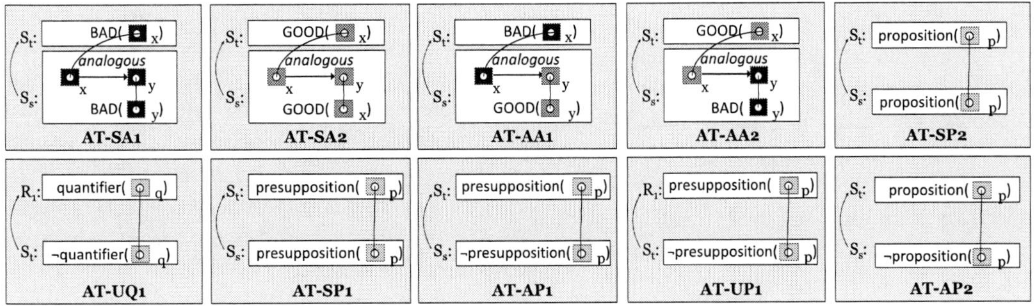

Figure 3: Argument templates for non-AC reasoning.

AT-A1: S_t implies/states that x is GOOD and should be brought about, but S_s implies/states that x is BAD because when x exists/happens (or happened), y, a GOOD entity/event, will be (or was) SUPPRESSED (or NOT PROMOTED).

In Example 2, the reasoning is instantiated by AT-A3, with x="*corporate income tax*", a BAD thing, and y="*better education quality*", a GOOD thing.

Additional templates We create a few ATs to capture minor, non-AC reasoning for each relation, including UNDERCUT relations. In total, we create four additional types of ATs: *presupposition, argument from analogy, proposition,* and *quantifier*. We create four templates (not shown) for an UNDERCUT relation. We thus assume S_t as a link, denoted as R_t. An example is as follows:

AT-U1: R_t supports the goodness of x, but S_s implies/states that x is BAD because when x happens (or happened), y, a GOOD thing, will be (or was) SUPPRESSED (or NOT PROMOTED).

Figure 3 shows *analogous* and *propositional* templates for SUPPORT (AT-SA1 and AT-SA2) and ATTACK (AT-AA1 and AT-AA2) relations. The template is as follows (e.g. AT-AA1):

AT-AA1: S_t states that x is BAD, and S_s states that x is BAD because y is BAD and is analogous to x.

For the UNDERCUT relation, our analysis revealed that a quantifier in a relation could be attacked. Thus, we create the template AT-UQ1 for UNDERCUT, represented as:

AT-UQ1: R_1 assumes a quantifier q, but S_s disagrees with it.

(3) R_{1S_x}: *Intelligent services must urgently be regulated more tightly by parliament;*
R_{1S_y}: *this should be clear to everyone after the disclosures of Edward Snowden.*
S_s: *Granted, those concern primarily the British and American intelligence services,*

In Example 3, R_1, a SUPPORT(S_x,S_y) relation, assumes that *all* intelligent services should be regulated more tightly; however, S_s states that *only* two services are concerned.

To capture the argument where the underlying assumptions in one segment are supported or attacked by another, we introduce the relations AT-SP1, AT-AP1, and AT-UP1 for SUPPORT, ATTACK, and UNDERCUT, respectively. The template can be interpreted as follows (e.g. AT-AP1):

AT-AP1: S_t assumes a presupposition p, but S_s agrees with it.

(4) S_t: *For dog dirt left on the pavement dog owners should by all means pay a bit more.*
S_s: *Indeed, it's not the fault of the animals*

In Example 4, S_t presupposes that dog dirt is the fault of the animals, but S_s disagrees. Thus, template AT-AP1 would be selected.[7]

We also create templates for propositional explanations, represented in templates AT-SP2 and AT-AP2. The templates can be interpreted as follows (e.g. AT-SP2):

AT-SP2: S_t states a proposition p, and S_s restates it.

---

[7] ¬presupposition means that S_s disagrees with the presupposition in S_t (R_1 in the case of UNDERCUT). This notion is similar for *quantifier* and *proposition*.

2.3 Annotation Study

For testing the feasibility of our templates, we observe two metrics using the test set: (i) inter-annotator agreement and (ii) template coverage. For our inter-annotator agreement study, we asked two fluent-English speakers with knowledge of ASs to explain each AR with an argument template and to fill in the template's slots using the annotation tool brat (Stenetorp et al., 2012). To study the coverage of relations which can be represented with an AT, we asked the annotators to mark a relation as the special pattern "OTHER" when any AT cannot be instantiated for a given relation. The annotators were given the original, segmented argumentative text, its ARs (i.e. SUPPORT, ATTACK, and UNDERCUT relations), and the predefined list of ATs. As a training phase, both of the annotators were asked to annotate the development set and to discuss disagreements amongst each other.

Next, the annotators were instructed to individually annotate all 270 relations in the test set. As we were aware that an annotation may consist of two or more compatible instantiations, one being more salient than the others, we wanted to regard all semantically compatible templates as correct. For example, consider the following text from the annotation: S_t: *The death penalty should be abandoned.* S_s: *Innocent people are convicted.* Both of the annotators agreed that an AT from Figure 2 was appropriate and slot x was "*death penalty*". However, one annotator chose AT-A3 with y = "*Innocent people*", a GOOD entity, and the other annotator chose AT-A4 with y = "*Innocent people are convicted*", a BAD event. The annotators agreed with each other's annotation because PROMOTE(*death penalty, Innocent people are convicted*) and SUPPRESS(*death penalty, Innocent people*) are semantically compatible.

Therefore, when analyzing the inter-annotator agreement, we categorized each pair of template instantiations as "*agreeable*" if the following conditions were met: (i) the ATs selected by both annotators are exactly the same *and* the phrases associated with the template slots are exactly the same or overlapped, *or* (ii) if (i) was not met, each of the annotators agreed on the other's annotation.[8] 46.3% (125/270) of the relations were categorized as "*agreeable*" for (i) only. For both (i) and (ii),

85.9% (232/270) of the relations were categorized as "*agreeable*". The Cohen's Kappa (κ) score is 0.80, indicating a good agreement. This difference in agreement signifies the variety of semantically compatible instances for a given pair of argumentative relations. This also indicates the importance of conducting a large-scale annotation, where a pair of ARs may have two or more semantically compatible instances.

The coverage of relations representable with an AT for the test set is 74.6% (173/232).[9]. Although our set of ATs is small, we cover a majority of patterns on a test set consisting of multiple, diverse topics. Our results support our hypothesis that ATs are not uniformly distributed but highly skewed.

3 Instantiating ATs with Constrained Structured Prediction

3.1 Overview

The full-fledged task of automatically instantiating ATs for two argumentative segments is computationally challenging due to a large amount of arbitrary slot-fillers x and y for an AT. As a first step towards full-fledged parsing, due to the small size of our corpus, we simplify this challenge in our current task setting by (i) limiting AT instantiations to ATTACK and SUPPORT relations instantiated with an AC template (i.e. 8 templates in Figure 2) due to the low distributions of other ATs (e.g. *undercut, presupposition*, etc) and (ii) assuming slot-fillers x and y have already been identified. In our future work, we will relax these conditions by testing against arbitrary slot-filler pairs and reasoning which may not be instantiated using ATs.

Let us formally define the simplified task of AT instantiation. Our input is two argumentative segments S_t, S_s and slot-fillers x in S_t and y in S_s. Our output is an appropriate AT representing the writer's reasoning behind S_t and S_s in terms of slot-fillers x, y. To represent an AT instantiation, we use the notation $\langle r, v_x, c, v_y \rangle$, where $r \in \{\text{SUPPORT}, \text{ATTACK}\}$, $v_x, v_y \in \{\text{GOOD}, \text{BAD}\}$ and $c \in \{\text{PROMOTE}, \text{SUPPRESS}\}$ represent an argumentative relation, a VJ of slot-fillers x and y, and the type of causality from x to y, respectively (e.g. $\langle \text{SUPPORT}, \text{BAD}, \text{PROMOTE}, \text{BAD} \rangle$ for AT-S4). We refer to r, v_x, c, v_y as *AT ingredients*.

The core idea of the proposed method is as follows. Observing the AT dev set, we found that

---

contextual clues are typically not available for *all* AT ingredients but for *some* AT ingredients. Thus, we hypothesize that AT ingredients with no explicit clue can be inferred using the knowledge of ATs their ingredients identified by explicit clues. In Example 1, for instance, if we already know that (i) the value judgment v_x of *"charge tuition fees"* is BAD, (ii) the value judgment v_y of *"a right to education"* is GOOD, and (iii) the argumentative relation r is SUPPORT, then we can uniquely identify that the causality is SUPPRESS.

3.2 Models for AT ingredients

We create three models $m_{\text{arg}}, m_{\text{val}}$, and m_{cau} for identifying an AR, VJ, and causality, each of which returns a confidence score of their decision. As this is the first attempt at automating the instantiation of ATs, we use simple models for identifying AT ingredients rather than developing sophisticated models. This makes the framework transparent and analysis simple while allowing us to examine the effectiveness of template constraints.

Value Judgment (m_{val}) We train a Support Vector Machine (SVM)-based binary classifier (Cortes and Vapnik, 1995) to identify the VJ of the given slot-fillers x, y (i.e. GOOD or BAD). From observation of the AT dev set, we found the following features useful for VJ identification: (i) auxiliary verbs (e.g. *should, must, ought*) and (ii) negated auxiliary verbs (e.g. *should not, must not*).[10] We also found that adjectives, both inside and outside a slot-filler, are useful. For example, consider the following text: *"Yes, it is annoying and cumbersome **to separate your trash$_x$**"*. The keywords *annoying* and *cumbersome* explicitly indicate that the VJ of the slot-filler x (i.e. *to separate your trash*) is *bad*. Simultaneously, we discovered that slot-fillers had clues themselves for indicating VJ (e.g. *Innocent* in *"Innocent people"*). Thus, we introduce two additional features: (iii) the average sentiment of each adjective outside the slot-filler and (iv) inside the slot-filler.[11]

Causal Relations (m_{cau}) We develop a simple rule-based classifier for identifying causal relations between the given slot-fillers x and y. We use a predefined list of causal phrases (i.e. *causes, will lead to*, etc. for PROMOTE, and *destroy,*

kill, etc. for SUPPRESS) composed from Reisert et al. (2015). We use the AT development set to expand the phrase list for any PROMOTE or SUPPRESS phrases not in the list. Given the source S_s and target S_t segments, we use the following rules: If a PROMOTE phrase appears *after* x in S_t, then predict PROMOTE with a confidence score of *1.0*, namely $m_{\text{cau}}(\text{PROMOTE}) = 1.0, m_{\text{cau}}(\text{SUPPRESS}) = 0.0$. The same rule is applied to a SUPPRESS phrase. Else if a PROMOTE phrase appears *before* y in S_s, then predict PROMOTE with a confidence score of *1.0*. The same rule is applied to a SUPPRESS phrase. Otherwise (i.e. there are no PROMOTE or SUPPRESS phrases), we predict PROMOTE, the majority relation (66%) in the AT development set. Since we are less confident than other ingredients if there is no contextual clue for the causality, we set the confidence scores to $m_{\text{cau}}(\text{PROMOTE}) = \varepsilon, m_{\text{cau}}(\text{SUPPRESS}) = 0.1\varepsilon$. ε is a number less than all confidence scores given by AR and VJ models.

Argumentative Relations (m_{arg}) We replicate a simple classification model (Peldszus and Stede, 2015b) for identifying the argumentative relation between given segments S_s and S_t (as either SUPPORT or ATTACK). The classifier is based on a logistic regression and uses surface features such as lemma, part-of-speech tags, and segment length from the source and target segments.

3.3 Putting all things together

To instantiate an AT, we use a standard linear model constrained by ATs as follows:

$$\underset{r, v_x, c, v_y}{\arg\max} \mathbf{w} \cdot \Phi(r, v_x, c, v_y) \text{s.t.} \langle r, v_x, c, v_y \rangle \in T,$$

where $\mathbf{w}$ is a weight vector, Φ is a feature function of an AT instantiation $\langle r, v_x, c, v_y \rangle$ and T represents the SUPPORT and ATTACK templates from Figure 2. The feature function $\Phi(r, v_x, c, v_y)$ returns an 8-dimensional feature vector characterizing an AT instantiation as follows: $\{m_{\text{arg}}(\text{SUPPORT}), m_{\text{arg}}(\text{ATTACK}), m_{\text{val}}(x, \text{GOOD}), m_{\text{val}}(x, \text{BAD}), m_{\text{cau}}(\text{PROMOTE}), m_{\text{cau}}(\text{SUPPRESS}), m_{\text{val}}(y, \text{GOOD}), m_{\text{val}}(y, \text{BAD})\}$. We use the confidence values of each AT ingredient calculated by the separate models described in Section 3.2. For instance, given an AT instantiation $\langle \text{SUPPORT}, \text{BAD}, \text{PROMOTE}, \text{BAD} \rangle$, we create the following feature vector: $\{m_{\text{arg}}(\text{SUPPORT}), 0, 0, m_{\text{val}}(x, \text{BAD}), m_{\text{cau}}(\text{PROMOTE}), 0, 0, m_{\text{val}}(y, \text{BAD})\}$. We

---

[10] We parse each segment using Spacy (Honnibal and Johnson, 2015).

[11] We use an existing sentiment lexicon (Warriner et al., 2013) to extract the sentiment polarity of each adjective.

learn $\mathbf{w}$ on training data by using an averaged structured perceptron (Collins, 2002). We call this a *template-constrained inference model*, or **TCI**. To see the effectiveness, we consider the model without $\langle r, v_x, c, v_y \rangle \in T$, which we call *non-constrained inference model*, or **NI**. If the NI model's output does not match an AT, we output $\langle \text{SUPPORT}, \text{GOOD}, \text{PROMOTE}, \text{GOOD} \rangle$ (AT-S1), the majority AT in the dev set.

The advantage of TCI is that if a model of each ingredient is not confident about its prediction and the most-likely AT is invalid, the wrong prediction can be fixed by combining the knowledge of ATs and other confident AT ingredient predictions. The NI model entirely depends on the independent decision of each ingredient model, regardless of whether the predictions are confident or not, which is compensated by TCI.

4 Evaluation

4.1 Setting

In Section 2, the annotators were given an argumentative relation and instructed to instantiate an AT. Towards fully automating the task of AT instantiation, we also test our system when no argumentative relation is given. Therefore, we consider two settings: (i) predict an AT with the gold-standard argumentative relation (G) and (ii) with no gold-standard relation (N). Thus, we examine four models: *NI-G, NI-N, TCI-G*, and *TCI-N*.[12]

For all models for AT instantiation, we conduct a 5x10-fold cross validation using 231 unique SUPPORT and ATTACK AC instantiations collected from the annotations on the 69 texts (270 relations) from our test set.[13] In each fold, we create a validation set consisting of one-fifth of the training data. We then oversample the training data. We employ early stopping with a patience of 2 and measure its performance using the accuracy of predictions on the validation set.

4.2 Results and discussion

The results (F_1 score) for the $m_{\text{arg}}, m_{\text{val}}$, and m_{cau} subtask models are as follows: 0.59, 0.65, 0.42. The results indicate that the rule-based causality classifier has lower performance. We attribute this

---

[12]For m_{val}, we estimate the hyperparameters of SVM by performing an exhaustive grid search with a 3-fold cross-validation on the AT dev set instances (Radial Basis Function (RBF) kernel, c=1000, gamma=0.005).

[13]One relation may have two unique, semantically compatible instantiations amongst our two annotators.

Table 1: Performance of our AT instantiation models with standard deviation across 5-folds.

Model	Precision	Recall	F1
Majority	0.03±0.00	0.12±0.00	0.05±0.00
Random	0.02±0.01	0.12±0.00	0.04±0.01
NI-N	0.17±0.06	0.17±0.02	0.13±0.01
TCI-N	**0.23±0.01**	**0.21±0.02**	**0.19±0.01**
NI-G	0.35±0.08	0.24±0.01	0.21±0.02
TCI-G	**0.44±0.02**	**0.41±0.02**	**0.38±0.01**

Table 2: The performance of implicit causality (CS) and value judgment (VJ) ingredients between NI-G / TCI-G.

Ing.	Precision	Recall	F1
CS	0.48 / **0.88**	0.43 / **0.88**	0.38 / **0.88**
VJ	0.59 / **0.61**	**0.65** / 0.62	0.57 / **0.60**

to the lack of explicit contextual clues indicating the causality between slot-fillers. Through a subjective analysis, we found that roughly 88% of causal relations are implicit in the AT test set, thus PROMOTE is mainly predicted.

Table 1 shows the results of AT instantiation. The low performance of a majority and random baseline indicates that the AT instantiation task is not simple. The proposed models (NI, TCI) clearly outperform these baseline models. The TCI model consistently outperforms the NI model in both settings G and N. This indicates that template constraints are useful for instantiating ATs.

To further test our hypothesis that AT ingredients without an explicit contextual clue (i.e. implicit) can be inferred with a template constraint, we manually analyzed all 231 of the testing instances and label whether or not an explicit contextual clue exists for VJ and causality. We then compared the accuracies of each ingredient on implicit problem instances for NI-G and TCI-G. Shown in Table 2 are our results which indicate that our model is able to infer ingredients with no explicit contextual clue more reasonably with the introduction of a template constraint, especially in the case of causality.

The following shows an AT without an explicit contextual clue for causality that was predicted correctly using TCI-G: "S_t: *Nevertheless, everybody should contribute to the funding of **the public broadcasters**$_x$ in equal measure, S_s: for we need general and independent media$_y$.*", where explicit clues (i.e. *should contribute to* and *we need*) indicate the VJ of x, y, both GOOD, but the causality between x and y is implicit. Combining this with the SUPPORT relation, the template constraints indicate that AT-S1 is the only possibility.

5 Related Work

ATs   Reed (2006) annotated the Araucaria corpus (Reed, 2006) with Walton et al. (2008)'s argumentation schemes (AS), and successive work (Feng and Hirst, 2011) created a machine learning-model to classify an argument into five sets of schemes. However, Reed (2006) does not report the inter-annotator agreement. Lawrence and Reed (2016) created a model for instantiating ASs with a natural language representation, whereas we instantiate using templates and slot-fillers. Green (2015) conducted work on identifying new ASs used in biomedical articles.

Several argumentative corpora have been created for argumentation mining fields such as argument component identification, argument component classification, and structure identification (Reed et al., 2008; Rinott et al., 2015; Stab and Gurevych, 2014). Earlier work on discourse structure analysis includes discourse theories such as Rhetorical Structure Theory (Mann and Thompson, 1987). The Penn Discourse TreeBank, the largest manually annotated corpus for discourse relations, targeted both implicit and explicit relation detection for either adjacent sentences or clauses (Prasad et al., 2008). However, these studies do not aim for capturing implicit reasoning behind arguments.

AT ingredients   Although we adopted a simple approach for AT ingredient identification for our first attempt (see Section 3.2), many sophisticated approaches have been proposed. Shallow discourse analysis of ARs has been extensively studied (Cocarascu and Toni, 2017; Niculae et al., 2017; Peldszus and Stede, 2015a,b). VJ identification is similar to targeted sentiment analysis (Mitchell et al., 2013; Dong et al., 2014). Somasundaran and Wiebe (2010) developed an annotation method for targeted sentiment. However, we aim to expand the annotation to other types of arguments, and their work only considers the task setting of stance classification. Finally, causal relation identification between an entity pair in a sentence has been studied (Zhang and Wang, 2015). In the future, we will incorporate these sophisticated techniques into our model.

6 Conclusion and future work

In this work, we propose a feasible annotation scheme for capturing a writer's reasoning in argumentative texts. We first developed a small list of predefined templates (ATs) for capturing the reasoning of ARs, where each template encodes a causal label that enables annotators to avoid manual generation of natural language slot-fillers, and conducted a corpus study. Our results indicate that ATs are highly skewed, and even with a small set of ATs, we can capture a majority of reasoning (74.6%) for multiple, diverse policy topics. We believe that the design decision to leave a wide variety of long-tailed, minor classes of reasoning as "OTHER" helps keep the AT instantiation simple. Furthermore, our results can be considered a good achievement (Cohen's κ=0.80). The annotated corpus is made publicly available.[14] We then created several preliminary models for automatically instantiating ATs. We discovered that template-constrained inference helps towards instantiating ATs with implicit ingredients necessary for understanding the reasoning behind an argument.

In the future, we will extend our work by conducting a large-scale annotation of ATs using methods such as crowdsourcing, and we will experiment with full-fledged parsing via recent neural models for capturing argumentative component features (Eger et al., 2017; Schulz et al., 2018; Ajjour et al., 2017). We plan to use other available argumentative corpora for conducting our experiments. We will also work towards expanding our templates and integrating them into the argument reasoning task proposed in SemEval2018 (Habernal et al., 2017). Finally, we plan to capture the causal information lost by annotating other factors of the causality such as severity, truthfulness, likelihood, to name a few.

Acknowledgements

This work was supported by JSPS KAKENHI Grant Number 15H01702 and JST CREST Grant Number JPMJCR1513. We would like to thank Jan Šnajder and all reviewers of this work for their useful comments and feedback.

---

[14] https://github.com/preisert/argument-reasoning-patterns

References

Yamen Ajjour, Wei-Fan Chen, Johannes Kiesel, Henning Wachsmuth, and Benno Stein. 2017. Unit segmentation of argumentative texts. In *Proceedings of the 4th Workshop on Argument Mining*, pages 118–128. Association for Computational Linguistics.

Oana Cocarascu and Francesca Toni. 2017. Identifying attack and support argumentative relations using deep learning. In *Proceedings of the 2017 Conference on EMNLP*, pages 1385–1390.

Michael Collins. 2002. Discriminative training methods for hidden markov models: Theory and experiments with perceptron algorithms. In *Proceedings of the ACL-02 conference on EMNLP*, pages 1–8.

Corinna Cortes and Vladimir Vapnik. 1995. Support-vector networks. *Machine learning*, 20(3):273–297.

Li Dong, Furu Wei, Chuanqi Tan, Duyu Tang, Ming Zhou, and Ke Xu. 2014. Adaptive recursive neural network for target-dependent twitter sentiment classification. In *Proceedings of ACL*, pages 49–54.

Steffen Eger, Johannes Daxenberger, and Iryna Gurevych. 2017. Neural end-to-end learning for computational argumentation mining. In *Proceedings of the ACL*, pages 11–22.

Vanessa Wei Feng and Graeme Hirst. 2011. Classifying arguments by scheme. In *Proceedings of ACL*, pages 987–996.

Debanjan Ghosh, Aquila Khanam, Yubo Han, and Smaranda Muresan. 2016. Coarse-grained argumentation features for scoring persuasive essays. In *Proceedings of ACL*, volume 2, pages 549–554.

Nancy L Green. 2015. Identifying argumentation schemes in genetics research articles. *Proceedings of the Second Workshop on Argumentation Mining*, pages 12–21.

Ivan Habernal, Henning Wachsmuth, Iryna Gurevych, and Benno Stein. 2017. The argument reasoning comprehension task. *arXiv preprint arXiv:1708.01425*.

Kazi Saidul Hasan and Vincent Ng. 2014. Why are you taking this stance? identifying and classifying reasons in ideological debates. In *Proceedings of EMNLP*, pages 751–762.

Chikara Hashimoto, Kentaro Torisawa, Stijn De Saeger, Jong-Hoon Oh, and Jun'ichi Kazama. 2012. Excitatory or inhibitory: A new semantic orientation extracts contradiction and causality from the web. In *Proceedings of the 2012 Joint Conference on EMNLP and CoNLL*, pages 619–630.

Matthew Honnibal and Mark Johnson. 2015. An improved non-monotonic transition system for dependency parsing. In *Proceedings of the 2015 Conference on EMNLP*, pages 1373–1378.

John Lawrence and Chris Reed. 2016. Argument mining using argumentation scheme structures. In *Computational Models of Argument*, pages 379–390.

William C Mann and Sandra A Thompson. 1987. Rhetorical structure theory: Description and construction of text structures. In *Natural Language Generation*, pages 85–95.

Margaret Mitchell, Jacqui Aguilar, Theresa Wilson, and Benjamin Van Durme. 2013. Open Domain Targeted Sentiment. In *Proceedings of EMNLP*, pages 1643–1654.

Elena Musi, Debanjan Ghosh, and Smaranda Muresan. 2016. Towards feasible guidelines for the annotation of argument schemes. In *Proceedings of the Third Workshop on Argument Mining*, pages 82–93.

Vlad Niculae, Joonsuk Park, and Claire Cardie. 2017. Argument mining with structured svms and rnns. *arXiv preprint arXiv:1704.06869*.

Rudi Palmieri. 2014. *Corporate argumentation in takeover bids*, volume 8. John Benjamins Publishing Company.

Andreas Peldszus and Manfred Stede. 2015a. An annotated corpus of argumentative microtexts. In *Proceedings of the First Conference on Argumentation*, pages 801–815.

Andreas Peldszus and Manfred Stede. 2015b. Joint prediction in mst-style discourse parsing for argumentation mining. In *Proceedings of EMNLP*, pages 938–948.

Isaac Persing and Vincent Ng. 2016. Modeling Stance in Student Essays. In *Proceedings of ACL*, pages 2174–2184.

Rashmi Prasad, Nikhil Dinesh, Alan Lee, Eleni Miltsakaki, Livio Robaldo, Aravind K Joshi, and Bonnie L Webber. 2008. The penn discourse treebank 2.0. In *Proceedings of LREC*, pages 2961–2968.

Chris Reed. 2006. Preliminary results from an argument corpus. *Linguistics in the twenty-first century*, pages 185–196.

Chris Reed, Raquel Mochales Palau, Glenn Rowe, and Marie-Francine Moens. 2008. Language resources for studying argument. In *Proceedings of LREC*, pages 91–100.

Paul Reisert, Naoya Inoue, Naoaki Okazaki, and Kentaro Inui. 2015. A computational approach for generating toulmin model argumentation. In *In Proceedings of the Second Workshop on Argumentation Mining*, pages 45âĂŞ55.

Eddo Rigotti. 2006. Relevance of context-bound loci to topical potential in the argumentation stage. *Argumentation*, 20(4):519–540.

Ruty Rinott, Lena Dankin, Carlos Alzate, Mitesh M Khapra, Ehud Aharoni, and Noam Slonim. 2015. Show me your evidence–an automatic method for context dependent evidence detection. In *Proceedings of the 2015 Conference on EMNLP*, pages 17–21.

Claudia Schulz, Steffen Eger, Johannes Daxenberger, Tobias Kahse, and Iryna Gurevych. 2018. Multi-task learning for argumentation mining in low-resource settings. In *Proceedings of NAACL*, pages 35–41. Association for Computational Linguistics.

Swapna Somasundaran and Janyce Wiebe. 2010. Recognizing stances in ideological on-line debates. In *Proceedings of the NAACL HLT 2010 Workshop on Computational Approaches to Analysis and Generation of Emotion in Text*, pages 116–124. Association for Computational Linguistics.

Yi Song, Michael Heilman, Beata Beigman Klebanov, and Paul Deane. 2014. Applying argumentation schemes for essay scoring. *Proceedings of the First Workshop on Argumentation Mining*, pages 69–78.

Christian Stab and Iryna Gurevych. 2014. Annotating argument components and relations in persuasive essays. In *Proceedings of COLING*, pages 1501–1510.

Christian Stab and Iryna Gurevych. 2017. Parsing argumentation structures in persuasive essays. *Computational Linguistics*, 43(3):619–659.

Pontus Stenetorp, Sampo Pyysalo, Goran Topić, Tomoko Ohta, Sophia Ananiadou, and Jun'ichi Tsujii. 2012. Brat: a web-based tool for nlp-assisted text annotation. In *Proceedings of EACL*, pages 102–107.

Henning Wachsmuth, Khalid Al-Khatib, and Benno Stein. 2016. Using argument mining to assess the argumentation quality of essays. In *Proceedings of COLING*, pages 1680–1691.

Douglas Walton, Christopher Reed, and Fabrizio Macagno. 2008. *Argumentation schemes*. Cambridge University Press.

Amy Beth Warriner, Victor Kuperman, and Marc Brysbaert. 2013. Norms of valence, arousal, and dominance for 13,915 english lemmas. *Behavior research methods*, 45(4):1191–1207.

Dongxu Zhang and Dong Wang. 2015. Relation classification via recurrent neural network. *arXiv preprint arXiv:1508.01006*.

A   Supplemental Material

A.1   Corpus distribution

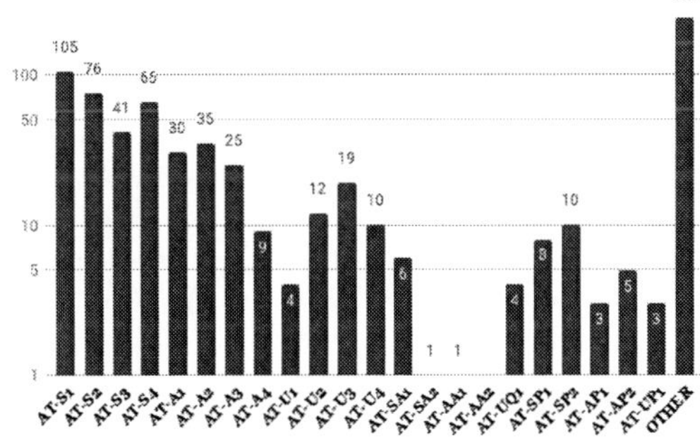

Figure 4: Distribution of argumentation templates in our full corpus (i.e. dev and test set).

Frame- and Entity-Based Knowledge for
Common-Sense Argumentative Reasoning

Teresa Botschen[*]   **Daniil Sorokin**[*]   **Iryna Gurevych**

Ubiquitous Knowledge Processing Lab (UKP) and Research Training Group AIPHES
Department of Computer Science, Technische Universität Darmstadt
`www.ukp.tu-darmstadt.de`

Abstract

Common-sense argumentative reasoning is a challenging task that requires holistic understanding of the argumentation where external knowledge about the world is hypothesized to play a key role. We explore the idea of using event knowledge about prototypical situations from FrameNet and fact knowledge about concrete entities from Wikidata to solve the task. We find that both resources can contribute to an improvement over the non-enriched approach and point out two persisting challenges: first, integration of many annotations of the same type, and second, fusion of complementary annotations. After our explorations, we question the key role of external world knowledge with respect to the argumentative reasoning task and rather point towards a logic-based analysis of the chain of reasoning.

1 Introduction

Recently, Habernal et al. (2018) introduced a challenging dataset for Argument Reasoning Comprehension (ARC) used in the SemEval-2018 shared task. After reviewing the participating systems, they hypothesize that *external world knowledge may be essential for ARC*.[1] We explore enriching models with event and fact knowledge on ARC to investigate into this hypothesis.

Semantic tasks profit from external knowledge: language understanding requires more complex knowledge than that contained in current systems and word embeddings. For the task of semantic plausibility, Wang et al. (2018) reveal the failure of models only relying on distributional data, whilst the injection of world knowledge helps. Glockner et al. (2018) point out the deficiency of state-of-the-art approaches for understanding entailment on

the large-scale SNLI corpus (Stanford Natural Language Inference) (Bowman et al., 2015). In their study, the model incorporating external lexical information from WordNet, KIM (Knowledge-based Inference Model) (Chen et al., 2018), does not yield the awaited improvements — where the crucial point might be WordNet (Miller, 1995) which does not contain explicit world knowledge in the form of event- and fact-based knowledge. Previous work argues that information in WordNet overlaps with word embeddings (Zhai et al., 2016), therefore we focus on other types of knowledge in our work.

Complementary sources of external knowledge: we experiment using the lexical-semantic resource FrameNet (FN) and the knowledge base Wikidata (WD). These resources provide information beyond the lexical relations encoded in WordNet and thus have a potential to enhance the underlying model with other kind of external world knowledge. On the one hand, FN provides qualitative event-knowledge about prototypical situations. Thus, identifying frames (FrameId) unveils the situation or action that is happening. On the other hand, WD provides fact-knowledge about the concrete entities. So, linking entities to a knowledge base (EntLink) disambiguates the participants. Furthermore, both resources provide meta-knowledge about how their frames or entries relate to each other.

Multiple levels of knowledge processing help: combining several kinds of annotations benefits question answering (Khashabi et al., 2018), external knowledge about synonyms enhances inference (Chen et al., 2018), and jointly modeling several tasks (e.g., frame-semantic parsing and dependency parsing) is fruitful (Peng et al., 2018). In particular, the idea of connecting event semantics and fact knowledge was confirmed by Guo et al. (2016): they jointly formalize semantic role labeling and relation classification and thereby improve upon PropBank semantic role labeling.

---

[*] First and second authors contributed equally to this work.

[1] SemEval-2018 Task 12: `https://competitions.codalab.org/competitions/17327`

90

Proceedings of the 5th Workshop on Argument Mining, pages 90–96
Brussels, Belgium, November 1, 2018. ©2018 Association for Computational Linguistics

Outline In this paper, we investigate whether external information in terms of event-based frames (FN) and fact-based entities (WD) can contribute to holistic understanding of the argumentation in the ARC task. First, we examine the effect of both annotations separately and second, we explore whether a joint annotation benefits from the inherent complementarity of the schemata in FN and WD and eventually leads to a better annotation coverage. We enhance the baseline model provided with the ARC task in order to contrast three system configurations: '+FN', '+WD' and '+FN/WD'.

Contributions We *(1)* present a proof of concept for semantic enrichment for the ARC task, *(2)* identify the importance of advanced combinations of complementary semantic annotations and *(3)* question the key role of external world knowledge with respect to ARC.

Code The code for the experiments with the enriched model is available online: `https://github.com/UKPLab/emnlp2018-argmin-commonsense-knowledge`

2 Our Approach: Semantic Enrichment for Argument Reasoning Comprehension (ARC)

First, we explain the ARC task together with the baseline that we will build upon (cf. Sec. 2.1). Second, we review our two external knowledge sources, FN and WD, and comment on their complementarity (cf. Sec. 2.2, 2.3, 2.4). Finally, we present our approach with preprocessing and the actual model enrichment (cf. Sec. 2.5, 2.6).

2.1 ARC Task

The ARC task (Habernal et al., 2018) is formulated as follows: given a debate title (a), claim (b) and reason (c), a system chooses the correct warrant (i) over the other (ii), see Figure 1. The warrants vary only slightly, e.g., by a single negation. The argumentation chain is sophisticated and uses logical reasoning and language understanding. In order to automatically draw the correct decision, a holistic

(a)	<u>title</u>: Can companies be trusted?
(b)	<u>claim</u>: Companies can't be trusted.
(c)	<u>reason</u>: Corporations have only goal: to make a profit.
(i)	**warrant**: they do not have to satisfy customers to make a profit
(ii)	<u>warrant</u>: they have to satisfy customers to make a profit

Figure 1: An instance of the ARC corpus, illustrating title (a), claim (b), reason (c) and the warrants (i) and (ii).

understanding of the context of both, claim and reason, is crucial – for which Habernal et al. (2018) recommend the inclusion of external knowledge.

Baseline The baseline provided by Habernal et al. (2018) is an intra-warrant attention model that reads in *Word2Vec* vectors (Mikolov et al., 2013) of all words in (a-c) and adapts attention weights for the decision between (i) and (ii).

Shared task winner The shared task winner, GIST (Choi and Lee, 2018), transfers inference knowledge (SNLI, Bowman et al., 2015) to the task of ARC and benefits from similar information in both datasets.

Our approach in contrast to GIST Our approach extends the baseline model with two external knowledge schemata, FN and WD, to explore their effects. The intuition can be explained with the instance in Figure 1: FN could be helpful by disambiguating 'companies' and 'corporations' to the same frame with meta-knowledge how it relates to other frames and WD could be of additional help by mapping them to entities with detailed information and examples for such institutions. We focus on utilizing the two knowledge schemata of FN and WD and thus, our interest is orthogonal to GIST. The advantage of our approach is independence of domain and task, which becomes especially relevant in scenarios lacking large-scale support data.

2.2 FrameNet's Event Knowledge

The Berkeley FrameNet (Baker et al., 1998; Ruppenhofer et al., 2016) is an ongoing project for manually building a large lexical-semantic resource with expert annotations. It embodies the theory of frame semantics (Fillmore, 1976): frames capture units of meaning corresponding to prototypical situations. It consists of two parts, a lexicon that maps predicates to frames they can evoke, and fully annotated texts. For example, the verb *buy* can evoke either the frame *Commerce_buy* or *Fall_for*, depending on the context (buying goods versus buying a lie). Furthermore, the lexicon gives access to frame-specific role-labels (e.g., *Buyer, Goods* or *Deception, Victim*) as applied in semantic role labeling. Finally, FN specifies high-level relations (e.g., *inherit, precede*) between frames, forming a hierarchy with a collection of *(frame,relation,frame)*-triples. We use FN 1.5 which contains ∼1K frames and ∼12K distinct predicate-frame combinations.[2]

---

[2] `framenet.icsi.berkeley.edu/fndrupal`

2.3 Wikidata's Fact Knowledge

Wikidata is a collaboratively constructed knowledge base that encodes world knowledge in the form of binary relations. It contains more than 40 million entities and 350 million relation instances.[3] The binary relations express both semantic and ontological connections between the entities (e. g. CAPITAL (Hawaii, Honolulu); INSTANCE OF (Hawaii, location)). Wikidata includes an ontology of fine-grained classes and is interlinked with other semantic web resources. A broad community curation, similar to Wikipedia, ensures a higher data quality compared to other knowledge bases (Färber et al., 2015). Formally, Wikidata can be described as a graph $W = (E, R, I)$, where E is a set of entities, R is a set of binary relation types and I is a collection of relation instances encoded as $r(e_1, e_2), \ r \in R, \ e_1, e_2 \in E$.

2.4 Complementarity of Annotations

Work on event semantics hints at two annotation types complementing each other: additional information about participants benefits event prediction (Ahrendt and Demberg, 2016; Botschen et al., 2018) and context information about events benefits the prediction of implicit arguments and entities (Cheng and Erk, 2018). The complementarity is further affirmed by efforts on aligning WD and the FN lexicon: the best alignment approach only maps 37% of the total WD properties to frames (Mousselly-Sergieh and Gurevych, 2016). The complementarity of FN an WD annotations is the reason for also testing a model with the joint annotation '+FN/WD'.

2.5 Preprocessing - Obtaining Annotations

We use two freely available systems to obtain semantic annotations for the claim (b), the reason (c) and the alternative warrants (i, ii): the frame identifier by Botschen et al. (2018) for frame annotations and the entity linker by Sorokin and Gurevych (2018). We employ pre-trained vector representations to encode information from FN and WD. We use the pre-trained frame embeddings (50-dim.) that are learned with *TransE* (Bordes et al., 2013) on the structure of the FN hierarchy with the collection of *(frame, relation, frame)*-triples (Botschen et al., 2017). We also use *TransE* to pre-train entity embeddings (100-dim.) on the WD graph. The an-

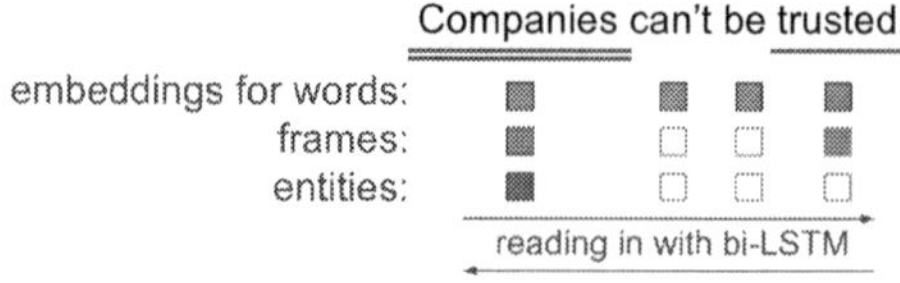

Figure 2: Different embeddings from layers of annotations for a sentence: words, frames, entities.

notation of the ARC data leads to more frames per sentence (6.6 on avg.) than entities per sentence (0.7 on avg.).

2.6 Model - Enriching with Semantics

We extend the baseline model by Habernal et al. (2018) with embeddings for frames and entities (cf. Sec. 2.5 for frame embeddings and entity embeddings). The baseline model is an intra-warrant attention model that only uses conventional pre-trained word embeddings as an input. We apply a *late fusion* strategy: obtain the annotations separately and combine them afterwards by appending the frame and entity embeddings to the word vectors on the token level. Each input sentence is processed by a bi-directional long short-term memory (LSTM) network that reads not only word embeddings, but also frame embeddings for all event mentions and entity embeddings for all entity mentions (Figure 2). Now, the attention weights for the decision between the two warrants are adapted based on the semantically enriched representation of claim (b) and reason (c).[4]

We optimize hyperparameters on the development set with random search. All models are trained using the Adam optimizer (Kingma and Ba, 2014) with a batch size of 16. For our evaluation, we perform ten runs and report the mean and max accuracy together with the standard deviation.

3 Results

In Table 1 we report our results on the ARC task. Our extended approaches '+FN' and '+WD' for semantic enrichment with information about frames and entities increase the averaged performance by more than one percentage point against the baseline. For the best run, the advantage of '+FN' and '+WD' becomes even clearer (+2.2 pp.). On the other hand, the straightforward combination of the two external knowledge source, '+FN/WD', does not lead to further improvements. This points out the

---

[3] www.wikidata.org/wiki/Special: Statistics

[4] We refer to Habernal et al. (2018) for more details.

Approach	Dev.	mean (±)	Test	(±)	max Test
Habernal et al. (2018) (reimpl.)	0.6712	0.0155	0.5570	0.0184	0.5878
+WD	0.6623	0.0071	**0.5680**	0.0235	0.6036
+FN	**0.6741**	0.0119	**0.5676**	0.0257	**0.6104**
+FN/WD	0.6630	0.0088	0.5592	0.0164	0.5946

Table 1: Mean and max accuracy over ten runs on the ARC dev. and test sets (best results highlighted in bold).

need for advanced models that are able to fuse annotations of different types. Albeit positive the results do not seem be a strong support for the hypothesis of (Habernal et al., 2018) about external knowledge being beneficial for the defined task, as we observe only moderate improvements. Overall, the enriched models ('+WD', '+FN' and '+FN/WD') make mostly the same predictions as the baseline system. For instance, for '+WD' there is $79,5\%$ overlap of the predictions with the baseline, and for '+FN', it is 76.6%. In the following section, we try to identify the reasons why the structured knowledge in the form of FN and WD does not further improve the results.

3.1 Error analysis

The amount of semantic information that the model can utilize is dependent on the number of annotations for a test instance[5]. We analyze the performance of the enriched models by the number of annotations for '+WD' and for '+FN'.

Figure 3 shows the performance of '+WD' in comparison to the baseline against the number of WD entities per test instance. As expected, there is no difference in performance for the instances

without WD annotations. We can see a clear improvement for the instances with one or two entities, which indicates that some semantic knowledge is helping to draw the decision between the two warrants. Contrary, '+WD' performs equal to the baseline for three or more annotations.

The performance of the '+FN' model against the number of the frame annotations is plotted in Figure 4. Whilst the difference between '+FN' and baseline varies more, we can observe a similar tendency: once some semantic annotations are available the enriched model outperforms the baseline, whereas with the growing number of frames the difference in performance decreases.

Both annotation tools, the WD entity linker as well as the FN frame identifier, introduce some noise: for the entity linker, Sorokin and Gurevych (2018) report 0.73 F-score and the frame identifier has an accuracy of 0.89 (Botschen et al., 2018). We perform a manual error analysis on 50 instances of the test set to understand the effect of the noisy WD annotation.[6] In 44% of errors, no WD annotation was available and in 52%, the annotations were (partially) incorrect. Only 4% of errors oc-

---

[5]Each instance is four sentences: a claim, a reason, a debate title and a candidate warrant.

[6]Judging if a predicted frame is correct requires deep linguistic expertise and special training on the FrameNet guidelines. Therefore, we excluded FN from this first study.

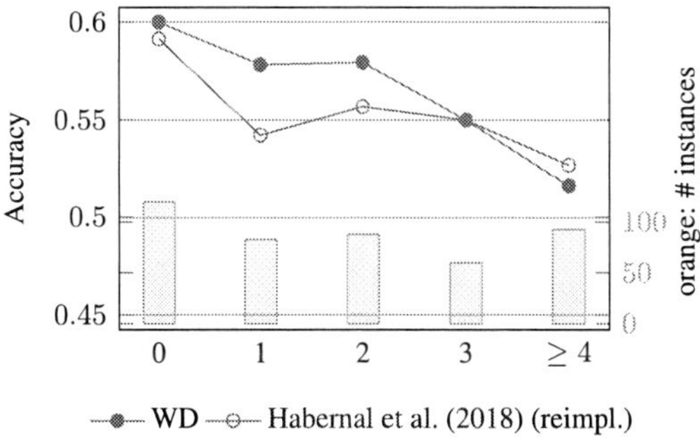

Figure 3: Performance for the '+WD' approach by the number of WD entities in a test set instance.

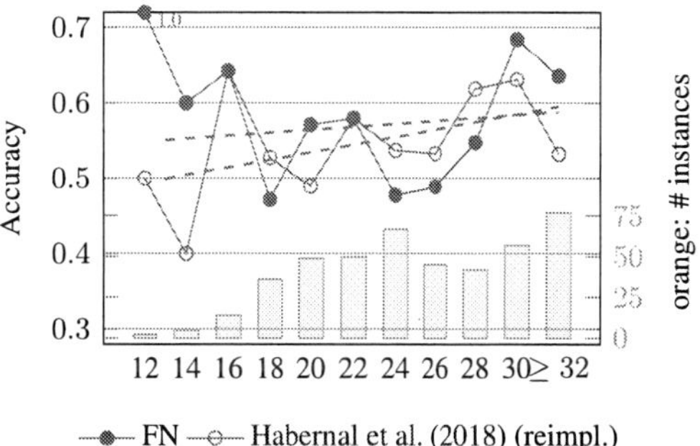

Figure 4: Performance for the '+FN' approach by the number of frames in a test set instance.

cur despite correct entities being available to the model. Notably, in 65% of the cases a correct entity annotation leads to a correct prediction.

Taken together, for instances with little context and therefore only some annotations with frames or entities, the semantic enrichment helps to capture a broader context of the argumentation chain which in turn benefits the classification. However, for instances with more context and therefore more annotations with frames or entities, the benefit is turned down by a worse precision of the annotation tools. Interestingly, the effect of improved performance only for shorter sequences with less annotations is in line with findings of research on information retrieval (Müller et al., 2008), where the trade-off between some annotations that increase the accuracy and more annotations that can hurt the performance is known as precision-recall balance (Riedel et al., 2010; Manning et al., 2008).

3.2 Qualitative analysis

When manually inspecting the annotations of frames and entities, it becomes questionable whether these actually have the potential of contributing to a clear distinction between the two warrants. Figure 5 shows two instances of the ARC corpus with FN and WD annotations. Both annotation layers contribute useful information about the world, which is not contained in the textual input. For instance, 'companies' and 'corporations' are correctly disambiguated and linked to the same frame and the phrase 'use of force' is mapped to the entity Q971119 for a legal concept. Nevertheless, when manually inspecting the annotations of frames and entities it becomes apparent that the provided background knowledge is not sufficient to draw the distinction between the two warrants. In the first example in Figure 5, the key difference between the two warrants is the negation (and similar in the second example). Even if our approach performs a semantic enrichment of the context, the crucial capability of performing reasoning is still missing. This means, our input representation is semantically enriched, but is not parsed into a logic-based representation.

To sum up, in the previous Section 3.1, we show that our approach is of help by successfully enriching the context with semantics for shorter instances; and in this Section 3.2, we analyze why our approach is too limited to solve some key challenges of the ARC task. We conclude with the

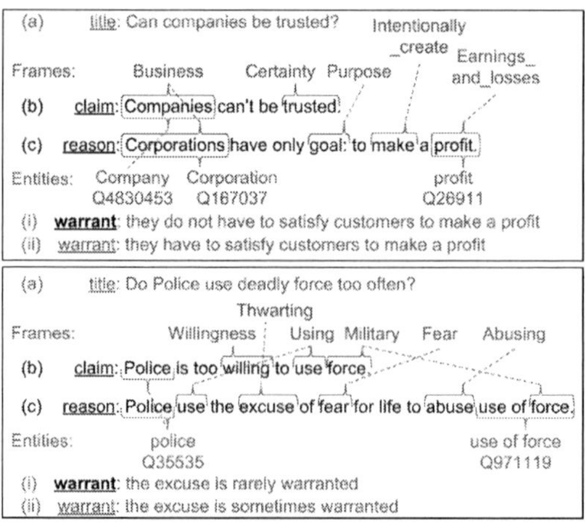

Figure 5: Instances of ARC corpus, with claim (b) and reason (c) annotated with frames and entities.

key challenge of ARC not being lexical-semantic gaps between warrants but rather different phenomena such as negation and that this challenge is to be resolved with logical analysis rather than with integrating world knowledge.

4 Conclusion

We integrate world knowledge from FrameNet and Wikidata into the task of common-sense argumentative reasoning and achieve an improvement in performance compared to the baseline approach. Based on the experiments and the manual analysis, we conclude that external world knowledge might not be enough to gain significant improvements in argumentative reasoning, and we rather point towards logical analysis.

Starting from the hypothesis of the evaluators of the shared task about world knowledge being essential for the Argument Reasoning Comprehension task, we show the potential of semantic enrichment of the context for shorter instances. Our results offer a first perspective on using external resources for the Argument Reasoning Comprehension task. More broadly, our approaches '+FN' (events) and '+WD' (facts) showcase the contribution of semantic enrichment to high-level tasks requiring common sense knowledge.

FrameNet and Wikidata are open-domain resources and our enrichment approach is task-independent. Consequently, we encourage utilizing event- and fact-knowledge in further language understanding tasks, e.g., Story Cloze (Mostafazadeh et al., 2016) or Semantic Textual Similarity (Agirre et al., 2012), using our freely available model.

Acknowledgments

This work has been supported by the DFG-funded research training group "Adaptive Preparation of Information form Heterogeneous Sources" (AIPHES, GRK 1994/1).

References

Eneko Agirre, Mona Diab, Daniel Cer, and Aitor Gonzalez-Agirre. 2012. Semeval-2012 task 6: A pilot on semantic textual similarity. In *Proceedings of the First Joint Conference on Lexical and Computational Semantics-Volume 1: Proceedings of the main conference and the shared task, and Volume 2: Proceedings of the Sixth International Workshop on Semantic Evaluation*, pages 385–393. Association for Computational Linguistics.

Simon Ahrendt and Vera Demberg. 2016. Improving event prediction by representing script participants. In *Proceedings of the 16th Annual Conference of the North American Chapter of the Association for Computational Linguistics: Human Language Technologies (NAACL)*, pages 546–551, San Diego, USA. Association for Computational Linguistics.

Collin F. Baker, Charles J. Fillmore, and John B. Lowe. 1998. The Berkeley FrameNet project. In *Proceedings of the 36th Annual Meeting of the Association for Computational Linguistics and 17th International Conference on Computational Linguistics - Volume 1*, pages 86–90, Stroudsburg, PA, USA.

Antoine Bordes, Nicolas Usunier, Alberto Garcia-Durán, Jason Weston, and Oksana Yakhnenko. 2013. Translating embeddings for modeling multi-relational data. In *Proceedings of the 26th International Conference on Advances in Neural Information Processing Systems (NIPS)*, pages 2787–2795.

Teresa Botschen, Iryna Gurevych, Jan-Christoph Klie, Hatem Mousselly Sergieh, and Stefan Roth. 2018. Multimodal Frame Identification with Multilingual Evaluation. In *Proceedings of the 16th Annual Conference of the North American Chapter of the Association for Computational Linguistics: Human Language Technologies (NAACL)*, pages 1481–1491. Association for Computational Linguistics.

Teresa Botschen, Hatem Mousselly-Sergieh, and Iryna Gurevych. 2017. Prediction of Frame-to-Frame Relations in the FrameNet Hierarchy with Frame Embeddings. In *Proceedings of th 2nd Workshop on Representation Learning for NLP (RepL4NLP, held in conjunction with ACL)*, pages 146–156.

Samuel R. Bowman, Gabor Angeli, Christopher Potts, and Christopher D. Manning. 2015. A large annotated corpus for learning natural language inference. In *Proceedings of the 2015 Conference on Empirical Methods in Natural Language Processing (EMNLP)*, pages 632–642. Association for Computational Linguistics.

Qian Chen, Xiaodan Zhu, Zhen-Hua Ling, Diana Inkpen, and Si Wei. 2018. Neural Natural Language Inference Models Enhanced with External Knowledge. In *Proceedings of the 56th Annual Meeting of the Association for Computational Linguistics (ACL)*, pages 2406–2417, Melbourne, Australia. Association for Computational Linguistics.

Pengxiang Cheng and Katrin Erk. 2018. Implicit argument prediction with event knowledge. In *Proceedings of the 16th Annual Conference of the North American Chapter of the Association for Computational Linguistics: Human Language Technologies (NAACL)*, pages 831–840. Association for Computational Linguistics.

HongSeok Choi and HyunJu Lee. 2018. Gist at semeval-2018 task 12: A network transferring inference knowledge to argument reasoning comprehension task. In *Proceedings of the 16th Annual Conference of the North American Chapter of the Association for Computational Linguistics: Human Language Technologies (SemEval-Workshop)*, page (to appear), New Orleans, LA, USA. Association for Computational Linguistics.

Michael Färber, Basil Ell, Carsten Menne, and Achim Rettinger. 2015. A Comparative Survey of DBpedia, Freebase, OpenCyc, Wikidata, and YAGO. *Semantic Web Journal*, 1:1–5.

Charles J. Fillmore. 1976. Frame semantics and the nature of language. *Annals of the New York Academy of Sciences*, 280:20–32.

Max Glockner, Vered Shwartz, and Yoav Goldberg. 2018. Breaking NLI Systems with Sentences that Require Simple Lexical Inferences. In *The 56th Annual Meeting of the Association for Computational Linguistics (ACL)*, Melbourne, Australia.

Jiang Guo, Wanxiang Che, Haifeng Wang, Ting Liu, and Jun Xu. 2016. A unified architecture for semantic role labeling and relation classification. In *Proceedings of the 26th International Conference on Computational Linguistics: Technical Papers (COLING)*, pages 1264–1274.

Ivan Habernal, Henning Wachsmuth, Iryna Gurevych, and Benno Stein. 2018. The Argument Reasoning Comprehension Task: Identification and Reconstruction of Implicit Warrants. In *Proceedings of the 16th Annual Conference of the North American Chapter of the Association for Computational Linguistics: Human Language Technologies (NAACL)*, pages 1930–1940, New Orleans, LA, USA. Association for Computational Linguistics.

Daniel Khashabi, Tushar Khot, Ashish Sabharwal, and Dan Roth. 2018. Question Answering as Global Reasoning over Semantic Abstractions. In *Proceedings of the 32nd Conference of Association for the Advancement of Artificial Intelligence (AAAI)*, pages 1905–1914. AAAI Press.

Diederik Kingma and Jimmy Ba. 2014. Adam: A Method for Stochastic Optimization. *arXiv preprint arXiv:1412.6980*.

Christopher D. Manning, Prabhakar Raghavan, and Hinrich Schütze. 2008. *Introduction to Information Retrieval*. Cambridge University Press, New York, NY, USA.

Tomas Mikolov, Kai Chen, Greg Corrado, and Jeffrey Dean. 2013. Efficient Estimation of Word Representations in Vector Space. *arXiv preprint arXiv:1301.3781*.

George A Miller. 1995. WordNet: a lexical database for English. *Communications of the ACM*, 38(11):39–41.

Nasrin Mostafazadeh, Nathanael Chambers, Xiaodong He, Devi Parikh, Dhruv Batra, Lucy Vanderwende, Pushmeet Kohli, and James Allen. 2016. A Corpus and Cloze Evaluation for Deeper Understanding of Commonsense Stories. In *Proceedings of the 2016 Conference of the North American Chapter of the Association for Computational Linguistics: Human Language Technologies (NAACL)*, pages 839–849, San Diego, California. Association for Computational Linguistics.

Hatem Mousselly-Sergieh and Iryna Gurevych. 2016. Enriching Wikidata with Frame Semantics. In *Proceedings of the 5th Workshop on Automated Knowledge Base Construction (AKBC, held in conjunction with NAACL)*, pages 29–34.

Christof Müller, Iryna Gurevych, and Max Mühlhäuser. 2008. Closing the Vocabulary Gap for Computing Text Similarity and Information Retrieval. *International Journal of Semantic Computing*, 2(02):253–272.

Hao Peng, Sam Thomson, Swabha Swayamdipta, and Noah A Smith. 2018. Learning joint semantic parsers from disjoint data. *arXiv preprint arXiv:1804.05990*.

Sebastian Riedel, Limin Yao, and Andrew McCallum. 2010. Modeling Relations and Their Mentions without Labeled Text. In *Proceedings of the European Conference on Machine Learning and Knowledge Discovery in Databases*, pages 148–163, Barcelona, Spain.

Josef Ruppenhofer, Michael Ellsworth, Miriam R.L. Petruck, Christopher R. Johnson, and Jan Scheffczyk. 2016. *FrameNet II: Extended Theory and Practice*, revised november 1, 2016 edition. International Computer Science Institute, Berkeley, USA.

Daniil Sorokin and Iryna Gurevych. 2018. Mixing Context Granularities for Improved Entity Linking on Question Answering Data across Entity Categories. In *Proceedings of the 7th Joint Conference on Lexical and Computational Semantics (*SEM, held in conjunction with NAACL)*, pages 65–75. Association for Computational Linguistics.

Su Wang, Greg Durrett, and Katrin Erk. 2018. Modeling Semantic Plausibility by Injecting World Knowledge. In *Proceedings of the 16th Annual Conference of the North American Chapter of the Association for Computational Linguistics: Human Language Technologies (NAACL)*, pages 303–308. Association for Computational Linguistics.

Michael Zhai, Johnny Tan, and Jinho D Choi. 2016. Intrinsic and extrinsic evaluations of word embeddings. In *Proceedings of the 30th Conference of Association for the Advancement of Artificial Intelligence (AAAI)*, pages 4282–4283. AAAI Press.

Incorporating Topic Aspects for Online Comment Convincingness Evaluation

Yunfan Gu[1], Zhongyu Wei[1,*], Maoran Xu[1], Hao Fu[1],
Yang Liu[2], Xuanjing Huang[3]

[1]School of Data Science, Fudan University, China
[2]Liulishuo Company
[3]School of Computer Science, Fudan University, China
{17210980015, zywei, 14300180099, 14307130013}@fudan.edu.cn,
yang.liu@liulishuo.com,xjhuang@fudan.edu.cn

Abstract

In this paper, we propose to incorporate topic aspects information for online comments convincingness evaluation. Our model makes use of graph convolutional network to utilize implicit topic information within a discussion thread to assist the evaluation of convincingness of each single comment. In order to test the effectiveness of our proposed model, we annotate topic information on top of a public dataset for argument convincingness evaluation. Experimental results show that topic information is able to improve the performance for convincingness evaluation. We also make a move to detect topic aspects automatically.

1 Introduction

With the popularity of online forums such as idebate[1] and convinceme[2], researchers have been paying increasing attention to analyzing persuasion content (Wei et al., 2016a,b). Argument convincingness assessment plays an important role in persuasion content analysis. Previous researchers attribute the convincingness of arguments to argument structure (Potash et al., 2017; Peldszus and Stede, 2015), strong evidence (Hasan and Ng, 2014; Park and Cardie, 2014), specific argument components (Habernal and Gurevych, 2016a; Persing and Ng, 2015), interactions (Ji et al., 2018), domain knowledge (Wei et al., 2017) and so on. Most efforts of convincingness evaluation focus on using explicit linguistic features, such as words (Chalaguine and Schulz, 2017) and part-of-speech (POS) (Wachsmuth et al., 2017a) etc. Considering people construct their arguments based on different topic aspects, we thus argue that topic information can be crucial for convincingness evaluation.

---

*Corresponding author
[1]https://idebate.org/
[2]http://convinceme.net/

	Argument1	**Argument2**
Content	The American Water companies are Aquafina (Pepsi), Dasani (Coke), Perrier (Nestle) which provide jobs for the american citizens.	If bottled water did not exist, more people would be drinking sweetened liquids because it would be the only portable drinks! People would become fat!
Topic Aspect	Economy	Convenience and health

Table 1: Example of an argument pair and corresponding topic aspects. **Debate:** Ban plastic water bottles **Stance:** No; **Label:** A1>A2

To illustrate this idea, Table 1 gives a brief example of an argument pair. Both arguments express opinions against the banning of plastic water bottles. *Argument 1* is expressed from the topic aspect of *economy* while *Argument 2* makes the point from the aspect of *convenience and health*. As we can see, for a specific discussion subject, different aspects might reveal various degree of convincingness. Wang et al. (2017) has already made attempt to make use of latent persuasive strengths of topic aspects for quality evaluation on a formal debate dataset. However, there is still no further research on online debating texts, which is un-structured with multiple participants.

In this paper, we propose to incorporate latent topic aspects information to evaluate the convincingness of comments in online forum. We make use of graph convolutional networks (GCN) to utilize the latent topic information of comments for a specific subject. We assume that arguments sharing the same topic aspect are more likely to have similar degree of convincingness, and GCN is able to make use of the topic similarity among arguments. Bi-directional long short-term memory (Bi-LSTM) is used to encode each argument. We annotate topic aspects information on top of a public dataset collected from online forum Habernal and Gurevych (2016b) to evaluate our proposed model.

Main contribution of this article are three folds:

Proceedings of the 5th Workshop on Argument Mining, pages 97–104
Brussels, Belgium, November 1, 2018. ©2018 Association for Computational Linguistics

(1) we annotate topic aspects for each argument in an existing dataset over 16 discussion threads (2 stances for each subject); (2) we propose a BiLSTM-GCN model and prove the effectiveness of topic aspects in convincingness evaluation; (3) we implement several baseline models to detect the topic aspect automatically.

2 Data Description

Our experiments are conducted on *UKPConvArg1* corpus released by Habernal and Gurevych (2016b). The source argument is from 16 debates on Web debate platforms `createdebate.com` and `convinceme.net`. Each debate is about a specific topic and has two stances. We call each (debate,stance) tuple a "split", so there are 32 splits in total. The dataset includes sets of argument pairs according to 32 splits, and each argument pair is annotated with a binary relation (0 and 1) which represents the pairwise convincingness relationship (more/less convincing), 11,650 in total. Since we take the *UKPConvArg1Strict* version as our dataset, the equal instances are removed. The topic aspect annotations are not from the initial dataset, but from our own annotations.

In order to extract topic aspects from each topic, we manually annotate each argument by two annotators. The annotation process is as follows. First, two annotators have a discussion and then determine possible topic aspect candidates for each split. Second, two annotators independently check every argument and summarize one main topic aspect. As for arguments carrying multiple aspects, we pick the primary topic aspect. Third, after all the annotations are made, they are asked to rank the topic aspects under a split according to topic aspect strength by discussion. Due to the quality of the corpus, some arguments have to be assigned to the aspect None if it (1) has nothing to do with the topic, or (2) has no point of view, or (3) is contradictory/ambiguous. Results of topic aspect annotations are shown in Appendix.

To clarify the annotations of topic aspects, we will take the annotation process for comments under the topic of "banning plastic water bottles" as an example. Comments from the con-side of the this debating might hold different topic aspects. Some of them concern about the economic decay after banning plastic water bottles. And some of them suggest that we can recycle plastic water bottles instead of banning them. The others care more about the inconvenience and safety after banning plastic water bottles. After reading all these arguments, annotators conclude that there should be three main topic aspects, "economics", "bottle recycling" and "convenience and health" respectively. There are some arguments which have no point of view or seem ambiguous, and the topic aspects of these arguments will be set as "None". Since the average length of arguments is relatively short, so most of the arguments hold a single topic aspect. Therefore, each argument only has one label to simplify the problem. The dataset is available here[3].

3 Proposed Model

In this paper, we propose a BiLSTM-GCN model to solve the convincingness evaluation task. The BiLSTM acts as the the foundation to generate the representation of each argument, and GCN is built upon BiLSTM to make use of the inter-relationships of similar arguments. The architecture of our model is shown in Figure 1. In general, Our aim is predicting a binary relation (0 and 1) representing more/less convincing given an argument pair. All the arguments in the same split are considered as a batch.

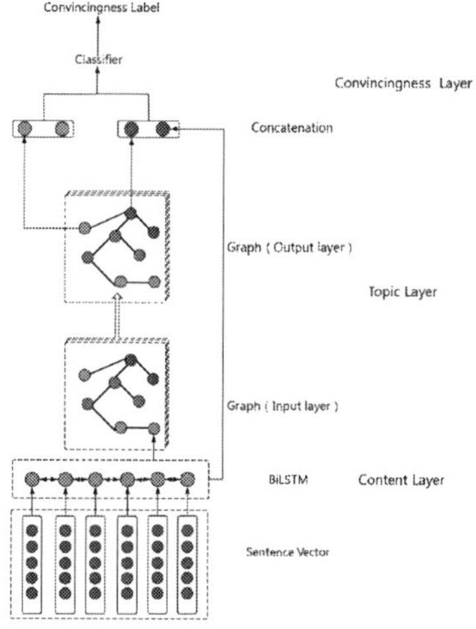

Figure 1: BiLSTM-GCN model architecture

3.1 Content Layer

The input of the content layer is the word embedding matrix of each argument and the output of

[3]`http://www.sdspeople.fudan.edu.cn/ zywei/data/5thargmine-topic-convince.zip`

content layer is the representation vector of each argument. BiLSTM plays the role of encoder in this layer, and it has been proved effective to encode sentences (Goodfellow et al., 2016; Dyer et al., 2015; Wang and Jiang, 2016).

We simply employ the word embeddings released by Glove (Pennington et al., 2014), and we choose the 840B tokens, 300 dimensional vector version. As to the word which is absent in the Glove vocabulary, we randomly generate a 300 dimensional vector to represent those out of vocabulary vectors. These vectors are then put into BiLSTM to get the basic representation of each argument. The dimension of argument representation is set to 64 after tuning.

3.2 Topic Layer

The input of topic layer is the representation vector of each argument. The output of topic layer is the updated representation vector of each argument. The core of our topic layer is GCN (Kipf and Welling). The main function of this layer is utilizing the topic aspect information.

We consider a single-layer GCN for better argument representation. The GCN layer propagates the information of a node onto its nearest neighbours.

Our GCN model simply takes the following form. A represents the adjacency matrix, X represents the feature matrix, which is a stacked version of raw argument representations generated from BiLSTM. W is a parameter matrix which can be trained in the training process. We add self connected edges to A to keep the information of the original argument itself. $\hat{A}$ is the normalized form of A. Normalization is a compulsory part for combining information, since we have to keep the ratio of self information and neighbours' information the same for each argument. Z is the final feature matrix, and each row represents the new representation of each argument.

$$Z = f(X, A) = Relu(\hat{A}XW) \qquad (1)$$

The normalization process is described below:

$$\hat{A} = D^{-\frac{1}{2}}(A + I_N)D^{\frac{1}{2}} \qquad (2)$$

Here, I_N is the identity matrix, which represents the self-connections. $D_{ii} = \sum_j A_{ij}$ is a diagonal matrix and each element on the diagonal represents the degree of argument i. The self-connections are not normalized since we think that

original argument is more useful than other arguments.

3.2.1 Adjacency Matrix

The adjacency matrix represents whether there is an edge between two nodes, but the graph structure among the arguments is implicit. We can capture the implicit structure by making use of argument similarity or topic aspect.

Argument similarity: We can calculate the similarity of two arguments by distance under embedding setting and use threshold to decide whether there is an edge.

Topic aspects: When two arguments share the same topic aspect, they are supposed to have an edge between corresponding nodes.

3.2.2 Feature Matrix

Feature matrix is built upon BiLSTM, and is a stacked version of argument representation. The argument representation is the mean pooling of the BiLSTM result. In fact, the result of graph convolutional network is still a feature matrix which absorbs information from neighbours. The feature dimension is set to 64, and the dimension of each matrix is fixed over 32 splits by setting the maximum argument quantities as the row dimension. Default arguments are filled by zero vectors. The result of graph convolutional network is still a feature matrix, which involves related nodes' information.

3.3 Convincingness Layer

The input of convincingness layer is the updated representation vector of each argument. The output of convincingness layer is a binary label (0 and 1) representing more/less convincing given an argument pair. As a result the core of this convincingness layer is a classifier.

We can simply apply the softmax classifier. However, inspired by DistMult (Yang et al., 2014), we design a classifier which will perform better. Our classifier takes the following form. e_s represents the representation of argument 1, and e_o represents the representation of argument 2, and W is a parameter matrix. We set the parameter matrix as a real antisymmetric matrix. Therefore, the result of comparing argument 1 and argument 2 will be opposite to the result of comparing argument 2 and argument 1.

$$f(s, r, o) = e_s^T R e_o \qquad (3)$$

Our parameter matrix is better than the normal linear layer mainly because it can capture the interactive relationship between different feature dimensions.

4 Experiments

4.1 Experiment Setup

We test our model on the dataset depicted in Section 2 to evaluate convincingness of arguments. To compare with the algorithms applied in the initial task (Habernal and Gurevych, 2016b), we still use 32-fold cross-split cross-validation, which means 31 splits are training data and the other one is test data. The preprocessing part is the same as the original task as well. And we train our BiLSTM-GCN model as described in Section 3 and evaluate prediction accuracy on the test split.

In this paper, we implement our BiLSTM-GCN model by Pytorch. Each split is considered as a batch to train and test. The loss function we use is simply the quadratic loss function. We have tried the cross entropy loss and the quadratic loss, and latter performs better when using our classifier. The batch loss is calculated by summing the loss of each argument pair. The weights of the parameter matrix classifier are initialized randomly from the normal distribution, and the initial hidden state of our BiLSTM is set to zero. And we take topic aspects to build adjacency matrix in convincingness evaluation task.

4.2 Baselines

The baselines for convincingness evaluation include: (1) **SVM** (Habernal and Gurevych, 2016b): The SVM with RBF kernel is based on a number of linguistic features. (2) **BiLSTM** (Habernal and Gurevych, 2016b): The input word embedding is as depicted in Section 3.1, and hidden dimension is 64. (3) **BiLSTM+argument length**: Since BiLSTM will transform all the arguments into same dimension, the information of argument length will be lost to some extent. Here we mention argument length since it can handle this task quite well. The accuracy of judging convincingness by its length can be 0.73, which is not mentioned in the original work. As a result, we take it as a useful feature to help our model work better.

Here, we don't list the baseline with our topic aspects annotations because the topic aspects among different debates are not the same, so it can't play the role of an explicit feature. We have

to encode the topic aspect information, that is also a reason of applying Graph Convolutional Network in our work.

We also try different methods to build the adjacency matrix as depicted in Section 3.2.1, including unit matrix, Jaccard similarity, cosine similarity, word mover's distance and topic aspects. (1) **Unit matrix**: Unix matrix means that the adjacency matrix is just a unit matrix, and the GCN here act as a single linear layer. (2) **Jaccard similarity**: Jaccard similarity is calculated by the following form. A and B means the argument 1 and argument 2 in an argument pair. In our experiments we find that use threshold to build adjacency is better than use weighted adjacency matrix. As a result , we all use the threshold to build a zero-one adjacency matrix in the following building methods.The threshold of Jaccard similarity is set to 0.5 after normalizing.

$$J(A, B) = \frac{|A \cap B|}{|A \cup B|} \tag{4}$$

(3) **Cosine similarity**: Cosine similarity is represented using a dot product and magnitude as the following form. The threshold of cosine similarity is set to 0.95 after normalizing.

$$C(A, B) = \frac{A \cdot B}{\|A\| \|B\|} \tag{5}$$

(4) **Word mover's distance**(Kusner et al., 2015): The word mover's distance calculating is reproduced by reading the original paper. And the threshold is set to 0.35 after adjusting.

4.3 Experimental Results

This part, we compare our BiLSTM-GCN model with baselines mentioned above. Table 2 lists the results of convincingness evaluation task. The adjacency matrix of our BiLSTM-GCN model in Table 2 is based on our topic aspects annotations. In Table 3, We test other adjacency matrix building methods as described above and analyze the results.

The result shows that our BiLSTM-GCN model performs better than best baseline model, and obviously better than models utilized in the initial task. What's more, we have proved that the inter-relationships of arguments can help us evaluate the convincingness better by using GCN.

The results in Table 3 show that our annotations perform the best among all the metrics, which

Model	Accuracy
SVM	0.78
BiLSTM	0.76
BiLSTM+argument length	0.797
BiLSTM-GCN+argument length (topic aspects)	**0.811**

Table 2: Results of convincingness evaluation task

Adjacency metric	Accuracy
Unit matrix	0.800
Jaccard similarity	0.799
Cosine similarity	0.793
Word mover's distance	0.808
Topic aspects	**0.811**

Table 3: Results of BiLSTM-GCN model with various adjacency matrix building methods

means topic aspect is an excellent way to evaluate the relationship between arguments. And we can know that some state-of-the-art text similarity metric like word mover's distance performs better than classical text similarity metrics like Jaccard similarity and cosine similarity.

4.4 Further analysis of topic detection

We know that the topic aspects are not labeled in most data. Since we already have the annotations of topic aspects, so we can set a classification task, which can be further used for automatic annotation. The training data and test data are the same as convincingness evaluation. However, the labels will change. Here, if two arguments in an argument pair share the same topic aspect, the label will be set to 1, or it will be set to 0. We also suggest that None type is different from all other types including None type itself. We test some baseline models and our BiLSTM-GCN model on this task and evaluate F-score on the test split. We don't use accuracy since the labels are imbalanced here, only about thirty percent of argument pairs have positive labels.

The baselines for topic aspect detection include: (1) **Random classification**: Select zero or one randomly. (2) **LDA clustering** (Blei et al., 2003): Automatically cluster the arguments by LDA over each split into the number of topic aspects we annotate. (3) **SVM**: The SVM with RBF kernel is based on a number of linguistic features.

We choose word mover's distance to build adjacency matrix instead of our annotations, since it

is the kind of the latest metric of text similarity calculation. The word mover's distance calculation is reproduced by reading the original paper (Kusner et al., 2015). The threshold is set to 0.35 after adjusting. Table 4 lists the results of topic aspect detection task.

Model	F-score
Random classification	0.425
LDA clustering	0.524
SVM	0.589
BiLSTM-GCN	**0.612**

Table 4: Results of topic aspect detection task

The result shows that our BiLSTM-GCN model performs the best among all the methods, and supervised training methods like SVM performs better than unsupervised methods like LDA clustering. All these models perform significantly better than the lower bound given by random classification.

5 Conclusions and Future works

In this paper, we apply BiLSTM-GCN model on a convincingness evaluation task and the model performs 3-5% better than the original method on the online debate dataset. Our model utilizes not only the explicit argument features like length but also topic aspects which are latent features. Our experiments proves that topic information is able to improve the performance for convincingness evaluation. In future, we will consider to utilize external knowledge to further improve the performance of convincingness evaluation. The possible external knowledge can be similar arguments from other websites, or argument search engine (Wachsmuth et al., 2017b).

Acknowledgements

The work is partially supported by National Natural Science Foundation of China (Grant No. 61702106), Shanghai Science and Technology Commission (Grant No. 17JC1420200, Grant No. 17YF1427600 and Grant No.16JC1420401).

References

David M Blei, Andrew Y Ng, and Michael I Jordan. 2003. Latent dirichlet allocation. *Journal of machine Learning research*, 3(Jan):993–1022.

Lisa Andreevna Chalaguine and Claudia Schulz. 2017. Assessing convincingness of arguments in online debates with limited number of features. In *Proceedings of the Student Research Workshop at the 15th Conference of the European Chapter of the Association for Computational Linguistics*, pages 75–83.

Chris Dyer, Miguel Ballesteros, Wang Ling, Austin Matthews, and Noah A Smith. 2015. Transition-based dependency parsing with stack long short-term memory. *arXiv preprint arXiv:1505.08075*.

Ian Goodfellow, Yoshua Bengio, Aaron Courville, and Yoshua Bengio. 2016. *Deep learning*, volume 1. MIT press Cambridge.

Ivan Habernal and Iryna Gurevych. 2016a. What makes a convincing argument? empirical analysis and detecting attributes of convincingness in web argumentation. In *Proceedings of the 2016 Conference on Empirical Methods in Natural Language Processing*, pages 1214–1223. Association for Computational Linguistics.

Ivan Habernal and Iryna Gurevych. 2016b. Which argument is more convincing? analyzing and predicting convincingness of web arguments using bidirectional LSTM. In *Proceedings of the 54th Annual Meeting of the Association for Computational Linguistics (Volume 1: Long Papers)*, pages 1589–1599. Association for Computational Linguistics.

Kazi Saidul Hasan and Vincent Ng. 2014. Why are you taking this stance? identifying and classifying reasons in ideological debates. In *Proceedings of the 2014 Conference on Empirical Methods in Natural Language Processing (EMNLP)*, pages 751–762. Association for Computational Linguistics.

Lu Ji, Zhongyu Wei, Xiangkun Hu, Yang Liu, Qi Zhang, and Xuanjing Huang. 2018. Incorporating argument-level interactions for persuasion comments evaluation using co-attention model. In *Proceedings of the 27th International Conference on Computational Linguistics*, pages 3703–3714. Association for Computational Linguistics.

Thomas N Kipf and Max Welling. Semi-supervised classification with graph convolutional networks. In *arXiv:1609.02907*.

Matt Kusner, Yu Sun, Nicholas Kolkin, and Kilian Weinberger. 2015. From word embeddings to document distances. In *International Conference on Machine Learning*, pages 957–966.

Joonsuk Park and Claire Cardie. 2014. Identifying appropriate support for propositions in online user comments. In *Proceedings of the First Workshop on Argumentation Mining*, pages 29–38. Association for Computational Linguistics.

Andreas Peldszus and Manfred Stede. 2015. Joint prediction in MST-style discourse parsing for argumentation mining. In *Proceedings of the 2015 Conference on Empirical Methods in Natural Language Processing*, pages 938–948. Association for Computational Linguistics.

Jeffrey Pennington, Richard Socher, and Christopher Manning. 2014. Glove: Global vectors for word representation. In *Proceedings of the 2014 Conference on Empirical Methods in Natural Language Processing (EMNLP)*, pages 1532–1543. Association for Computational Linguistics.

Isaac Persing and Vincent Ng. 2015. Modeling argument strength in student essays. In *Proceedings of the 53rd Annual Meeting of the Association for Computational Linguistics and the 7th International Joint Conference on Natural Language Processing (Volume 1: Long Papers)*, pages 543–552. Association for Computational Linguistics.

Peter Potash, Alexey Romanov, and Anna Rumshisky. 2017. Here's my point: Joint pointer architecture for argument mining. In *Proceedings of the 2017 Conference on Empirical Methods in Natural Language Processing*, pages 1364–1373. Association for Computational Linguistics.

Henning Wachsmuth, Nona Naderi, Ivan Habernal, Yufang Hou, Graeme Hirst, Iryna Gurevych, and Benno Stein. 2017a. Argumentation quality assessment: Theory vs. practice. In *Proceedings of the 55th Annual Meeting of the Association for Computational Linguistics (Volume 2: Short Papers)*, pages 250–255. Association for Computational Linguistics.

Henning Wachsmuth, Martin Potthast, Khalid Al Khatib, Yamen Ajjour, Jana Puschmann, Jiani Qu, Jonas Dorsch, Viorel Morari, Janek Bevendorff, and Benno Stein. 2017b. Building an argument search engine for the web. In *Proceedings of the 4th Workshop on Argument Mining*, pages 49–59. Association for Computational Linguistics.

Lu Wang, Nick Beauchamp, Sarah Shugars, and Kechen Qin. 2017. Winning on the merits: The joint effects of content and style on debate outcomes. *Transactions of the Association of Computational Linguistics*, 5:219–232.

Shuohang Wang and Jing Jiang. 2016. Learning natural language inference with LSTM. In *Proceedings of the 2016 Conference of the North American Chapter of the Association for Computational Linguistics: Human Language Technologies*, pages 1442–1451. Association for Computational Linguistics.

Zhongyu Wei, Chen Li, and Yang Liu. 2017. A joint framework for argumentative text analysis incorporating domain knowledge. In *arXiv preprint arXiv:1701.05343*.

Zhongyu Wei, Yang Liu, and Yi Li. 2016a. Is this post persuasive? ranking argumentative comments in online forum. In *Proceedings of the 54th Annual Meeting of the Association for Computational Linguistics (Volume 2: Short Papers)*, volume 2, pages 195–200.

Zhongyu Wei, Yandi Xia, Chen Li, Yang Liu, Zachary Stallbohm, Yi Li, and Yang Jin. 2016b. A preliminary study of disputation behavior in online debating forum. In *Proceedings of the Third Workshop on Argument Mining (ArgMining2016)*, pages 166–171.

Bishan Yang, Wen Tau Yih, Xiaodong He, Jianfeng Gao, and Li Deng. 2014. Embedding entities and relations for learning and inference in knowledge bases. In *arXiv:1412.6575*.

Debate	Stance	Aspects
BAN	No	[A1] Economy; [A2] Bottle recycling; [A3] Convenience and health; [A4] None
	Yes	[A1] Environment; [A2] High price of bottled water; [A3] Health; [A4] None
CHR	Atheism	[A1] Challenging Christianity/God; [A2] Atheism is more scientific; [A3] None
	Christianity	[A1] Faith and belief; [A2] Attacking Atheism; [A3] None
EVO	Creation	[A1] Paradox of evolution; [A2] Religion; [A3] None
	Evolution	[A1] Evidence of evolution; [A2] Challenging Creation/God; [A3] None
FIR	Firefox	[A1] Extensions; [A2] Poor performance of IE; [A3] IE copies other browsers; [A4] None
	IE	[A1] Universality; [A2] Useful functions; [A3] Poor performance of Firefox; [A4] None
GAY	Right	[A1] Gay marriage is ones right; [A2] It is none of others business; [A3] None
	Wrong	[A1] Gay marriage is unnatural; [A2] Religion; [A3] Ethics; [A4] Law
SPA	No	[A1] Spanking makes children behave; [A2] Only last resort
	Yes	[A1] Parents can use other ways; [A2] It will hurt children; [A3] Children will think hitting others is alright; [A4] Bad for relationship; [A5] Children are too young to know what is right; [A5] None
SPO	No	[A1] Love/relationship; [A2] It depends on what happened; [A3] People make mistakes; [A4] None
	Yes	[A1] Murder is wrong; [A2] Self security; [A3] Unwillingness to live with a murderer
IND	No	[A1] Politics; [A2] Economy; [A3] Diplomacy; [A4] Population; [A5] None
	Yes	[A1] Economy; [A2] Education and talents; [A3] Politics; [A4] Culture; [A5] Patriotism; [A6] None
LOU	Fatherless	[A1] Lousy father is harmful to kids growth; [A2] Lousy father is a stain ; [A3] Fatherless kids can still be fine
	Lousy Father	[A1] Lousy father still helps; [A2] Lousy father can get better; [A3]Lousy father motivates one to be better; [A4] None
POR	No	[A1] Sexual desires; [A2] Entertainment; [A3] Porn does no harm; [A4] None
	Yes	[A1] Health and addiction; [A2] Porn does no good; [A3] Women rights; [A4] Religion; [A5] None
SCH	Bad	[A1] Creativity; [A2] Futility; [A3]Low quality; [A4] None
	Good	[A1] Equality; [A2] Uniforms make students concentrate on study; [A3] Logo of school; [A4] None
PER	Common Good	[A1] Helping others is better; [A2] It also helps oneself; [A3] None
	Personal Pursuit	[A1] Helping oneself is prerequisite; [A2] Human nature; [A3] Personal fulfillment
PRO	Pro-Choice	[A1] Right of decision; [A2] Unwanted pregnancy; [A3] None
	Pro-Life	[A1] No right to kill; [A2] Adoption;[A3] None
PHY	No	[A1] PE is useless; [A2] Studies; [A3]PE is tiring; [A4] PE causes bullying; [A5] None
	Yes	[A1] Health and obesity; [A2] Students can develop good habits, attitudes, etc.; [A3] None
TVB	Books	[A1] Books are better for learning; [A2] TV does harms to health; [A3] Books save money; [A4] None
	TV	[A1] TV provides richer information; [A2] Convenience; [A3] None
WIL	No	[A1] Raffles contributions; [A2] Farquhar was a subordinate
	Yes	[A1] Farquhar solved problems; [A2] Reputation; [A3] None

Table 5: (1) BAN: Banning plastic water bottles; (2) CHR: Christianity or Atheism; (3) EVO: Evolution vs. Creation; (4) FIR: Firefox vs. Internet Explorer; (5) GAY: Gay marriage: Right or wrong; (6) SPA: Should parents use spanking as an option to discipline? (7) SPO: If your spouse committed murder and he or she confided in you, would you turn them in? (8) IND: India has the potential to lead the world; (9) LOU: Is it better to have a lousy father or to be fatherless? (10) POR: Is porn wrong? (11) SCH: Is the school uniform a good or bad idea? (12) PER: Which type of endeavor is better, a personal pursuit or advancing the common good? (13) PRO: Pro-Choice vs. Pro-Life; (14) PHY: Should physical education be mandatory in schools? (15) TVB: TV is better than Books; (16) WIL: William Farquhar ought to be honored as the rightful founder of Singapore.

Proposed Method for Annotation of Scientific Arguments in Terms of Semantic Relations and Argument Schemes

Nancy L. Green
University of North Carolina Greensboro
Greensboro, N.C. 27402, U.S.A.
nlgreen@uncg.edu

Abstract

This paper presents a proposed method for annotation of scientific arguments in biological/biomedical journal articles. Semantic entities and relations are used to represent the propositional content of arguments in instances of argument schemes. We describe an experiment in which we encoded the arguments in a journal article to identify issues in this approach. Our catalogue of argument schemes and a copy of the annotated article are now publically available.

1 Introduction

This paper presents our current work on semantic annotation of scientific arguments in full-text biological/biomedical journal articles. The goal is to provide a method for semantic representation of arguments that can be used in empirical studies of scientific discourse as well as to support applications such as argument mining (Lippi and Torroni, 2016). Computational research on scientific discourse has focused on classification of text segments in terms of rhetorical goals (Teufel, 2010), experimental science activities (Liakata et al., 2012), or coherence relations (Prasad et al., 2011). Although some categories of those classification schemes are related to argumentation, those approaches are inadequate for representation of argumentation. Focusing mainly on non-technical literature and social media, argument mining researchers have investigated automatic classification of text segments in terms of argumentation concepts, e.g., premise/ conclusion, support/attack (Peldszus and Stede, 2016; Stab and Gurevych, 2016).

However, the propositional content of scientific arguments does not map neatly to text segments: two distinct arguments may be expressed in overlapping or embedded text; argument premises and conclusions may occur in non-contiguous text segments of varying granularity, and sometimes they may be implicit. As an alternative, we proposed a semantics-informed approach to argument mining in the biological/biomedical sciences as follows (Green, 2018). First, BioNLP tools could be used to derive a partial semantic interpretation of a text; next, argument schemes implemented as logic programs could be used to identify the propositional content of arguments, including implicit conclusions.

Consistent with that approach, we created a publically available catalogue of 15 argument schemes that we identified in journal articles on health effects of genetic variants. The schemes are expressed in terms of domain concepts used in our logic programs, rather than by generic definitions as in, e.g., (Walton et al., 2008). Here we describe an experiment in which we manually encoded the arguments in the "Results/Discussion" section of an article from that domain. The goals were to evaluate the feasibility of the task and to identify issues in the semantic representation of the arguments, as a step towards building a publically available corpus of argument-annotated full-text scientific journal articles. There are currently

Proceedings of the 5th Workshop on Argument Mining, pages 105–110
Brussels, Belgium, November 1, 2018. ©2018 Association for Computational Linguistics

no corpora of argument-annotated articles from the natural sciences research literature. The information gained will be used to refine our approach as we build a corpus. The catalogue and annotated article are available at https://github.com/ greennl/BIO-Arg.

2 Method

An article (van de Leemput et al., 2007) was selected from the open-access CRAFT corpus[1] in case the syntactic and concept annotations of that corpus (Bada et al. 2012; Verspoor et al. 2012) might be useful in the future in combination with our argument annotations. We annotated the arguments in the first eight paragraphs of the ten-paragraph "Results/ Discussion" section. (Although not participating in the annotation, a domain expert had previously helped interpret the article.) Encoded in XML, annotations were added using a text editor. (We adopted a lightweight approach to annotation tools due to the experimental nature of this work.) Part of the DTD for argument-related tags is shown in Figure 1.

```
<!ELEMENT DSEG (content* | entities-props* |
        argument* )* >
<!ATTLIST   DSEG  ID CDATA #REQUIRED >
<!ELEMENT entities-props (entity* | prop*)* >
<!ATTLIST   entity ID CDATA #REQUIRED >
<!ATTLIST   entity paraphrase CDATA >
<!ELEMENT argument (premise-list, conclusion ) >
<!ATTLIST   argument ID CDATA #REQUIRED >
<!ATTLIST   argument scheme CDATA #REQUIRED >
<!ELEMENT premise-list (premise+ ) >
<!ATTLIST   premise prop CDATA >
<!ATTLIST   premise domain-prop CDATA >
<!ATTLIST   premise paraphrase CDATA >
<!ATTLIST   premise conclusion-of CDATA >
<!ATTLIST   conclusion prop CDATA >
<!ATTLIST   conclusion inferred-prop CDATA >
<!ATTLIST   conclusion paraphrase CDATA >
```

Figure 1: Part of DTD

---

[1] Article 17590087 in http://bionlp-corpora.sourceforge.net/CRAFT/

For illustration, Figure 2 shows an excerpt of the annotated document. (Text of some <content> elements has been elided to save space.)

```
<DSEG ID="Observation" >
<content> During the generation of a line of mice
with knockout of the gene Park7 we noted an early
movement disorder that was inherited
independently of targeting vector transmission. Our
initial observations suggested the affected mice
suffered from an apparently paroxysmal movement
disorder, often induced by touch ... At initial
examination, ... likened the disorder to episodic
intermittent ataxia ... </content>
<entities-props>
 <entity ID="group1"
    paraphrase="the affected mice" />
 <entity ID="pheno1"
    paraphrase="ataxia-like movement disorder" />
<prop>have_pheno(group1, pheno1)</prop>
</entities-props>
</DSEG>
<DSEG ID="Experiment 1">
<content> To map the location of the disease-
causing lesion, we performed genome-wide linkage
analysis ... Analysis of these data showed a single
genomic region with significant linkage to disease,
providing a two-point LOD score of 5.13 at marker
20.MMHAP85FLG2 Chromosome 6qE1 ...</content>
<entities-props>
<entity ID="geno1"
    paraphrase="homozygous mutation on
    chromosome 6qE1" />
<prop>have_geno(group1,geno1)</prop>
</entities-props>
<argument ID="1" scheme="Agreement">
<premise-list>
   <premise prop="have_pheno(group1, pheno1)" />
   <premise prop="have_geno(group1,geno1)"/>
</premise-list>
<conclusion inferred-prop=
    "cause(geno1, pheno1, group1)"
    paraphrase="A homozygous mutation on
    chromosome 6qE1 may be the cause of the
    ataxia-like disorder in the affected mice" />
</argument>
</DSEG>
```

Figure 2: Annotated excerpt

The article presents a narrative of scientific discovery: a fortuitous observation followed by a series of experiments, intermediate conclusions, more experiments and final conclusions. To preserve this contextual information we divided the Results section into narrative <DSEG> (discourse segment) elements correspondingly. Fig. 2 illustrates the first two <DSEG>s. Each <DSEG> may contain several types of elements: <content>, <entities-props>, and <argument>. In our proposed annotation approach, the text of an article is enclosed within <content> elements of variable length -- from one to nine sentences in this annotated article.

Immediately following a <content> element, a partial semantic interpretation of that content may be given in an <entities-props> element. This element may contain <entity> tags for entities that have been introduced into the discourse in the preceding <content> element. The ID attribute of an <entity> uniquely identifies it in the discourse. Since an entity may have been introduced earlier, the annotator must determine if mentions are coreferential. In Figure 2 the first <entities-props> element shown describes the preceding <content> as introducing two discourse entities, assigned the IDs *group1* and *pheno1* by the annotator. The paraphrase attribute of <entity> and other elements is used to help the human reader.

An <entities-props> element also may contain propositions, marked <prop>. A proposition consists of a relation name used in the definition of argument schemes in our catalogue and the entity ID of its arguments, e.g., *have_pheno(group1, pheno1)*. A set of six semantic relations is used: *have_geno, have_pheno, have_protein, difference, similar*, and *cause*. Propositions may be negated. Although entities and relations were manually extracted, this is a stop-gap approach until NLP tools can assist in semantic extraction.

After <entities-props> elements are added, any arguments conveyed in the preceding <content> element are added. Argument annotations are not added inside of <content> elements due to the problems noted in the Introduction. In other words, separating annotation of semantic interpretations from the source text, and separating annotation of arguments from semantic interpretations provides the flexibility to overcome those problems. The decision was made to place <argument> elements immediately following the elements conveying them (rather than, e.g., at the end of the document) to preserve the context of the argument, since context informs dialectical structure and may constrain recognition of argument schemes.

A key attribute of an <argument> is the name of the scheme in our catalog of argument schemes. To assist the annotator, the schemes in the catalog are organized in a taxonomy (shown in Figure 3), defined, and accompanied by one or two examples. Most of the schemes involve causation; the causal schemes are differentiated first by whether the conclusion is based upon observation of one group or a comparison of two groups of individuals.

1. Causation
    1.1 One Group
        1.1.1   Agreement Arguments
            1.1.1.1   Agreement
            1.1.1.2   Failed Method of Agreement (effect)
            1.1.1.3   Failed Method of Agreement (cause)
        1.1.2   Eliminate Candidates
        1.1.3   Explanation-Based
            1.1.3.1   Effect to Cause
            1.1.3.2   No Effect to No Cause
            1.1.3.3   Consistent with Predicted Effect
    1.2 Two Group
        1.2.1   Difference
        1.2.2   Analogy (Causal)
        1.2.3   Explanation-Based
            1.2.3.1   Consistent Explanation
            1.2.3.2   Difference Consistent Explanation
2. Other
    2.1 Classification
    2.2 Confirmation

Figure 3: Taxonomy of argument schemes

An <argument> element consists of the <premise-list>, a list of <premise>s, and a <conclusion>. For example, Argument 1 shown in Figure 2 is an instance of the Agreement argument scheme from our catalogue. Its premises are copies of two

<prop> elements, derived from two different <content> elements. Its conclusion, labeled *inferred-prop*, has been inferred by the annotator based upon constraints of the Agreement argument scheme. To paraphrase the first premise, the phenotype[2] of group1 (a certain group of mice) is pheno1 (an ataxia-like disorder). The second premise is that the genotype of group1 is geno1 (a mutation on chromosome 6qE1). According to this argument scheme, one may defeasibly conclude that the cause of pheno1 in group1 is geno1. Note that all of the annotated conclusions are of the type *cause(genotype, phenotype, group)*.

Other aspects of our annotation scheme not illustrated in Figure 2 are illustrated (and underlined) in Figure 4. Implicit premises marked as *domain-prop* are reconstructed by the annotator based on domain knowledge that the reader is assumed to possess and which are required by the argument scheme. In Figure 4, the annotator supplied the domain knowledge that geno2a (a homozygous mutation of Itpr1, a gene on chromosome 6qE1) is similar to geno1 (a homozygous mutation on 6qE1). Some premises may be tagged with an optional *conclusion-of* attribute to indicate when the premise is a conclusion of a preceding argument. In Figure 4, the second premise is the inferred conclusion of argument 1.

```
<argument ID="2" scheme="Analogy">
<premise-list>
<premise prop="have_pheno(group1, pheno1)" />
<premise prop="cause(geno1, pheno1, group1)"
        conclusion-of="ARG 1 " />
<premise  prop="have_pheno(group2, pheno2)"  />
<premise prop="similar(pheno2,pheno1)" />
 <premise prop="cause(geno2, pheno2, group2)" />
 <premise domain-prop="similar(geno2a,geno1)" />
<conclusion inferred-prop="cause(geno2a, pheno1,
        group1)" />
</argument>
```

Figure 4: Argument with two implicit premises

---

[2] *Phenotype* describes a deleterious effect on an organism. *Genotype* describes a variation at the level of chromosome or gene that may have a deleterious effect.

Due to the preliminary, experimental nature of this annotation effort, it did not seem essential to adopt a particular tag set used by other researchers. However the <entities-props> elements were designed so that they could be automatically transformed into a Prolog knowledge base like the one used in (Green, 2018) for argument mining, and the structure of <argument> elements reflects the structure of logic programming rules used for argument mining in that work. Furthermore, at this stage of our research, we were more concerned with identifying relevant argumentation features to be annotated, rather than XML coding style.

3   Results and Discussion

We annotated 15 arguments in the Results/Discussion section of the article -- instances of seven schemes from our catalogue. In decreasing order, the number of instances of each are as follows: Agreement (4), Difference (4), Analogy (2) Consistent Explanation (2), Failed Method of Agreement (effect) (1), Eliminate Difference (1), Difference Consistent Explanation (1). In addition, we found two fairly domain-specific arguments, e.g. about the proportion of phenotypes predicted by Mendelian genetics, not represented in the catalogue.

In order to annotate the arguments, we also annotated 27 discourse <entity> elements (instances of nine entity types: *human, mouse, chromosome, gene, variant, gene product, gene function, disorder*), and 41 proposition (<prop>) elements. Two (implicit) premises of arguments were marked as *domain-prop* and five premises were conclusions of previous arguments. Nine of the 15 arguments had implicit conclusions.

Practically speaking, manual annotation of discourse entities was the most difficult aspect of the annotation process. It was difficult to keep track of coreferential entity IDs due to the number of <entity> elements. Furthermore, it was sometimes necessary to annotate discourse entities which were indirectly introduced. For example, the text introduced a discourse entity that could be described as a specific mutation of the gene Itpr1, namely Itpr1opt/opt; then a subsequent argument referred to the related entity, some mutation of Itpr1, i.e., a generalization of Itpr1opt/opt.

We are aware of limitations of this work, due to a lack of resources (annotators and domain experts), and welcome collaboration with other researchers to address them. First, the schemes in the catalogue have not been rigorously evaluated for inter-annotator agreement. However, a previous study (Green, 2017) suggested that some of the schemes, such as Agreement, as well as implicit conclusions of arguments, could be consistently identified. The current catalogue improves upon the materials used in our previous study. Still, work remains to evaluate (and possibly refine) the definitions of the argument schemes in the new catalogue.

Second, as noted earlier we have employed manual annotation of entities and propositions as a stop-gap effort until the articles can be preprocessed by NLP tools. BioNLP is an active area of research and our hope is that in the near future this step can be automated or semi-automated. Also, after annotating this article we became aware of BEL (Fluck et al., 2016), a formal language for describing causal relationships in biology, and are interested in exploring its use for expressing the propositional content of arguments in this domain.

In future work, we would like to analyze arguments in other articles in this subfield as well as in another subfield of genetics, such as evolutionary biology, and extend the present argument scheme catalogue as required. We welcome collaborators to work with us on that as well. The corpus could be used to derive semantic rules for argument mining.

4   Related Work

Most previous computational research on arguments in scientific discourse addressed something different than what we mean by 'argument'. That work is concerned with how an author justifies the publication of his article and positions it with respect to previous claims in his field (Teufel, 2010). It also covers the different functions of text segments in scientific communication, such as reporting the method or results (Liakata et al., 2011). In contrast, we are interested in arguments that present the author's scientific reasoning for validation by other scientists.

There are some correspondences between argument structure and discourse structure induced by certain text coherence relations in models such as Rhetorical Structure Theory (RST) (Mann and Thompson, 1988). However, standard text coherence models are challenged by the existence of arguments with non-contiguous, overlapping, embedded, or implicit components. Also, coherence relation definitions do not encode distinctions among argument schemes. Identification of argument schemes is necessary for evaluating argument acceptability, and for inferring implicit components. In earlier work (Green, 2010), we tried to adapt RST to overcome these problems for the description of arguments in short documents for non-experts about medical conditions. In addition to relaxing text constraints of RST, we annotated the RST analyses with argument schemes. It is not clear though whether this approach could adequately represent the structure of a full-text scientific journal article.

There has been little work addressing argument mining of scientific journals. White et al. (2011) annotated part of the CRAFT corpus with functional labels similar to those of (Liakata et al., 2011) and suggested that patterns of labels might be used to recognize arguments. Mercer's group (2016) is attempting to mine text of biomedical publications as a step towards extracting components of the Toulmin (1998) model of argument. Kirschner et al. (2015) annotated text segments in a corpus of educational research articles. Argument schemes were not annotated. It would be interesting to re-analyze that corpus to compare the types of arguments in it with the types of biological/biomedical arguments identified in our catalogue.

Acknowledgments

The analysis of the CRAFT article was done with the help of Michael Branon and Bishwa Giri, who were supported by a UNCG 2016 Summer Faculty Excellence Research Grant.

References

M. Bada, M. Eckert, D. Evans, et al. 2012. Concept annotation in the CRAFT corpus. *BMC Bioinformatics*, 13:161.

J. Fluck, S. Madan, S. Ansari, et al. 2016. Training and evaluation corpora for the extraction of causal relationships encoded in biological expression language (BEL). *Database* Vol. 2016. Article ID baw113; doi:10.1093/database/baw133.

N.L. Green. 2010. Representation of argumentation in text with Rhetorical Structure Theory. *Argumentation*, 24(2): 181-196.

N.L. Green. 2017. Manual identification of arguments with implicit conclusions using semantic rules for argument mining. In *Proc. of 4th Argument Mining Workshop*, pages 73-78.

N.L. Green. 2018. Towards mining scientific discourse using argumentation schemes. *Argument and Computation*, 9(2):121-135. DOI 10.3233/AAC-180038.

C. Kirschner, J. Eckle-Kohler, and I. Gurevych. 2015. Linking the thoughts: analysis of argumentative structures in scientific publications. In *Proc. NAACL/HLT*, pages 1-11.

J. van de Leemput, J. Chandran, M. Knight, et al. 2007. Deletion at ITPR1 underlies ataxia in mice and spinocerebellar ataxia 15 in humans. *PLoS Genetics*, 3(6, e108):113-129.

M. Liakata et al. 2012. Automatic recognition of conceptualization zones in scientific articles and two life science applications. *Bioinformatics*, 28(7): 2012.

M. Lippi and P. Torroni. 2016. Argumentation mining: state of the art and emerging trends. *ACM Transactions on Internet Technology*, 16(2): Article 10.

W. Mann and S. Thompson. 1988. Rhetorical structure theory: Towards a functional theory of text organization. *Text*, 8(3):243-281.

R. Mercer. 2016. Locating and extracting key components of argumentation from scholarly scientific writing. In E. Cabrio, G. Hirst, S. Villata and A. Wynder (eds.), *Natural Language Argumentation Mining: Processing and Reasoning over Textual Arguments*, Dagstuhl Seminar 16161, April 17-22, 2016.

A. Peldszus and M. Stede. 2016. An annotated corpus of argumentative microtexts. In *Proc. 1st European Conference on Argumentation*, Lisbon 2015, v. 2, pages 801-816.

R. Prasad, S. McRoy, N. Frid, A. Joshi, and H. Yu. 2011. The Biomedical Discourse Relation Bank. *BMC Bioinformatics*, 12:188.

C. Stab and I. Gurevych, 2014. Annotating argument components and relations in persuasive essays. In *Proc. COLING 2014*, pages 1501-1510.

S. Teufel. 2010. *The Structure of Scientific Articles: Applications to Citation Indexing and Summarization.* CSLI Publications, Stanford, CA.

S. Toulmin. 1998. *The Uses of Argument*. Cambridge University Press, Cambridge, UK.

K. Verspoor, K.B. Cohen, A. Lanfranchi, et al. 2012. A corpus of full-text journal articles is a robust evaluation tool for revealing differences in performance of biomedical natural language processing tools. *BMC Bioinformatics* 2012, 13:207.

D. Walton, C. Reed, and F. Macagno. 2008. *Argumentation Schemes.* Cambridge University Press, Cambridge, UK.

E. White, K.B. Cohen, and L. Hunter. 2011. The CISP annotation schema uncovers hypotheses and explanations in full-text scientific journal articles. In *Proc. of the 2011 Workshop on Biomedical Natural Language Processing*, ACL-HLT 2011, Portland, OR, USA, June 23-24, 2011, pages 134-135.

Using context to identify the language of face-saving

Nona Naderi
Department of Computer Science
University of Toronto
Toronto, Ontario, Canada
nona@cs.toronto.edu

Graeme Hirst
Department of Computer Science
University of Toronto
Toronto, Ontario, Canada
gh@cs.toronto.edu

Abstract

We created a corpus of utterances that attempt to save face from parliamentary debates and use it to automatically analyze the language of reputation defence. Our proposed model that incorporates information regarding threats to reputation can predict reputation defence language with high confidence. Further experiments and evaluations on different datasets show that the model is able to generalize to new utterances and can predict the language of reputation defence in a new dataset.

1 Introduction

Goffman (1967) defines *face*, or *reputation*, as "the positive social value a person effectively claims for himself by the line others assume he has taken during a particular contact. Face is an image of self delineated in terms of approved social attributes". Criticisms and persuasive attacks pose threats to reputation or face and they are common in all social interactions. Allegations are often made against organizations (e.g., companies and governments) and individuals (e.g., medical practitioners and politicians), and various argumentation tactics and persuasive strategies are used in response to these allegations to attempt to defend the respondent's reputation and thereby save face. Previous studies on reputation defence mostly use manual content analysis, such as the studies by Benoit and Henson (2009) and Zhang and Benoit (2009) on political cases, and by Penman (1990) and Tracy (2011) on courtroom cases. While these studies reveal much about reputation defence strategies in various social settings, they do not analyze in detail the actual language used in the defence of reputation.

Here, we examine political speeches and investigate whether we can detect the language of reputation defence. We created a corpus of reputa-

tion defence,[1] in which the annotations are based on the structure of parliamentary debate. This corpus is based on the oral question period of a Westminster-style parliamentary system, specifically that of Canada, where the government of the day is held accountable for its actions and tries to defend its reputation.[2] Using this naturally annotated data lets us avoid the subjectivity of manual analysis, any interpretation by the annotators, and any annotation inconsistencies. We investigate whether we can predict the language of reputation defence and whether the context in which the reputation defence occurs can help in identifying this language. We first perform experiments on a sampled dataset from Canadian parliamentary proceedings of 1994–2014. We then explore the performance of our approaches on two different governments. We show that the context of reputation defence is effective in its recognition.

2 Related work

Reputation defense is more broadly related to Aristotelian ethos (Aristotle, 2007) or one's credibility that is reflected through the use of language. Previous studies on face-saving and reputation management focused on identifying various persuasive strategies and their effectiveness (Benoit, 1995; Coombs and Holladay, 2008; Burns and Bruner, 2000; Sheldon and Sallot, 2008). In the NLP field, Naderi and Hirst (2017) performed a manual annotation analysis on reputation defence strategies in Parliament and proposed a computational model to identify strategies of denial, excuse, justification, and concession. Naderi and Hirst (2018) further proposed two approaches to

---

[1]The data is freely available at http://www.cs.toronto.edu/~nona/data/data.html
[2]https://www.ourcommons.ca/About/Compendium/Questions/c_d_principlesguidelinesoralquestions-e.htm

Proceedings of the 5th Workshop on Argument Mining, pages 111–120
Brussels, Belgium, November 1, 2018. ©2018 Association for Computational Linguistics

automatically annotate unlabeled speeches with defence strategies. Another related NLP study focuses on extracting ethos from the United Kingdom's parliamentary debates; Duthie and Budzynska (2018) used a set of features, such as sentiments and part-of-speech tags, to extract negative and positive references. Here, instead, we are interested in studying whether we can classify a speech as reputation defence or not, and whether the context can improve this classification.

3   Reputation defence

The main purpose of the oral question period in a Westminster-style parliamentary system is to hold the government accountable for its actions and to highlight the inadequacies of the government.[3] Members of the opposition and government backbenchers both may ask questions, and government ministers must respond. The questions asked by the opposition members are confrontational, intended to criticize or embarass the government, and are considered reputation threats; the answers to these questions by government ministers try to defend the government's choices and the ministers' reputations. Therefore, these questions and answers are a rich dataset for characterizing the language of reputation attack and the language of reputation defence. Government backbenchers can also pose questions. However, these questions are most often friendly and promotional questions, and the answers given to these questions try to promote the government's plans. Thus these questions and their answers are ordinary reputation-building or reputation-enhancing pairs. They thus act as negative examples.

This dichotomy between the two types of questions in Parliament is supported by qualitative studies such as those of Peŕez de Ayala (2001), Ilie (2006), and Bates et al. (2012). Peŕez de Ayala (2001) describes Question Time in the U.K. House of Commons as a "face-threatening genre" and examines politeness strategies used in the face-threatening language of a set of questions. Bates et al.'s (2012) analysis shows that government backbenchers ask either questions that allow the minister to talk about the government's policies and positions, or questions that are straightforward to answer. While concerns with reputation are of particular importance not only for politicians but are salient in all social encounters, gathering a dataset of reputation threats and defences from encounters other than parliamentary settings is challenging. Hence, we use the available parliamentary proceedings for characterizing these languages.

The following question posed by the opposition in the Canadian Parliament and the Minister's reply to it is an example of a reputation threat and the defence made in response. In the example, the [Deputy] Prime Minister is confronted by an opposition member with a persuasive attack, and he tries to defend and justify the actions of the government:[4]

Example 3.1 *Q. Mr. Speaker, the former finance minister continues to amaze the crowds with his dance of the veils, with the ethics counsellor standing just off stage catching whatever is shed. The first layer was the blind trust that no one could see through. Next came blind management. Now we are down to the last and flimsiest layer, the supervisory agreement. Could the Prime Minister explain why the former finance minister was allowed the opportunity for hands on management by the ethics counsellor while all other ministers adhered to the stricter blind trust or blind management agreements?*

A. Mr. Speaker, the arrangements that were in place were those that were appropriate to the circumstances and, in fact, reflect the views of the Parker commission that reviewed these matters in the past. The former minister complied entirely with the requirements before him.

The next example shows a non-threatening question and answer pair, where the question is posed by a government backbencher.[5]

Example 3.2 *Q. Mr. Speaker, my question is for the Minister of the Environment. Recently we have been reading more and more articles in the media concerning high levels of sulphur in fuels, air pollution and health problems that result from these high levels. On this issue could the minister tell the*

---

[3]The Westminster system originated in the United Kingdom and is used in Commonwealth nations, such as Canada, Australia, India, and New Zealand. The tradition of question time for government accountability is practiced under different names in these countries; in the United Kingdom, it is known as *oral questions*, in Canada as *oral question period*, in Australia and New Zealand as *question time*, and in India as *question hour*.

[4]2003-02-20, John Reynolds (Q) and John Manley, Deputy Prime Minister, representing the Prime Minister (A).

[5]2001-06-04, Shawn Murphy (Q) and David Anderson (A).

House what actions are being taken to deal with the issue of high sulphur levels in fuels in Canada?

A. Mr. Speaker, the announcement I made earlier this year covers gasoline, diesel and fuel oils outside road fuels. It will reduce the amount of sulphur in gasoline from its average now of 360 parts per million to 30 parts per million. In on road diesel, the figure will go from 500 parts per million to 15. The dates for this are the end of 2004 for gasoline and June 1, 2006, for diesel.

4 Data

We extracted our Canadian data from the Lipad[6] dataset of the Canadian parliamentary proceedings (Hansard) from 1994 to 2014. This data consists of the proceedings of the 35th to 41st Canadian parliaments. We focused on only the first question and answer pair of each topic of discussion during the oral question period of parliament sessions in order to minimize dependency on the broader topical context. We created a balanced corpus by randomly sampling the same number of questions posed by the opposition members (reputation threats) as those asked by the government backbenchers (friendly non-threats). This resulted in 9,048 pairs of questions and answers on more than 1,600 issues over the 20-year period.

To further analyze reputation defence strategies used by different governments, we extracted the question and answer pairs from parliaments with different governing parties. The Liberal Party was the government in the 36th, 37th, and 38th Parliaments, and the Conservative Party was the government in the 39th, 40th, and 41st Parliaments. This allows us to examine the language of reputation defence used by different political ideologies. Furthermore, by training and testing models on parliaments with different governing parties, we can ensure that the models are not affected by the ideology of the speaker and the topic of day or interest of the accuser. Table 1 shows the statistics of these datasets, which, unlike the 1994–2014 dataset, are not balanced.

5 Reputation threat analysis

A principled analysis of the language of face-threats or accusations themselves falls outside the scope of this work, but here we characterize the

---

6LInked PArliamentary Data, `https://www.lipad.ca`

Party	Parliaments	Opposition	Government
Liberal	36, 37, 38	11,090	1,736
Conservative	39, 40, 41	11,504	2,004

Table 1: Corpus statistics; *Party* shows the governing party; *Opposition* shows the number of questions asked by the opposition members and their respective answers, *Government* shows the number of questions asked by the government backbenchers and their respective answers.

differences between the questions asked by opposition members (reputation threats) and questions asked by government backbenchers (friendly non-threats). We randomly sampled 3,400 questions asked by the oppositions and 3,400 questions asked by the government backbenchers. We performed our analysis using Linguistic Inquiry and Word Count (LIWC) (Tausczik and Pennebaker, 2010), which is widely used in social science studies. Table 2 presents the ratio of averages between reputation threats and non-threat questions for a set of LIWC features, including *anger*, *negative* and *positive* emotions, *achievement*, and *cognitive processes*. Ratios greater than 1.0 indicate features that are more prominent in reputation threats and ratios less than 1.0 indicate features that are more prominent in non-threats. The results show that, unsurprisingly, anger and negative emotions used more in reputation threats than non-threats, whereas positive emotions are used more in non-threats. These features are motivated by theories, such as Brown and Levinson (1987) and Partington (2003) that recognize varying degrees of politeness in threatening or saving the addressee's face. Achievements are used more in non-threats and cognitive processes are used more in reputation threats. This is consistent with theories (Mulholland, 2003) that recognize mentioning the consequences of the fault as one mode of accusation.

6 Approach

Convolutional Neural Networks (CNN) have been shown to be effective for classification tasks (Kim, 2014). Here, we used a CNN model to represent the question and answer pairs for binary classifications of face-saving language. We first represented each word in the question and the answer with its associated pre-trained embedding. We then applied a convolution operation to each possible window of x words from the question and the answer to produce a feature map, similar to the ap-

113

Feature	Ratio	Text
Anger	1.15	**Opp:** Prime Minister has the **annoying** habit of blindly exonerating …
Negative emotion	1.35	**Opp:** We all know there is a **nasty** trade dispute going on between …
Positive emotion	0.69	**Gov:** … presenting new and exciting **opportunities** …
Achievement	0.82	**Gov:** … foundation has **successfully** concluded agreements with …
Cognitive processes	1.20	**Opp:** … Minister of the Environment **ought to** read the U.S. …

Table 2: Ratios of linguistic features in opposition questions to government backbenchers' questions. Text shows an example for each feature. **Opp** shows an opposition question and **Gov** shows a government backbencher's question.

proach of Kim (2014). We then applied a sliding Max Pooling and concatenated the representation of the question and the answer. We used 20 and 10 filters for the five-fold cross-validation and cross-parliament experiments, respectively. We used filter windows of 3 and 4, a dropout of 0.8, and mini-batch sizes of 32 and 50 for five-fold cross-validation and cross-parliament experiments, respectively.

Recurrent neural networks have been used effectively in NLP for sequence modeling. Here, we further used two long short-term memory (LSTM) (Hochreiter and Schmidhuber, 1997) networks[7] with 128 units to represent questions and answers, separately. The LSTM layers were then passed to a dropout layer (Hinton et al., 2012) with a rate of 0.6. We then merged the two representations. For all our Neural Network models, we initialized our word representations using the publicly available GloVe pre-trained word embeddings (Pennington et al., 2014)[8] (300-dimensional vectors trained on Common Crawl data), and restricted the vocabulary to the 5,000 most-frequent words. The models were trained with binary cross-entropy with the Adam optimizer (Kingma and Ba, 2014) for 10 and 5 epochs for five-fold cross-validation and cross-parliament experiments, respectively. We also tried encoding the questions and answers using a layer of Gated Recurrent Units (GRU) (Cho et al., 2014) with shared parameters, but this model performed worse than the other models, and for brevity we do not report the results here.

We further trained an SVM classifier (using the scikit-learn package (Pedregosa et al., 2011)) with all possible combinations of words extracted from the cross-product of questions and answers to capture the interaction between reputation threat and reputation defence. The features are tuples of word pairs from question and answer pairs. We removed word pairs that occurred fewer than 80 times in the datasets. Our use of this set of features is inspired by the effectiveness of word pairs in classifying discourse relations (Biran and McKeown, 2013; Pitler et al., 2009) regardless of their sparsity issue.

7 Evaluation and results

We approach the recognition of the face-saving language as a binary supervised classification task. Our baselines are majority class (which is always answers given to the opposition questions), an SVM model trained with answer unigram vectors (weighted using *tf–idf*, represented with the notation '-Answers' in the result tables), and one layer of GRU to model answer sequences. Since reputation defence is expressed in response to the reputation threat, we further considered the question as the context of the reputation defence and trained an SVM model with question and answer unigrams (weighted using *tf-idf*, represented by the notation '-Questions&Answers' in the result tables). For comparison, we further include the results of an SVM model trained on only unigrams from questions ('-Questions'). We also use one layer of GRU to model the concatenation of question and answer pairs as one sequence. The SVM model trained on word pairs is represented with the notation '-Questions×Answers' in the result tables.

In the cross-parliament setting, we used the 36th, 37th, and 38th parliaments with Liberal governments and the 39th, 40th, and 41st parliaments with Conservative governments. We first performed a five-fold cross-validation on the Liberal and Conservative governments individually (three parliaments each), and then performed a

---

[7]Using https://keras.io/

[8]https://nlp.stanford.edu/projects/glove/

Model	Accuracy	F_1	Precision	Recall
(1) Canada 1994–2014; Opposition: 4,524; Government: 4,524				
Majority	50.00			
Unigrams-Answers	76.57	76.57	76.59	76.57
Unigrams-Question&Answers	88.00	88.00	88.01	88.00
Unigrams-Questions	90.10	90.10	90.11	90.10
1 GRU(128)-Answers	81.60	82.64	77.27	89.99
1 GRU(128)-Questions&Answers	**94.39**	**94.23**	**93.94**	**94.91**
CNN(128)-Questions&Answers	91.40	91.16	90.54	92.41
2 LSTMs(128)-Questions&Answers	92.26	91.92	93.34	91.04
Word-pairs-Questions×Answers	91.46	91.46	91.47	91.46
(2) Parliaments 36, 37, 38; Opposition: 11,090; Government: 1,736				
Majority	86.47			
Unigrams-Answers	88.57	88.26	88.10	88.57
Unigrams-Questions&Answers	92.77	92.59	92.50	92.77
Unigrams-Questions	93.59	93.43	93.43	93.59
1 GRU(128)-Answers	90.89	94.91	91.53	98.70
1 GRU(128)-Questions&Answers	**95.72**	**97.52**	96.52	98.66
CNN(128)-Questions&Answers	94.50	96.87	95.12	**98.81**
2 LSTMs(128)-Questions&Answers	94.11	96.52	**97.23**	95.99
Word-pairs-Questions×Answers	95.06	94.95	94.98	95.06
(3) Parliaments 39, 40, 41; Opposition: 11,504; Government: 2,004				
Majority	85.16			
Unigrams-Answers	87.27	86.95	86.82	87.27
Unigrams-Questions&Answers	95.87	95.75	95.78	95.87
Unigrams-Questions	97.45	97.41	97.42	97.45
1 GRU(128)-Answers	91.05	94.93	91.63	98.63
1 GRU(128)-Questions&Answers	**98.33**	**99.02**	98.77	**99.30**
CNN(128)-Questions&Answers	97.10	98.31	97.50	99.20
2 LSTMs(128)-Questions&Answers	97.11	98.27	**98.98**	97.63
Word-pairs-Questions×Answers	97.48	97.43	97.45	97.48

Table 3: The performance of different models for binary classification of reputation defence language using five-fold cross-validation on (1) a balanced set from 1994–2014; (2) three Liberal governments; (3) three Conservative governments.

cross-parliament classification. For all datasets and models, we randomly used 10% of the training data as the development set. We evaluated the performance of reputation defence classification using the metrics *Accuracy, Precision, Recall,* and F_1. Table 3 shows the results of five-fold cross-validation on a balanced set from all parliaments in the period 1994–2014, on just the Liberal governments, and on just the Conservative governments. Both CNN and LSTM models improve the classification compared to the baselines. In general, we can see that all the models that rely only on the answer or reputation defence perform poorer than the models that rely also on the questions. The best model achieves an accuracy and F_1 measure of above 98% on the parliaments with Conservative governments. The highest accuracy and F_1 measure on the Liberal dataset is above 95% and 97%, respectively.

Table 4 shows the results of the cross-parliament classification. We trained the models on all Liberal parliaments, and tested them on all Conservative governments, and then vice versa. The SVM model trained using question-and-answer unigrams is a strong baseline. Both the CNN and LSTM models improved F_1 measure compared to the baseline models. On the cross-parliament classification setting, again the models trained on both questions and answers perform better. The overall performance of the neural net models across parliaments is poorer than the classification performance within parliaments. This can be explained by the differences in framing strategies used in the language of defence by the two parties, which each defend their actions and choices from their own point of view. The SVM model trained on the words extracted from the cross-product of questions and answers (word-pairs) achieves the best accuracy, reaching an accuracy and F_1 measure above 92% across parliaments. These results show that reputation defence language can be detected with high accuracy regardless of differences in ideologies and framing strategies.

An error analysis shows that most errors occurred in the classification of answers to non-threat questions. One reason for this is that while the government ministers do not defend themselves in the answers in response to the government backbenchers, they do try to enhance their

image. Consider the following example[9]:

Example 7.1 *Q. Mr. Speaker, my question is for the Minister of the Environment. Over the weekend, the leader of the Bloc Québécois had the temerity to claim that the 2005 budget did not serve the interests of the people in Quebec. I know full well that the environment is very important to the people in my riding. Could the minister tell the House how the environmental initiatives contained in the budget will benefit Quebec?*

A. Mr. Speaker, Quebeckers are impatiently awaiting the greenest budget since Confederation. Very successful contacts have been established with the Government of Quebec for the use of the partnership fund. Projects are sprouting up all over for the climate fund, for new investments, for national parks and for investment in renewable and wind energy. Mayors are waiting for green investments for cities and municipalities through the new deal, the green municipal fund, the Ener-Guide program for cities and so on. Quebec must not be blocked, but greened even more.

We further examined the cases where a reputation defence was erroneously assigned a non-defence label. These cases require real-world knowledge to determine that they are indeed reputation defence. Here is an example[10]:

Example 7.2 *Q. Mr. Speaker, this country was built upon common interests by and for the people here. We cannot allow the House of Commons to introduce a bill which, in reality, provides a recipe for destroying this country. Does the government realize that this draft bill is an avowal of failure by this government as far as the future of the federation is concerned?*

A. No, Mr. Speaker. This bill is a follow-up to the Supreme Court judgment referring back to the political stakeholders the responsibility to establish the conditions of clarity under which they would agree to negotiate the secession of a province from Canada, and it seems to me that one of those stakeholders is the Canadian House of Commons.

The models that rely on only the answer have particular difficulty in distinguishing these cases.

---

[9]2005-05-31, David Smith (Q) and Stéphane Dion (A).
[10]1999-12-13, André Bachand (Q) and Stéphane Dion (A).

Model	Accuracy	F_1	Precision	Recall
Train 36, 37, 38 (Opp: 11,090; Gov: 1,736) and test 39, 40, 41 (Opp: 11,504; Gov: 2,004)				
Majority	85.16			
Unigram-Answers	82.22	82.63	83.10	82.22
Unigrams-Questions&Answers	89.60	89.23	89.02	89.60
Unigrams-Questions	91.56	91.07	91.04	91.56
GRU(128)-Answers	84.02	91.21	85.23	98.25
GRU(128)-Questions&Answers	83.48	90.83	85.65	96.84
CNN(128)-Questions&Answers	85.86	92.32	86.53	**99.10**
2 LSTMs(128)-Questions&Answers	85.27	91.88	86.10	98.66
Word-pairs-Questions×Answers	**93.59**	**93.36**	**93.33**	93.59
Train 39, 40, 41 (Opp: 11,504; Gov: 2,004) and test 36, 37, 38 (Opp: 11,090; Gov: 1,736)				
Majority	86.47			
Unigram-Answers	86.95	85.44	84.87	86.95
Unigrams-Questions&Answers	90.34	89.10	89.40	90.34
Unigrams-Questions	91.14	90.52	90.42	91.14
GRU(128)-Answers	86.29	92.58	86.49	**99.71**
GRU(128)-Questions&Answers	85.58	92.14	86.49	98.75
CNN(128)-Questions&Answers	86.75	92.73	87.67	98.55
2 LSTMs(128)-Questions&Answers	86.72	**92.78**	87.10	99.45
Word-pairs-Questions×Answers	**92.95**	92.31	**92.62**	92.95

Table 4: The performance of different models for binary classification of reputation defence in the cross-parliament setting. **Opp** shows the number of opposition members' questions and their respective answers and **Gov** shows the number of government backbenchers' questions and their respective answers.

Model	Accuracy	F_1	Precision	Recall
Train 36, 37, 38 and test 39, 40, 41 (balanced, 3400 instances train and 3400 test)				
Majority	50.00			
Unigrams-Answers	67.94	67.92	67.99	67.94
+NRC Emotion (anger+pos+neg)	69.77	69.70	69.94	69.77
+Bigrams	73.41	73.33	73.73	73.41
+Vagueness cue words	73.85	73.75	74.22	73.85
Word-pairs-Questions×Answers	83.97	83.95	84.14	83.97
Train 39, 40, 41 and test 36, 37, 38 (balanced, 3400 instances train and 3400 test)				
Majority	50.00			
Unigrams-Answers	71.24	70.68	72.99	71.24
+NRC Emotion (anger+pos+neg)	71.71	71.14	73.57	71.71
+Bigram	73.71	72.91	76.88	73.71
+Vagueness cue words	73.88	73.91	76.98	73.88
Word-pairs-Questions×Answers	83.77	83.67	84.82	83.77

Table 5: The performance of different models for binary classification of reputation defence in the cross-parliament setting with the balanced data (1700 instances of each class).

8 Analyzing the language of defence

To help discover more about the underlying structure of the data, we conducted an exploratory feature analysis. We created two balanced datasets from the two governments, where each dataset consists of 3,400 question and answer pairs (1,700 questions asked by opposition members and 1,700 questions asked by government backbenchers). The question and answer pairs were selected randomly. In this setting, we focused only on the text of the answers or reputation defence.

We consider emotions, such as positive, negative, and anger. For extracting these features, we used the NRC Word-Emotion Association Lexicon (NRC Emotion lexicon)[11]. This lexicon provides manually assigned association scores for basic emotions including *anger, fear, joy, sadness, disgust, anticipation, trust, surprise*, and sentiments (*positive* and *negative*) (Mohammad and Turney, 2013). It consists of 14,182 unigrams that are manually annotated through crowdsourcing. We compute the total association scores of the lexicon words in the answer for each class of emotions and sentiments.

We further examined the NRC VAD Lexicon[12] for our analysis. This lexicon provides valence (positiveness–negativeness / pleasure / displeasure), arousal (active–passive), and dominance (dominant–submissive) scores for 20K English words (Mohammad, 2018). These dimensions have been used for analysis of human interaction (Burgoon and Hale, 1984). We use the total score of each dimension in the answer as a feature. We also consider vagueness cue words (Bhatia et al., 2016; Lebanoff and Liu, 2018). This set of features (40 cue words) is represented by the frequency of the vagueness cues in the answer. The use of these features is motivated by theories such as that of Fraser (2012) that suggest that hedge words can be used to avoid face-threatening acts. We also use bigrams as additional features. We performed the classification using SVM. The results of the binary classification of face-saving language on the balanced data of the cross-parliament setting is presented in Table 5.

The only emotion that contributed to the classification was anger. The positive impact of anger

		Predicted	
		Non-defence	Defence
Actual	Non-defence	1,360	340
	Defence	549	1,151

Table 6: Confusion matrix for the best performing model that relies only on features extracted from answers, including unigrams and bigrams, NRC emotions (anger+pos+neg), and vagueness cues. Trained on 36,37,38 (3,400 instances) and tested on 39,40,41 (3,400 instances).

		Predicted	
		Non-defence	Defence
Actual	Non-defence	1,368	332
	Defence	213	1,487

Table 7: Confusion matrix for the model trained on word pairs. Trained on 36,37,38 (3,400 instances) and tested on 39,40,41 (3,400 instances).

on the classification performance is in line with theories such as those of Mulholland (2003) and Benoit (1995) that find that attacking the accuser is a type of face-saving strategy. Both positive and negative sentiments also improved the performance of the classification, as did vagueness cues and bigrams. However, using valence, arousal, and dominance hurt the performance.

The confusion matrices for the best model trained on the features extracted from the answers (unigrams and bigrams + NRC Emotions including negative and positive sentiments and anger + vagueness cues) and the model trained on word pairs are presented in Tables 6 and 7, respectively. Both models are trained on 3,400 instances from the 36th, 37th, and 38th parliaments and tested on 3,400 instances from the 39th, 40th, and 41st parliaments.

9 Conclusion

Face-saving language is employed in everyday human interaction. In this study, we introduced the task of automatically recognizing the language of face-saving. We created a corpus of reputation-defence language on various issues from parliamentary proceedings that is freely available. We further presented two neural network approaches to classify this language. We showed that the context of reputation defence is important for this classification task. Our results supported our annotation decision based on the adversarial struc-

---

[11] http://saifmohammad.com/WebPages/ NRC-Emotion-Lexicon.htm

[12] http://saifmohammad.com/WebPages/ nrc-vad.html

ture of the parliament and showed that our corpus is appropriate for analyzing the language of reputation defence. A practical application of our model will be to analyze human behavior and to examine the effectiveness of reputation defence in various social settings.

Acknowledgements

This research is financially supported by an Ontario Graduate Scholarship, the Natural Sciences and Engineering Research Council of Canada, and the University of Toronto. We thank the anonymous reviewers for their thoughtful comments and suggestions.

References

Aristotle. 2007. *On Rhetoric: A Theory of Civic Discourse* (translated by G.A. Kennedy). Oxford University Press.

Soledad Peŕez de Ayala. 2001. FTAs and Erskine May: Conflicting needs? Politeness in question time. *Journal of Pragmatics*, 33(2):143–169.

Stephen R. Bates, Peter Kerr, Christopher Byrne, and Liam Stanley. 2012. Questions to the Prime Minister: A comparative study of PMQs from Thatcher to Cameron. *Parliamentary Affairs*, 67(2):253–280.

William L. Benoit. 1995. *Accounts, Excuses, and Apologies: A Theory of Image Restoration Strategies.* State University of New York Press, Albany.

William L. Benoit and Jayne R. Henson. 2009. President Bush's image repair discourse on Hurricane Katrina. *Public Relations Review*, 35(1):40–46.

Jaspreet Bhatia, Travis D. Breaux, Joel R. Reidenberg, and Thomas B. Norton. 2016. A theory of vagueness and privacy risk perception. In *Requirements Engineering Conference (RE), 2016 IEEE 24th International*, pages 26–35. IEEE.

Or Biran and Kathleen McKeown. 2013. Aggregated word pair features for implicit discourse relation disambiguation. In *Proceedings of the 51st Annual Meeting of the Association for Computational Linguistics (Volume 2: Short Papers)*, pages 69–73, Sofia, Bulgaria. Association for Computational Linguistics.

Penelope Brown and Stephen C. Levinson. 1987. *Politeness: Some Universals in Language Usage*, volume 4. Cambridge University Press.

Judee K. Burgoon and Jerold L. Hale. 1984. The fundamental topoi of relational communication. *Communication Monographs*, 51(3):193–214.

Judith P. Burns and Michael S. Bruner. 2000. Revisiting the theory of image restoration strategies. *Communication Quarterly*, 48(1):27–39.

KyungHyun Cho, Bart van Merrienboer, Dzmitry Bahdanau, and Yoshua Bengio. 2014. On the properties of neural machine translation: Encoder-decoder approaches. *arXiv preprint arXiv:1409.1259,*.

W. Timothy Coombs and Sherry J. Holladay. 2008. Comparing apology to equivalent crisis response strategies: Clarifying apology's role and value in crisis communication. *Public Relations Review*, 34(3):252–257.

Rory Duthie and Katarzyna Budzynska. 2018. A Deep Modular RNN Approach for Ethos Mining. In *Proceedings of the Twenty-Seventh International Joint Conference on Artificial Intelligence, IJCAI-18*, pages 4041–4047. International Joint Conferences on Artificial Intelligence Organization.

Bruce Fraser. 2012. Pragmatic competence: The case of hedging. In Gunther Kaltenböck, Wiltrud Mihatsch, and Stefan Schneider, editors, *New Approaches to Hedging*, pages 15–34. Brill.

Erving Goffman. 1967. *Interaction Ritual: Essays on face-to-face interaction.* Aldine.

Geoffrey E. Hinton, Nitish Srivastava, Alex Krizhevsky, Ilya Sutskever, and Ruslan R. Salakhutdinov. 2012. Improving neural networks by preventing co-adaptation of feature detectors. *arXiv preprint arXiv:1207.0580*.

Sepp Hochreiter and Jürgen Schmidhuber. 1997. Long short-term memory. *Neural Computation*, 9(8):1735–1780.

Cornelia Ilie. 2006. Parliamentary discourses. In Keith Brown, Anne H. Anderson, Laurie Bauer, Margie Berns, Graeme Hirst, and Jim Miller, editors, *Encyclopedia of Language and Linguistics*, second edition, pages 188–196. Elsevier, Oxford.

Yoon Kim. 2014. Convolutional neural networks for sentence classification. In *Proceedings of the 2014 Conference on Empirical Methods in Natural Language Processing (EMNLP)*, pages 1746–1751, Doha, Qatar. Association for Computational Linguistics.

Diederik Kingma and Jimmy Ba. 2014. Adam: A method for stochastic optimization. *arXiv preprint arXiv:1412.6980*.

Logan Lebanoff and Fei Liu. 2018. Automatic detection of vague words and sentences in privacy policies. In *Proceedings of the 2018 Conference on Empirical Methods in Natural Language Processing*, Brussels, Belgium. Association for Computational Linguistics.

Saif Mohammad. 2018. Obtaining reliable human ratings of valence, arousal, and dominance for 20,000 English words. In *Proceedings of the 56th Annual Meeting of the Association for Computational Linguistics (Volume 1: Long Papers)*, pages 174–184. Association for Computational Linguistics.

Saif M. Mohammad and Peter D. Turney. 2013. Crowdsourcing a word-emotion association lexicon. *Computational Intelligence*, 29(3):436–465.

Joan Mulholland. 2003. *A Handbook of Persuasive Tactics: A Practical Language Guide*. Routledge.

Nona Naderi and Graeme Hirst. 2017. Recognizing reputation defence strategies in critical political exchanges. In *Proceedings of the International Conference Recent Advances in Natural Language Processing, RANLP 2017*, pages 527–535, Varna, Bulgaria.

Nona Naderi and Graeme Hirst. 2018. Automatically labeled data generation for classification of reputation defence strategies. In *Proceedings of the Eleventh International Conference on Language Resources and Evaluation (LREC 2018)*, Paris, France. European Language Resources Association (ELRA).

Alan Partington. 2003. *The linguistics of political argument: The spin-doctor and the wolf-pack at the White House*. Routledge.

F. Pedregosa, G. Varoquaux, A. Gramfort, V. Michel, B. Thirion, O. Grisel, M. Blondel, P. Prettenhofer, R. Weiss, V. Dubourg, J. Vanderplas, A. Passos, D. Cournapeau, M. Brucher, M. Perrot, and E. Duchesnay. 2011. Scikit-learn: Machine learning in Python. *Journal of Machine Learning Research*, 12:2825–2830.

Robyn Penman. 1990. Facework & politeness: Multiple goals in courtroom discourse. *Journal of Language and Social Psychology*, 9(1-2):15–38.

Jeffrey Pennington, Richard Socher, and Christopher D. Manning. 2014. GloVe: Global vectors for word representation. In *Proceedings of the 2014 Conferene on Empirical Methods in Natural Language Processing (EMNLP)*, pages 1532–1543.

Emily Pitler, Annie Louis, and Ani Nenkova. 2009. Automatic sense prediction for implicit discourse relations in text. In *Proceedings of the Joint Conference of the 47th Annual Meeting of the ACL and the 4th International Joint Conference on Natural Language Processing of the AFNLP: Volume 2-Volume 2*, pages 683–691. Association for Computational Linguistics.

Catherine A. Sheldon and Lynne M. Sallot. 2008. Image repair in politics: Testing effects of communication strategy and performance history in a faux pas. *Journal of Public Relations Research*, 21(1):25–50.

Yla R. Tausczik and James W. Pennebaker. 2010. The psychological meaning of words: LIWC and computerized text analysis methods. *Journal of Language and Social Psychology*, 29(1):24–54.

Karen Tracy. 2011. A facework system of minimal politeness: Oral argument in appellate court. *Journal of Politeness Research. Language, Behaviour, Culture*, 7(1):123–145.

Ernest Zhang and William L. Benoit. 2009. Former Minister Zhang's discourse on SARS: Government's image restoration or destruction? *Public Relations Review*, 35(3):240–246.

Dave the debater: a retrieval-based and generative argumentative dialogue agent

Dieu Thu Le
Institute for Natural
Language Processing (IMS)
University of Stuttgart
thu@ims.uni-stuttgart.de

Cam-Tu Nguyen
National Key Laboratory for
Novel Software Technology
Nanjing University
ncamtu@nju.edu.cn

Kim Anh Nguyen
FPT Technology
Research Institute
FPT University
anhnk14@fpt.com.vn

Abstract

In this paper, we explore the problem of developing an argumentative dialogue agent that can be able to discuss with human users on controversial topics. We describe two systems that use retrieval-based and generative models to make argumentative responses to the users. The experiments show promising results although they have been trained on a small dataset.

1 Introduction

Research in argument mining has mainly focused on the problem of identifying claims, premises (Boltužić and Šnajder, 2014, 2015; Levy et al., 2014), assessing arguments, classifying stances, detecting political beliefs (Hasan and Ng, 2013; Iyyer et al., 2014; Bamman and Smith, 2015) or finding connection between claims (Stab and Gurevych, 2014). Very few research has addressed the problem of generating arguments directly in a conversational form.

To study and analyse debates, it is important to understand how to formulate claims, how arguments develop and relate to each other, what factors influence the next argument. In this work, we explore the question whether we can teach computers to make or generate arguments and follow the ideas/stances/sides of actors in a debate. To start inspecting this challenging problem, we develop two debate dialogue systems, a retrieval-based and a generative model. The aim of the system is to mimic a debater, make arguments and give relevant responses to users on given topics.

Such argumentative dialogue systems could be useful in a lot of future applications, such as in information campaigns, where the users can get objective answers for controversial topics to make evidence-based decisions; in an interactive argumentative dialogue system, where the users can practice making arguments, learning to persuade people.

2 Related work

Analyzing public debates about controversial issues is a well-studied area in social and political science. Natural language processing and machine learning could help building a scalable and data-driven predictive modelling for public debates. In this rapidly growing field, most of the work has focused on the identification of claims and justifications in text (Boltužić and Šnajder, 2014, 2015; Levy et al., 2014), connecting claims (Stab and Gurevych, 2014), actors with discourse analysis (Peldszus and Stede, 2015), stance detection (Hasan and Ng, 2013), or the categorization of political beliefs (Iyyer et al., 2014; Bamman and Smith, 2015).

Most of these studies have focused on public debates which can be found in newspaper articles, written essay (Stab and Gurevych, 2017) or parliament debates (Koehn, 2005). Another line of research works on Internet dialogues such as those in social networks, online forum debates (Walker et al., 2012a). The dialogic language used in these forms is usually different from that found in newspapers. While it also contains stances, arguments, opinions, this language is usually more informal, can contain typos and subjective acts such as sarcasm (Justo et al., 2014; Swanson et al., 2017). There are a number of studies focusing on this kind of data, working on sarcasm and nastiness detection (Justo et al., 2014; Swanson et al., 2017) as well as topic stance classification (Walker et al., 2012b).

Little research has been done on using machine learning to generate arguments in a conversation. The most relevant idea is the one reported in (Rakshit et al., 2017; Rach et al., 2018). In (Rakshit et al., 2017), the authors describe Debbie, a debate bot of the future. It is an initial working prototype, in which the system retrieves the most appropriate counter-arguments using a similarity al-

Proceedings of the 5th Workshop on Argument Mining, pages 121–130
Brussels, Belgium, November 1, 2018. ©2018 Association for Computational Linguistics

gorithm. In particular, they used Latent Semantic Similarity for word similarity and Wordnet, together with hierarchical agglomerative clustering to retrieve the most similar responses. Evaluation has been done based on the time the system took to retrieve the results. While this work is the most similar to our ideas, it is currently an initial prototype and fully-retrieved based. Our work on the other hand explores several options focusing on the currently challenging direction, generative model in argumentative dialogue systems.

Research on conversational systems has two main directions: task-oriented dialogue systems (Williams et al., 2017; Bordes and Weston, 2016; Eric and Manning, 2017) and general/open-domain chatting systems such as those described in (Vinyals and Le, 2015; Zhou et al., 2017; Li et al., 2016a; Serban et al., 2016). For the task-oriented dialogue systems, it is usually important to have an intent classifier together with a dialogue state tracker that keeps track of which information is needed to be requested and finally a language generation module (Williams et al., 2017; Bordes and Weston, 2016). Our work is more related to the second direction, a general/open-domain chatting system. Besides the common retrieval-based approach, a growing interest in the research area focuses on a generative, end-to-end system. One of the first study using sequence to sequence model for building conversational models is described in (Vinyals and Le, 2015). These systems can generate new responses in daily conversational topics, but are still quite limited in making sense of these responses. The main problem often lies in the decoder and objective parts, where usually the most generic and *safe* responses such as "I don't know" are selected. To deal with this problem, (Li et al., 2016a) proposed using another objective function to promote diversity in responses. Some other work investigates the problem of integrating emotion and persona into the conversational agents such as (Zhou et al., 2017; Li et al., 2016b).

3   The debater system

In this section, we describe our argumentative conversational system, which can give responses in two different modes: using a retrieval-based approach and using a generative model.

3.1   Format of a debate

The aim of the chatbot is to be able to carry a conversation with humans to debate about a given topic. At the initial step, the system suggests a topic (Table 1) and the user can decide to debate on this topic or move on to another one. When a topic is selected, the user can give her opinions and the system should generate coherent responses to the user's message. Ideally, the system's response should be meaningful, relevant to previous messages and present opinions/arguments about the given topic.

3.2   Dataset

In the demo, we use the Internet Argument Corpus (Abbott et al., 2016), which is a collection of 65K posts in 5.4K debate topics (Table 1) retrieved from Convinceme website[1]. While debates from medias such as those in newspapers, broadcast news are more officially and formally written, online debate posts are often more colorful, personal and may be rational, contain emotional languages. Such kinds of debates tend to be more subjective and naturally present how humans debate with each other. Topics of discussion in this online forum are various, ranging from political debates (e.g., *should guns be controlled?*) to everyday life topics (e.g., *How much should I tip the pizza man for my 20$ lunch order?*).

Star Wars vs. Lord of the Rings
Pepsi vs. Coke, the true taste test
A billboard saying "There is no God and life is still great" is offensive?
Is atheism a taboo in the USA?
Should .50 Cals be allowed in warfare?
Pencils vs. Pens
Should the Government allow NAZI rallies in neighborhoods where Holocaust survivors live?
Pronunciation: The letter Z, 'Zed' or 'Zee"?
Would you be more disappointed to find out that your child cheated on a test or smoked a cigarette?
How much should I tip the pizza man for my 20$ lunch order?
Cellphones While Driving
Smoking should be banned?
Should we judge motives or actions?

Table 1: Examples of debate topics

A debate can contain multiple posts from several users. We use each debate as a training sample of a dialogue for the argument system, where two consecutive posts are served as a quote and response pair.

To build the conversational argument system,

---

[1]http://www.convinceme.net/

we employ two typical approaches: a retrieval and a generative method.

3.3 The retrieval-based system

In the retrieval-based system, the task is to select the most relevant response given a user's message and the context of the conversation. While limited in the sense that it cannot generate new responses, retrieval-based systems are still often selected as a base method for many applications including summarisation, tasked-oriented dialogue systems. The aim of the system is to learn how to select the best argument from a pre-defined topic that matches the current user's response and the history of the conversation. The architecture of the system is depicted in Figure 1.

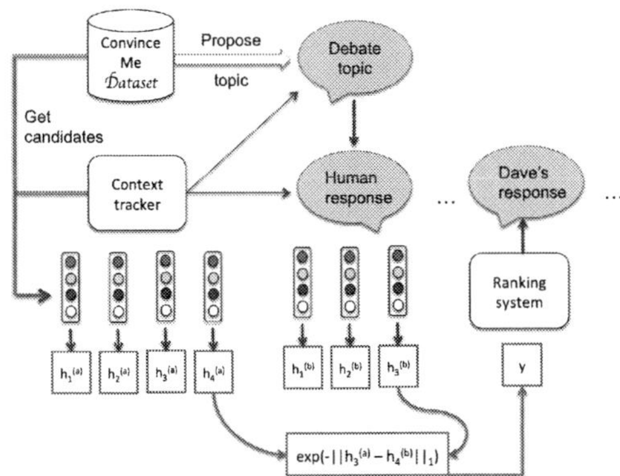

Figure 1: The debater retrieval system architecture

We use a siamese adaption of the LSTM network, which is called the Manhattan LSTM (MaL-STM) model (Mueller and Thyagarajan, 2016) to learn the similarity representation of two given messages. Common approaches usually use neural networks to represent sentences whose word vectors are trained on large corpora (Mikolov et al., 2013b; Le and Mikolov, 2014). The MaL-STM model on the other hand learns the semantic similarity directly with its representation learning objective function. It is reported to achieve state-of-the-art results on the task of assessing semantic similarity between sentences (Mueller and Thyagarajan, 2016).

The model is composed of two networks $LSTM_a$ and $LSTM_b$, where the weights of these two networks are shared. The first $LSTM_a$ represents candidate responses taken from the dataset, while the second $LSTM_b$ represents the current human's response. A context tracker helps keep-

ing track of which responses have been retrieved before to avoid repetition. The current user's message is compared to all candidates from the given debate to find the most relevant one r_{top}^k, where k is the index of the response in the dataset. Finally, r_{top}^{k+1}, the next response of r_{top} is selected to become Dave's response. Based on this approach, the first response r^1 will never be selected. To avoid irrelevant responses (when the user's message is not similar to any of the posts in the debate), we set a similarity threshold τ. For cases when the system cannot find a response that is similar (i.e., similarity value $\mathcal{S} < \tau$), the system will select the first post to return since the first post is usually the most general one that describes the topic of the debate. After a new response is selected, the context tracker will add the response to the context and only reset it when all responses have been achieved to promote diversity in the whole conversation.

For similarity metric, we use the simple function $\mathcal{S}(h_{T_a}^{(a)}, h_{T_b}^{(b)}) = \exp(-||h_{T_a}^{(a)} - h_{T_b}^{(b)}||_1)$ where $h_{T_a}^{(a)}$ and $h_{T_b}^{(b)}$ are representation of posts and user's messages respectively. The similarity value $\mathcal{S} \in [0, 1]$. l_1 norm is used in the similarity function instead of l_2 in order to avoid the problem of correcting errors in early stages due to vanishing gradients of the Euclidean distance (Chopra et al., 2005). It has also been reported to perform slightly better than other metrics such as cosine similarity (Mueller and Thyagarajan, 2016; Yih et al., 2011).

To train the MaLSTM, one needs to have a parallel corpus with similarity annotation between pairs of sentences. Unfortunately, there is no such corpus that is directly representing posts' similarities in debates and is large enough for training. We therefore use the Quora question pairs Kaggle competition dataset[2] which contains 404,302 question pairs annotated with similarity information (i.e., whether they are having the same meaning or not). Examples of questions in the training set is given in Table 2. This dataset has an open domain with questions covering many topics, which are suitable to be applied to our online post similarity assessment task. As can be seen from Table 2, computing similarity between sentences requires more than just word/word meaning matching. A similarity classifier should be able to do reasoning and take into account the struc-

---

[2]https://www.kaggle.com/c/quora-question-pairs

ture of the sentences. For the embedding layer, we use the pre-trained word2vec of Google News dataset[3](Mikolov et al., 2013a).

Questions that are equal
How can I be a good geologist?
What should I do to be a great geologist?
How do I read and find my YouTube comments?
How can I see all my Youtube comments?
What can make Physics easy to learn?
How can you make physics easy to learn?
Questions that are not equal
What are the types of immunity?
What are the different types of immunity in our body?
What is abstract expressionism in painting?
What are major influences of abstract expressionism?
Why do girls want to be friends with the guy they reject?
How do guys feel after rejecting a girl?

Table 2: Examples of Quora questions used for training the MaLSTM for the retrieval-based approach

3.4 The generative system

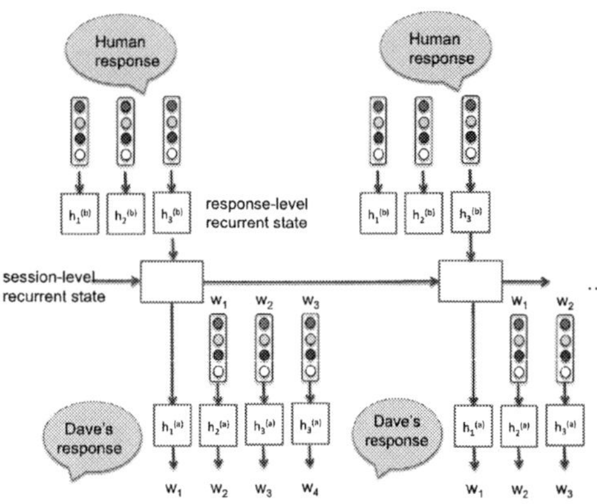

Figure 2: The debater generative system architecture

Although retrieval-based method is straightforward and guarantee to produce high quality messages, it is limited to only arguments that are available in the dataset and cannot adapt or tailor to every new responses from the users. A common trend in dialogue system community is to push towards generative models, where they are able to generate new messages based on the context and/or current states of the conversation (Vinyals and Le, 2015; Li et al., 2016a; Zhou et al., 2017).

Debating is different from normal open-domain conversation: argumentative responses may present attributes such as emotion, agreement, disagreement, sarcasm and stance.

[3]https://code.google.com/archive/p/
word2vec/

To study if an end-to-end model could generate such responses, we use a hierarchical recurrent (RNN) encoder-decoder architecture as depicted in Figure 2. The original hierarchical RNN was introduced in (Sordoni et al., 2015) for the task of generating context-aware query suggestion for search engines. Its model attempts to capture the context of user queries based on sessions and sample suggestion one word at a time.

Applying to the task of generating debater responses, this architecture could take into account previous users' responses and is context sensitive. The order of messages in history is captured and encoded in a session-level recurrent state and the current response is represented in a response level recurrent state.

A given topic is treated as the first message starting a conversation. When the user submits the first response, it is fed into a bidirectional RNN (Jain and Medsker, 1999), in our case using GRU cells (Cho et al., 2014). Each word in the response is embedded using the pre-trained word embeddings. The encoder RNN then updates its internal vector, the *response-level* recurrent state. To capture the context of the previous messages in the dialogue and condition the next response generation based on the context, the *session-level* recurrent state is updated using another RNN on top of the previously computed current response-level encoder. This therefore forms a hierarchical architecture that could be able to capture the deep dialog context together with the current response encoder.

Given a set of responses $\mathcal{R} = \{r^1, r^2, ..., r^M\}$ where M is the number of responses in the given session and the responses are submitted in a chronological order. Each response is represented by a set of words $r^m = \{w_1^m, w_2^m, ..., w_{N_m}^m\}$, where N_m is the total number of words in that response.

Response-level encoder. For each word w_n, the response-level recurrent encoder state $h_{(enc),n}^m$ is computed based on the previous state and the current word:

$$h_{(enc),n}^m = g_{(enc)}(h_{(enc),n-1}^m, w_n^m) \qquad (1)$$

The first initial state h_0 is set to 0. $h_{(enc),n}^m$ stores information about the current response r_m and word w_n^m.

Session-level encoder. In the session-level encoder, we encode the context of the previous re-

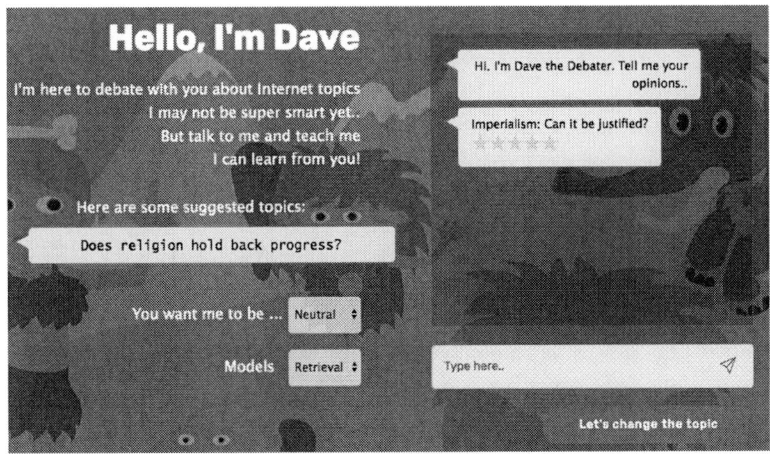

Figure 3: Dave the debater web demo

sponses in state c

$$c_{(enc)}^m = g_{(enc)}(c_{(enc)}^{m-1}, r^m) \qquad (2)$$

The session level encoder sums up the context of all responses that the network has seen so far in a chronological order. It additionally builds up on the response vector r^m.

Response decoder. In this model, the response is sampled one word at a time. In particular, the prediction of the next response r^m based on the context $r^{1:m-1}$ is based on the estimation of the probability:

$$P(r^m|r^{1:m-1}) = \prod_{n=1}^{N_m} (w_n|w_{1:n-1}, r^{1:m-1}) \qquad (3)$$

The current state d_n^m of the decoder is computed using another GRU:

$$d_{(dec),n}^m = g_{(dec)}(d_{(dec),n-1}^m, w_n^m) \qquad (4)$$

To embed the context information into the decoder space d^m, we initialize the first recurrent state d_0^m using a tanh function:

$$d_{(dec),0}^m = \tanh(D_0 c^{m-1} + b_0) \qquad (5)$$

where D_0 projects the context summary vector c^{m-1} into the decoder space and b_0 is a bias vector.

Finally, the probability of a word w_n^m takes the form u is computed based on the previous words and given context as:

$$P(w_n^m = u|w_{1:n-1}^m, r^{1:m-1}) =$$
$$\frac{\exp(e_u^T f(d_{n-1}^m, w_{n-1}^m))}{\sum_k \exp(e_k^T f(d_{n-1}^m, w_{n-1}^m))}$$

where e_u and e_k are the word embeddings of word u and k; f is the function that is computed based on both response-level and session-level states, similar to those used in (Sordoni et al., 2015; Cho et al., 2014).

$$f(d_{n-1}^m, w_{n-1}^m) = H_0 d_{n-1}^m + E_0 w_{n-1}^m + b_0 \quad (6)$$

Objective function. In this framework, we use the maximum mutual information (MMI) as proposed in (Li et al., 2016a) instead of the tradition likelihood function. As reported in (Li et al., 2016a), MMI objective function helps produce more diverse and interesting responses.

The likelihood objective function is computed as:

$$r^* = \arg\max_r \{\log P(r|r^{1:m})\} \qquad (7)$$

while the MMI objective function is defined as:

$$r^* = \arg\max_r \{\log P(r|r^{1:m}) - \log P(r)\} \quad (8)$$

Generation and reranking. We use sampling method, where each word is sampled based on the output distribution. The results are finally reranked based on the log likelihood or the MMI score.

4 Web Demo for Dave the debater

A demo of the system described in the previous sections is available at `http://114.212.80.16:8000/debate/`. The interface is illustrated in Figure 3. A topic is randomly selected for a user, he or she can start talking about this topic by

125

giving own arguments. The user can also select to switch to a new debate topic with the button "Let's change the topic".

There are two different modes depending on which debater system the user wants to talk to. In the retrieval mode, each topic has a pre-defined list of responses. Note that these responses are ordered chronically. The selected responses are chosen based on the comparison of the user's current message and the history of the debate. In particular, the message from the user is being compared to every responses in the pre-defined set and the response coming after the most similar one is going to be selected. We keep track of all responses that have been retrieved to not get repeated responses again. More details about the approach is explained in section 3.3.

For the generative mode, the user can talk about the given topic or any other topics. The responses are generated based on the current message (encoded in the response-level recurrent state) and the context, which is the history of the whole conversation from the beginning (encoded in the session-level recurrent state) (section 3.4).

To collect feedbacks for each response to retrain the models, users are able to rate each response with rating from 1 (very bad) to 5 (very good). These ratings are stored in the database together with the responses and their contexts to use in the future so the models can learn from them.

5   Experiments and results

In this section, we report the first evaluation results we have so far for both retrieval-based and generative argumentative dialogue system.

5.1   Retrieval-based model

We evaluate the MaLSTM as describe in section 3.3 for the similarity assessment task on the Quora dataset. As we do not have directly gold standard data for similarity evaluation performing on the argumentation dataset, we use the Quora as a measurement of the similarity assessment for the MaLSTM. We used 50 hidden layers, word embedding length of 300, batch size of 2048, dropout rate of 30%. For the loss function, we used the mean square error and Adam Optimizer (Kingma and Ba, 2014). After several experiments, we observe that the model accuracy and loss converge at around 50 epochs. The model accuracy and loss on the train and validation dataset are plotted in

Figure 4. The final result obtained on the test set is 81.92%.

Topic: Is anything in this world free?
Human: Nothing in this world is completely free, there must always be a cost somewhere
Dave: Nothing in this world is free.. Everybody has to pay a price for anything they want or recieve.. Life is not free.. Death is not free.. Happiness is not free.. No matter what it is, there will always be a toll.. Nothing in this world is free..
Human: I totally agree with you
Dave: Close, there is no energy cost to giving up life, entropy takes care of that.. But there is an energy cost to having life to give up.. I was running under the assumption that "free" was referring to currency, not energy.. If we're going to argue that energy is a currency for the purposes of this debate, then there's really no debate to be had at all..
Human: Happiness is free
Dave: I'm sorry to ruin your fun, but "picking up a penny on the street" is MOST definitely not free, the effort to bend down and grab that penny costs you energy loss etc.. of course on minuscule level but still causes some sort of work.. In general for one thing to be free another has to lose true, BUT there is still never anything free for the one that is receiving the "gift", even the portion of receiving is some sort of exchange!
Human: how about dead?
Dave: Death comes with many expense's there is a energy cost, you have to give up life to gain death, Death can come at the price of pain..

Table 3: Examples of a conversation in the retrieval mode

5.2   Generative model

Evaluation metric. To evaluate the responses from the generative model, following (Vinyals and Le, 2015; Li et al., 2016a; Zhou et al., 2017), we use the perplexity metric PP evaluated on the test data:

$$PP = 2^{-\sum_y \log P(y)} \tag{9}$$

Usually the lower the perplexity the better the model is, and more specialized corpus also often obtains lower perplexity.

To measure the degree of diversity of responses, we use the *distinct-1* and *distinct-2* metrics following (Li et al., 2016a). They are the number of distinct unigrams and bigrams in generated responses, scaled by total number of tokens.

Settings. In our experiments, for both encoder and decoder, the number of recurrent layers is set to two, the number of dimensions for the recurrent layer is 512 and the drop-out ratio is 0.2. We use the batch size of 192, the Adadelta method for adapting learning rate (Zeiler, 2012).

For the decoder, we examine two methods: the Sampling method, in which responses are sampled from output distribution token by token. For each

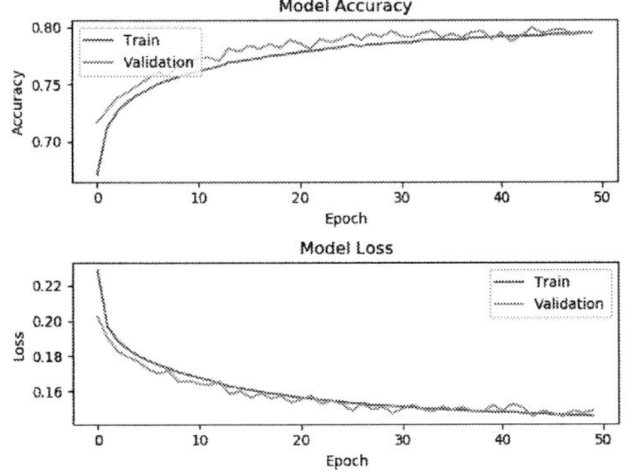

Figure 4: Retrieval-based model: MaLSTM results

token, the temperature transform is performed prior to sampling. Generally, the low temperature sample is more grammatically correct while the high temperature sample represents greater linguistic variety. In our experiments, we set the default temperature to 0.5. The second model is Sampling with MMI re-ranking. In this model, the sampling procedure is done the same as the other one, but candidates are ranked according to their MMI-score (see section 3.4).

Human: I think guns should be banned **Dave:** So, if you want to ban guns, then they're not completely legitimate. I don't think that the government should start a legal system..
Topic: There are no good arguments for the non-existence of God. **Human:** sure, I believe in God. **Dave:** I am not a christian but there are so many of the bible.. The bible has written to it, and if a dog do have the same in the existence of god, then that would be the only true gods..
Human: it does not make much sense what you are saying **Dave:** I think they are..
Topic: evolution: scientific or unscientific? **Human:** scientific should be better **Dave:** Well i'm not to say he was the first person who would have been on the same - life **Human:** alright.. **Dave:** You are a good debater!
Human: which one would you pick? **Dave:** I am a fan of both..

Table 4: Random context-sensitive examples in the generative mode

Finally, to prevent the model from generating the same tokens over and over again, we use a penalized coefficient method, in which tokens that have been generated before will have their probabilities lower down by a factor of 10.0. Tokens

that are not penalized including modifiers (such as *a*, *an*, *the*) and punctuations.

Testing data. For testing the perplexity of the model and the distinctness metrics, we prepare two datasets: a context free dataset that contains 200 argumentative sentences and a context sensitive dataset containing 200 consecutive argumentative responses from an online debate.

The results are reported in table 5. The context sensitive perplexity is higher than the context free perplexity. In both cases, the reranking method helps reducing the perplexity of the model by 13% (in context sensitive case) and 3.1% (in context free case). Reranking also helps increasing the diversity of the responses: the *distinct-1* increased by 3.8% and the *distinct-2* increased by 13.16%.

While these metrics may not be the most useful in evaluating conversational systems, they are most widely used metrics and could somehow give a reflection on how different models perform.

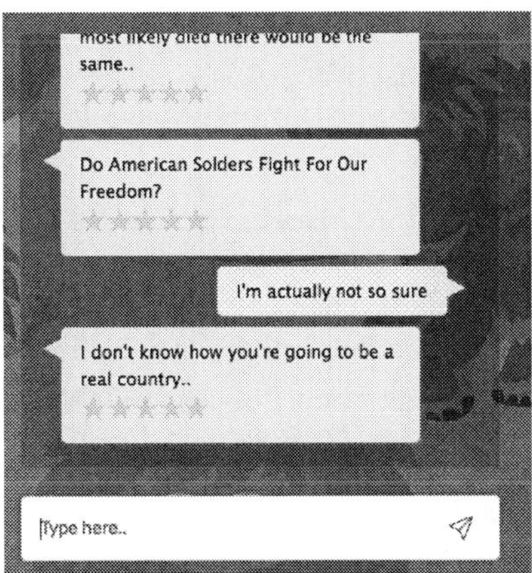

Figure 5: Generative model on random army topic: white bubbles (left) are responses from Dave

6 Conclusion and future work

In this paper, we have described an argumentative dialogue agent, whose aim is to be able to debate with human on a given topic. We explored two approaches, using a retrieval-based and a generative system. The systems have been trained on a limited open-domain dataset, but have shown interesting and promising results. Still there is a lot of work that can be done to improve the system, including training on a much larger dataset, combining both retrieving and generating methods alternatively to give interesting responses to the users based on different scenarios. For the retrieval-

Model	Sampling	Sampling & MMI re-ranking
Context-sensitive Perplexity	88.51	76.97 (-13.0%)
Context-free Perplexity	75.53	73.17 (-3.1%)
Distinctness *distinct-1*	0.708 %	0.736 (+3.8%)
Distinctness *distinct-2*	5.94%	6.84% (+13.16%)

Table 5: Perplexity and distinctness for the sampling method and sampling with MMI re-ranking method

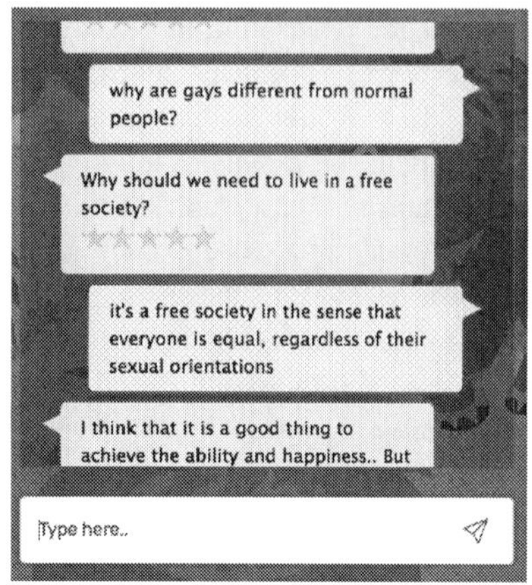

Figure 6: Generative model on random gay/society topic: white bubbles (left) are responses from Dave

based system, one can try the un-tied version of the Manhattan LSTM, since responses could vary in length and may not be symmetric. In the generative system, different decoding methods could be applied such as a traditional beam search, sampling output based on topics, increasing the depth and power of the model. One can also integrate argument strategies as those described in (Rosenfeld and Kraus, 2016) to the generative system to have a more structural and persuasive conversation. Such system can put the first milestones in developing a machine that can someday fully engage in a debate and discussion with human on controversial topics.

References

Rob Abbott, Brian Ecker, Pranav Anand, and Marilyn Walker. 2016. Internet argument corpus 2.0: An sql schema for dialogic social media and the corpora to go with it. In *Proceedings of the Tenth International Conference on Language Resources and Evaluation (LREC 2016)*, Paris, France. European Language Resources Association (ELRA).

David Bamman and Noah A. Smith. 2015. Open extraction of fine-grained political statements. In *Proceedings of the 2015 Conference on Empirical Methods in Natural Language Processing*, pages 76–85, Lisbon, Portugal. Association for Computational Linguistics.

Filip Boltužić and Jan Šnajder. 2014. Back up your stance: Recognizing arguments in online discussions. In *Proceedings of the First Workshop on Argumentation Mining*, pages 49–58, Baltimore, Maryland. Association for Computational Linguistics.

Filip Boltužić and Jan Šnajder. 2015. Identifying prominent arguments in online debates using semantic textual similarity. In *Proceedings of the First Workshop on Argumentation Mining*, Denver, Colorado, USA. Association for Computational Linguistics.

Antoine Bordes and Jason Weston. 2016. Learning end-to-end goal-oriented dialog. *CoRR*, abs/1605.07683.

Kyunghyun Cho, Bart van Merriënboer, Çalar Gülçehre, Dzmitry Bahdanau, Fethi Bougares, Holger Schwenk, and Yoshua Bengio. 2014. Learning phrase representations using rnn encoder-decoder for statistical machine translation. *ArXiv e-prints*, abs/1406.1078.

Sumit Chopra, Raia Hadsell, and Yann LeCun. 2005. Learning a similarity metric discriminatively, with application to face verification. In *Proceedings of the 2005 IEEE Computer Society Conference on Computer Vision and Pattern Recognition (CVPR'05) - Volume 1 - Volume 01*, CVPR '05, pages 539–546, Washington, DC, USA. IEEE Computer Society.

Mihail Eric and Christopher D. Manning. 2017. A copy-augmented sequence-to-sequence architecture gives good performance on task-oriented dialogue. *CoRR*, abs/1701.04024.

Kazi Saidul Hasan and Vincent Ng. 2013. Stance classification of ideological debates: Data, models, features, and constraints. In *Proceedings of the Sixth International Joint Conference on Natural Language Processing*, pages 1348–1356.

Mohit Iyyer, Peter Enns, Jordan Boyd-Graber, and Philip Resnik. 2014. Political ideology detection using recursive neural networks. In *Proceedings of the 52nd Annual Meeting of the Association for Computational Linguistics (Volume 1: Long Papers)*, pages 1113–1122. Association for Computational Linguistics.

L. C. Jain and L. R. Medsker. 1999. *Recurrent Neural Networks: Design and Applications*, 1st edition. CRC Press, Inc., Boca Raton, FL, USA.

Raquel Justo, Thomas Corcoran, Stephanie M. Lukin, Marilyn Walker, and M. Inés Torres. 2014. Extracting relevant knowledge for the detection of sarcasm and nastiness in the social web. *Know.-Based Syst.*, 69(1):124–133.

Diederik P. Kingma and Jimmy Ba. 2014. Adam: A method for stochastic optimization. *CoRR*, abs/1412.6980.

Philipp Koehn. 2005. Europarl: A Parallel Corpus for Statistical Machine Translation. In *Conference Proceedings: the tenth Machine Translation Summit*, pages 79–86, Phuket, Thailand. AAMT, AAMT.

Quoc Le and Tomas Mikolov. 2014. Distributed representations of sentences and documents. In *Proceedings of the 31st International Conference on International Conference on Machine Learning - Volume 32*, ICML'14, pages II–1188–II–1196. JMLR.org.

Ran Levy, Yonatan Bilu, Daniel Hershcovich, Ehud Aharoni, and Noam Slonim. 2014. Context dependent claim detection.

Jiwei Li, Michel Galley, Chris Brockett, Jianfeng Gao, and Bill Dolan. 2016a. A diversity-promoting objective function for neural conversation models. In *Proceedings of the 2016 Conference of the North American Chapter of the Association for Computational Linguistics: Human Language Technologies*, pages 110–119. Association for Computational Linguistics.

Jiwei Li, Michel Galley, Chris Brockett, Georgios P. Spithourakis, Jianfeng Gao, and Bill Dolan. 2016b. A persona-based neural conversation model. Cite arxiv:1603.06155Comment: Accepted for publication at ACL 2016.

Tomas Mikolov, Kai Chen, Greg Corrado, and Jeffrey Dean. 2013a. Efficient estimation of word representations in vector space. *CoRR*, abs/1301.3781.

Tomas Mikolov, Ilya Sutskever, Kai Chen, Greg Corrado, and Jeffrey Dean. 2013b. Distributed representations of words and phrases and their compositionality. *CoRR*, abs/1310.4546.

Jonas Mueller and Aditya Thyagarajan. 2016. Siamese recurrent architectures for learning sentence similarity. In *Proceedings of the Thirtieth AAAI Conference on Artificial Intelligence*, AAAI'16, pages 2786–2792. AAAI Press.

Andreas Peldszus and Manfred Stede. 2015. Joint prediction in mst-style discourse parsing for argumentation mining. In *Proceedings of the 2015 Conference on Empirical Methods in Natural Language Processing*, pages 938–948. Association for Computational Linguistics.

Niklas Rach, Saskia Langhammer, Wolfgang Minker, and Stefan Ultes. 2018. Utilizing argument mining techniques for argumentative dialogue systems. In *Proceedings of the 9th International Workshop On Spoken Dialogue Systems (IWSDS)*.

Geetanjali Rakshit, Kevin K. Bowden, Lena Reed, Amita Misra, and Marilyn A. Walker. 2017. Debbie, the debate bot of the future. *CoRR*, abs/1709.03167.

Ariel Rosenfeld and Sarit Kraus. 2016. Strategical argumentative agent for human persuasion. In *ECAI*, volume 285 of *Frontiers in Artificial Intelligence and Applications*, pages 320–328. IOS Press.

Iulian V. Serban, Alessandro Sordoni, Yoshua Bengio, Aaron Courville, and Joelle Pineau. 2016. Building end-to-end dialogue systems using generative hierarchical neural network models. In *Proceedings of the Thirtieth AAAI Conference on Artificial Intelligence*, AAAI'16, pages 3776–3783. AAAI Press.

Alessandro Sordoni, Yoshua Bengio, Hossein Vahabi, Christina Lioma, Jakob Grue Simonsen, and Jian-Yun Nie. 2015. A hierarchical recurrent encoder-decoder for generative context-aware query suggestion. In *Proceedings of the 24th ACM International on Conference on Information and Knowledge Management*, CIKM '15, pages 553–562, New York, NY, USA. ACM.

Christian Stab and Iryna Gurevych. 2014. Identifying argumentative discourse structures in persuasive essays. In *Proceedings of the 2014 Conference on Empirical Methods in Natural Language Processing (EMNLP)*, pages 46–56. Association for Computational Linguistics.

Christian Stab and Iryna Gurevych. 2017. Parsing argumentation structures in persuasive essays. *Comput. Linguist.*, 43(3):619–659.

Reid Swanson, Stephanie M. Lukin, Luke Eisenberg, Thomas Chase Corcoran, and Marilyn A. Walker. 2017. Getting reliable annotations for sarcasm in online dialogues. *CoRR*, abs/1709.01042.

Oriol Vinyals and Quoc V. Le. 2015. A neural conversational model. *CoRR*, abs/1506.05869.

Marilyn Walker, Jean Fox Tree, Pranav Anand, Rob Abbott, and Joseph King. 2012a. A corpus for research on deliberation and debate. In *Proceedings of the Eight International Conference on Language Resources and Evaluation (LREC'12)*, Istanbul, Turkey. European Language Resources Association (ELRA).

Marilyn A. Walker, Pranav Anand, Rob Abbott, Jean E. Fox Tree, Craig H. Martell, and Joseph King. 2012b. That is your evidence?: Classifying stance in online political debate. *Decision Support Systems*, 53:719–729.

Jason D. Williams, Kavosh Asadi, and Geoffrey Zweig. 2017. Hybrid code networks: practical and efficient end-to-end dialog control with supervised and reinforcement learning. *CoRR*, abs/1702.03274.

Wen-tau Yih, Kristina Toutanova, John C. Platt, and Christopher Meek. 2011. Learning discriminative projections for text similarity measures. In *Proceedings of the Fifteenth Conference on Computational Natural Language Learning*, CoNLL '11, pages 247–256, Stroudsburg, PA, USA. Association for Computational Linguistics.

Matthew D. Zeiler. 2012. ADADELTA: an adaptive learning rate method. *CoRR*, abs/1212.5701.

Hao Zhou, Minlie Huang, Tianyang Zhang, Xiaoyan Zhu, and Bing Liu. 2017. Emotional chatting machine: Emotional conversation generation with internal and external memory. *CoRR*, abs/1704.01074.

PD3: Better Low-Resource Cross-Lingual Transfer
By Combining Direct Transfer and Annotation Projection

Steffen Eger, Andreas Rücklé, Iryna Gurevych
Ubiquitous Knowledge Processing Lab (UKP-TUDA)
Department of Computer Science
Technische Universität Darmstadt
`www.ukp.tu-darmstadt.de`

Abstract

We consider unsupervised cross-lingual transfer on two tasks, viz., sentence-level argumentation mining and standard POS tagging. We
combine direct transfer using bilingual embeddings with annotation projection, which
projects labels across unlabeled parallel data.
We do so by either merging respective source
and target language datasets or alternatively by
using multi-task learning. Our combination
strategy considerably improves upon both direct transfer and projection with few available
parallel sentences, the most realistic scenario
for many low-resource target languages.

1 Introduction

In recent years, interest in multi- and cross-lingual
natural language processing (NLP) has steadily increased. This has not only to do with the recognition that performances of newly introduced systems
should be robust across several tasks (in several languages), but more fundamentally with the idea of
truly 'universal' NLP methods which should not
only suit English, an arguably particularly simple
exemplar of the world's roughly 7,000 languages.

A further motivation for cross-lingual approaches is the fact that many labeled datasets are
to this date only available in English and labeled
data is generally costly to obtain—be it via expert
annotators or through crowd-sourcing. Therefore,
methods which are capable of training on labeled
data in a resource-rich language such as English
and which can then be applied to typically resource-
poor other languages are highly desirable.

Two standard cross-lingual approaches are projection (Yarowsky et al., 2001; Das and Petrov,
2011; Täckström et al., 2013; Agic et al., 2016)
and direct transfer (McDonald et al., 2011). Direct transfer trains, in the source language L1, on
language-independent or shared features and then

directly applies the trained system to the target language of interest L2. In contrast, projection trains
and evaluates on L2 itself. To do so, it uses parallel data, applies a system trained on L1 to its
source side and then projects the inferred labels
to the parallel L2 side. This projection step may
involve word alignment information. After projection, an annotated L2 dataset is available on which
L2 systems can be trained.

Projection and direct transfer each ignore important information, however. For example, standard
projection ignores the available data in L1 once
the L2 dataset has been created and standard direct
transfer does not use any L2 information.

In this work, we investigate whether the inclusion of both L1 and L2 data outperforms transfer
approaches that exploit only one type of such information, and if so, under what conditions. More
precisely, we first train a system on shared features as in standard direct transfer on labeled L1
data. Then, we make use of two further datasets.
One is based on the source side of parallel unlabeled data; it is derived similarly as in self-training
(Yarowsky, 1995) by applying the trained system
to unlabeled data, from which a pseudo-labeled
dataset is derived. The other is based on its target
side—using annotation projections—as in standard
projection. Thus, we explore the effects of combining *P*rojection and *D*irect transfer using three
datasets (PD3). Our approach is detailed in §2.

We report results for two L2 languages (French,
German) on one sentence-level problem (argumentation mining) and one token-level problem (POS
tagging). We find that our suggested approach PD3
substantially outperforms both direct transfer and
projection when little parallel data is available, the
most realistic scenario for many L2 languages.

While our approach is general, our focus is
particularly on argumentation mining (ArgMin),
a rapidly growing research field in NLP. Cross-

131

Proceedings of the 5th Workshop on Argument Mining, pages 131–143
Brussels, Belgium, November 1, 2018. ©2018 Association for Computational Linguistics

lingual transfer is majorly important for ArgMin because it is inherently costly to get high-quality annotations for ArgMin due to: (i) subjectivity of argumentation as well as divergent and competing ArgMin theories (Daxenberger et al., 2017; Schulz et al., 2018), leading to disagreement among crowd-workers as well as expert annotators (Habernal and Gurevych, 2017), (ii) dependence of argument annotations on background knowledge and parsing of complex pragmatic relations (Moens, 2017). Thus, in order not to reproduce the same annotation costs for new languages, cross-lingual ArgMin methods are required. These techniques should both perform well with little available parallel data, to address many languages, and with general (non-argumentative) parallel data, because this is much more likely to be available. Our experiments address both of these requirements.[1]

2 PD3

Let $\mathcal{L}_S = \{(x^S, y^S)\}$ denote a set of L1 data points in which each x^S is an instance and y^S its corresponding label. We assume that x^S is either a sentence or a sequence of tokens, and y^S is either a single label or contains one label for each token in the sequence. We assume access to a set $\mathcal{U}^{S,T} = \{(x^S, x^T)\}$ of unlabeled L1 and L2 data points in which target and source instances x^T and x^S are translations of each other. We let $\mathcal{U}_S = \mathcal{U}_S^{S,T}$ stand for the L1 part of $\mathcal{U}^{S,T}$, i.e., $\mathcal{U}_S$ consists of the data points x^S only: $\mathcal{U}_S = \{x^S \mid (x^S, x^T) \in \mathcal{U}^{S,T}\}$. We let $\mathcal{U}_T = \mathcal{U}_T^{S,T}$ be analogously defined. Finally, we assume that our instances x^S and x^T have a shared representation, e.g., that their words have a bilingual vector space representation in which mono- and cross-lingually similar words are close to each other. Table 1 (a),(b) illustrates our resource assumptions.

PD3 is described in Algorithm 1. We first train a classifier C (e.g., a neural network) on our labeled L1 data $\mathcal{L}_S$. Then we apply the trained model on the unlabeled x^S instances from $\mathcal{U}_S$, yielding pseudo-labeled dataset $\hat{\mathcal{D}}_S$. Next, we create another pseudo-labeled L2 data set $\hat{\hat{\mathcal{D}}}_T$ by projecting the label $\hat{y}^S$ of x^S in a pair $(x^S, x^T) \in \mathcal{U}^{S,T}$ to the instance x^T. We note that projection is trivial and 'loss-less' for sentence classification tasks because there is exactly one label for the whole sentence.

Algorithm 1: PD3

Input: $\mathcal{L}_S, \mathcal{U}^{S,T}, C$: labeled L1 data and unlabeled L1-L2 translations, and a classifier C

Output: $M_{S \circledast \hat{S} \circledast \hat{\hat{T}}}$: a model trained (using C) on $\mathcal{L}_S$ as well as pseudo-labeled data derived from $\mathcal{U}^{S,T}$

1 $M_S \leftarrow \text{train}_C(\mathcal{L}_S)$;

2 $\hat{Y}_S \leftarrow \text{predict}_{M_S}(\mathcal{U}_S)$; $//$ $\hat{\mathcal{D}}_S = \{(x^S, \hat{y}^S)\}$

3 $\hat{\hat{\mathcal{D}}}_T \leftarrow \{(x^T, \hat{y}^S) \mid (x^S, x^T) \in \mathcal{U}^{S,T}, (x^S, \hat{y}^S) \in \hat{\mathcal{D}}_S\}$;

4 $M_{S \circledast \hat{S} \circledast \hat{\hat{T}}} \leftarrow \text{train}_C(\mathcal{L}_S \circledast \hat{\mathcal{D}}_S \circledast \hat{\hat{\mathcal{D}}}_T)$;

In contrast, for sequence tagging problems, projection typically requires word alignment information, which is an error prone process. This is the reason why we use a 'double hat' for $\hat{\hat{D}}_T$ to indicate that there may be two sources of noise: one from prediction and one from projection.

Finally, we combine our original dataset $\mathcal{L}_S$ with the two pseudo-labeled dataset $\hat{\mathcal{D}}_S$ and $\hat{\hat{\mathcal{D}}}_T$ and train our classifier C on it; after training, our goal in cross-lingual transfer is to apply the trained classifiers to L2 data.

We denote this combination operation by $\circledast$. A simple approach is to let $\circledast$ be the "merging" (or, concatenation) of both datasets (**PD3-merge**). In this variant of PD3, $\mathcal{L}_S$, $\hat{\mathcal{D}}_S$ and $\hat{\hat{\mathcal{D}}}_T$ are merged into one big dataset on which training takes place.

A more sophisticated approach is to let $\circledast$ represent a multi-task learning (MTL) scenario (Caruana, 1993; Søgaard and Goldberg, 2016) in which L1 and L2 instances represent one task each (**PD3-MTL**). Here, rather than merging $\mathcal{L}_S$, $\hat{\mathcal{D}}_S$ and $\hat{\hat{\mathcal{D}}}_T$, we treat source language datasets ($\mathcal{L}_S$ and $\hat{\mathcal{D}}_S$) as one task and target language datasets ($\hat{\hat{\mathcal{D}}}_T$) as another task, each having a dedicated output layer. This leads to a different network architecture than in PD3-merge, in which we now have two separate output layers (i.e., one for each language); this distinction is also illustrated in Figure 1 below. Thus, for each input instance, we predict two outputs (e.g., two ArgMin labels), one in the source language and one in the target language.[2]

The general idea behind MTL is to learn several

---

[2]During training, we update parameters for the 'correct' task as well as for all shared weights. At test time, we only pick the output corresponding to the target language task, if we focus on cross-lingual transfer, or corresponding to the source language, if we focus on in-language evaluation.

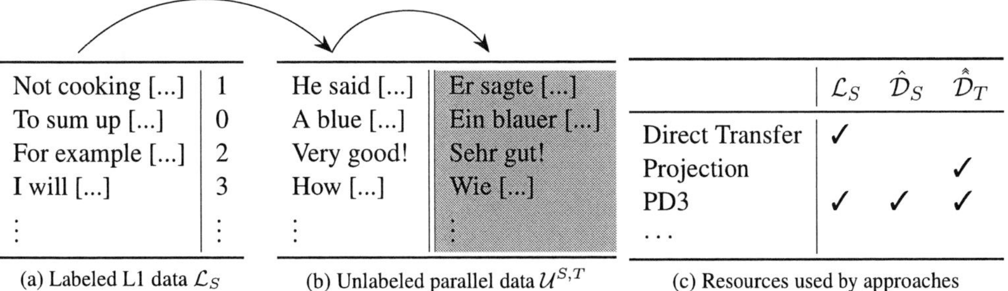

<table>
<tr><td colspan="2">Not cooking [...]   1</td><td colspan="2">He said [...]   Er sagte [...]</td><td></td><td>$\mathcal{L}_S$</td><td>$\hat{\mathcal{D}}_S$</td><td>$\hat{\mathcal{D}}_T$</td></tr>
</table>

Not cooking [...]	1	He said [...]	Er sagte [...]		$\mathcal{L}_S$ $\hat{\mathcal{D}}_S$ $\hat{\mathcal{D}}_T$	

(a) Labeled L1 data $\mathcal{L}_S$	(b) Unlabeled parallel data $\mathcal{U}^{S,T}$	(c) Resources used by approaches

Table 1: Illustration of resources used for PD3: (a) labeled source language data; (b) unlabeled parallel data; (c) comparison with Direct Transfer and annotation projection. Arrows indicate the information flow: we use $\mathcal{L}_S$ to label the source side of parallel data and then project to its target side. Note that both variants of PD3 (PD3-merge and PD3-MTL) use the same resources but utilize/combine them differently, as described in the text.

tasks jointly, in one architecture with shared parameters, so that generalized representations can be learned (in the hidden layers of a neural network) that benefit multiple tasks. In our case, the two tasks solve the same problem (e.g., ArgMin), but in different languages. A general advantage of MTL over merging arises when tasks have different output spaces, in which case merging may confuse a learner due to heterogeneous labels across the two tasks. We do not face this situation. However, in our context, an advantage of MTL over merge may still be that the MTL paradigm has more capacity because it has connecting weights between the task-specific output layers and the network's last (common) hidden layer. Further, MTL can accommodate task-specific losses, which can be used to, e.g., down-weight one of the two tasks, besides further conceptual differences (Caruana, 1993). In our situation, splitting original and pseudo-labeled datasets by languages, in MTL, may also better account for syntactic and semantic idiosyncrasies of individual languages than merge, where such distinctions are blurred.

Table 1 (c) compares the different resource assumptions of direct transfer, annotation projection, and PD3. Note that other selections of resources might be possible (e.g., 'PD2', using only $\mathcal{L}_S$ and $\hat{\mathcal{D}}_T$, or even differently annotated L2 data). We discuss some of these in the supplementary material.

3 Data

Table 2 gives dataset statistics for our two tasks, which we describe in the following.

ArgMin Our focus task is ArgMin on the sentence-level: the task is to determine whether a sentence contains one of the argumentative constructs major claim, claim, premise, or else is non-argumentative (Peldszus and Stede, 2013; Stab and Gurevych, 2014). We use the latest version of an English student essay corpus (Stab and Gurevych, 2017), which has recently also been translated to German by student crowd-workers (Eger et al., 2018). We give four examples from the English ArgMin dataset in Table 3. The majority of all instances is labeled as premise (47%). We use 3,000 sentences of the original training split as our parallel corpus and only train on the remaining 2,086 sentences (this is the set $\mathcal{L}_S$). We additionally evaluate our approaches with parallel data from TED (Hermann and Blunsom, 2014), where we train on the full 5,086 sentences from the ArgMin training split. TED contains a collection of talks on science, education, and related fields, transcribed into written English and translated by crowd-workers into different languages. We take two sources of parallel data here because the domain of the parallel data intuitively has an influence on results in tasks such as argumentation mining. That is, while standard NLP tasks such as POS tagging are relatively stable across different domains, arguments may be very differently realized across different datasets (Daxenberger et al., 2017). Frequency aspects also play a role, since argumentation may be prominent in domains such as student essays or debate portal, but much less ubiquitous in, e.g., news articles.

POS Tagging We also include a standard NLP task, namely, POS tagging. We use subsets of the Universal Dependency Treebanks (Nivre et al., 2016) with English as L1 and German and French as L2s. For English, we select 800 random sentences from the corresponding English treebank as training data and 200 sentences as development

Task	Task type	$|\mathcal{Y}|$	Train-EN		Dev-EN		Test-DE		Test-FR	
			Sent.	Tokens	Sent.	Tokens	Sent.	Tokens	Sent.	Tokens
POS	Token-Level	18	800	13,292	200	3,174	799	12,512	1,478	35,766
AM	Sentence-Level	4	5,086	105,990	607	12,658	1,448	29,234	-	-

Table 2: Statistics for datasets used in this work. $|\mathcal{Y}|$ denotes the size of the label space.

data.[3] We evaluate the system that transfers from English to German or French on the original development data provided in the corresponding treebank splits. As our unlabeled parallel data, we use subsets of various sizes from the TED parallel corpus for English-French and English-German.

4 Experimental Setup

Sentence level network architecture: In our **sentence-level ArgMin** experiments, we use a convolutional neural network (CNN) with 1-max pooling to learn a representation of the input sentence and feed this representation into a softmax regression classifier.[4] We use 800 CNN filters with a window size of 3. For optimization, we use Adam with a learning rate of 0.001. Training sentences are processed in minibatches of size 16. We do not apply dropout or ℓ_2 regularization.

We report average macro F1 scores over 20 runs with different random initializations. For PD3-merge, we shuffle the merged data before training—i.e., mini-batches can contain $\mathcal{L}_S$, $\hat{\mathcal{D}}_S$, and $\hat{\mathcal{D}}_T$ data. For PD3-MTL, we shuffle L1 and L2 data individually and during training we sample each mini-batch from either task according to its size. In the MTL setup, we share the CNN layer across tasks and use task-specific softmax regression layers.

Sequence tagging network architecture: For **token-level POS tagging**, we implement a bidirectional LSTM as in Ma and Hovy (2016) and Lample et al. (2016) with a CRF output layer. This is a state-of-the-art system for sequence tagging tasks such as POS and NER. Our model uses pretrained word embeddings and optionally concatenates these with a learned character-level representation. For all experiments, we use the same network topology: we use two hidden layers with 100 hidden units each, applying dropout on the hidden units and on the word embeddings. We use

Adam as optimizer. Our network uses a CRF output layer rather than a softmax classifier to account for dependencies between successive labels.

In the MTL setup, we use the same architecture, but connect the last hidden layer to individual output layers, one for each task. Our MTL architecture extends the architecture of Søgaard and Goldberg (2016) by replacing the softmax output layer with a CRF output layer, and by including character-level word representations. The difference between MTL and single-task learning (STL) is illustrated in Figure 1. STL is a network with only one task, as in PD3-merge, direct transfer and standard projection.

We report average accuracy over five (or 10, in case of very little data) random weight matrix initializations. In the MTL setup, we choose a mini-batch randomly in each iteration (containing instances from only one of the tasks as in our sentence-level ArgMin experiments).

Cross-lingual Embeddings: For token-level experiments, we initially train 100-d BIVCD embeddings (Vulić and Moens, 2015) from Europarl (Koehn, 2005) (for EN-DE) and the UN corpus (Ziemski et al., 2016) (for EN-FR), respectively. For sentence-level experiments, we use 300-d BIVCD embeddings. This means that we initially assume that high-quality bilingual word embeddings are readily available for the two languages involved. At first sight, this appears a realistic assumption since high-quality bilingual embeddings can already be obtained with very little available *bilingual* data (Zhang et al., 2016; Artetxe et al., 2017). In low-resource settings, however, even little *monolingual* data is typically available for L2 and we address this setup subsequently.

Upper bound: For both ArgMin and POS, we report the in-language upper bound, i.e., when the model is trained and evaluated on L2. For this, we choose random L2 train sets of size $|\mathcal{L}_S|$.

Projection strategy for sequence tagging: We first word-align parallel data using fast-align (Dyer et al., 2013). When an L2 word is uniquely aligned to an L1 word, we assign it the L1 word's unique

---

[3]We choose only 800 sentences in order to keep overall computational costs of our experiments smaller. Note that 800 sentences yield an in-language performance of roughly 90%.

[4]An alternative would have been to directly work on sentence-level representations using cross-lingual sentence embeddings (Rücklé et al., 2018).

Not cooking fresh food will lead to lack of nutrition	Claim
To sum up, [...] the merits of animal experiments still outweigh the demerits	Major claim
For example, tourism makes up one third of Czech's economy	Premise
I will mention some basic reasoning as follows	O

Table 3: Simplified examples (EN) from our AM corpus, one for each of the four classes.

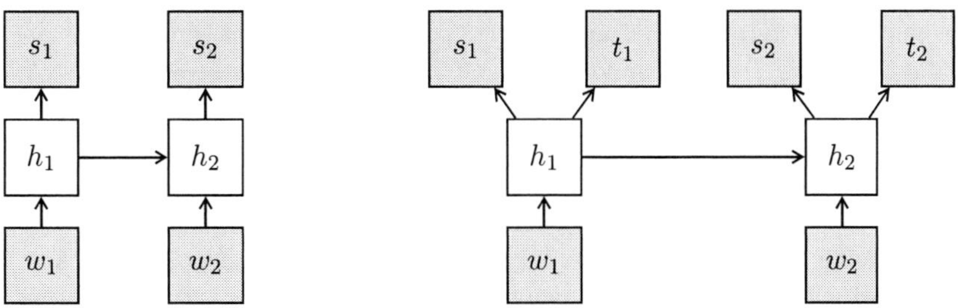

Figure 1: Sequence tagging STL vs. MTL with two tasks. For readability, character-level representations and CRF connections in the output layers are omitted. Bidirectional connections in the hidden layers are also missing. Here, w are the input words and s and t denote different tasks; h are the hidden layers.

label. When an L2 word is aligned to several L1 words, we randomly draw one of the aligned source labels. When an L2 word is not aligned to any L1 word, we draw a label randomly from its unique labels in the remainder of the corpus. Our projection strategy is standard, cf. Agic et al. (2016).

5 Experiments

5.1 Results

Detailed results for PD3-merge, PD3-MTL, standard projection, and direct transfer as a function of the available parallel data are given in Table 4 in the appendix. Condensed and averaged results (over DE and FR) are shown in Figure 2.

ArgMin Results are shown in Figure 2 (right), ranging over $\{50, 100, 500, 1000, 2000, 3000\}$ parallel sentences. PD3 is consistently more effective than projection and outperforms direct transfer with at least 100 parallel sentences. In particular, PD3-merge outperforms direct transfer already with 50 parallel sentences ($\sim$44% for PD3-merge vs. $\sim$39% for direct transfer) and quickly closes the gap towards the in-language upper-bound ($\sim$54% vs. $\sim$59% with 500 parallel sentences). PD3-MTL on the other hand only slightly (but consistently) improves upon projection. With an increased number of parallel sentences, we observe that all methods reach performances very close to the in-language upper bound.

POS Tagging Figure 2 (left) shows POS results, averaged across DE and FR, when transferring from English. Tagging accuracies are given as a function of the size of the available parallel data, ranging over $\{50, 100, 500, 1000, 5000\}$ parallel sentences. As for ArgMin, PD3 is consistently better than projection and improves upon direct transfer with more than 50 parallel sentences. As the number of parallel sentences increases, PD3-MTL, PD3-merge and standard projection become indistinguishable, indicating that it does not pay out anymore to use the more resource-intensive approach PD3. However, most importantly, with little parallel data, gains of PD3 over standard projection are substantial: for 50 parallel sentences performance values are roughly doubled ($\sim$30% accuracy for projection vs. >55% for PD3). For little available parallel data, PD3-MTL can also considerably improve upon PD3-merge. For example, with 100 parallel sentences, PD3-MTL achieves an accuracy of $\sim$65%, whereas PD3-merge achieves $\sim$60% and direct transfer achieves $\sim$61%.

5.2 Analysis

We now analyze several aspects of our approach, such as the errors it commits and the differences between PD3-MTL and PD3-merge, as well as whether we observe the same trends for high- and low-quality bilingual embeddings.

PD3-MTL vs. PD3-merge For POS, the better performance of PD3-MTL in some cases compared to PD3-merge may be due PD3-MTL having more parameters due to independent connection weights between the CRF classifier and the last hidden layer. Moreover, some authors have also argued that MTL is "fundamentally different" from simply adding auxiliary data (Bollmann and Søgaard, 2016). In contrast, for ArgMin, we observed that PD3-merge substantially outperforms PD3-MTL in many cases. We hypothesize that the reason is the model selection for PD3-MTL, which chooses the model with best performance on the dev portion of $\mathring{\mathcal{D}}_T$. Since the model trained on the small $\mathcal{L}_S$ train set tends to overpredict the majority class here, the label distribution on the parallel data differs substantially from that of the test data. The effects in PD3-merge are not as pronounced since it also contains parts of data with the true label distribution.

Direct Transfer vs. PD3   Direct transfer sometimes outperforms PD3 for very few available parallel sentences because PD3 uses noisy data in the form of projected labels, which are particularly unreliable when parallel data is scarce (see our error analysis below). This is not true for ArgMin, however, because projection is loss-less here, as remarked above. Accordingly, direct transfer never outperforms PD3 for ArgMin.

Domain shift of parallel data   Using TED as parallel corpus in ArgMin rather than a held-out portion of the ArgMin dataset itself, we observe the following, see Figure 3 (top) and Table 4: (i) PD3-merge still outperforms all other methods; (ii) PD3-MTL more strongly outperforms projection; (iii) the in-language upper-bound is harder to reach. Overall, however, our curves follow a very similar trend as they do when parallel data comes from ArgMin itself, even though argumentation in TED is certainly much less pronounced than it is in student essays. This means that our approach appears robust to changes in domain of the parallel data even for domain-specific problems such as ArgMin, and can still outperform direct transfer in these cases. This is important since parallel data is generally sparse and most likely there is a substantial domain gap to the original L1 train data. The TED results are also interesting insofar as PD3-merge using 1K parallel sentences performs similarly as standard projection does using 100K.

Error Analysis   For **POS**, the projection system that uses only 50 parallel sentences suffers not only from a tiny L2 training corpus (50 sentences, 783 tokens). Because the parallel corpus is tiny, getting high-quality alignments from fast-align on it is also more difficult because the aligner lacks statistical evidence. We checked alignment quality on 11 randomly chosen short translation pairs (both pairs shorter than 10 tokens) and on 3 long pairs (both longer than 20 tokens) for EN-DE. On the short pairs, 26% of the alignment decisions of fast-align were wrong. On the long pairs, 46% were wrong. In contrast, with 5000 parallel sentences error rates were considerably lower: 11% and 16%, respectively. Hence, projection uses a tiny corpus with considerable noise in the case of very small amount of parallel data, causing it to commit all kinds of errors (e.g., tagging verbs as numbers, etc.). In contrast, PD3 uses a larger and much cleaner amount of L1 data besides the tiny and noisy L2 corpus, which causes it to perform substantially better.

Direct transfer systems suffer mostly from two sources of noise: "syntactic shift" due to the L2 language having a different word order than the L1 counterpart on which they have been trained; "semantic shift" due to the test words being all OOV (this is analogous to monolingually replacing words by OOV synonyms). The latter effect may be understood as a "blurring" of the input. Accordingly, direct transfer easily confuses similar classes: for example, the EN→DE direct transfer system has a low F1-score on AUX (confusing auxiliary verbs with actual verbs) of 35% and on NOUN (confusing nouns with proper nouns) of 37%. Adding L2 data to the train set, as in PD3, quickly alleviates this: the F1-score on AUX for 100 parallel sentences is 37% and it is 62% for NOUN for PD3-merge. For 5000 parallel sentences, corresponding numbers are 56% and 76% respectively.

For **ArgMin** and tiny amounts of parallel data, projection predicts all classes but has a very strong tendency to predict the majority class 'premise'. The reason is not that projected labels are noisy—in contrast, they are very good, because projection is error-free, as stated above. The problem is rather that the amount of training data for standard projection is tiny in this case (size of $\mathring{\mathcal{D}}_T$). PD3 in contrast trains on much more data and mimics the true distribution much better. Common errors for PD3 and direct transfer are confusing claims with major claims; these often have very similar surface realizations.

Low-resource shared representations   In our main experiments, we assumed access to high qual-

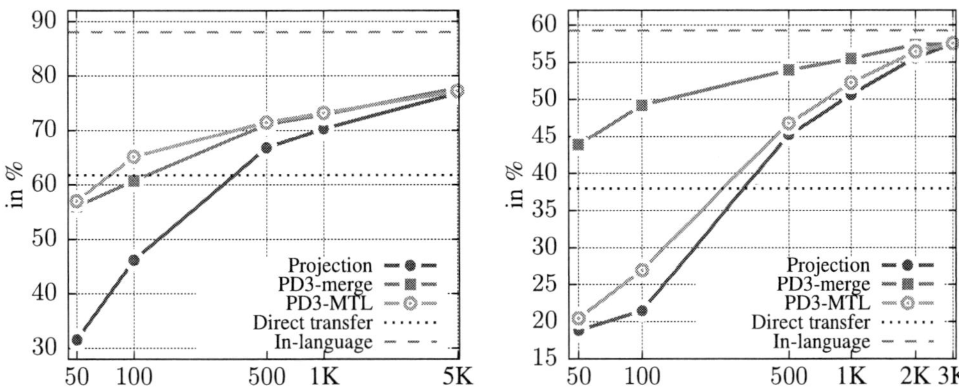

Figure 2: Left: POS accuracies in % as a function of available parallel sentences. Right: Sentence-level ArgMin F1 scores in % as a function of available parallel sentences.

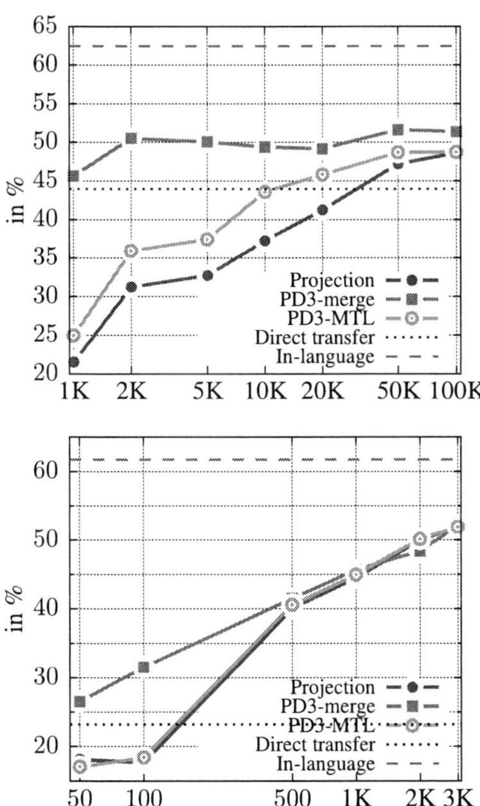

Figure 3: Top: Sentence-level ArgMin F1 scores in % as a function of available parallel sentences (sampled from the parallel TED corpus). Bottom: Sentence-level ArgMin F1 scores in % as a function of available parallel sentences (low-quality bilingual word embeddings).

ity bilingual word embeddings. This may not be justified when the L2 language is low-resource. Hence, we investigated performances when little monolingual data in L2 is available. That is, we limited monolingual data to only 30K sentences in L2. Given that we assumed 50-3000 parallel sentences for projections and given that monolingual data is typically much more plentiful than parallel data, we deemed 30K plausible. We report trends for the ArgMin sentence classification problem.

Hence, we trained a monolingual word2vec model on 30K DE sentences (randomly sampled from the German Wikipedia). For English, we trained a similar model on the whole of the English Wikipedia (since L1 is not low-resource). To induce a bilingual vector space, we then mapped English and German in a common space via the method of Artetxe et al. (2017). This approach iteratively expands a small seed lexicon of matched word pairs, thereby successively improving vector space alignment across two languages. It has been reported to induce good bilingual representations even when only common digits in the two languages or a few dictionary entries are available as initial seed lexicon. We induced a seed dictionary from our parallel sentences (ranging over $\{50, 100, 500, 1000, 2000, 3000\}$ pairs) using fast-align and then applied the technique of Artetxe et al. (2017). We subsequently re-ran PD3 and all other models with the resulting low-quality bilingual word embeddings. The results, for ArgMin, are shown in Figure 3 (bottom). As can be seen, direct transfer becomes considerably worse in this case, which is expected, since the embedding space is of much lower quality now. The performance drop is from 37% macro-F1 with high-quality embeddings to 23%. However, all trends stay the same, e.g., PD3-merge remains the top performer for the sentence-level experiments, followed by PD3-MTL and standard projection. A difference is that PD3-merge now becomes indistinguishable from standard projection for 1K parallel sentences already, rather than 2K as before.

In the extreme case when the bilingual vector space separates into two independent spaces, one for each language, then standard projection is at least as good as PD3, for all sizes of parallel data. This is because the L1 data cannot improve the L2 model since both operate on independent representations. However, it is likely that the added noise may then even confuse a PD3 system if it is not well-regularized.

We experimented with further reductions to 10K monolingual sentences in L2 and still saw a similar trend as in Figure 3 (bottom). Below 10K sentences, we found that, somewhat surprisingly, word2vec could not induce meaningful monolingual embedding spaces, though it is conceivable that other representation learning techniques, such as those based on co-occurrence matrices, would have performed better.

Comparison For POS, we note that our numbers are generally incomparable to other works because we use 800 monolingual sentences to train an English tagger from and (more importantly) treat the number of parallel sentences as a variable whose influence we investigate. Still, to give a reference: Täckström et al. (2013) report cross-lingual tagging accuracies of up to 90% for German and French as L2 using a constraint feature-based CRF. They use up to 5M parallel sentences and 500K size training data in L2, massively more than we use.

For ArgMin, we also have no direct comparisons, because we are the first, to our knowledge, to explore the student essay corpus of Stab and Gurevych (2017) on sentence- rather than token-level. Sentence-level annotation may be preferable because it is sometimes both conventional as well as difficult to decide which exact tokens should be part of an argument component (Persing and Ng, 2016). In terms of cross-language drop, Eger et al. (2018) report a similar drop of roughly 20pp when training an argumentation mining system on English and applying it to similarly annotated German data, for direct transfer. They close this gap using machine translation, while we close it under much milder assumptions using small amounts of parallel data and a more sophisticated transfer approach.

6 Related Work

Our work connects to different strands of research.

Multi-Task Learning MTL was shown to be particularly beneficial when tasks stand in a natural hierarchy and when they are syntactic in nature (Søgaard and Goldberg, 2016). Moreover, it has been claimed that further main benefits for MTL are observed when data for the main task is sparse, in which case the auxiliary tasks may act as regularizers that prevent overfitting (Ruder et al., 2017). The latter is the case for PD3-MTL with little available parallel data.

MTL has also been made use of for *supervised cross-lingual transfer* techniques (Cotterell and Heigold, 2017; Yang et al., 2017; Kim et al., 2017; Dinh et al., 2018). These assume small training sets in L2, and a system trained on them is regularized by a larger amount of training data in L1. In contrast to these, we assume no gold labels in L2 (*unsupervised transfer*), which necessitates a projection step. Our approach could also be combined with these supervised ones, by adding this small gold data to the three different datasets that we use in PD3.

Argumentation Mining ArgMin is a fast-growing field in NLP with applications in decision making and the legal domain (Palau and Moens, 2009) and can be solved on sentence-level (Daxenberger et al., 2017; Niculae et al., 2017; Stab et al., 2018) or token-level (Eger et al., 2017; Schulz et al., 2018). Cross-lingual ArgMin has recently attracted interest (Aker and Zhang, 2017; Eger et al., 2018). The proposed approaches mostly used machine translation, which is unavailable for the vast majority of the world's languages.

Low-resource transfer Low-resource language transfer has recently become very popular, e.g., when relying on only very few translation pairs for bilingual embedding space induction (Artetxe et al., 2017; Zhang et al., 2016) or in unsupervised machine translation using no parallel sources at all (Artetxe et al., 2018; Lample et al., 2018). Low-resource transfer (on a level of domains rather than languages) has also been considered in ArgMin (Schulz et al., 2018), assuming little annotated data in a new target domain due to annotation costs of ArgMin as a subjective high-level task.

7   Concluding Remarks

We combined direct transfer with annotation projection, addressing short-comings of both methods and combining their strengths. We saw consistent gains over either of the two methods in isolation, particularly in the small dataset scenario with 50-500 parallel sentences. This is arguably the most realistic scenario for a good portion of the world's languages, for which several dozens of parallel sentences are readily available e.g. from Bible translations (Christodoulopoulos and Steedman, 2015). We also note that while translating 50 sentences by hand may be as easy as labeling 50 sentences in L2, provided the problem requires no expert knowledge, parallel data serves many NLP problems, while the cost of labeling multiplies by the number of problems.

We also analyzed our approach under changes to external factors such as the bilingual embeddings and the domain of the parallel data, and found it to perform stable under such shifts, consistently outperforming the two baselines it is built upon in the setting of little available parallel sentences. This is particularly important for tasks such as ArgMin, for which it is inherently difficult to get domain specific parallel data, let alone for many languages.

Future work should consider further extensions: E.g., for cross-lingual approaches, it is also possible to select predictions on the source side of parallel data into the train sets only if the classifier's confidence exceeds a certain threshold, or to apply this process iteratively (Täckström, 2012). This can be immediately applied and extended to the PD3 approach. Another extension is to perform self-training on L2 data, which we briefly discuss in the supplementary material. Moreover, PD3 should also be applied in scenarios where L2 is a more distant language to English than considered here, or to setups where L1 is another language than English, although it is unlikely that the general trends we detected here would not persist under L1 and L2 variations. Further, while we did not observe consistent gains of PD3-MTL (sometimes considerable losses) over PD3-merge, we note that there are refinements of the MTL paradigm (e.g., Liu et al. (2017)) which might yield better results in our situation.

Acknowledgments

This work has been supported by the German Federal Ministry of Education and Research (BMBF) under the promotional reference 01UG1816B (CEDIFOR) and 03VP02540 (ArgumenText) and by the German Research Foundation as part of the QA-EduInf project (grant GU 798/18-1 and grant RI 803/12-1).

References

Zeljko Agic, Anders Johannsen, Barbara Plank, Héctor Martínez Alonso, Natalie Schluter, and Anders Søgaard. 2016. Multilingual projection for parsing truly low-resource languages. *Transactions of the Association of Computational Linguistics (TACL)*, 4:301–312.

Ahmet Aker and Huangpan Zhang. 2017. Projection of argumentative corpora from source to target languages. In *Proceedings of the 4th Workshop on Argument Mining, ArgMining@EMNLP 2017, Copenhagen, Denmark, September 8, 2017*, pages 67–72.

Mikel Artetxe, Gorka Labaka, and Eneko Agirre. 2017. Learning bilingual word embeddings with (almost) no bilingual data. In *Proceedings of the 55th Annual Meeting of the Association for Computational Linguistics (ACL 2017)*, pages 451–462.

Mikel Artetxe, Gorka Labaka, Eneko Agirre, and Kyunghyun Cho. 2018. Unsupervised neural machine translation. *ICLR*.

Marcel Bollmann and Anders Søgaard. 2016. Improving historical spelling normalization with bidirectional lstms and multi-task learning. In *Proceedings of the 26th International Conference on Computational Linguistics (COLING 2016)*, pages 131–139.

Rich Caruana. 1993. Multitask learning: A knowledge-based source of inductive bias. In *Proceedings of the 10th International Conference on Machine Learning (ICML 1993)*, pages 41–48.

Christos Christodoulopoulos and Mark Steedman. 2015. A massively parallel corpus: the bible in 100 languages. *Language Resources and Evaluation*, 49(2):375–395.

Ryan Cotterell and Georg Heigold. 2017. Cross-lingual character-level neural morphological tagging. In *Proceedings of the 2017 Conference on Empirical Methods in Natural Language Processing (EMNLP 2017)*, pages 759–770.

Dipanjan Das and Slav Petrov. 2011. Unsupervised part-of-speech tagging with bilingual graph-based projections. In *Proceedings of the 2011 Conference of the North American Chapter of the Association for Computational Linguistics: Human Language Technologies (NAACL-HLT 2011)*, pages 600–609.

Johannes Daxenberger, Steffen Eger, Ivan Habernal, Christian Stab, and Iryna Gurevych. 2017. What is the Essence of a Claim? Cross-Domain Claim Identification. In *Proceedings of the 2017 Conference on Empirical Methods in Natural Language Processing*, pages 2045–2056.

Erik-Lân Do Dinh, Steffen Eger, and Iryna Gurevych. 2018. Killing four birds with two stones: Multi-task learning for non-literal language detection. In *Proceedings of the 27th International Conference on Computational Linguistics (COLING 2018)*, pages 1558–1569.

Chris Dyer, Victor Chahuneau, and Noah A. Smith. 2013. A simple, fast, and effective reparameterization of ibm model 2. In *Proceedings of the 2013 Conference of the North American Chapter of the Association for Computational Linguistics: Human Language Technologies (NAACL-HLT 2013)*, pages 644–648.

Steffen Eger, Johannes Daxenberger, and Iryna Gurevych. 2017. Neural end-to-end learning for computational argumentation mining. In *Proceedings of the 55th Annual Meeting of the Association for Computational Linguistics (Volume 1: Long Papers)*, pages 11–22, Vancouver, Canada. Association for Computational Linguistics.

Steffen Eger, Johannes Daxenberger, Christian Stab, and Iryna Gurevych. 2018. Cross-lingual argumentation mining: Machine translation (and a bit of projection) is all you need! In *Proceedings of the 27th International Conference on Computational Linguistics (COLING 2018)*.

Ivan Habernal and Iryna Gurevych. 2017. Argumentation mining in user-generated web discourse. *Computational Linguistics*, 43(1):125–179.

Karl Moritz Hermann and Phil Blunsom. 2014. Multilingual Models for Compositional Distributed Semantics. In *Proceedings of the 52nd Annual Meeting of the Association for Computational Linguistics (ACL 2014)*, pages 58–68.

Joo-Kyung Kim, Young-Bum Kim, Ruhi Sarikaya, and Eric Fosler-Lussier. 2017. Cross-lingual transfer learning for pos tagging without cross-lingual resources. In *Proceedings of the 2017 Conference on Empirical Methods in Natural Language Processing (EMNLP 2017)*, pages 2822–2828.

Philipp Koehn. 2005. Europarl: A Parallel Corpus for Statistical Machine Translation. In *In Proceedings of the tenth Machine Translation Summit*, pages 79–86. AAMT.

Guillaume Lample, Miguel Ballesteros, Sandeep Subramanian, Kazuya Kawakami, and Chris Dyer. 2016. Neural architectures for named entity recognition. In *Proceedings of the 2016 Conference of the North American Chapter of the Association for Computational Linguistics: Human Language Technologies (NAACL-HLT 2016)*, pages 260–270.

Guillaume Lample, Ludovic Denoyer, and Marc'Aurelio Ranzato. 2018. Unsupervised machine translation using monolingual corpora only. *ICLR*.

Pengfei Liu, Xipeng Qiu, and Xuanjing Huang. 2017. Adversarial multi-task learning for text classification. In *Proceedings of the 55th Annual Meeting of the Association for Computational Linguistics (ACL 2017)*, pages 1–10.

Xuezhe Ma and Eduard H. Hovy. 2016. End-to-end sequence labeling via bi-directional lstm-cnns-crf. In *Proceedings of the 54th Annual Meeting of the Association for Computational Linguistics (ACL 2016)*, pages 1064–1074.

Ryan McDonald, Slav Petrov, and Keith Hall. 2011. Multi-source transfer of delexicalized dependency parsers. In *Proceedings of the 2011 Conference on Empirical Methods in Natural Language Processing (EMNLP 2011)*, pages 62–72.

Marie-Francine Moens. 2017. Argumentation mining: How can a machine acquire common sense and world knowledge? *Argument & Computation*. Accepted.

Vlad Niculae, Joonsuk Park, and Claire Cardie. 2017. Argument mining with structured svms and rnns. In *Proceedings of the 55th Annual Meeting of the Association for Computational Linguistics (Volume 1: Long Papers)*, pages 985–995. Association for Computational Linguistics.

Joakim Nivre, Marie-Catherine de Marneffe, Filip Ginter, Yoav Goldberg, Jan Hajic, Christopher D. Manning, Ryan McDonald, Slav Petrov, Sampo Pyysalo, Natalia Silveira, Reut Tsarfaty, and Daniel Zeman. 2016. Universal dependencies v1: A multilingual treebank collection. In *Proceedings of the Tenth International Conference on Language Resources and Evaluation (LREC 2016)*.

Raquel Mochales Palau and Marie-Francine Moens. 2009. Argumentation mining: The detection, classification and structure of arguments in text. In *Proceedings of the 12th International Conference on Artificial Intelligence and Law*, ICAIL '09, pages 98–107, New York, NY, USA. ACM.

Andreas Peldszus and Manfred Stede. 2013. From Argument Diagrams to Argumentation Mining in Texts: A Survey. *International Journal of Cognitive Informatics and Natural Intelligence*, 7(1):1–31.

Isaac Persing and Vincent Ng. 2016. End-to-end argumentation mining in student essays. In *Proceedings of the 2016 Conference of the North American Chapter of the Association for Computational Linguistics: Human Language Technologies*, pages 1384–1394, San Diego, California. Association for Computational Linguistics.

Andreas Rücklé, Steffen Eger, Maxime Peyrard, and Iryna Gurevych. 2018. Concatenated power mean word embeddings as universal cross-lingual sentence representations. *CoRR*, abs/1803.01400.

Sebastian Ruder, Joachim Bingel, Isabelle Augenstein, and Anders Søgaard. 2017. Sluice networks: Learning what to share between loosely related tasks. In *arXiv preprint*.

Claudia Schulz, Steffen Eger, Johannes Daxenberger, Tobias Kahse, and Iryna Gurevych. 2018. Multi-task learning for argumentation mining in low-resource settings. In *Proceedings of the 16th Annual Conference of the North American Chapter of the Association for Computational Linguistics: Human Language Technologies*, pages 35–41. Association for Computational Linguistics.

Anders Søgaard and Yoav Goldberg. 2016. Deep multi-task learning with low level tasks supervised at lower layers. In *Proceedings of the 54th Annual Meeting of the Association for Computational Linguistics (ACL 2016)*, pages 231–235.

Christian Stab, Johannes Daxenberger, Chris Stahlhut, Tristan Miller, Benjamin Schiller, Christopher Tauchmann, Steffen Eger, and Iryna Gurevych. 2018. Argumentext: Searching for arguments in heterogeneous sources. In *Proceedings of the 2018 Conference of the North American Chapter of the Association for Computational Linguistics: System Demonstrations*, pages 21–25.

Christian Stab and Iryna Gurevych. 2014. Annotating argument components and relations in persuasive essays. In *Proceedings of the 25th International Conference on Computational Linguistics (COLING 2014)*, pages 1501–1510.

Christian Stab and Iryna Gurevych. 2017. Parsing argumentation structures in persuasive essays. *Computational Linguistics*, 43(3):619–659.

Oscar Täckström. 2012. Nudging the envelope of direct transfer methods for multilingual named entity recognition. In *Proceedings of the NAACL-HLT Workshop on the Induction of Linguistic Structure*, pages 55–63.

Oscar Täckström, Dipanjan Das, Slav Petrov, Ryan T. McDonald, and Joakim Nivre. 2013. Token and type constraints for cross-lingual part-of-speech tagging. *Transactions of the Association of Computational Linguistics (TACL)*, 1:1–12.

Oscar Täckström, Ryan McDonald, and Joakim Nivre. 2013. Target language adaptation of discriminative transfer parsers. In *Proceedings of the 2013 Conference of the North American Chapter of the Association for Computational Linguistics: Human Language Technologies (NAACL-HLT 2013)*, pages 1061–1071.

Ivan Vulić and Marie-Francine Moens. 2015. Bilingual word embeddings from non-parallel document-aligned data applied to bilingual lexicon induction. In *Proceedings of the 53rd Annual Meeting of the Association for Computational Linguistics and the 7th International Joint Conference on Natural Language Processing (ACL-IJCNLP 2015)*, pages 719–725.

Zhilin Yang, Ruslan Salakhutdinov, and William W. Cohen. 2017. Transfer learning for sequence tagging with hierarchical recurrent networks. *5th International Conference on Learning Representations (ICLR 2017)*.

David Yarowsky. 1995. Unsupervised word sense disambiguation rivaling supervised methods. In *Proceedings of the 33rd Annual Meeting on Association for Computational Linguistics (ACL 1995)*, pages 189–196.

David Yarowsky, Grace Ngai, and Richard Wicentowski. 2001. Inducing multilingual text analysis tools via robust projection across aligned corpora. In *Proceedings of the First International Conference on Human Language Technology Research (HLT 2001)*, pages 1–8.

Yuan Zhang, David Gaddy, Regina Barzilay, and Tommi Jaakkola. 2016. Ten pairs to tag – multilingual pos tagging via coarse mapping between embeddings. In *Proceedings of the 2016 Conference of the North American Chapter of the Association for Computational Linguistics: Human Language Technologies (NAACL-HLT 2016))*, pages 1307–1317.

Micha Ziemski, Marcin Junczys-Dowmunt, and Bruno Pouliquen. 2016. The united nations parallel corpus v1.0. In *Proceedings of the Tenth International Conference on Language Resources and Evaluation (LREC 2016)*. European Language Resources Association (ELRA).

A Supplemental Material

In Table 4, we show detailed results across languages and tasks, as well as different transfer strategies. Below, we discuss another transfer strategy named L2-ST.

Further approaches When systems are trained on shared features as in direct transfer, then another approach for unsupervised cross-lingual transfer is self-training on L2 data (Täckström, 2012; Täckström et al., 2013). The idea is to train a system on labeled source language data $\mathcal{L}_S$, and then directly apply this trained system to the parallel target language data (this is possible because of the shared feature representation), rather than its source side and merge this newly obtained "self-labeled" dataset with $\mathcal{L}_S$.

We found this strategy, named L2-ST in Table 4 in the appendix, to perform substantially below our considered transfer strategies when there is a sufficient amount of L2 data available. Only with very little target L2 data (50 parallel sentences) did we observe some gains over PD3 in POS tagging. The reason is that for very little parallel data, alignment links are very noisy, as discussed above, so that the projected labels are of low quality. In this case, however, the best strategy is then to combine PD3 with self-training in L2, and thus to combine four datasets: two of them in L1 and two of them in L2. This strategy, which we dub PD4 in Table 4, outperforms L2-ST, but is worse than PD3 for high- and medium-sized parallel corpora. The reason is that the system trained on $\mathcal{L}_S$ is typically much better when applied to L1 data than when applied to L2—see our discussion on direct transfer—and thus the L2 predictions resulting from labeling the source side of parallel data and then projecting to L2 are better than those from directly predicting on L2, provided the projection step is sufficiently good.

This is also the reason why PD4-merge always underperforms PD3-merge for ArgMin—since projection is error-free for sentence level classification.

Task Parallel Sentences	Projection	PD3-merge	PD3-MTL	L2-ST	PD4-merge	Direct Transfer	In-Language (upper bound)
Token-level POS tagging with TED as parallel corpus (EN→DE)							
50	37.86	53.63	55.21	53.56	56.09	55.63	86.29
100	45.37	60.84	61.27	55.81	60.14		
500	67.07	70.16	70.18	57.60	64.68		
1,000	70.74	72.30	72.24	57.27	66.18		
5,000	76.04	77.22	76.55	56.28	66.67		
Token-level POS tagging with TED as parallel corpus (EN→FR)							
50	25.16	58.36	58.78	67.21	67.55	67.87	92.67
100	46.97	60.64	68.96	70.02	71.42		
500	66.49	72.00	72.79	70.34	73.81		
1,000	69.86	73.51	74.14	70.07	73.23		
5,000	77.41	78.29	77.81	68.92	74.37		
Sentence-level AM with 3K sentences of AM as parallel corpus (EN→DE)							
50	18.80	43.89	20.45	39.95	41.13	37.94	59.25
100	21.46	49.20	26.95	36.55	45.89		
500	45.18	53.93	46.75	39.18	49.53		
1,000	50.62	55.45	52.20	38.24	49.87		
2,000	55.55	57.32	56.39	38.47	50.29		
3,000	57.47	57.42	57.52	38.35	51.41		
Sentence-level AM with TED as parallel corpus (EN→DE)							
1,000	21.51	45.61	24.93	42.32	46.59	43.93	62.42
2,000	31.21	50.48	35.93	41.63	45.87		
5,000	32.71	50.03	37.40	43.57	46.85		
10,000	37.22	49.35	43.57	44.42	47.24		
20,000	41.23	49.13	45.78	45.08	48.02		
50,000	47.16	51.57	48.66	43.18	50.20		
100,000	48.58	51.32	48.72	45.05	50.53		

Table 4: Individual results for all tasks, languages, and number of parallel sentences. We report the accuracy for our token-level POS tagging experiments and F1 scores for our sentence-level AM experiments. L2-ST denotes cross-lingual transfer with self-training using L2 data as in (Täckström, 2012; Täckström et al., 2013). PD4-merge combines PD3 with self-training in L2.

Cross-Lingual Argumentative Relation Identification:
from English to Portuguese

Gil Rocha[*] and **Christian Stab**[†] and **Henrique Lopes Cardoso**[*] and **Iryna Gurevych**[†]

[*] LIACC/DEI, Faculdade de Engenharia, Universidade do Porto
Rua Dr. Roberto Frias, 4200-465 Porto, Portugal
[†] Ubiquitous Knowledge Processing Lab (UKP-TUDA)
Department of Computer Science, Technische Universität Darmstadt
`https://www.ukp.tu-darmstadt.de/`

Abstract

Argument mining aims to detect and identify argument structures from textual resources. In this paper, we aim to address the task of argumentative relation identification, a subtask of argument mining, for which several approaches have been recently proposed in a monolingual setting. To overcome the lack of annotated resources in less-resourced languages, we present the first attempt to address this subtask in a cross-lingual setting. We compare two standard strategies for cross-language learning, namely: projection and direct-transfer. Experimental results show that by using unsupervised language adaptation the proposed approaches perform at a competitive level when compared with fully-supervised in-language learning settings.

1 Introduction

The aim of argument mining (AM) is the automatic detection and identification of argumentative structures contained within natural language text. In general, arguments are justifiable positions where pieces of evidence (premises) are offered in support of a conclusion. Most existing approaches to AM build upon supervised machine learning (ML) methods that learn to identify argumentative content from manually annotated examples. Building a corpus with reliably annotated arguments is a challenging and time-consuming task, due to its complexity (Habernal et al., 2014). Consequently, training data for AM is scarce, in particular for less-resourced languages. To overcome the lack of annotated resources for AM in less-resourced languages, we explore cross-language learning approaches (Xiao and Guo, 2013). The aim of cross-language learning is to develop ML techniques that exploit annotated resources in a source language to solve tasks in a target language. Eger et al. (2018) propose the first attempt

to address the identification of argumentative components in a cross-language learning setting. In this paper, we aim to employ existing state-of-the-art cross-language learning techniques to address the task of *argumentative relation identification*, leveraging knowledge extracted from annotated corpora in English to address the task in a less-resourced language, such as Portuguese. As it may be costly to produce small amounts of training data in many different languages, we employ unsupervised language adaptation techniques, which do not require labeled data in the target language.

The aim of argumentative relation identification, the last subtask of the AM process (Peldszus and Stede, 2015), is to classify each argumentative discourse unit (ADU) pair as argumentatively related or not. We assume that the subtask of text segmentation in ADUs is already solved (although no ADU classification is assumed). The task is formulated as a binary classification problem: given a tuple $\langle ADU_s, ADU_t \rangle$, we aim to classify the relation from ADU_s to ADU_t as "support" (where ADU_s plays the role of premise and ADU_t plays the role of conclusion), or "none" (unrelated ADUs). This is a consistent way of formulating the problem (*i.e.* the premise on the left and conclusion on the right side of the tuple), which is an important requirement for the learning process as the relation we aim to capture is a directional relation (*i.e.* ADU_s supports/refutes ADU_t and not on the way around).

We hypothesize that good semantic representations of text, capturing argumentative relations between ADUs, can be independent of the text language. By capturing the semantics of such relations in a higher-level representation (through sentence encoding and aggregation techniques) that is agnostic of the input language, we believe that transfer learning (Pratt and Jennings, 1996) is feasible and, consequently, encouraging results can

144

Proceedings of the 5th Workshop on Argument Mining, pages 144–154
Brussels, Belgium, November 1, 2018. ©2018 Association for Computational Linguistics

be obtained for less-resourced languages. For that, we propose employing cross-language learning techniques, such as *projection* (Yarowsky et al., 2001) and *direct transfer* (McDonald et al., 2011). We show promising results following the approach presented in this paper, by obtaining performance scores in an unsupervised cross-language setting that are competitive (and in some settings better) than fully-supervised in-language ML approaches.

To the best of our knowledge, this is the first approach to consider the task of argumentative relation identification in a cross-lingual setting.

2   Related Work

The full process of AM can be decomposed into several subtasks (Peldszus and Stede, 2015), namely: text segmentation, identification of ADUs, ADU type classification, relation identification, and relation type classification.

Addressing argumentative relation identification in isolation, Nguyen and Litman (2016) adopt a feature-based approach including lexical (unigrams), syntactic (part-of-speech, production rules), discourse indicators (PDTB relations) and topic-context features. Recent works address the task through deep learning architectures. Bosc et al. (2016) employ an encoder-decoder architecture and two distinct LSTMs to identify support and attack relations on tweets. Cocarascu and Toni (2017) follow architectures used for the recognizing textual entailment task, reporting results that substantially improve accuracy as compared to a feature-based ML approach on the same corpus.

Other approaches model the problem jointly with previous subtasks of AM. Stab and Gurevych (2017) follow a feature-based approach employing features at different levels of abstraction and integer linear programming for joint optimization of the subtasks. Eger et al. (2017) propose an end-to-end AM system by framing the task as a token-level dependency parser and sequence tagging problem. Potash et al. (2017) use an encoder-decoder problem formulation by employing a pointer network based deep neural network architecture. The results reported by Potash *et al.* (0.767 macro F1-score) constitute the current state-of-the-art on the Persuasive Essays corpus (Stab and Gurevych, 2017) for the subtask of argumentative relation identification.

Related work aiming to capture relations between elementary units of texts is closely re-lated to our task. For instance, recognizing textual entailment (RTE) also focuses on pair classification (Sammons et al., 2012). State-of-the-art systems explore complex sentence encoding techniques using a variety of approaches, such as recurrent (Bowman et al., 2015a) and recursive (Bowman et al., 2015b) neural networks, followed by a set of hidden layers (including aggregation functions (Chen et al., 2017; Peters et al., 2018) and attention mechanisms (Rocktäschel et al., 2015)). In another line of work, discourse parsing approaches aim to identify the structure of the text in terms of discourse or rhetorical relations between elementary units of text (*e.g.* propositions). Recent work focuses on building good representations of text relying on neural network architectures (Braud et al., 2017). Some attempts exist to address these related tasks in cross-lingual settings. For RTE there has been work using parallel corpora (Mehdad et al., 2011) and lexical resources (Castillo, 2011), as well as shared tasks (Camacho-Collados et al., 2017). Typically, these systems explore projection approaches and abstract representations that do not require prior translation, namely bilingual dictionaries, syntactic information, statistical knowledge and external knowledge from lexical resources (*e.g.* ConceptNet, WordNet, BabelNet). More recently, Agic and Schluter (2018) provide multilingual test data for four major languages (Arabic, French, Spanish and Russian) and baseline cross-language RTE models. Preliminary work shows that projection approaches work better in cross-lingual settings than direct transfer.

Despite the similarity between the tasks of argumentative relation identification and RTE, since both tasks are grounded in different conceptual frameworks, the inherent semantic relations that the tasks aim to capture is conceptually different (as detailed by Cabrio and Villata (2013)). In this respect, it is important to notice that the SNLI corpus (Bowman et al. (2015a), the reference corpus for RTE) is composed of literal descriptions of scenes depicted in images, where pairs were manually created. Compared to the Argumentative Essays corpus and, more specifically, to ADU pairs extracted from it, we observe that the latter tend to require higher-level semantic reasoning (this is apparent when comparing the example provided in Table 2 with the following example extracted from the SNLI corpus: "A soccer game with multiple

Lang	Corpus	#Docs	#Rel	#None	#Support	#Attack	Arg. Schema	Type
EN	Argumentative Essays	402	22,172	17,923	3,918	331	Premise, Claim, Major Claim	Essays
PT	ArgMine	75	778	621	153	4	Premise, Claim	Opinion Articles

Table 1: Corpora Statistics

Lang.	Source ADU	Target ADU	Label
EN	Teachers are not just teachers, they are also friends and conseilieurs	In conclusion, there can be no school without a teacher	support
	computers need to be operated by people	no one can argue that technological tools are must-haves for the classroom	none
PT	Durante a última década, a saúde, o meio ambiente, a biodiversidade, assim como a evolução humana tem sido temas recorrentes em todos os meios de comunicação. *(During the last decade, health, environment, biodiversity, as well as human evolution have been recurring topics in all sorts of media)*	O século XXI é sem sombra de dúvida a era da Biologia *(The 21st century is undoubtedly the era of biology)*	support
	Seria da mais elementar prudência não voltar a precisar de lhe pedir dinheiro *(It would be most prudent not to need asking it money again)*	O fluxo de migrantes agravou o peso do euroceptismo nos governos *(The flow of migrants has increased the weight of euroscepticism in governments)*	none

Table 2: Annotated examples extracted from the Argumentative Essays (EN) (Stab and Gurevych, 2017) and ArgMine corpus (PT) (Rocha and Lopes Cardoso, 2017)

males playing." entails "Some men are playing a sport.").

To the best of our knowledge, Eger et al. (2018) present the first work exploiting cross-lingual techniques for argument mining. The authors address component extraction and classification and show that machine translation and (naïve) projection work considerably better than direct transfer. More details regarding cross-language learning techniques are presented in Section 4.3.

3   Corpora

To address the task of argumentative relation identification in a cross-language setting, argument-annotated corpora are required in different languages. Such corpora should, ideally, (a) contain annotations of arguments in different languages, (b) follow the same argumentation theory and (c) belong to the same genre of text and similar domains. Currently, there are resources for English (Stab and Gurevych, 2017) and Portuguese (Rocha and Lopes Cardoso, 2017) that follow the premise-conclusion argumentation model and contain annotations of argumentative relations between ADUs, and thus fulfill the first and the second criteria listed above. However, the corpora collected for this work (Table 1) do not meet the third criterion because they contain annotations from different types of texts: persuasive essays and opinionated articles. We focus our attention on the language adaptation of the models proposed in this paper, even though we are aware that this domain shift might play an important role in the performance of our proposed methods.

3.1   Data Preparation

Since we focus on a specific subtask of AM, argumentative relation identification, we need to generate appropriate datasets from the corpora listed in Table 1. As input, we receive texts annotated with argumentative content at the token level following a specific argumentation theory (*i.e.* premise-conclusion model). For the task at hand, we construct a dataset containing ADU pairs annotated with "none", "support" or "attack". We start by splitting each document into paragraphs, for the following reasons: (a) in all corpora used in this work, arguments are constrained to paragraph boundaries; (b) paragraph splitting reduces the number of "none" relations in the final dataset and, therefore, leads to a less skewed class distribution of the labels.

For each paragraph with ADUs $c_1, ..., c_n$, we generate tuples $\langle c_i, c_j \rangle$, with $i \neq j$ and $i, j \in [1, n]$ as argument component pairs, and label them with "support"/"attack" if the original annotation contains a direct argumentative relation from c_i to c_j, or with "none" otherwise. As shown in Table 1, label distribution is skewed towards "none" relations. Given the low number of "attack" relations, we disregard them for this paper. Hence, we formulate the task as a binary classification problem: each tuple is classified as "none" or "support".

Table 2 shows an example of the content available in the corpora for each of the labels.

4 Methods

Similarly to approaches that aim to learn universal sentence representations able to capture the semantics of the sentence (Bowman et al., 2015b; Conneau et al., 2017), we explore different deep learning architectures to encode the meaning of ADUs for the task of argumentative relation identification. To help replicate our results, we publish the code used in this work[1]. We propose five neural network architectures that differ in the sentence encoding techniques employed (as described in Section 4.1), to which we add a fully-connected hidden layer with the same dimension as the output of the sentence encoding component, followed by a softmax layer to obtain the final predictions. To prevent the model from overfitting, we apply dropout (Srivastava et al., 2014) in each model after the sentence encoding component.

4.1 Sentence Encoding

We explore different ways of encoding the meaning of ADU pairs.

LSTM. LSTMs (Hochreiter and Schmidhuber, 1997) are recurrent neural networks (RNN) that process each word at a time and decide which information to keep in order to produce a concise representation of the word sequence. We concatenate word embedding representations of the words in ADU_s and ADU_t with a special delimiter token $delim$ (with its embeddings randomly initialized). The role of this delimiter is to indicate the RNN that a transition from ADU_s to ADU_t is being made. Then, the LSTM cell processes the entire sequence. The final hidden state representation is used as the sentence representation.

BiLSTM. Traditional LSTMs process the text in a single direction and do not consider contextual information of future words in the current step. Bidirectional LSTMs use both previous and future context by processing the input sequence in two directions. We follow the same procedure described for LSTM by concatenating ADUs using a

special token. The final representation is the concatenation of the forward and backward step.[2]

Conv1D. Both ADUs are encoded separately using a convolutional neural network (CNN) (LeCun et al., 1998), with a fixed kernel size of 2, stride 1 and a max pooling layer to obtain the final fixed-length representation. The motivation for using CNNs is the fact that they can model the sequence of words by processing subsequences in parallel to obtain a final higher-level representation of the sentence. This is a promising approach when dealing with text in different languages, where the order of words are different.

Inner-Att. Inspired by previous successful work using attention (Bahdanau et al., 2014; Stab et al., 2018) in several NLP applications, we propose an attention-based sentence encoding that learns the importance of weighting ADU_t depending on the content of ADU_s. We adopt an innerattention mechanism as proposed by Wang et al. (2016). First, we encode ADU_s using a LSTM. Then, we determine the importance weighting on the input sequence ADU_t instead of on the hidden states of the $LSTM(ADU_t)$: this has been shown to prevent biased importance weights towards the end of a sequence (Wang et al., 2016). This attention mechanism uses the information encoded in $LSTM(ADU_s)$ to inform which of the words in ADU_t the model should pay more attention to, given ADU_s. By employing this attention mechanism, we obtain a weighted input embeddings representation of ADU_t, represented as $\widetilde{x}_t$ The final hidden state used as the encoding of the tuple is obtained by applying a LSTM over the weighted representation of ADU_t: $LSTM(\widetilde{x}_t)$.

4.2 In-Language Baseline Models

As in-language baselines, we present experiments using the following models: (a) logistic regression employing a bag-of-words encoding (1 to 3 n-grams) for feature extraction based on word counts, without employing weighting techniques[3] (*BoW+LR*); (b) Chen et al. (2017): propose the enhancement of sequential inference models based on chain networks to address the task of RTE. The authors propose two models: a sequential model

---

[1] https://github.com/GilRocha/
emnlp2018-argmin-workshop-xLingArgRelId

[2] For both LSTM and BiLSTM sentence encoding, we also tried to encode ADU_s and ADU_t separately using two distinct RNNs followed by a concatenation of both representations, obtaining a consistently lower performance.

[3] we also tried using TF-IDF encoding, obtaining lower performance metrics consistently.

ESIM and a model that incorporates syntactic parsing information in tree LSTMs, Tree-LSTM. Since the Tree-LSTM requires preprocessing tools to obtain the syntactic parsing information, which we argue are not suited for cross-lingual settings targeting less-resourced languages, we only explore the ESIM model in this work. The neural inference model is composed by three major components: input encoding (based on BiLSTMs), local inference modeling, and inference composition; and (c) Peters et al. (2018): a re-implementation of the widely used decomposable attention model developed by Parikh et al. (2016). At the time of development of this work, models (b) and (c) constitute current state-of-the-art models for RTE. We used the code publicly available for both approaches with small modifications in order to make predictions in our binary classification task[4]. These baseline models were employed to obtain a lower-bound for our task and to determine how well existing approaches perform. Since all baselines were originally developed in a monolingual setting, there is no trivial way to employ them as baselines in a cross-lingual setting.

4.3 Cross-Language Learning Techniques

Several approaches have been presented for cross-language learning, including *projection*, *direct transfer*, and *feature space analysis*. As a convention, L_S denotes the source language (in which most of the annotated data is available) and L_T the target language (in which the capability of the system to perform cross-language adaptation will be evaluated, typically containing few or no labeled data).

In projection approaches (Yarowsky et al., 2001; Hwa et al., 2005), annotated data in L_S is projected (by translation) to L_T. More concretely, the learning instances originally in L_S are translated (*e.g.* using machine translation tools or using parallel data) to L_T and the corresponding labels are projected to the new learning instances in L_T. Then, a ML system is trained and evaluated on the projected data in L_T. Typically, fine-grained word alignment techniques are employed to obtain high quality translations and to better preserve the annotation's token-level boundaries. The majority of cross-language learning approaches follow the projection approach. Recent studies, namely (Eger et al., 2018), point out that the quality of current machine translation systems and word alignment tools provide a good basis for projection approaches.

In a direct transfer approach (McDonald et al., 2011), the system is fully trained on the source language L_S, and then the learned model is used to initialize a new model that will work on the target language L_T. If few or no annotated data is available in L_T, the model is used after updating the embedding layer for the target language (using multilingual word embeddings), to make predictions on L_T (unsupervised direct transfer learning). If enough (according to the task) annotated data is available in L_T, the model can be retrained on L_T (after supervised training in L_S) for better adaptation to the target language (supervised direct transfer learning).

Feature space approaches (Bell et al., 2014) perform subspace analysis to find a feature space that can be employed across different languages and at the same time is suitable for the target language.

In this work, we explore the projection and direct transfer approaches. We leave for future work exploring feature space approaches. Regarding the projection approach, we machine translate the ADUs obtained from the Argumentative Essays corpus (Stab and Gurevych, 2017), originally in English, to the target language (*i.e.* Portuguese) using the Google Translator API[5]. Since we formulated the problem as a classification task given two ADUs, the projection of the labels is trivial (no token level alignment is required). Mandatory for the direct transfer approach is the existence of cross-lingual word embeddings, which are trained to obtain a shared embedding space representation of words in different languages. With them, we are able to employ techniques based on word embeddings across different languages. Similarly to monolingual word embeddings, various approaches for learning cross-lingual word embeddings have been proposed in recent years (Ruder, 2017). In this paper, we use pre-trained multilingual embeddings publicly available (Ferreira et al., 2016). The embeddings were obtained by combining parallel data from the TED Corpus with pre-trained English GloVe embeddings[6]. Each embedding contains 300 dimensions.

---

[4]RTE considers three labels: "neutral", "entailment", and "contradiction".

4.4 Dealing with unbalanced datasets

As shown in Table 1, the distribution of labels is skewed towards the "none" class. In the presence of unbalanced datasets, ML algorithms tend to favor predictions of the majority class. Aiming to improve the results for the "support" label (minority class), we explore two widely used techniques to deal with unbalanced datasets in ML problems (He and Garcia, 2009): *random undersampling* and *cost-sensitive learning*.

Random undersampling consists of randomly removing examples from the majority class until a predefined number of examples, determined to obtain a balanced dataset in the end of process. In cost-sensitive learning, each class is assigned a weight that works as a penalty cost. Higher/lower costs are used for examples of the minority/majority class, respectively. The ML model is then trained to minimize the total cost, which will become more sensitive to misclassification of examples in the minority class. To determine the weight matrix for each class we follow the heuristic proposed by King and Zeng (2001).

For all the experiments presented in the following sections, these techniques are only applied to the training set (random undersampling) or during the training phase (cost-sensitive learning).

5 Evaluation

In order to validate the main hypothesis proposed in this paper – that the proposed models can capture argumentative relations between ADUs at a semantic-level that is transferable across languages – we have run a set of in-language and cross-language experiments.

Our cross-language experiments use 80% of ADU pairs originally available in L_S as training data and the remaining 20% as test data. In order to tune the parameters of the model, we sample 10% of the training set as the validation data. All splits of the datasets are made at the document-level (*i.e.*, ADU pairs belonging to document $\mathcal{D}$ are not spread in different partitions) and keeping the original distribution of labels in each partition (stratified splitting). Then, the models are evaluated on the full dataset in L_T without retraining (unsupervised language adaptation).

In-language experiments aim to establish baseline scores for a supervised ML system that can make use of annotated resources in L_T. We perform 5-fold cross-validation for in-language experiments. Final scores correspond to the sum of the confusion matrix from the test set predictions in each fold (Forman and Scholz, 2010). Following this procedure, we obtain final evaluation metrics for the full dataset in L_T that are directly comparable with the scores reported on the full dataset for L_T in cross-language experiments, as the evaluation scores are obtained from exactly the same data in both settings. Cross-validation splits are also at the document-level and keep the original label distribution.

Since reporting single performance scores is insufficient to compare non-deterministic learning approaches (Reimers and Gurevych, 2017), we report average scores of 10 runs with different random seeds. Due to the unbalanced nature of the datasets, evaluation metrics reported in the experiments are average macro F1-scores over all 10 runs. All models are trained using the Adam optimizer, using the default parameters suggested in the original paper (Kingma and Ba, 2014), and cross-entropy loss function. The activation function used in all the layers was ReLU (Glorot et al., 2011). To find the best model in each run, we stop training once the accuracy on the validation set does not improve for 5 epochs (early-stop criterion) or 50 epochs are completed. The batch size used in the experiments was set to 32 learning instances. The dimension of the LSTM cell, used by some of the models, was set to 96 after hyperparameter tunning (we tried with 32, 64, 96 and 128). Finally, to accelerate training, we set the maximum length for all ADUs to 50 tokens[7].

5.1 In-Language Results

Table 3 summarizes in-language results obtained for the Argumentative Essays corpus, which contains essays written in English.

Without using any technique to deal with the unbalanced nature of the dataset (upper part of Table 3), results show that all neural network models outperform the baselines. Surprisingly, state-of-art models adopted from the RTE community, namely Peters et al. (2018) and Chen et al. (2017), perform poorly in our task. These results were unexpected because: (a) the tasks are similar (both approaches aim to classify pairs of propositions in similar classes) and (b) the results reported for RTE are quite impressive, namely 0.893 and 0.886

---

[7]Only 0.2% of ADUs in ArgEssays (Stab and Gurevych, 2017) and 4.5% of ADUs in ArgMine Corpus (Rocha and Lopes Cardoso, 2017) exceed this length.

of accuracy on the SNLI test set, respectively. We hypothesize that despite the similarity of the tasks, the fact that texts have inherently different genres and the datasets different characteristics (label distribution and number of examples) prevents the models proposed for RTE from generalizing well to our task. Results show that the baseline *BoW+LR* is very competitive compared to the neural network architectures. In this setting, the best performing system is *Conv1D*.

Model	*Macro-F1*	*F1-None*	*F1-Supp*
Random	.447	.625	.269
Peters et al. (2018)	.512	.903	.121
Chen et al. (2017)	.577	.879	.275
BoW+LR	.604	.898	.311
LSTM	.606	.877	.336
BiLSTM	.624	.867	.381
Conv1D	.634	.879	.390
Inner-Att	.621	.882	.360
Cost Sensitive Learning			
BoW+LR	**.641**	.875	.407
LSTM	.616	.822	.410
BiLSTM	.634	.835	**.434**
Conv1D	.631	.832	.430
Inner-Att	.606	.822	.410
Random Undersampling			
BoW+LR	.574	.748	.401
LSTM	.566	.734	.399
BiLSTM	.609	.796	.422
Conv1D	.598	.786	.410
Inner-Att	.586	.775	.397

Table 3: In-Language Scores - Arg. Essays (EN). Bold numbers indicate the highest score in the column.

As expected, the skewed nature of the dataset plays an important role in the reported results: scores for the "support" relation are very low compared with scores for "none". We also report experiments conceived to address the unbalanced nature of the dataset, as explained in Section 4.4. We can observe that using cost-sensitive learning we obtained better results for *BoW+LR*, *LSTM* and *BiLSTM*. It is notable that the simple *BoW+LR* approach obtains better results than more complex neural network techniques. We believe this is due to the fact that the number of examples in the dataset is not sufficient to explore the full capabilities of the neural network techniques proposed here (and that have been successful in many other scenarios). Finally, in the cost-sensitive learning setting we obtain the best performance scores for the "support" label, in all models. Regarding random undersampling, results are consistently below those reported using the cost-sensitive learning approach.

The first column in Table 4 summarizes in-language results on the Portuguese ArgMine corpus. We observe similar results compared to the English results reported above. The only exceptions are: (a) *Inner-att* model obtains better results without using balancing techniques, and (b) random undersampling performs better than cost-sensitive learning.

Existing state-of-the-art work on the Argumentative Essays corpus for the subtask of argumentative relation identification reports, as macro F1-scores, 0.751 (Stab and Gurevych, 2017), 0.756 (Nguyen and Litman (2016), in an initial release of the Argumentative Essays corpus containing 90 essays) and 0.767 (Potash et al., 2017). Finally, Eger et al. (2017) reported a F1-score of 0.455 (100% token level match) and 0.501 (50% token level match), but these scores are dependent on the classification of the components in the previous steps (the problem was modeled differently). Therefore, the results reported in Table 3 are worse than state-of-the-art work. The aim of this work is to address the task for a less-resourced language using cross-language learning approaches. Consequently, the main goal is not to propose a novel approach for argumentative relation identification in a monolingual setting. It is important to notice that some of the previous approaches proposed in a monolingual setting do not comply with the proposed approach in this paper: Stab and Gurevych (2017) and Nguyen and Litman (2016) employ different types of features which we argue not to be suitable for cross-language learning targeting less-resourced languages, as extracting these features requires complex linguistic preprocessing tools which cannot be reliably employed in less-resourced languages; and Eger et al. (2017) and Potash et al. (2017) modeled the problem differently by jointly modeling different subtasks of the argumentation mining process.

5.2 Cross-Language Results

Table 4 includes results obtained for cross-language experiments, exploring unsupervised language adaptation techniques (English to Portuguese). Comparing direct transfer and projection approaches, we can observe that projection performs slightly better in most cases. Comparing the scores obtained in the in-language and cross-language settings, we observe that, in general, performance in the cross-language setting improves

	In-Language			Direct Transfer			Projection		
Model	*Macro*	*None*	*Supp*	*Macro*	*None*	*Supp*	*Macro*	*None*	*Supp*
Random	.448	.613	.283	-	-	-	-	-	-
BoW+LR	.457	.888	.025	-	-	-	-	-	-
Peters et al. (2018)	.485	.887	.082	-	-	-	-	-	-
Chen et al. (2017)	.522	.856	.188	-	-	-	-	-	-
LSTM	.489	.868	.110	.461	.887	.036	.462	.884	.041
BiLSTM	.510	.840	.180	.463	.870	.057	.466	.877	.055
Conv1D	.459	.882	.035	.459*	.880	.038	.462*	.884	.039
Inner-Att	**.534**	.764	.305	.454	.883	.025	.456	.882	.030
Cost Sensitive Learning									
BoW+LR	.520	.846	.193	-	-	-	-	-	-
LSTM	.496	.680	.312	.489	.870	.109	.493	.849	.137
BiLSTM	.523	.786	.259	.485	.861	.109	.503	.845	**.162**
Conv1D	.503	.827	.178	.497	.854	.141	.494	.841	.147
Inner-Att	.479	.637	.321	.477	.867	.088	.484*	.844	.123
Random Undersampling									
BoW+LR	.264	.191	.337	-	-	-	-	-	-
LSTM	.494	.668	.321	.494*	.870	.118	.495*	.859	.131
BiLSTM	.464	.581	.348	**.500***	.856	**.145**	**.512***	.865	.158
Conv1D	.423	.554	.292	.499*	.855	.144	.492*	.849	.134
Inner-Att	.487	.621	**.352**	.482	.878	.087	.495*	.861	.128

Table 4: In and Cross-Language scores on the Portuguese (PT) corpus. Bold numbers indicate the highest score in the column. ⋆ = equal or above in-language scores. All metrics correspond to F1-scores.

for the "none" relation and, conversely, drops for the "support" relation. In general, we can observe that the macro-f1 scores of in-language and cross-language approaches are very similar and, in some settings, cross-language macro F1-scores are equal or above in-language scores (marked with the ⋆ symbol in Table 4). Compared to fully-supervised approaches on the target language, such cross-language approaches are able to perform similarly without any annotated data in the target language. These results suggest that transfer learning across languages is possible using the proposed models and that the hypothesis (*i.e.* the argumentative relations between ADUs can be captured in higher-level representations that are transferable) explored in this work is valid.

Regarding the balancing techniques in a cross-language settings, results show that random undersampling works generally better than cost-sensitive learning. Finally, balancing techniques improved the overall scores for all the models.

Similarly to the findings of Eger et al. (2018), we observed better results following the projection approach. As discussed by the authors, it seems that current neural machine translation models have reached a level that makes approaches relying on automated translations feasible and very promising. In this work, the drop in performance using direct transfer was less severe than that of Eger et al. (2018) and very close to the results obtained using the projection approach.

5.3 Error Analysis

To better understand the errors, in particular in cross-lingual scenarios, we selected 5 documents from the ArgMine Corpus (randomly sampled from the set of documents but manually selected to contain false-positive and false-negative examples), comprising a total of 56 ADU pairs for each setting (in-language and cross-language experiments were manually compared).

We noticed that the ArgMine Corpus lacks linguistic indicators of argumentative content (*e.g.* "therefore", "thus", "firstly") that prevail in the Argumentative Essays corpus. This constitutes a consequence of the domain shift between the corpora with potential impact on the performance loss reported in this work. Furthermore, the ArgMine Corpus contains opinionated news articles, which typically require common-sense knowledge and temporal reasoning to identify relations of support (*e.g.* ADU_s: "Greece, last year, tested the tolerance limits of other European taxpayers" and ADU_t: "The European Union of 2016 is no longer the one of 2011.". This example was manually translated from Portuguese to English).

Finally, we also noticed that our deliberative choice of not distinguishing between *linked* and *convergent* arguments (Peldszus and Stede, 2013) led to the problem of including in our dataset linked arguments with p premises as p ADU pairs. Linked arguments seem to be more prevalent in the ArgMine corpus, and treating them simply as convergent brings us to a problem of partial argumentative relation detection, for which further premises are needed.

6 Conclusions and Future Work

We have presented the first attempt to address the task of argumentative relation identification in a cross-lingual setting. By performing cross-language learning experiments for Portuguese using two popular transfer learning approaches – projection and direct transfer – we have shown that competitive results can be obtained using unsupervised language adaptation, when compared to a fully-supervised machine learning approach on the target language. Experimental results have shown that the cross-lingual transfer loss is relatively small (always below 10%) and, in some settings, transfer learning approaches achieve better scores than fully supervised in-language approaches. These findings demonstrate that suitable higher-level representations of argumentative relations can be obtained that, combined with cross-lingual word embeddings, can be transferred across languages.

In future work, we aim to evaluate the proposed approaches in other languages and explore featurespace analysis techniques recently proposed to address related NLP tasks. Furthermore, we intend to explore multi-task learning techniques, to leverage the knowledge gathered from related tasks (*e.g.* training the models both in argument relation identification and RTE datasets).

Acknowledgments

The first author was partially supported by an Erasmus Placements grant. Part of this work has been supported by the German Federal Ministry of Education and Research (BMBF) under the promotional reference 03VP02540 (ArgumenText).

References

Zeljko Agic and Natalie Schluter. 2018. Baselines and test data for cross-lingual inference. In *Proceedings of the Eleventh International Conference on Language Resources and Evaluation (LREC 2018)*, Paris, France. European Language Resources Association (ELRA).

Dzmitry Bahdanau, Kyunghyun Cho, and Yoshua Bengio. 2014. Neural machine translation by jointly learning to align and translate. *CoRR*, abs/1409.0473.

Peter Bell, Joris Driesen, and Steve Renals. 2014. Cross-lingual adaptation with multi-task adaptive networks. In *INTERSPEECH 2014, 15th Annual Conference of the International Speech Communication Association, Singapore, September 14-18, 2014*, pages 21–25.

Tom Bosc, Elena Cabrio, and Serena Villata. 2016. Tweeties squabbling: Positive and negative results in applying argument mining on social media. In *Computational Models of Argument - Proceedings of COMMA 2016, Potsdam, Germany, 12-16 September, 2016*, pages 21–32.

Samuel R. Bowman, Gabor Angeli, Christopher Potts, and Christopher D. Manning. 2015a. A large annotated corpus for learning natural language inference. In *EMNLP*, pages 632–642. The Association for Computational Linguistics.

Samuel R. Bowman, Christopher Potts, and Christopher D. Manning. 2015b. Recursive neural networks can learn logical semantics. In *Proceedings of the 3rd Workshop on Continuous Vector Space Models and their Compositionality*, pages 12–21. Association for Computational Linguistics.

Chloé Braud, Maximin Coavoux, and Anders Søgaard. 2017. Cross-lingual rst discourse parsing. In *Proceedings of the 15th Conference of the European Chapter of the Association for Computational Linguistics: Volume 1, Long Papers*, pages 292–304. Association for Computational Linguistics.

Elena Cabrio and Serena Villata. 2013. A natural language bipolar argumentation approach to support users in online debate interactions. *Argument & Computation*, 4(3):209–230.

Jose Camacho-Collados, Mohammad Taher Pilehvar, Nigel Collier, and Roberto Navigli. 2017. Semeval-2017 task 2: Multilingual and cross-lingual semantic word similarity. In *Proceedings of the 11th International Workshop on Semantic Evaluation (SemEval-2017)*, pages 15–26. Association for Computational Linguistics.

Julio Javier Castillo. 2011. A wordnet-based semantic approach to textual entailment and cross-lingual textual entailment. *Int. J. Machine Learning & Cybernetics*, 2(3):177–189.

Qian Chen, Xiaodan Zhu, Zhen-Hua Ling, Si Wei, Hui Jiang, and Diana Inkpen. 2017. Enhanced lstm for natural language inference. In *Proceedings of the 55th Annual Meeting of the Association for Computational Linguistics (Volume 1: Long Papers)*, pages 1657–1668. Association for Computational Linguistics.

Oana Cocarascu and Francesca Toni. 2017. Identifying attack and support argumentative relations using deep learning. In *Proceedings of the 2017 Conference on Empirical Methods in Natural Language Processing, EMNLP 2017, Copenhagen, Denmark, September 9-11, 2017*, pages 1374–1379.

Alexis Conneau, Douwe Kiela, Holger Schwenk, Loïc Barrault, and Antoine Bordes. 2017. Supervised learning of universal sentence representations from natural language inference data. In *Proceedings of the 2017 Conference on Empirical Methods in Natural Language Processing*, pages 670–680. Association for Computational Linguistics.

Steffen Eger, Johannes Daxenberger, and Iryna Gurevych. 2017. Neural end-to-end learning for computational argumentation mining. In *Proceedings of the 55th Annual Meeting of the Association for Computational Linguistics (ACL 2017)*, volume Volume 1: Long Papers, pages 11–22. Association for Computational Linguistics.

Steffen Eger, Johannes Daxenberger, Christian Stab, and Iryna Gurevych. 2018. Cross-lingual argumentation mining: Machine translation (and a bit of projection) is all you need! In *Proceedings of the 27th International Conference on Computational Linguistics*, pages 831–844. Association for Computational Linguistics.

Daniel C. Ferreira, André F. T. Martins, and Mariana S. C. Almeida. 2016. Jointly learning to embed and predict with multiple languages. In *Proceedings of the 54th Annual Meeting of the Association for Computational Linguistics (Volume 1: Long Papers)*, pages 2019–2028. Association for Computational Linguistics.

George Forman and Martin Scholz. 2010. Apples-to-apples in cross-validation studies: Pitfalls in classifier performance measurement. *SIGKDD Explor. Newsl.*, 12(1):49–57.

Xavier Glorot, Antoine Bordes, and Yoshua Bengio. 2011. Deep sparse rectifier neural networks. In *Proceedings of the Fourteenth International Conference on Artificial Intelligence and Statistics*, volume 15 of *Proceedings of Machine Learning Research*, pages 315–323, Fort Lauderdale, FL, USA. PMLR.

Ivan Habernal, Judith Eckle-Kohler, and Iryna Gurevych. 2014. Argumentation mining on the web from information seeking perspective. In *Proceedings of the Workshop on Frontiers and Connections between Argumentation Theory and Natural Language Processing*, pages 26–39. CEUR-WS.

Haibo He and Edwardo A. Garcia. 2009. Learning from imbalanced data. *IEEE Trans. on Knowl. and Data Eng.*, 21(9):1263–1284.

Sepp Hochreiter and Jürgen Schmidhuber. 1997. Long short-term memory. *Neural Comput.*, 9(8):1735–1780.

Rebecca Hwa, Philip Resnik, Amy Weinberg, Clara Cabezas, and Okan Kolak. 2005. Bootstrapping parsers via syntactic projection across parallel texts. *Nat. Lang. Eng.*, 11(3):311–325.

Gary King and Langche Zeng. 2001. Logistic regression in rare events data. *Political Analysis*, 9:137–163.

Diederik P. Kingma and Jimmy Ba. 2014. Adam: A method for stochastic optimization. *CoRR*, abs/1412.6980.

Y. LeCun, L. Bottou, Y. Bengio, and P. Haffner. 1998. Gradient-based learning applied to document recognition. *Proceedings of the IEEE*, 86(11):2278–2324.

Ryan McDonald, Slav Petrov, and Keith Hall. 2011. Multi-source transfer of delexicalized dependency parsers. In *Proceedings of the Conference on Empirical Methods in Natural Language Processing*, EMNLP '11, pages 62–72, Stroudsburg, PA, USA. Association for Computational Linguistics.

Yashar Mehdad, Matteo Negri, and Marcello Federico. 2011. Using bilingual parallel corpora for cross-lingual textual entailment. In *Proceedings of the 49th Annual Meeting of the Association for Computational Linguistics: Human Language Technologies - Volume 1*, HLT '11, pages 1336–1345, Stroudsburg, PA, USA. Association for Computational Linguistics.

Huy Nguyen and Diane J. Litman. 2016. Context-aware argumentative relation mining. In *Proceedings of the 54th Annual Meeting of the Association for Computational Linguistics, ACL 2016, August 7-12, 2016, Berlin, Germany, Volume 1: Long Papers*.

Ankur Parikh, Oscar Täckström, Dipanjan Das, and Jakob Uszkoreit. 2016. A decomposable attention model for natural language inference. In *Proceedings of the 2016 Conference on Empirical Methods in Natural Language Processing*, pages 2249–2255. Association for Computational Linguistics.

Andreas Peldszus and Manfred Stede. 2013. From argument diagrams to argumentation mining in texts: A survey. *Int. Journal of Cognitive Informatics and Natural Intelligence (IJCINI)*, 7(1):1–31.

Andreas Peldszus and Manfred Stede. 2015. Joint prediction in mst-style discourse parsing for argumentation mining. In *Proc. Conf. on Empirical Methods in NLP*, pages 938–948, Lisbon, Portugal. ACL.

Matthew Peters, Mark Neumann, Mohit Iyyer, Matt Gardner, Christopher Clark, Kenton Lee, and Luke Zettlemoyer. 2018. Deep contextualized word representations. In *Proceedings of the 2018 Conference of NAACL: Human Language Technologies, Volume 1 (Long Papers)*, pages 2227–2237. Association for Computational Linguistics.

Peter Potash, Alexey Romanov, and Anna Rumshisky. 2017. Here's my point: Joint pointer architecture for argument mining. In *Proceedings of the 2017 Conference on Empirical Methods in Natural Language Processing*, pages 1364–1373. Association for Computational Linguistics.

Lorien Pratt and Barbara Jennings. 1996. A survey of transfer between connectionist networks. *Connection Science*, 8(2):163–184.

Nils Reimers and Iryna Gurevych. 2017. Reporting score distributions makes a difference: Performance study of lstm-networks for sequence tagging. In *Proceedings of the 2017 Conference on Empirical Methods in Natural Language Processing*, pages 338–348. Association for Computational Linguistics.

Gil Rocha and Henrique Lopes Cardoso. 2017. Towards a relation-based argument extraction model for argumentation mining. In *Statistical Language and Speech Processing: 5th International Conference, SLSP 2017, Le Mans, France, October 23–25*, pages 94–105, Cham. Springer International Publishing.

Tim Rocktäschel, Edward Grefenstette, Karl Moritz Hermann, Tomás Kociský, and Phil Blunsom. 2015. Reasoning about entailment with neural attention. *CoRR*, abs/1509.06664.

Sebastian Ruder. 2017. A survey of cross-lingual embedding models. *CoRR*, abs/1706.04902.

Mark Sammons, V.G.Vinod Vydiswaran, and Dan Roth. 2012. Recognizing textual entailment. In Daniel M. Bikel and Imed Zitouni, editors, *Multilingual Natural Language Applications: From Theory to Practice*, pages 209–258. Prentice Hall.

Nitish Srivastava, Geoffrey Hinton, Alex Krizhevsky, Ilya Sutskever, and Ruslan Salakhutdinov. 2014. Dropout: A simple way to prevent neural networks from overfitting. *Journal of Machine Learning Research*, 15:1929–1958.

Christian Stab and Iryna Gurevych. 2017. Parsing argumentation structures in persuasive essays. *Comput. Linguist.*, 43(3):619–659.

Christian Stab, Tristan Miller, and Iryna Gurevych. 2018. Cross-topic argument mining from heterogeneous sources using attention-based neural networks. *CoRR*, abs/1802.05758.

Bingning Wang, Kang Liu, and Jun Zhao. 2016. Inner attention based recurrent neural networks for answer selection. In *Proceedings of the 54th Annual Meeting of the Association for Computational Linguistics (Volume 1: Long Papers)*, pages 1288–1297. Association for Computational Linguistics.

Min Xiao and Yuhong Guo. 2013. A novel two-step method for cross language representation learning. In C. J. C. Burges, L. Bottou, M. Welling, Z. Ghahramani, and K. Q. Weinberger, editors, *Advances in Neural Information Processing Systems 26*, pages 1259–1267. Curran Associates, Inc.

David Yarowsky, Grace Ngai, and Richard Wicentowski. 2001. Inducing multilingual text analysis tools via robust projection across aligned corpora. In *Proceedings of the First International Conference on Human Language Technology Research*, HLT '01, pages 1–8, Stroudsburg, PA, USA. Association for Computational Linguistics.

More or less controlled elicitation of argumentative text: Enlarging a microtext corpus via crowdsourcing

Maria Skeppstedt[1,3]**, Andreas Peldszus**[2]**, Manfred Stede**[3]
[1]Department of Computer Science and Media Technology, Linnaeus University, Växjö, Sweden
`maria.skeppstedt@lnu.se`
[2]Retresco GmbH, Berlin, Germany
`andreas.peldszus@retresco.de`
[3]Applied Computational Linguistics, University of Potsdam, Potsdam, Germany
`stede@uni-potsdam.de`

Abstract

We present an extension of an annotated corpus of short argumentative texts that had originally been built in a controlled text production experiment. Our extension more than doubles the size of the corpus by means of crowdsourcing. We report on the setup of this experiment and on the consequences that crowdsourcing had for assembling the data, and in particular for annotation. We labeled the argumentative structure by marking claims, premises, and relations between them, following the scheme used in the original corpus, but had to make a few modifications in response to interesting phenomena in the data. Finally, we report on an experiment with the automatic prediction of this argumentation structure: We first replicated the approach of an earlier study on the original corpus, and compare the performance to various settings involving the extension.

1 Introduction

As with most areas in NLP, progress on Argumentation Mining hinges on the availability of data, and in the case of this field, this is generally taken to be *annotated* data. Up to now, only few corpora labelled with full argumentation structure (i.e., argument components and relations between them) are available; prominent ones are the persuasive essay corpus of Stab and Gurevych (2014), the web text corpus of Habernal and Gurevych (2017), and the argumentative microtext corpus of Peldszus and Stede (2016).[1] The latter is interesting because it has in parallel been annotated with various other linguistic layers, as will be described in Section 2. The microtexts are relatively "clean" text, and the annotation of argumentation structure was generally easy, leading to reasonable annotator agreement, as reported by Peldszus and

Stede (2016). However, a drawback is the relatively small corpus size: 112 texts of about five argumentative text units on average. While this data has proven to be useful for various purposes (see Section 2), for machine learning it is clearly desirable to have a larger corpus of this kind.

In this paper, we turn to crowdsourcing as a means to generate more text. We used essentially the same instructions as used by Peldszus and Stede (2016), and recruited writers via Amazon Mechanical Turk. Naturally, the set of resulting texts is not identical in nature to the original ones, and thus the first contribution of this paper is an analysis of how the different text elicitation scenarios influences the outcome, i.e., to evaluate the pros and cons of crowdsourcing for this type of task. The second contribution is an evaluation of the annotation scheme that was used for argumentation: Which modifications are necessary in order to produce adequate analyses of the text? Finally, the third contribution is to report on results of an automatic classification experiment: We replicated the Minimum Spanning Tree approach proposed by Afantenos et al. (2018), and we compare the results that have already been achieved on the original corpus to those stemming from the new sections of the corpus. We regard this as valuable information on the influence of corpus size on classification results.

In the following, as background we briefly describe the original corpus, and then explain our approach to crowdsourcing the text production task. This is followed by a description of the annotation phase, and the lessons learned. Finally, we report on the classification experiment, and then sum up.

The new corpus data, with its annotation of argumentation structure, is available on the website of the arg-microtext corpus (see below).

---

[1]Many other corpora are available with more lean or more specific annotations; see Section 4 of (Lippi and Torroni, 2016).

Proceedings of the 5th Workshop on Argument Mining, pages 155–163
Brussels, Belgium, November 1, 2018. ©2018 Association for Computational Linguistics

2 Background: The 'argumentative microtext corpus'

2.1 Data

We start from the arg-microtext corpus (Peldszus and Stede, 2016), a freely available[2] parallel corpus of 112 short texts with 576 argumentative discourse units (henceforth: segments). The texts are authentic discussions of controversial issues, which were given to the writers as prompts. They were originally written in German and have been professionally translated to English, preserving the segmentation and if possible the usage of discourse markers. The texts have been collected in a controlled text generation experiment, in a classroom setting with students, using a short instruction. This had the result that all of the texts fulfill the following criteria: (i) The length of each text is about 5 segments; (ii) one segment explicitly states the central claim; (iii) each segment is argumentatively relevant; (iv) at least one objection to the central claim is considered (in order to produce more interesting argumentation).

Finally, all texts have been checked for spelling and grammatical problems, which have been corrected by the annotators. The reason underlying this decision was the intended role of the corpus as a resource for studying argumentation in connection with other linguistic phenomena (see Section 2.3), where plain errors can lead to undesired complications for parsers, etc. Hence, "authenticity" on this level was considered as less important. In this respect the corpus differs from web-text corpora that have been collected for argumentation mining purposes, such as the Internet Argument Corpus (Abbott et al., 2016), the ABCD corpus (Rosenthal and McKeown, 2015) and others.

2.2 Annotation scheme

The argumentation structure of every text was annotated according to a scheme proposed by Peldszus and Stede (2013), which in turn had been based on Freeman's theory of argumentation structures (Freeman, 2011). This annotation scheme has already been proven to yield reliable structures in annotation and classification experiments, for instance by (Peldszus and Stede, 2015; Potash et al., 2017). (Stab and Gurevych, 2017) use a similar scheme for their corpus of persuasive essay, and they also provide classification results for the

microtext corpus.

The argumentation structure of a text is defined as a tree with the text segments as nodes. Each node is associated with one argumentative role: the *proponent* who presents and defends the central claim, or the imaginary *opponent* who critically questions the proponent's claims. Edges between the nodes represent argumentative relations: *support* or *attack*. The scheme allows to discriminate between 'rebutting' attacks, targeting another node and thereby challenging its acceptability, and 'undercutting' attacks, targeting an edge and thereby challenging the acceptability of the inference from the source to the target node. It can also represent linked support, where multiple premises jointly support a claim, i.e., one of the premises would not be able to play the support role in isolation. Another category is 'example support', where the supporting material is a concrete instance of some abstract proposition, serving as evidence. Finally, it is possible to identify two segments as saying essentially the same thing, hence the second being a restatement of the first. (This typically occurs with central claims, which are sometimes being rephrased at the end of the text.)

For illustration, sample analyses are shown below in Figures 1 and 2.

2.3 Other annotation layers

In contrast to other argumentation corpora, the microtext corpus is unique in that it is already annotated with further layers of linguistic information, which makes it usable for systematic correlation studies. Stede et al. (2016) described the annotation of discourse structure according to RST and SDRT, and Becker et al. (2016) added information on *situation entity types*, which Smith (2003) had proposed as a linguistic tool for identifying different 'discourse modes', viz. Narrative, Description, Report, Information, and Argument. Reisert et al. (2017) annotated part of the corpus with information on argumentation schemes, in the spirit of Walton et al. (2008). Also, an alternative approach to schemes, that of Rigotti and Greco Morasso (2010), was annotated on the microtexts by Musi et al. (2018).

Given these extra layers, we regard the extension of the microtext corpus as especially useful, as the annotations of the other layers may now also be added, resulting in a much more valuable re-

---

[2]http://angcl.ling.uni-potsdam.de/resources/argmicro.html

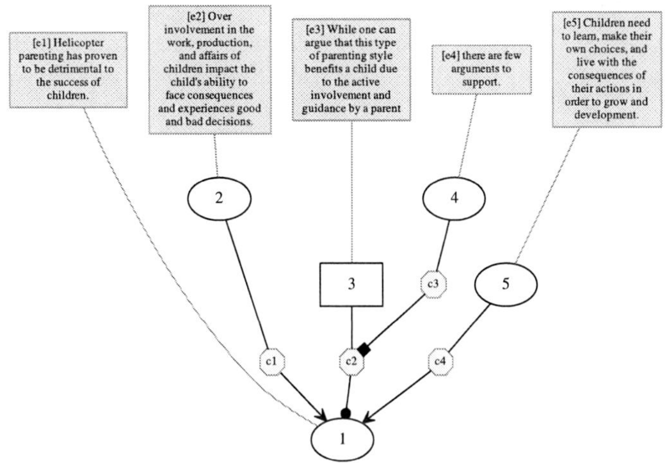

Figure 1: An example text and its argumentation structure: Text segments, proponent (round) and opponent (box) nodes, supporting (arrow-head) and attacking (circle-head) relations.

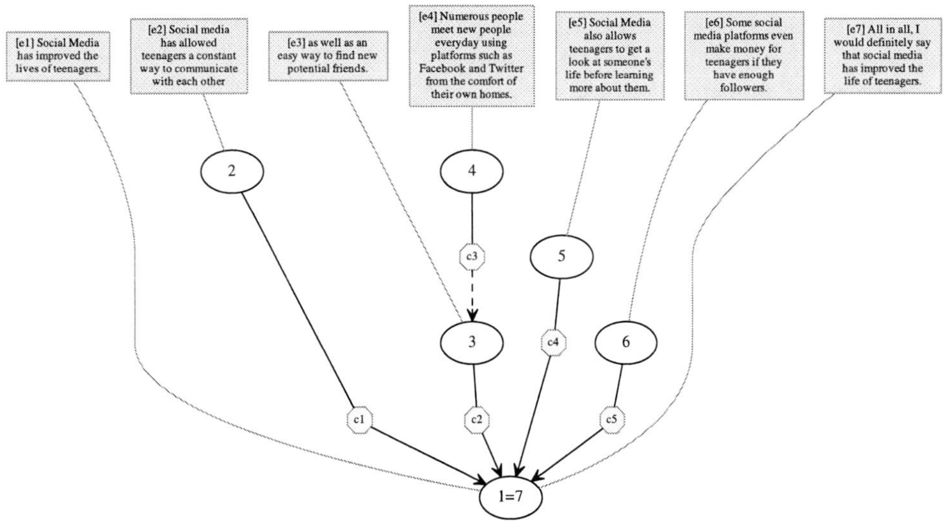

Figure 2: An example of an argumentation structure for which the main claim is repeated in the text. Each segment has been annotated as an independent argumentative discourse unit, all of them directly supporting the main claim, with the exception of one unit which gives support by example.

source, both in terms of volume and in terms of phenomena that can be investigated.

3 Crowdsourcing the production of argumentative texts

3.1 Setting

We recruited authors via Amazon Mechanical Turk, making sure (as far as possible) that they were High School Graduates and living in the U.S. (to increase the chances for language competence). The authors were given the task of producing a short text that argued for or against a general debate topic, the prompt. Everybody was given one from the set of 36 prompts and wrote no more than one text for the experiment. Prompts were gathered from publicly available essay-writing exercises, making sure that they do not presuppose local or temporally-restricted knowledge that our Turkers might not have. For illustration, here are three of the prompts we used:

- Should car drivers be strictly prohibited from using their cell phones?

- Does recycling really make a difference?

- Do older people make good or bad parents?

We calculated the time it takes authors on average by means of a pilot study, and then decided to pay the authors 1.10$ for their effort. Like in the original setting descibed in the previous section, authors were instructed to use about 5 sentences, to clearly take a stance and make it explicit by means of a claim statement, and to also include at least one argument for the opposite view in their text.

3.2 Filtering

As to be expected, not all of the texts that were produced did, however, fulfill all the criteria. First, a number of them did not mention the opposing view; since this does not lead to degenerate data in any way, we decided to leave those texts in the corpus. In contrast, texts in which no clear stance towards the debate topic was taken were excluded from further annotation. Such texts typically listed a number of conditions for agreeing with the topic at hand, gave recommendations for solving an issue, or simply listed a few arguments for and against the topic, without indicating a winning side. Also, we removed texts where authors took a stance, but mainly wrote things unrelated to the debate. Likewise, texts that were not understandable (for grammatical and/or content reasons), and texts that were very long or very short (more than eight or less than four argumentative discourse units) were excluded. Since the debate topics given were very general, the authors sometimes voiced a more specific opinion on a topic. For instance, for the prompt "Do long distance relationships work?", two of the authors argued for the more specific stance: "long-distance relationships work in the short run but not in the long run". These texts, being otherwise faithful to our criteria, were kept in the corpus for annotation.

3.3 Cleaning

The texts that we kept after the filtering phase were manually cleaned, i.e., minor misspellings and grammatical errors were corrected. Furthermore, some of the authors have taken a clear stance on the given prompt question by simply starting their text with "yes" or "no", before presenting their arguments. This violates the guidelines, which ask for texts that should be understandable without actually having the question as headline. For these cases, the answer was replaced with a statement that paraphrased the prompt question and indicated the "yes" or "no" polarity. In addition, text-initial anaphors (referring to parts of the question) were replaced with their intended antecedents.

We are aware that cleaning and repairing are potentially controversial moves. Our main motivation was that the data be comparable to that of the original corpus, and therefore we largely followed the 'cleaning' procedure described by Peldszus and Stede (2016). However, all "raw" versions of the texts will also be part of the corpus release, as for certain experiments it might be important to be confronted with authentic language containing mistakes of various kinds.

3.4 Statistics

A total of 205 texts had been originally collected, and from these, 34 were excluded from further consideration, for the reasons given above (but still part of the corpus to be distributed). Thus, we altogether moved 83% of the crowdsourced texts to the next phase: annotation of argumentation structure. We see this rate as rather encouraging, demonstrating that crowdsourcing is a viable approach for this type of text elicitation task.

4 Annotating the crowdsourced texts

We applied the annotation guidelines (mentioned in Section 2) and used the freely available graph annotation tool GraPAT[3] (Sonntag and Stede, 2014) to annotate the 171 texts that passed our filtering step. Two annotators (one of them being a co-author of this paper) shared the work, and a third person (another co-author) joined in discussions of difficult cases. At the present stage, we did not run an inter-annotator agreement study, because this had already been done on the original corpus and guidelines (see Peldszus and Stede (2016)), thereby verifying the usability of the scheme. However, the annotation process was not entirely straightforward. In the following, we describe specifically the challenges posed by the different type of text, in comparison to the original microtexts and the annotation scheme. We regard most of the phenomena as not just specific to this project, but to be relevant for empirical work on argumentation mining, especially for designing annotation guidelines, in general.

4.1 Implicit claims

The first observation concerns the presence of an explicit "central claim". Authors were encouraged to state it in their text, but we did not filter texts that lack it (because, in fact, many "natural" argumentative texts have no explicit claim, as for instance found by Habernal and Gurevych (2017)). As long as the argumentative structure and content of the text suggested some segment to be a viable candidate for main claim, our annotators chose it. This had the effect that—in contrast to the original corpus with its rather crisp claims—both specific refinements of the writing prompt (e.g., "As long as the kids are provided with a stable home life, divorce does not have to be an enormous trauma from which there is no recovering") and relatively vague statements (e.g., "There are many benefits to using LED lights") can now be central claims. However, when the text argued clearly, but did not supply any reasonable candidate for explicit claim, annotators added this as an extra statement, which will then serve as the root of the argumentation tree. A manually added statement serving as the main claim was added in 34 texts. One example is the following text, where the last sentence is the manually added claim:

<hr>

[3] http://angcl.ling.uni-potsdam.de/resources/grapat.html

(1) Do we need fracking, depite its risks? Fracking has uncovered cheap natural gas. The aggregate savings to the American household are then passed on to the economy in the way of spending. Also, the coal industry has imploded as a consequence which is more of a pollutant than natural gas. The potential contamination damage caused by the fracking process is outweighed by the reduction of energy costs to the American household. Yes, we need fracking despite its risks.

4.2 Restatements

Another phenomenon that did not occur in the previously published corpus, was that the authors restated a claim, typically the main claim. These restatements were annotated through connecting the text segments that restated the claim to the same argumentative discourse unit, as shown in Figure 2 (node '1 = 7'). In the annotated corpus, 29 argumentative units are restatements of previously mentioned ones, and 19 of them restate the main claim.

4.3 Direct versus indirect support

Another difficulty concerned the attachment point of support relations. It can be difficult to decide whether a statement supports or opposes directly the central claim, or a separate statement (thus affecting the claim only indirectly). This kind of ambiguity was also reported for the arg-microtext corpus by Peldszus and Stede (2016). We noted that it appears quite frequently in the crowdsourced texts. For instance, in Figure 2, all segments, except one, are annotated as direct support of the main claim, as there are no surface markers (or clear semantic cues involving background knowledge) in the text which would signal that any of these arguments support any other argument. However, the author may have intended additional supporting relations.

4.4 Argument support versus causal connection

Another challenge stems from drawing the line between relations in the texts that are argumentative, and those that describe a (non-pragmatic) causal connection of events. The example below may be viewed as one single argumentative discourse unit, which includes one long causal connection. Alternatively, it may be segmented into three sub-arguments, on the ground that it is possible to agree on or refute each one of these three segments separately. E.g., it is possible to agree that people go to the stores to recycle, but refute that this leads to more money being spent in the shop, or that this leads to economic growth.

(2) It is also a benefit as it encourages people to go to stores to recycle and then spend that money at the shop increasing the amount spent at the store and encouraging economic growth.

4.5 Implicit modality or evaluation

In many cases, annotation decisions turned out to be dependent on whether a certain modality or a positive or negative evaluation is added to a segment by the annotator's interpretation. In the (partial) text below, segment 2, 3 and 4 are annotated as supporting the claim 1. In turn, 5 supports 4, given that the annotator interprets "a heart rate that gets going" as a positive state of affairs, brought about by the desire to keep weight.

(3) [Spending time together as a family engaged in sports together is a good thing.]$_1$ [It increases a sense of family togetherness,]$_2$[gets people outside and into the fresh air and sunshine,]$_3$[and gets the heart rate going.]$_4$[This in turn helps to keep weight at a healthy level]$_5$ (...)

4.6 Non-argumentative text units

Finally, there were three cases in which the texts contained segments that the annotators deemed to be irrelevant for the argument, for instance because it provides only background information or reports some personal experience of the author that is only vaguely related. In the original corpus this was not the case and hence lead to tree structures spanning the entire text. Now in the crowd-sourced texts, we decided to leave those texts in the corpus and therefore now have segments that are not part of the graph. An example is the beginning of a text on the pros and cons of soft drink can deposits:

(4) I live in Michigan, where we have a deposit.

4.7 Summary

The annotation effort lead to a total of 932 argumentative units (segments). The distribution of relations is: convergent support (467); example sup-

port (23); rebutting attack (137); undercutting attack (77); linked support or attack (57); restatement (29).

5 Experiments on automatic classification

In the following, we will describe our experiments on automatically identifying the argumentative structures. This has already been done on the original version of the corpus, e.g., recently by Afantenos et al. (2018). In our experiments we replicate their approach, and test it on the texts we acquired and annotated as described above. Our aim is to get an understanding of how much the old and the new data sets differ in terms of achievable predictions, and to assess possible improvements by extending the size of the corpus.

Regarding the new phenomena pointed out in Section 4, we chose to ignore non-argumentative segments for the purposes of this experiment, similar as if they had been filtered out in a prior step of a pipeline. For one thing, this concerns only three texts, and, more importantly, if we want to compare our results to the earlier work, we should work with the same representations. Second, implicit claims that have been made explicit by the annotators are included when we predict argumentation structures.

5.1 Experimental Setup

For predicting argumentation structures, we replicated the MST model of Afantenos et al. (2018), which is an improved version of the model originally presented by Peldszus and Stede (2015). This approach learns four local models for various aspects of the argumentation structure: for identifying the central claim of the text (cc); for determining the argumentative role, i.e. proponent or opponent (ro), for classifying the function of a segment, such as support or attack (fu); and finally for identifying which units are 'attached' to each other, i.e. are connected by an argumentative relation (at). The predictions of these local models are then combined into a single edge score and decoded to a structure by selecting the minimum spanning tree (MST). This approach has been shown to yield competitive results when compared to ILP decoders; see the original papers for more details.

Similar to previous work, our experiment uses the argumentation graphs in a version that is converted to dependency structures. Also, the set of relations is reduced to merely 'support' and 'attack' by conflating the subcategories. This step is done in order to be compatible with earlier work (no other corpora use this set of fine-grained distinctions of support and attack so far) and to alleviate a potential sparse-data problem per specific relation. Restatements (which tend to occur only for the main claim) exist in the new data set but not in the original one; for compatibility, we converted them to support relations in order to maintain compatibility with the old corpus. Again, this is a purely technical decision made in order to allow a comparison with prior and related work. As an alternative, experiments with the fine-grained set of relation have been done (on the original corpus) by Peldszus (2018).

We adopt the evaluation procedure of previous work, i.e., we use 50 train-test splits, resulting from 10 randomized repetitions of 5-fold cross validation. For evaluations on the original corpus we use the published splits, for the new corpus we derive splits analogously. The correctness of predicted structures is measured separately for the four subtasks, reported as macro averaged F1, and more unified in a labelled attachment score (LAS) as it is commonly used for evaluation in dependency parsing (see Kübler et al., 2009, ch. 6.1). For significance testing, we use the Wilcoxon signed-rank test (Wilcoxon, 1945).

5.2 Evaluation Scenarios

We compare the results on the original dataset and those on the new one using three evaluation scenarios:

Single Corpus This is the standard scenario for evaluating the model on one single corpus, from which both training and test sets are sampled. We reproduce the results on the original corpus, and produce new results for the new corpus. Comparing these scores gives a first, but only tentative, impression whether the structures annotated in the new corpus are as easy or as hard to recognize as in the original corpus.

Cross Corpus When we train the model exclusively on one corpus and test it on the other, we can investigate the degree of generalization of the model. This is especially interesting, since the new corpus had different prompts and thus covers different topics. We expect a decrease in performance when compared to in-domain results as in the single-corpus setting.

Extend Corpus Finally, we use one corpus as additional training data when evaluating on the other. This helps us to understand to which degree new data can help achieve better results for the four subtasks and overall for the prediction of full structures. We expect improvements here, when compared with the single-corpus setting.

5.3 Results

The results are shown in Table 1. In the scenario, 'old' refers to the original corpus, and 'new' to the new one described in this paper.

Single Corpus The results reproduced on the original corpus are equivalent to published results. On the new corpus, we overall achieve similar scores. Differences are subtle: central claims are a bit harder to recognize (an absolute difference of -2.5 points) on the new corpus. This is to be expected, as the new corpus features restatements of the main claim which are competitors to the original main claim. The scores for argumentative role, function and attachment classification are quite equal. This leads us to assume that the structures annotated in the new corpus are not more or less complicated to be recognized than the structures in the original corpus.

Cross Corpus As expected, the cross-corpus results are in general lower than single-corpus scores for both directions. When training on the old corpus and testing on the new one, we observe a relative decrease of 7% compared to the average level score achieved when training and testing on the new corpus. The loss is slightly stronger for argumentative function and attachment than on the other levels. In the reverse direction, when training on new and testing on old, the average loss is even higher with 11%. Here, central claim and argumentative function exhibit the highest decrease. The exception is the attachment level, with only a minor drop of 3%.

Extend Corpus When using the "other" corpus as additional training data and comparing this with the 'single' scenario without extra training data, we find on average only mild improvements (which we again report as relative improvements). Interestingly, the gains per task differ across the directions: When evaluating on the old corpus using the new data for extra training, there is a small

scenario			results				
type	train	test	cc	ro	fu	at	LAS
single	old	old	.870	.768	.754	.719	.526
cross	new	old	.745	.695	.644	.698	.450
extend	both	old	.859	.779†	.757	.724	.532
single	new	new	.845	.766	.750	.714	.527
cross	old	new	.797	.731	.693	.665	.439
extend	both	new	.856†	.782†	.765‡	.712	.526

Table 1: Evaluation scores for the predicted structures reported as macro avg. F1 for the cc, ro, fu, and at levels, and as labelled attachment score (LAS). Results marked with a dagger are significant improvements over the corresponding 'single' score, with † for $p < 0.05$ and ‡ for $p < 0.01$.

drop (-1.3%) in central claim identification and a small raise in role classification (+1.4%). The remaining levels show minor improvements. In the other direction, i.e. when evaluating on the new corpus using the old corpus as additional training data, we observe improvements in role (+2.1%) and function classification (+2.0%), as well as a small raise in central claim identification (+1.3%). One possible explanation for this is the impact of the restatements in the new corpus. An improvement that is consistent across both directions is that in role classification. We presume that more training data really helped to recognize the less frequent opponent role.

6 Summary and Outlook

In order to extend an existing corpus of 112 short argumentative texts (which had been gathered in a classroom setting with students), we employed crowdsourcing for collecting a new dataset that can serve as an extension to the old one. We described our steps in assembling the data set in such a way that is compatible to the original corpus but at the same time is to some extent faithful to the "crowdsource complications". As a result, there are two changes in the corpus now: Texts may contain non-argmentative segments, and some "artificial" segments representing central claims have been added where authors left the claim implicit. Still, these are no dramatic steps, and overall, we claim that (i) crowdsourcing can be a viable method for collecting this type of data, and that (ii) the new corpus can be used in tandem with the old one as a coherent dataset.

Finally, to substantiate (ii), we reproduced an experiment on automatic prediction of the argu-mentation structure, which showed that predicting on the crowdsourced texts is generally not harder than on the old ones, and that overall, the task can benefit from the increased corpus size, though not dramatically. But we expect the increased corpus size to be useful for other machine learning experiments, especially for neural network approaches, such as those recently run by Potash et al. (2017) on the old corpus (albeit using only a small part of the annotations for a simplified setting).

An interesting question for future work concerns the viability of using crowdsourcing not just for collecting the texts, but also for annotation. Instead of having annotators draw graph structures, one would translate the process into a sequence of questions whose answers would imply the structural description. We plan to explore this path with suitable pilot experiments.

The corpus and annotations are available from the arg-microtexts website (see footnote 2 above).

Acknowledgements

We would like to thank Constanze Schmitt for carrying out annotations and for translating the annotation guidelines into English, and Anna Laurinavichyute for setting up and running the MTurk experiment. We would also like to thank the Swedish Research Council (Vetenskapsrådet) that partly funded this study through the project "Navigating in streams of opinions: Extracting and visualising arguments in opinionated texts" (No. 2016-06681). Finally, thanks to the anonymous reviewers for their constructive comments.

References

Rob Abbott, Brian Ecker, Pranav Anand, and Marilyn Walker. 2016. Internet Argument Corpus 2.0: An SQL schema for dialogic social media and the corpora to go with it. In *Proc. Language Resources and Evaluation*, pages 4445–4452.

Stergos Afantenos, Andreas Peldszus, and Manfred Stede. 2018. Comparing decoding mechanisms for parsing argumentative structures. *Argument and Computation*. (published online, February 2018).

Maria Becker, Alexis Palmer, and Anette Frank. 2016. Argumentative texts and clause types. In *Proceedings of the Third Workshop on Argumentation Mining*, Berlin. Association for Computational Linguistics.

James B. Freeman. 2011. *Argument Structure: Representation and Theory*. Argumentation Library (18). Springer, Berlin/New York.

Ivan Habernal and Iryna Gurevych. 2017. Argumentation mining in user-generated web discourse. *Computational linguistics*, 43(1):125–179.

Sandra Kübler, Ryan McDonald, and Joakim Nivre. 2009. Dependency Parsing. *Synthesis Lectures on Human Language Technologies*, 2(1):1–127.

Marco Lippi and Paolo Torroni. 2016. Argumentation mining: State of the art and emerging trends. *ACM Trans. Internet Technol.*, 16(2):10:1–10:25.

Elena Musi, Smaranda Muresan, and Manfred Stede. 2018. A multilayer annotated corpus of argumentative text: From argument schemes to discourse relations. In *Proceedings of LREC 2018*, Miyazaki, Japan.

Andreas Peldszus. 2018. *Automatic recognition of argumentation structure in short monological texts*. Ph.D. thesis, Universität Potsdam.

Andreas Peldszus and Manfred Stede. 2013. From argument diagrams to argumentation mining in texts: A survey. *International Journal of Cognitive Informatics and Natural Intelligence (IJCINI)*, 7(1):1–31.

Andreas Peldszus and Manfred Stede. 2015. Joint prediction in mst-style discourse parsing for argumentation mining. In *Proceedings of the 2015 Conference on Empirical Methods in Natural Language Processing*, pages 938–948, Lisbon, Portugal. Association for Computational Linguistics.

Andreas Peldszus and Manfred Stede. 2016. An annotated corpus of argumentative microtexts. In *Argumentation and Reasoned Action: Proceedings of the 1st European Conference on Argumentation, Lisbon 2015 / Vol. 2*, pages 801–816, London. College Publications.

Peter Potash, Alexey Romanov, and Anna Rumshisky. 2017. Here's my point: Joint pointer architecture for argument mining. In *Proceedings of the 2017 Conference on Empirical Methods in Natural Language Processing*, pages 1375–1384, Copenhagen, Denmark. Association for Computational Linguistics.

Paul Reisert, Naoya Inoue, Naoaki Okazaki, and Kentaro Inui. 2017. Deep argumentative structure analysis as an explanation to argumentative relations. In *Proceedings of The 23rd Annual Meeting of the Association for Natural Language Processing*, pages 38–41.

Eddo Rigotti and Sara Greco Morasso. 2010. Comparing the argumentum model of topics to other contemporary approaches to argument schemes: The procedural and material components. *Argumentation*, 24(4):489–512.

Sara Rosenthal and Kathy McKeown. 2015. I couldn't agree more: The role of conversational structure in agreement and disagreement detection in online discussions. In *Proceedings of the 16th Annual Meeting of the Special Interest Group on Discourse and Dialogue*, pages 168–177, Prague, Czech Republic. Association for Computational Linguistics.

Carlota Smith. 2003. *Modes of discourse. The local structure of texts*. Cambridge University Press, Cambridge.

Jonathan Sonntag and Manfred Stede. 2014. Grapat: a tool for graph annotations. In *Proceedings of LREC 2014*, Reykjavik.

Christian Stab and Iryna Gurevych. 2014. Annotating argument components and relations in persuasive essays. In *Proceedings of the 25th International Conference on Computational Linguistics (COLING 2014)*, pages 1501–1510. Dublin City University and Association for Computational Linguistics.

Christian Stab and Iryna Gurevych. 2017. Parsing argumentation structures in persuasive essays. *Computational Linguistics*, 43(3):619–659.

Manfred Stede, Stergos Afantenos, Andreas Peldszus, Nicholas Asher, and Jérémy Perret. 2016. Parallel discourse annotations on a corpus of short texts. In *Proceedings of the International Conference on Language Resources and Evaluation (LREC)*, Portoroz.

D. Walton, C. Reed, and F. Macagno. 2008. *Argumentation schemes*. Cambridge University Press, Cambridge.

Frank Wilcoxon. 1945. Individual comparisons by ranking methods. *Biometrics Bulletin*, 1(6):80–83.

Author Index